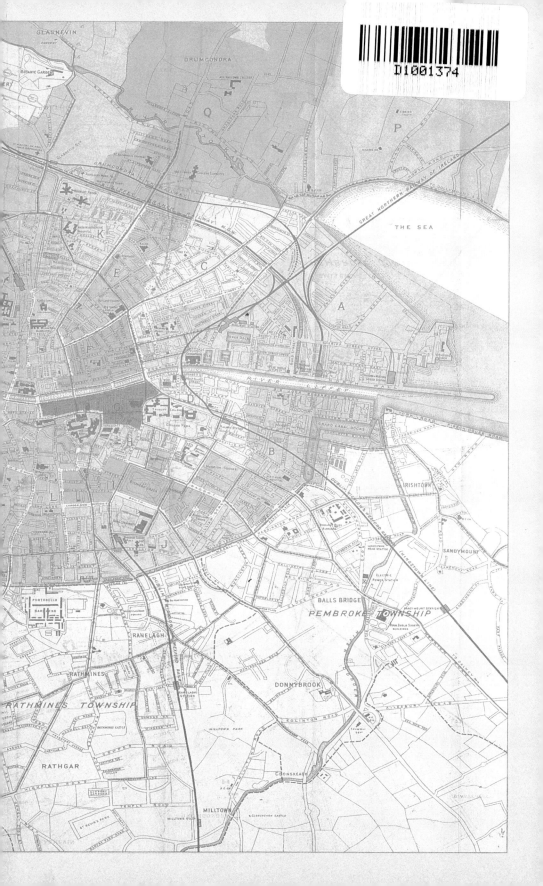

JOHN STANISLAUS JOYCE

JOHN STANISLAUS JOYCE

JOYCE

THE VOLUMINOUS LIFE AND GENIUS OF JAMES JOYCE'S FATHER

JOHN WYSE JACKSON AND PETER COSTELLO

St. Martin's Press ✺ New York

JOHN STANISLAUS JOYCE: THE VOLUMINOUS LIFE AND GENIUS OF JAMES
JOYCE'S FATHER. Copyright © 1997 by John Wyse Jackson and Peter Costello. All
rights reserved. Printed in the United States of America. No part of this book may
be used or reproduced in any man-ner whatsoever without written permission
except in the case of brief quotations embodied in critical articles or reviews. For
information, address St. Martin's Press, 175 Fifth Avenue, New York, N.Y. 10010.

Library of Congress Cataloging-in-Publication Data

Jackson, John Wyse.
  John Stanislaus Joyce : the voluminous life and genius of James Joyce's father
/ John Wyse Jackson and Peter Costello.–1st U.S. ed.
    p. cm.
  "First published in Great Britain by Fourth Estate Limited"–T.p. verso.
  Includes bibliographical references and index.
  ISBN 0-312-18599-5
  1. Joyce, John Stanislaus, 1849-1931. 2. Novelists, Irish–20th century–Family
relationships. 3. Joyce, James, 1849-1931–Family. 4. Fathers–Ireland–Biography.
5. Fathers and sons–Ireland. 6. Joyce family. I. Costello, Peter. II. Title.
PR6019.09Z6318 1998
823'.912–dc21   98-5495
[B]   CIP

First published in Great Britain by Fourth Estate Limited

First U.S. Edition: June 1998

10 9 8 7 6 5 4 3 2 1

To
the happy memory of our late friends and mentors

Patricia HUTCHINS
John RYAN
William Bedell STANFORD

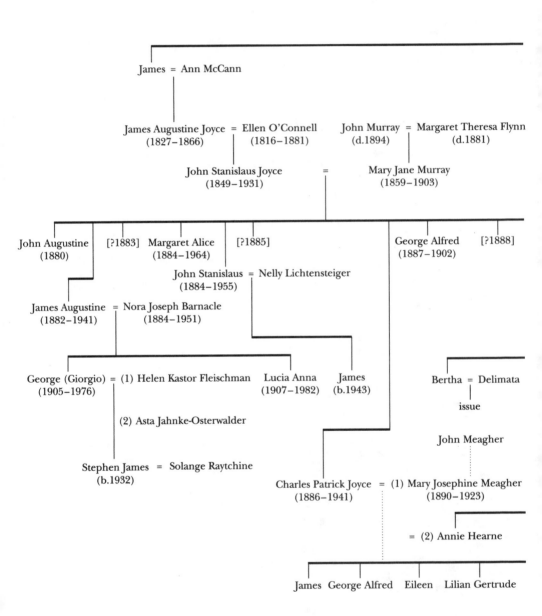

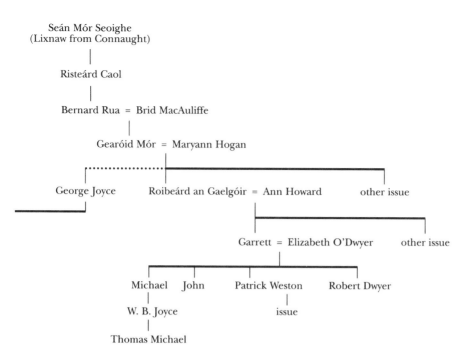

Seán Mór Seoighe
(Lixnaw from Connaught)
|
Risteárd Caol
|
Bernard Rua = Brid MacAuliffe
|
Gearóid Mór = Maryann Hogan

George Joyce   Roibeárd an Gaelgóir = Ann Howard   other issue

Garrett = Elizabeth O'Dwyer   other issue

Michael   John   Patrick Weston   Robert Dwyer
| |
W. B. Joyce   issue
|
Thomas Michael

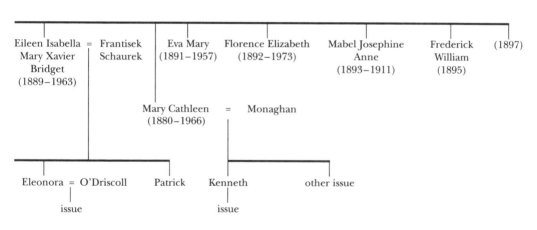

Eileen Isabella = Frantisek   Eva Mary   Florence Elizabeth   Mabel Josephine   Frederick   (1897)
Mary Xavier   Schaurek   (1891–1957)   (1892–1973)   Anne   William
Bridget   (1893–1911)   (1895)
(1889–1963)

Mary Cathleen   =   Monaghan
(1880–1966)

Eleonora = O'Driscoll   Patrick   Kenneth   other issue
| |
issue   issue

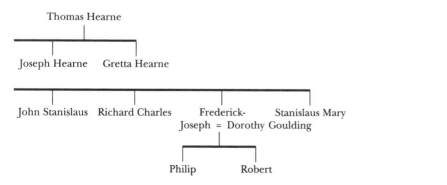

Thomas Hearne

Joseph Hearne   Gretta Hearne

John Stanislaus   Richard Charles   Frederick-   Stanislaus Mary
                                      Joseph = Dorothy Goulding

Philip   Robert

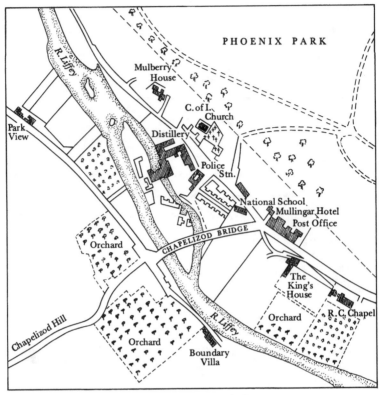

Chapelizod in 1876

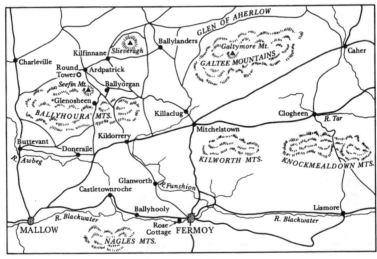

Fermoy and District

CONTENTS

A Note on Money

Whether he had it or not, money in John Stanislaus Joyce's day was denominated in pounds sterling (£). The pound was subdivided into 20 shillings (and so £1. 10s. is today's £1.50). Shillings in turn were subdivided into 12 pence (or d.). Thus a third of £4, £1. 6s. 8d., was a more accurate rendering of today's £1.33. (In the style of the day, two shillings might be written as '2/–', and two shillings and sixpence as '2/6'.)

Some charges – school fees, for example – were quoted in guineas, a guinea being twenty-one shillings, or £1. 1s. This was more lucrative (for the charger) and was a standard confirmation of professional status or 'swagger'. To this day, auctions for racehorses are conducted in guineas.

The Irish link with sterling lasted from the 1720s (shortly after the Wood's Ha'pence scandal brilliantly exploited by Swift in the *Drapier's Letters*) until 1979.

FOREWORD

Most biographies are written about those who were famous – or at least well-connected – during their lifetimes, or who achieved or perpetrated something notable in the eyes of the world. This book is not one of them. It is indeed the story of a most unusual man, but a man whose existence (like that of most of us) was centred around ordinary things, the family landmarks of births and deaths, getting money and spending it (not necessarily in that order), talking to friends, being young and growing old. John Stanislaus Joyce's lifetime was spent in Ireland from the 1840s to the 1930s, a period of operatic convulsion for the country. His life was divided between Cork in the south and Dublin in the east. In neither city was he ever very famous, but in each he was well known by acquaintance, sight and reputation to a large proportion of the citizenry. And John Stanislaus, as long as he drew breath, could never be ignored by anyone who knew him: his quick and witty tongue ensured that. All who came into close contact with him were affected to an extreme degree – especially the members of his own family. He generated both obsessive love and extreme hatred, sometimes in the same person. He inspired much devotion and at least as much dislike. He was a good companion, a relisher and raconteur of life, a font of humour, a blasphemer, a drinker of mythological stature. But the world, inasmuch as it knows him, would judge him to have been a failure.

Ireland between the Famine and the Free State, in the last turbulent years of British rule, was literally another country. John Stanislaus Joyce, simply by being there, was witness to the long birth of the modern nation, and he contrived to be personally close to many of the dramatic fluxes and alarms of the age. Though it is not for achievements that his life is memorable, it might be said that his greatest one was in making James Joyce into the man he was. From the moment this son was born until his own death almost fifty years later, John's first concern was James. Reciprocally, the world in which John Stanislaus lived would become the imaginative world where the writer James Joyce lived also. James's ebullient father was his prime inspiration and supplied the context (and often the text) to almost everything he ever wrote. This book is not one of literary criticism, but as it traces the erratic path of John Stanislaus through the years, it may also illuminate some of the fleeting and almost forgotten concerns – social, political and personal – that James Joyce drew upon to make his writing. His father's family, ancestry, character and the minute circumstances of his life became the bedrock from which the spring of Joyce's art flowed. Even the family's earliest roots in the Irish-speaking oral tradition of story-telling and song fed directly into the three great modernist novels that would transform the world's fiction in the twentieth century.

While the story of John Stanislaus Joyce may allow a new perspective, a 'parallax' view, perhaps, to emerge on Joyce the writer, James Joyce is not the hidden subject of this biography. Instead, we hope here to do final justice to the unique genius of the man his father was, a man of his times, reverberating in Irish history and culture, and through him also to learn something more about the other members of the teeming Joyce family – a family of separate and collective individuality – who are usually obscured from view like minor planets in orbit round a brilliant sun.

John Stanislaus was fond, as were so many of his generation and education, of quoting Latin tags. He would have been familiar with the original Roman concept of 'genius' – that guiding spirit allotted to each person at birth to influence his fortunes and character, and finally to conduct him out of the world. In a later meaning of the word, the genius of John Stanislaus was his dominating characteristic, a genius for being alive, a prevailing spirit of the age and of Ireland. The spirit of the Anchises-like begetter of that wandering Aeneas, James Joyce, 'his sire's familiar or genius haunting the shore' of his father's later life – the phrase is from an 1887 *Aeneid* (ed. Bowen) – was certainly a special one. John

Stanislaus Joyce was a prodigal son and a prodigal father, prodigal with his money, his repartee, his emotions, his love of music and lore and controversy. In his prodigality was his genius too. Yet this genius, as other Roman tradition had it, was divided into its good and its evil sides. For James Joyce, he was the ideal parent, the father incarnate; for the rest of his children he was a nightmare from which they struggled to awake.

The contradictions and mercurial charm of this strangest of Joyces are among the themes of this biography. How did this Irish Victorian gentleman descend into immortality? Intelligent and fiercely feckless, he resists encapsulation, but his life is deserving of attention for its own unlikely sake, quite apart from his role in literature. In this book we have made important use of an interview conducted with John Stanislaus Joyce as he lay in bed in Drumcondra during the last decade of his life. The work of an unidentified journalist or stenographer, it was found among James Joyce's papers after his death. With its cascading memories and asides, the interview captures evocatively and uniquely the colourful old gentleman's voice and, as such, in quoting from it, we have left intact its somewhat eccentric syntax and spelling. A caveat may be entered that these effervescent recollections, while always illuminating, are not always accurate. John Stanislaus Joyce, for decades a frock-coated fabulist on the streets of Dublin, understood the value of the artificer.

Lastly, the words of the eminent American Joycean, David Hayman, are also apposite here. Our findings too 'are tentative, hypothetical, audacious and incomplete' – and at times, no doubt, mistaken. This is true of all research, though readers and critics – as well as biographers – often forget it. There can never be such a thing as a definitive biography. No man or woman can be fully known.

Mr Stephen James Joyce, great-grandson of John Stanislaus, has in the past urged those writing about his family to abandon old-fashioned Freudianisms in favour of exploration of the Dublin and Irish mileux that informed his grandfather's work. This is precisely what this book attempts to do. Extracts from work still in copyright are used only where essential to the text, and have been kept to a minimum. For these minimal quotations we have observed the guidelines relating to 'fair dealing' laid down in 1987 by the Society of Authors in conjunction with the Publishers Association. Of course, we must thank the whole Joyce line for bearing the genius that gave the world both James Joyce and his father. As should be the case with any book on matters Joycean, it is to be hoped that some readers will feel drawn towards the (sometimes initially daunting) masterpieces of James Joyce. If so, this will be its own reward.

We are also grateful to Ken Monaghan, Bob Joyce, the representatives of the estate of Stanislaus Joyce, Philip Joyce of Cork, Arthur Walls, Paddy Joyce, Yvonne Conroy, Michael Dwyer Joyce and other descendants and relatives of John Stanislaus Joyce, whose kind help now extends over several years. The 'Dublin Joyces' in particular have not stinted in their support, directing us to many family documents and allowing us to quote extensively from them. We will always be indebted: it must not be assumed, however, that they agree with all we have written.

Very many other people have been generous with their advice, expertise, patience and Joyceana. We thank them warmly: Hector MacDonnell, Brenda Maddox, Fergal Little, J. B. Lyons, Fritz Senn and his friends at the Zürich James Joyce Foundation, Mr Carey Joyce of Acres, Co. Cork, David Pierce, Clive Priddle, the President of St Colman's College in Fermoy, Terence Moran, Arthur Garrett and members of the Devin and Lidwell families, Peggy Guinan, Andrew Gibson, Robert Hampson and the Charles Peake *Ulysses* Seminar, Peter Parker, Chris Rolfe and the James Joyce Society of London, Anthony Cronin, Ruth, Julie and Lucy Moller, David Norris, John Galvin of Fermoy, Robert Nicholson, John and Laura McCourt, and Liam too, C. R. Lacy of Ecuador and, at John Sandoe (Books) Ltd in Chelsea, all the staff and many of the customers. Inevitably, some (temporarily forgotten) friends and benefactors will have to content themselves with a bare mention in the notes, or even just the quiet knowledge that we will buy them a black beer when we next meet.

During the twenty-five years or so of research that lie behind this book, we have consulted more sources of information than can now be credited, but we would like particularly to thank Cornell University Library, to whose collections several allusions are made here. Other librarians in Ireland, England, Scotland and America have been most helpful, including those at the National Library of Ireland, the British Library (with the Official Publications section, the Manuscripts Room and the newspaper outpost at Colindale), the Gilbert Library in Pearse Street, Dublin, the Irish National Archives, the Dublin Civic Museum, the Mitchell Library in Glasgow, the Library of Southern Illinois University at Carbondale, Senate House Library in London, the James Joyce Cultural Institute, the James Joyce Tower at Sandycove, the Libraries of Trinity and University Colleges in Dublin, Fermoy Public Library, the Irish Architectural Archive, the Manuscripts Room at University College London, the Central Catholic Libraries of Dublin and London, the Kerry County Library in Tralee and the London Library.

The book would not have been written without the support of our families: Mary, Timothy and Patrick Costello, Ruth Jackson, Lois, Peter, Patrick, Michael, Margery – and even Conor, when he arrived – Wyse Jackson, Gwen and Daniel Mathews, and Michael and Margaret McGinley, *inter alios*. All of them have done a great deal more than merely listened: they have actively helped. We hope to have other subjects of conversation soon. And in this book about fathers, we thank our own fathers for their unique contributions and for their memories of John Stanislaus Joyce's lifetime.

The book owes its greatest debt of all, however, to Bernard McGinley, who was involved from the beginning and a great deal of whose research and writing have been made use of here: his name ought really to appear on the cover. He has our warmest thanks.

Finally, we would like to pay tribute to the three writers to whom this book is dedicated. They were among the first people in Ireland to appreciate and inquire, with passion as well as scholarship, into the significance and early background of James Joyce. Their combination of heart and mind is missed.

The Authors
Independence Day
4 July 1997

PART ONE

Son

'Mr Dedalus . . . parting his coat-tails,
stood with his back to the glowing fire.'
Drawing by Robin Jacques,
for *A Portrait of the Artist as a Young Man.*
Courtesy of Jonathan Cape.

CHAPTER 1

Ancestral Joyces

In the last decades of James Joyce's life, visitors to his Paris flats at 2 Square Robiac, and later at 7 rue Edmond Valentin, found themselves sitting under the benign gaze of a series of family portraits in heavy gilded frames. The most recent of these, by the young Irish artist Patrick Tuohy, displayed the passionate intensity of the author's father, John Stanislaus Joyce, his ruddy face aglow with the fire of life.

Tuohy had been commissioned by James Joyce, not so much for his talent, which was considerable, but for the past associations that his family had with the Joyces. His grandfather had been one of the reporters for the *Freeman's Journal* of the famous 1891 meeting in Committee Room 15 in the Houses of Parliament that brought about Parnell's downfall, while his doctor father had attended at the death of James's brother George. Such associations, with their echoes of long-vanished phases of Irish life, were important to James.

An emotive photograph taken in 1938 by Gisèle Freund shows the writer (exhausted by Work in Progress, his working title for *Finnegans Wake*) relaxing *en famille* with his son Giorgio and grandson Stephen beneath this very portrait of the infant's great-grandfather, which had by then been transferred to Giorgio's home in the rue Scheffer, in the fashionable Passy district of Paris. As the photographer herself recalled, this photograph was taken at James Joyce's own special request. *Afin d'éterniser quatre générations de Joyce, l'écrivain posa selon son propre désir avec Giorgio et Stephen sous le portrait de son père, John Stanislaus Joyce, peint par l'artiste irlandais, Patrick Tuohy.* Stephen Joyce remembers that his grandfather attached particular importance to this photograph, an importance consistent with his feelings about his family. The group portrait of the four generations was intended to serve as a family icon. Little Stephen had been born in February 1932, just after the demise of old John Stanislaus Joyce in December 1931, a fateful conjunction which James Joyce evoked in his tender poem 'Ecce Puer'.

After his father's death, James Joyce admitted to close friends just what he owed him, not only as a man but as a writer: much of his own work had come directly from his father, and from his father's circle of Dublin friends. Just how true this was we shall see in due course, for in a real sense John Stanislaus Joyce is the ur-author of *Ulysses* and *Finnegans Wake*.

Named in his father's will as his only heir, James Joyce inherited from John Stanislaus Joyce, among other notable characteristics, a very intense pride in their family name. That Joyce pride is still very much alive today in the person of Stephen Joyce. Yet the name of his dead grand-uncle George, given also to his father Giorgio, was a direct invocation of the earliest ancestor known to these Joyces.

John Stanislaus Joyce was able to trace his family line back to his great-grandfather, a certain George Joyce, who flourished about the end of the eighteenth century. But as John Stanislaus was the only son of an only son of an only son, there seemed to be no immediate Joyce relatives by whom the family traditions in which he set such great store could be confirmed. There were plenty of relatives on his mother's and his wife's sides – far too many, John Stanislaus thought – but James Joyce's childhood was curiously free of Joyce connections. A disappointing but convenient situation for his father.

There were (we can now establish) some true Joyce relatives, albeit oddly detached cousins. Before George Joyce the great mist of Irish history had descended, leaving unclear just who these Joyces were and where they came from. What was this family, exactly, in which James Joyce and his father took so much pride, and whose coat of arms was carried with care from home to home across the breadth of Europe?

* * *

All Irish Joyces come ultimately from the Joyce Country in the west of Ireland. This lies between the villages of Cong and Leenane along the banks of the Joyce river, in the Maum Valley to the west of Lough Mask in the northern part of County Galway. The Joyce river flows south along the valley and, joining with another stream, enters Lough Corrib. On the shores of this lake is Cong Abbey, burial place of Roderick O'Connor, the last High King of Ireland, whose name echoes through the pages of *Finnegans Wake*.

Nearby is Ashford Castle, once the seat of the Guinness family, who took one of their titles from a small island in the lake called Ardilaun. The Guinnesses as landlords had usurped the ancient patrimony of the Joyces: but John Stanislaus would live to claim that the first Lord Ardilaun, then Sir Arthur Edward Guinness, had been defeated for Parliament as a result of his campaigning. (John Stanislaus imagined that the Guinnesses were in fact originally from the same part of the country as the Joyces; but this is not true: the first of them was, it seems, a Cromwellian settler from Cornwall.)

Cong marks the eastern end of the Joyce Country. To the north it reaches to Maamtrasna Mountain, above the village where the Maamtrasna murders took place in 1882. Away to the west the border of the Joyce Country lies along the Maumturk Mountains, beyond which are the Twelve Pins (alluded to in the *Wake*.)

The Joyces ('of ancient and honourable English descent', according to Hardiman's *History of Galway*) were a family of Norman-Welsh origin. They came to Connaught in the thirteenth century, intermarried with the native O'Flahertys and became (as the saying was) more Irish than the Irish themselves. The first known of the name was Thomas Joyce, who married Nora O'Brien, daughter of the king of Thomond, in what is now County Clare. His brother Walter was Archbishop of Armagh, resigning the seat to another brother, Roland, in 1311. Roland was confessor to Edward II, England's most notorious homosexual king.

Later some Joyces settled in the town of Athenry and in Galway City – they were numbered among the famous 'Tribes of Galway', providing several mayors for the city. The coat of arms which both John and James made use of was based on the arms of these Joyces – the Joyces of Corgary. Not only did James Joyce own a copy of the arms framed as a decoration, he had them stamped on the binding of a volume of manuscript poems which he had specially made for Nora Joyce, after a difficult passage in their 'marriage'.

In the middle of the nineteenth century the nation-wide valuation records show that the vast majority of Joyces were still to be found either in Galway (some 427 households in eighteen locations), or in Mayo just to the north (214 households in nine locations). However, the third largest concentration of the family name was right down in the south of the country, in East County Cork, where there were eighty-three households in thirty-four locations. It was to these southern Joyces, so curiously separated from their ancestral home, that John Stanislaus belonged. Though the *Tithe Applotment* survey of the 1820s places the Joyces only in the northern part of East Cork, by the 1850s several families of them were found scattered further south, often around Youghal and especially in Cork City itself, where there were some fourteen households, in one of which John Stanislaus Joyce was already a bawling baby.

As there were Joyces recorded at only two locations in Clare, the county lying directly between Galway and Limerick, it is improbable that the clan had spread south through that county. By what roundabout route, then, had they got to Cork? It has been suggested that they were actually Joyes of Wexford, or had some connection with the English Joyces, perhaps even with the regicide George 'Cornet' Joyce, executioner of Charles I, who disappeared from Rotterdam in 1670. But these speculations are unfounded. The true story is a curious one.

To find the missing link in the chain it is necessary to turn south to County Kerry. Some time about 1680, William FitzMaurice, nineteenth of the Lords of Kerry (other more successful Anglo-Norman settlers), required a new steward for the household at his family seat at Lixnaw on the Brick river, a few miles south-west of Listowel in the Barony of Clanmaurice in North Kerry. He found Seán Mór Seoighe (Big John Joyce).

With that Irish form of his name, Seán Mór Seoighe came from Connemara, most likely from in or near the Irish-speaking Joyce Country itself, in that wild area south of Westport, County Mayo. Based close by, over the mountains from Leenane, one of the great families of Galway, the O'Malleys, were at both Westport

6

and Letterfrack, using Killary Harbour and Ballynakill Harbour for their maritime exploits along the west coast of Ireland. One of the O'Malleys was also establishing himself at Kilmeelickin, just north of Maam in the very heart of the Joyce Country. The O'Malleys – of whom the so-called pirate Queen, Grace O'Malley or Granuaile, was one – were friendly with the Kerry FitzMaurices, then a Jacobite family and later opposed to William and Mary. It is possible to surmise that the link was instrumental in bringing about Seán Mór Seoighe's move to the south-west corner of the country, from Connaught to Munster. Indeed, he may have undertaken the journey on an O'Malley vessel, after a recommendation. (There is a tradition, current among the Joyces of Acres, outside Fermoy, that in fact it was two brothers Joyce who had come to Kerry from the Kylemore-Ballynakill district close to Letterfrack. Perhaps it was.)

Seán Mór, with or without his brother, had arrived in Lixnaw twenty years before the eighteenth century began. It was a new world. He was probably something more than what the documentation terms a 'steward' There was real work to be done. It would have been strange to import into Kerry an overseer who knew nothing about local conditions or local families, unless he had some special skill. The family trade of the Joyces of Connaught was working with limestone, as lime-burners, stonemasons and builders; the family is still associated with the limestone and marble quarries of Connemara in the Maum Valley and around Kylemore. Both varieties of stone were found on the lands at Lixnaw (as well, unusually, as coal). Given how much building was to be done over the next years by the FitzMaurices, it is likely that Seán Mór followed the trade of Tim Finnegan in the ballad of 'Finnegan's Wake' and was set in charge of the work. He would prosper in the position.

The thirteenth-century castle at Lixnaw had been demolished in about 1600, to be replaced by a Jacobean mansion called Lixnaw Old Court on the other side of the Brick river. As his new steward arrived, William FitzMaurice began to transform the house into a lavish modern residence and to tame the wilderness around it. Within a generation or two there would be built a mock ruin which could be seen from the house, a building devoted to cockfighting, a family mausoleum and all the appurtenances of a grand country seat. The river was diverted to form scenic curves and a bathing place in the garden, and trees were planted along walks around the estate. Water parties were held and guests entertained lavishly. Old Court was not old, but it became a court in little.

In all this work Seán Mór and later his son Risteárd Caol (Richard the Thin) clearly made themselves indispensable to their masters, for they were given lands nearby to settle. Though the soil around Lixnaw was not rich, it could be much improved by dressing the fields with lime, and no doubt these enterprising and loyal Joyces made the best of what they had been given.

William FitzMaurice had died in March 1697 and was succeeded by Thomas FitzMaurice (who was created Viscount Clanmaurice and First Earl of Kerry on 17 January 1723). Thomas had been married in 1693 to Anne Petty, sister of the Earl of Shelburne and daughter of Sir William Petty of the Down Survey, which mapped the whole island of Ireland for the first time. Sir William held vast estates in south Kerry and, it was said, property in every county in Ireland. Miss Petty was described by Dean Swift, in a letter to Stella, as 'egregiously ugly, but perfectly well bred'. Though the new Earl of Kerry was a terrible tyrant, he was well managed by his prudent and exceedingly wealthy wife, who (according to Lord Lansdowne) 'furnished several houses, supported a style of living superior to any family whatever in Ireland, and with all this improved his fortune'.

His children did not love him, however. Nor did his servants, among whom were the Joyces. But Lixnaw was a special place to be, and the work continued, for Lady Anne further extended the house, adding two fine wings, an elegant library and a chapel with copies of much-admired Raphael cartoons at Hampton Court. Paintings by old masters such as van den Hagen hung in the house also. Tyrant or not, the First Earl of Kerry, who died in March 1742, would have been a good employer for the Joyces.

Seán Mór Joyce's son, Risteárd Caol, in turn had a son, Bernard Rua. Bernard Rua Joyce married a Bríd MacAuliffe of Newmarket, County Cork. In about 1750 some of the Lixnaw descendants of Seán Mór, including Bernard Rua and his family, moved out of Kerry to settle on better lands that the FitzMaurices had also given them at Athlacca, further to the east in County Limerick. (In the middle of the last century the surviving Kerry Joyces, a mere eight households, were nearly all in the Barony of Clanmaurice, the district around Lixnaw.) The reason for this shift may have been the death of William FitzMaurice, the Second Earl of Kerry, at Lixnaw on 4 April 1747, a mere five years after he succeeded. He was said by Lord Lansdowne in his autobiography to have been 'gentleman-like and spirited, but weak and debauched, and married into a very weak family, the Earl of Cavan's'.

His heir, Francis Thomas FitzMaurice, was only six, and was made a ward of court and educated at the direction of the Lord Chancellor of Ireland. Lixnaw went into decline. On coming of age in 1761 Francis Thomas, who did not care much for the old house, abandoned it and afterwards sold his Kerry estates in 1783 to the Hare family of Cork (later the Lords Listowel). All he retained was the family mausoleum at Lixnaw, but that, too, has now vanished. The house had impressed the topographer Charles Smith in 1750, with its extent and its lavish style, its canals and garden vistas; but twenty-five years later Arthur Young visited the estate on his famous tour of Ireland in October 1776 and found that 'All is desolation and everything in ruins' – the walls and roof were being removed by thieves and the trees cut down.

Francis FitzMaurice was 'a simple young Irish peer', according to Horace Walpole, 'who had married an elderly Irishwoman that had been divorced on his account, and had wasted a vast estate in the idlest ostentation'. Having married Mrs Daly, a Catholic heiress from Galway more than twenty years older, he went to live in France. According to his heir, Lord Lansdowne, 'after dissipating nearly all his property the 3rd Earl invested what was left, with equally bad judgement and fortune, in French *assignats*'. However, his surviving papers in the French National Archives reveal a careful and prudent man. He fled the French Revolution and died in England in 1818.

Of Lixnaw Old Court, that seat of culture and refinement which had been admired by so many, where the ancestors of John Stanislaus Joyce learnt the value of hard work and patronage, almost nothing now remains. Time has obliterated the work of Seán Mór Seoighe and his children, but the legacy of his days serving the rich and powerful would persist among the generations that followed. John Stanislaus Joyce was one day to congratulate his son James on 'his receiving such an Honour from his Majesty' when he was awarded a small grant from the Royal Literary Fund: Seán Mór would have felt similarly proud.

These Joyces were clearly not mere tillers of the soil. Given the almost princely importance since medieval times of the Lords of Kerry, patrons of Gaelic poets, friends and relations of those in high places, and the high style in which they lived in the seventeenth and eighteenth centuries, the trusted retainer and agent of the family was in a position that can only have bestowed on Seán Mór Seoighe's descendants a lingering sense of their unique importance in the great scheme of Irish life.

The Joyces established themselves at Athlacca, where they would have found that it was far easier to make a good living from the land than in either Kerry or Connemara. They were on the edge of the 'Golden Vale'; the soil was rich and the grass lush and green. It was great horse country, and it is surely here that the family began in earnest a long and fruitful interest in the horse, an aristocratic animal that brought status and authority to its owner in eighteenth-century Ireland. Whether or not they actually bred horses at this time, the Joyces themselves rapidly proliferated. (By the 1850s there would be some nineteen Joyce households in nine locations scattered along the Cork border in the south-east of County Limerick.) Gearóid Mór, a son of Bernard Rua (who had led the migration from Kerry), settled with his wife, a Maryann Hogan, at Ballyorgan, to the south of Athlacca. Their eldest son was Robert Joyce, known as Roibeárd an Gaelgóir, perhaps because he had a fund of traditional tales and poems (already becoming more precious as the use of Gaelic declined). Roibeárd married an Ann Howard and from her family, the Howards of Howardstown, got in 1783 a parcel of marginal land at Glenosheen (the Glen of Oisin), a hamlet in the northern foothills of the Ballyhoura Mountains, west of Ballyorgan.

Roibeárd an Gaelgóir, recalled by his descendants as a magnificent old gentleman, died in 1828. One of his sons was Garret Joyce (born in 1796), an 'occasionally employed' shoemaker, who married an Elizabeth O'Dwyer. The couple went in about 1826 to live at Lyre na Greinne, on the hillside above Ballyorgan and

Glenosheen. Their children were Michael, John, Patrick Weston and Robert Dwyer Joyce. From this isolated and impoverished beginning these last two brothers would go on to achieve nation-wide fame as writers.

Patrick Weston Joyce (1827–1914) became the celebrated author of *Irish Names of Places*, a book familiar to at least six generations of Irish readers, and of many other works on Irish history, folklore and music, including *Old Celtic Romances*. He was indubitably one of the great literary figures of nineteenth-century Ireland.

His younger brother, Robert Dwyer Joyce (1830–83), became a civil servant and then a doctor. Already known as a poet, he emigrated to Boston, where he practised medicine, at the same time achieving immense literary success with *Ballads of Irish Chivalry* (1872) and *Deirdre* (1876), which sold 10,000 copies in its first week of publication. He returned in 1883 to Dublin, where he died the same year. His patriotic songs were a staple of every nationally minded singer for three generations.

Dotted around the north side of the Ballyhouras there were other little groups of Joyce cousins. Patrick Weston in his *Old Irish Folk Music and Songs* described something of the life they shared, and remembered a typical outing:

My home in Glenosheen, in the heart of the Ballyhoura Mountains, was a home of music and song: they were in the air of the valley; you heard them everywhere – sung, played, whistled; and they were mixed up with the people's pastimes, occupations and daily life. Though we had pipers, fiddlers, fifers, whistlers and singers of our own, wandering musicians were welcomed; and from every one some choice air or song that struck our fancy was sure to be learned and stored up to form part of an ever-growing stock of minstrelsy.

... The people of the village turned out on a sunny day in June to 'foot' the half dry turf in the bog at the back of Seefin mountain which rises straight over Glenosheen; always a joyous occasion for us children. Dinner time came – about 1 o'clock: each family spread the white cloth on a chosen spot on the dry clean bog surface.

There might have been half a dozen groups in that part of the bog, all near each other, and they all sat down to dinner at the same time: glorious smoking hot floury savoury potatoes, salt herrings (hot like the potatoes) and good wholesome *bláthach,* i.e. skimmed thick milk slightly and pleasantly sour – a dinner fit for a hungry king.

After dinner there was always a short interval for rest and diversion – generally rough joyous romping. On this occasion Peggy Moynihan ... sat willingly on a turf bank ... and she gave us the 'Clár Bog Déil' in Irish, with intense passion, while the people, old and young – including myself and my little brother Robert – listened, mute and spellbound.

The habit of song would never desert the Joyces.

The connections of these Joyces are still prominent in Irish life (largely in medicine): a strong line of distinction through several generations. Allusions to both brothers are scattered through James Joyce's own writings. Indeed the image of Parnell as a stag flashing his antlers on the mountainside may have been suggested to him by his boyhood reading of one of Robert Dwyer Joyce's ballads about the area, or by the old tale of the 'uncatchable' stag of the Ballyhouras.

In about 1898 the eldest of the Glenosheen Joyces, Michael Joyce, established a family pedigree from which many of the above family details have been derived. His son was W. B. Joyce, educationalist and author, who also wrote about the history of Dublin. W. B. Joyce's son, Thomas Michael Joyce (1896–1958), was a dentist, who, after many years abroad in England and Wales, returned to Ireland in 1952 and practised in Pearse Street. On 16 June 1954, with Myles na Gopaleen (otherwise Brian O'Nolan and Flann O'Brien), John Ryan, Anthony Cronin, Patrick Kavanagh and Samuel Beckett's friend A. J. Leventhal of Trinity College, he went on the very first Bloomsday expedition, celebrating the fiftieth anniversary of the day on which *Ulysses* is set.

Tom Joyce was there to represent 'the family', being a cousin, however well removed, of James Joyce. Both John Ryan and Anthony Cronin recalled his fine tenor voice, a voice shared by both the Glenosheen Joyces and the Cork Joyces, and almost endemic in the extended Joyce family. During the jaunt, in a pub in Irishtown where they had paused hoping to hear a broadcast of the Ascot Gold Cup, Tom Joyce regaled the party with a beautiful rendering of one of James Joyce's favourite songs, 'Silent, O Moyle'.

In view of the interest which his grandfather had taken in his own lineage, it is very unlikely that Tom Joyce's claim to a relationship with the author of *Ulysses* was false: *these* Joyces had no doubts about who they were, given their family obsession with history. Tom Joyce (then an ex-soldier studying at Trinity College's Dental School) will have been the young man who called upon James Joyce in the autumn of 1922 in Paris and left his card. Joyce thought from his name that he was a son of another Tom Joyce, a cousin of his father's who strangely resembled him, last seen drunk and unsteady at a Clontarf regatta in the late 1890s. But by then the author of *Ulysses* was not anxious to encourage the attentions of remote relatives who might make demands upon him.

James Starkey, otherwise the poet 'Seumas O'Sullivan', an early friend of James Joyce, who lent him money, boots and a toothbrush when he left Ireland in 1904, was aware of the family resemblance between these branches of the Joyces. He later wrote of the striking colour of their eyes, 'a sea-blue which is found so often in the western Joyces. I had as a boy on many occasions met the historian, Patrick Weston Joyce; and [Robert Dwyer Joyce] the author of *The Boys of Wexford* had also this family characteristic, as I was told by my father who knew him intimately [as a medical student] in the sixties. And in James Joyce, author of *Ulysses*, although he may have come from a different branch of the clan, I found it once again.' Aside from the sea-blue eyes, perhaps, too, a similar cast of face had made him aware of a family connection, for Tom Joyce resembled both John Stanislaus Joyce and Stanislaus Joyce, and they in turn resembled P. W. and R. D. Joyce.

If they were all part of the same extended family, how had our Joyces become separated? As Roibeárd an Gaelgóir had got his land from his wife's people he cannot have been part of the main line of Athlacca Joyces with an interest in that family property. Our Joyces' remote ancestor, George Joyce of Fermoy, was recalled (by James Joyce for his first biographer Herbert Gorman) as 'a man of property' (an ambiguous phrase in the circumstances of eighteenth-century Ireland). Given the dates involved, it appears that George Joyce was the son of a John Joyce, the brother or cousin of Roibeárd an Gaelgóir. Certainly the relationship must have been a close one for it to have been recalled by Michael Joyce's side of the family, though the surviving documents in family hands do not detail it. (In the immediate family of the Ballyorgan Joyces what became of Michael's second brother John is unclear. John, though a family name among John Stanislaus Joyce's forebears, was not later used by the Joyces of Glenosheen, perhaps because it was in common use in another line of the family.)

Understandably, there was no room on the Limerick lands for all the members of the expanding Joyce clan. In time these landless Joyces began to cross the Ballyhoura Hills into north Cork, a mere matter of a few miles to the south, settling in the Blackwater Valley. There was soon a cluster of them around the new garrison town of Fermoy, which the entrepreneur John Anderson (who had bought the estate from Lord Fermoy in 1791) began to develop after 1797. The town was on the main route between Dublin and Cork, and busy with postal and military traffic. There are records of John Joyces and even a James there in early Victorian times, working as masons, lime-burners and publicans.

As the novelist Elizabeth Bowen observed, the Blackwater Valley was a very different world from Limerick or from Tipperary, over the mountains to the north. Her family seat, Bowen's Court, was just south of the Ballyhoura Hills. And in this different world, some of the Joyces would soon forget about their origins on the other side of the Ballyhouras.

These very valleys from which his ancestors came are alluded to by James Joyce in 'Davin's story' in *A Portrait of the Artist as a Young Man*. This suggests that he may well have had some inkling about their importance in his family's history. (The character of Davin was based on Joyce's Limerick friend, George Clancy, a keen supporter of Gaelic sports.) The setting of the incident, ten miles to the south of Killmallock on the road through the hills to Buttevant, places it almost exactly at Glenosheen. Could the peasant woman who tries to lure the sexual innocent to her bed ('Come in and stay the night here. You've no call to be frightened. There's no one in it but ourselves.') have been the unhappy wife of a Joyce – whom Stephen Dedalus sees as 'a type of her race and his own, a batlike soul waking to the consciousness of itself in darkness and secrecy and loneliness and, through the eyes and voice and gesture of a woman without guile, calling a stranger to her bed'?

*   *   *

Winding south from Ardpatrick and Glenosheen, the road passes over the Ballyhoura Mountains and down into a valley which opens out into the vale where the River Blackwater flows. On the road is Kildorrery, a little over a mile to the west of which lies Bowen's Court, where the Glenosheen Joyces often went for the fair, and beyond that is Doneraile, long the parish of novelist Canon Sheehan (in whom James Joyce was keenly interested). Here also was the home of Elizabeth St Leger, the daughter of the First Lord Doneraile, who overheard a Masonic ceremony in her father's house, and was enrolled as the first (but not the only) female Mason. The story, perhaps passed on by John, is alluded to in *Ulysses*. Near here, too, is Kilcolman Castle, once the property of the poet Spenser. But for most Irish people of the nineteenth century the town meant the Doneraile Conspiracy, the subject of Canon Sheehan's novel, *Glenanaar*.

Then the road goes south through Rockmills to Glanworth. Some of the Joyces settled here, others at Kilworth, others still at Acres. The road comes down from Glanworth to a place on the outskirts of Fermoy a little to the east of the grand house and estate of Castlehyde – celebrated in poetry as 'Sweet Castle Hyde', attributed to Robert Dwyer Joyce. Castlehyde had been sold by the Hydes in 1851 in the Encumbered Estates Court and had been bought by the brewer Arthur Guinness – the family here again crossing the traces of the Joyces. From him it was bought in 1856 by John Sadlier, the notorious Irish politician who brought about the demise of the first Irish Independent Party of the 1850s.

In the middle ages the main road crossed the River Blackwater by a bridge just to the west of present-day Fermoy. Even today the old medieval road can be followed down a narrow defile between the lands of Castlehyde and Grange Farm to the riverbank where the ancient wooden bridge once was. And it is on this old road that Rose Cottage (now called Grange Cottage) stands, where the father of John Stanislaus Joyce was born in 1827.

Today the farm buildings consist not only of the original cottage, but also of stables, yards and even a forge. The lane is still called Joyce's Lane. Nearby, there are extensive quarries and an abandoned lime kiln. Limestone working and horses were the dominant features of the life at Rose Cottage: the Joyces when they arrived took every advantage of both the presence of a large British military encampment and the rapid development of Fermoy town itself, supplying mounts to the one and building supplies to the other. Rose Cottage was in the heart of hunting country, and J. R. O'Flanagan's 1844 book on the Blackwater river – his family lived in Grange Farm House across the lane – is full of tales of the local hunt and its dashing ways.

George Joyce, the earliest Joyce to be mentioned by James and the one who moved to Rose Cottage, was likely to have been born in south Limerick in or soon after 1776, and to have been named after George Washington. (Washington remained something of a hero in Cork: Great Georges Street, named for the Hanoverians, was renamed Washington Street in the 1920s.) He had a son, James Joyce, who married an Ann McCann 'of Ulster'. Their son, James Augustine Joyce, was born here at Rose Cottage in 1827. He was the father in turn of John Stanislaus Joyce. Here at least is firmer ground, for his own father's birthday was the earliest date that John Stanislaus knew for certain in his family history.

James Joyce's statement to Gorman that his father came 'from an old Cork family that once possessed extensive holdings' leaves it unclear whether he was referring to some medieval context, or to the situation at about 1800, approximately when George Joyce's son James was born. For Catholics of the period, outside of certain classes, the idea of extensive holdings is nonsense. Probably what the writer had in mind was not landed property, but the later city properties in Cork.

On a visit to Cork as a child in 1894 with John Stanislaus, the young James was to hear his great-grandfather, James Joyce the elder, from whom his own name came, extolled by one of the older generation of Corkonians as a 'fierce old fire-eater'. In his youth he was said to have been a Whiteboy, one of those agrarian terrorists who ravaged Munster from 1760 onwards – this must have been in the early 1820s. There was at this time a great deal of disturbance in Munster.

A special Act of Parliament was passed to deal with the Whiteboys in 1822. Much of the province was in a state of armed insurrection: in north Cork bands of Whiteboys came down from the hills to raid the towns for arms and food. The military were called out and many arrests were made. At a special assize in Cork City in mid-February 1823 some 300 prisoners were dealt with, of whom thirty-six were sentenced to death. Mixed up with these agrarian troubles were the activities of Rockites, a group, strong in the vicinity, who were linked to the Whiteboys but had also been inspired by the writings of Pastorini into a millenarian belief that the end of the world was imminent and that all the Protestants would be destroyed. They gave history a helping hand by burning them out and killing them. The Anglican church at Athlacca was burnt, and much of Glenosheen was put to the torch at this time as well, as it contained a settlement of Palatine Protestants.

The family tradition was that James Joyce was to have been hanged; but the government in fact released most of the prisoners to assuage the widespread disaffection. His radicalism and fervent anticlericalism confirms the family's status as small tenant farmers. Catholic priests of the nineteenth century were nearly always the sons of gentry, strong farmers or merchants: their spiritual influence owed much to their social standing in the community. In a period when there were few professions for educated men, the priesthood offered opportunities to many younger sons of better families. The Joyces were not as yet in that class. It was from his resentful and embittered grandfather that John Stanislaus derived his own anticlericalism, which in turn was passed on to his sons James and Stanislaus.

The radical James (as the old Corkonian recalled also) was a keen rider to hounds. But as readers of Somerville & Ross will realise, to follow the local hunt was no real indication of superior social standing in rural Ireland; it demanded nothing more than the ability to keep a horse. Many farmers and others of the Joyces' class were as keen on the chase as any sprig of the big house. It was from him that the later Joyces inherited one of their most prized possessions, a hunting waistcoat decorated with the heads of dogs and stags. James Joyce the writer himself wore it on ceremonial family occasions such as his birthday.

James Augustine Joyce, that child born at Rose Cottage in 1827, who became the father of John Stanislaus, was the only son born to old James and Anne. This unusual fact (at a time when Irish families often ran to fifteen children) suggests that emotionally and sexually all may not have been well with the marriage. However, the Joyces prospered in Fermoy. The cottage's position and its extensive stabling suggests that the connection with horses was not only for the army but also for stage coaches, then the usual means of transport through Ireland. These were largely run by Charles Bianconi, a relation of the O'Connells, based in Clonmel.

At a later date Rose Cottage and further properties in Fermoy were held by various other Joyces. There were six brothers who worked on the new bridge over the river there, some of whom are said to have been among the immigrant builders of St Patrick's Cathedral in New York City. Other Joyce properties and businesses are also recorded. There was a John Joyce running a public house in King's Square in Fermoy. And the family remains in the area to this day.

Before dealing with the further migrations of the Joyces from country to city, we might pause and take stock of just what this family history reveals. First, that the father of the author of *Ulysses* came of stock that can be traced back with some certainty step by step to Gaelic-speaking Connaught. Second, that though some members of the family, such as those settled in the hill country at Glenosheen, were happy to retain and cultivate their Gaelic culture (which they then put to literary use), others were keener to take hold of the commercial advantages offered by the development of Ireland and Cork in the early nineteenth century. One detects a set of opportunists, perhaps in the mould of Seán Mór Seoighe.

Literature and music seem to have characterised the Joyces for generations. But more importantly, we can now place John Stanislaus exactly in the course of Irish history, in that culturally significant shift from the medieval Gaelic-speaking life of Seán Mór Seoighe in 1680 to the anglophone entrepreneurism fostered by the growth of commerce in Cork.

Within a couple of generations they had lost touch with their Gaelic roots and all memory of that past had seemingly evaporated. The vital love of language and music would take a different form, blossoming later in the vigour of John Stanislaus's witty speech, the precision of James Joyce's writings and the love both had for song, which reached down even to James's son Giorgio.

John Stanislaus and his son were happy to allude airily to remote Connaught ancestors with coat-armour, but not to the hill farmers and small tradesmen who were their immediate relatives. They wished to be gentlemen, not peasants.

Soon after the birth in 1827 of James Augustine Joyce at Rose Cottage, his father and grandfather left Fermoy and moved to Cork City. A deed of 16 July 1830 records the purchase by George Joyce of a property at White Street from Richard Gould, a salt and lime maker (listed in *Slater's Royal Directory* for 1846, still in the same area). The property consisted of a yard and a plot of land, then occupied by the stables of a Charles Connell (or O'Connell) and part of a bowling green running along forty-three feet of the street. This site was later to become 14 and 15 White Street and the seven adjoining houses down an alley would be called Joyce's Court. White Street connects George's Quay along the River Lee with Douglas Street and the actual site lies directly behind the Catholic church of St Finbarre South on Dunbar Street. White Street was named after the architect Henry White for whom James Joyce the elder acted as executor after his death in 1842. This deed of purchase is the last we hear of George Joyce; having settled his family in the great city, he vanishes from history.

The Joyces were well enough established by now to have their portraits painted. The famous gallery in James Joyce's Paris apartment began with a portrait of James Joyce the elder painted (according to expert opinion) in the 1840s, and one of Anne McCann Joyce. The significance of the pictures is that they embody the new bourgeois life of the Joyces. There is nothing backward-looking about these portraits, though in style they are stiff and provincial. They represent a self-made generation, anxious to demonstrate in paint and gilt their own prosperity.

And still their prosperity grew. There was much commercial activity. James Joyce and a business partner, Jeremiah Joseph O'Connor, leased in 1835 a salt and lime works at Carrigeeny; they were to sell it in 1842 for £500. The *Cork Post Office Directory* for 1842-3 lists 'James Joyce Horse Trainer, 12 Winthrop Street' and 'James Joyce Salt Lime Manufacturer, 16 White Street and South Terrace' – again the connection with horses and lime goes back to Rose Cottage and beyond. (Winthrop Street lay just off Cork's main thoroughfare, St Patrick's Street, while South Terrace was a new and respectable development on the edge of the city.)

By now it seems certain that old George Joyce was dead; his son James, as head of the family, continued to consolidate the Joyce assets, his name appearing frequently in the records at this time. *The County and City of Cork Almanack* for 1843 still lists the salt and lime works, but shows that the stables had been moved to 7 Caroline Street. This address soon disappears, however, and later directories mention only the premises at White Street and another acquisition at Anglesea Street.

This property, where James Joyce already had stables, was leased (on 7 January 1846) from Sir Thomas Deane for a period of 200 years. To the west were stables belonging to a Mr Pennefather. The directory for this year names James Joyce as both a Horse Dealer at 36 George's Street and a Lime Burner at South Terrace. This was the situation when in 1847 his only son, James Augustine Joyce, married Ellen O'Connell, the daughter of John O'Connell, whose family was connected with the great Daniel O'Connell, the Liberator. (It may be that the bride and groom were already in some way related: both of their mothers were McCanns from the north of Ireland.) It was believed later (by Stanislaus Joyce, the writer's brother) that the marriage had been arranged by the priest, 'to steady the young man'.

This period of Irish history was dominated by the figure of Daniel O'Connell, much as the latter part of the century would be by Parnell. In 1828 he had been elected MP for Clare, but was unable to take his seat until the next year, when the Catholic Emancipation Act was passed. The O'Connells were an old and extensive family; the name is a common one throughout Kerry and Cork. From the wealthy landed gentry of Derrynane, Daniel O'Connell's Kerry home, who could trace their pedigree back to the fourteenth century, sprang the O'Connells of Tarmons, also in Kerry. When the land at Tarmons was sold in 1785, these O'Connells moved into Cork where they became successful merchants, primarily in the drapery business. They fell into trade, just as the Joyces were hoping to rise out of it. Yet this was a relationship which Daniel O'Connell himself had been pleased to recognise. On his annual visits to Cork for the Assizes before his election to Parliament he always made a point of calling on his cousins in Fishamble Street near the Old Court House. There (in a vignette recalled by John Stanislaus's mother), the great man would walk arm in arm with her grand-father, Charles O'Connell, up and down the street between the Franciscan chapel and South Main Street, both men wearing the knee-breeches fashionable in those days.

Almost the last act of Daniel O'Connell's legal career was to defend at the Cork Assizes the Doneraile Conspirators, twenty-one men from the town who were charged with conspiracy to murder various Cork worthies. O'Connell saved many of them from the gallows by managing to have the all-Protestant jury replaced with a more balanced one. His arrival at short notice at the Court House was to form a key scene in Canon Sheehan's novel, *Glenanaar*. Few who could claim an immediate link with the Liberator were shy of proclaiming the fact: he was the most famous man in Ireland and the Joyces were proud to have married into his clan.

Ellen O'Connell, born in 1816, was a full decade older than her husband and was to have been a nun. She and her sister Alicia, educated by the Cork Ursulines, had entered South Presentation Convent, Cork, in October 1836, but Ellen left after four months. Alicia went on to take the habit on 13 April 1837 and two years later made her profession there before Bishop Murray of Cork and Fr Theobald Mathew, the Chaplain Superior of the convent. The reasons for Ellen's defection are preserved in the records there:

It was a matter of her own choosing. She became nervously and unnecess-arily anxious about her health, which was not, in reality *bad*. She had just finished the fourth month of her Postulantship. She was a nice, amiable and good girl – *too good*, to encounter the rough seas of this world; where she can scarcely escape the meeting of many a rock and many a breaker – but, little as her religious training has been, may she have learnt in her short Noviciate, to look up only to the *one eye*, that steadily and securely guides, each bark of this uncertain life.

It must remain a moot question whether the delicate, hysterical personality suggested by this record was ever really suited to married life. Her portrait certainly reveals an anxious and over-sensitive face, and her later years would be blighted by jealousy and bitterness.

Ellen O'Connell was (as Stanislaus Joyce later recalled) one of nineteen children. Her family believed in education. A brother, Charles, would be sent to Queen's College, Cork, where he was remembered by his contemporaries as a skilled botanist, and later became a priest. Ellen's schooling with the Ursuline nuns was the epitome of respectable education in those days, and her leather-bound French prayer books were still in the family attic in the 1880s, 'the symbol of culture in Cork when she was a girl.' Though James A. Joyce began as a fervent Catholic, he too became anticlerical, and in time would pass on this attitude to his son. Yet these clerical influences were always an important part of life in contemporary Cork.

James Augustine Joyce and Ellen O'Connell were married in the church of SS Peter and Paul, Paul Street, Cork, on 29 January 1847. As was then common, their marriage was followed by a post-nuptial settlement, signed on 28 February 1848; this was an agreement that was to have far-reaching consequences. Earlier that month James Joyce senior had acquired from William Pennefather (then of Island House) the property in Anglesea Street. Further property was bought on 24 February. By the terms of the settlement John O'Connell assigned £1000 to James Augustine Joyce as a marriage portion; and the bride's grandfather, out of the great love he bore him (according to the deed), gave him a half share in lands at Skahard (now a public park) and on Goat Island in the Douglas river. For his part James A. Joyce or his father put into trust the properties around White and Anglesea Streets. The trustees were a Michael Murphy and the bride's brother, William O'Connell, then a draper in Castle Street. The contributions of the Joyce and O'Connell families were about equal, though the O'Connell name carried more social prestige, and they had real wealth.

The family portrait gallery shows John Stanislaus's parents as they were close to the time of their marriage. The portrait of Ellen is likely to have been done about now; that of James Augustine as a young man perhaps a little earlier. The pictures make evident her maturity in comparison to his almost juvenile appearance. Some time in the early 1860s the mature James Augustine would have his portrait painted again, by a fashionable artist in Cork, to match more conventionally that of his wife. These three paintings would retain a special significance for their son, John Stanislaus, as they represented those who had really loved him. James Augustine was a man of 'angelic temper', but he was also a little shiftless. Ellen Joyce was a woman with a sharp tongue. Once as newly-weds they were out for a country walk when it came on to rain. They took refuge in a roadside cottage, but when the rain showed no sign of clearing, Ellen sent her husband to the nearest village for a car to take them back into Cork City. The woman of the house said mildly, looking after the disappearing figure: 'Sure that's a fine young man, God bless him. I suppose now, ma'am, you're his mother.' 'No, faith,' said the newly married wife, with bitter wit, 'I'm his grandmother.'

On 4 July 1849 Ellen Joyce was delivered of a son and James Augustine collected ten guineas from a friend whom he had bet that he would be the first to become a father. The boy was baptised two days later (sponsored by his relatives William and Ellen O'Connell) and was christened John Stanislaus Joyce. He was to be their only son, remarkably the third only son in succession. Here again a Joyce marriage appears to have foundered on the rocks of sexual feeling, or the lack of it. In his own life John Stanislaus would prove to have the fecundity for which the O'Connells rather than the Joyces were famous – and Daniel O'Connell infamous. In his own day it was said (untruly, modern historians believe) that one could not throw a stick over a workhouse wall in Cork or Kerry without striking a bastard offspring of the Liberator. Yet in later life John Stanislaus would treat his own eldest surviving child James as if he too were another only son. It was a privileged position, being the sole heir to a dynasty of Joyces, as John Stanislaus Joyce would soon learn.

CHAPTER 2

The Son of a Gentleman

John Stanislaus Joyce may have talked of those in the portraits as being the only people who had ever really loved him, but little is known about the details of his childhood. Though he delighted in children and in later life would often embarrass their parents by stopping to talk with them on the street, his own very early years were not a subject that interested him much as a source of anecdote. This alone suggests a childhood in which little Jack, as he was known, was the object of all adult attention in the family. But the family background can be built up in some detail, and this furnishes some idea of the circumstances in which the boy was reared and of the origin of attitudes he would carry to the end of his life.

Even before a child is aware of its relations, or of the wider world, it is conscious of the place where it is brought up. Thomas Hood's 'I remember I remember, the house where I was born' was a familiar recitation of the period. The Joyces resided now in Anglesea Street, just off South Terrace. This was then a most respectable address, with large, even grand, Georgian houses along it. The Joyce house had perhaps twelve or fourteen rooms and stood in its own grounds where Copley Street ran into Angelsea Street. Behind and beside it were the various other yards in which the business was carried on. Though the house has now disappeared, contemporary maps show an imposing double-fronted building with two curving paths round the front garden to a large entrance gate. The streets in the neighbourhood were still being developed: in the early 1850s this would have seemed a very nice address. Later the Corn Market, the Haymarket and the lines of tracks leading into one of the city's railway terminuses of the

Cork, Bandon and South Coast Railway would be built opposite, and beyond them the imposing gas holders of the Cork Gas Works.

It was here, among the strange mixture of lace curtains and polished silver, horse dung and bad drains that epitomised Victorian middle-class life, that John Stanislaus was raised. Though Anglesea Street stood on the edge of Cork City at that date, this was merely an indication that it was new and modern. Certainly it was a respectable enough area: the Church of Ireland Bishop of Cork had his palace on South Terrace, where there was also a Jewish Synagogue. The arrival of the railways and markets a little to the east may not (to Victorian eyes) have meant a great deal.

The city was also easy to escape from. There were relatives of John's mother living in some comfort at Sunday's Wells outside Cork; and at Monkstown on Cork Harbour there were places for holidays. Young John would also have been taken on trips to the seaside at Passage West and later perhaps as far as Blarney to visit its famous castle. Though James Joyce the writer, for all his words, never kissed the Blarney Stone there, it is highly probable that his father did.

The family house in Anglesea Street was called Rose Cottage, after the ancestral home in Fermoy. With its space and style, it may have marked John Stanislaus with an idea of what was due in life to a gentleman's son. What the family's possessions were is not now known, except for the paintings which were already an important part of the Joyce tradition. (No portrait of John Stanislaus was added during these Cork years and why he was not painted must be a mystery: it is likely that family troubles in the mid-1860s precluded such an extravagance.) However, in the house there would have been a good number of solid oak cupboards, tables and chairs made by rural craftsmen; some of these no doubt came with George Joyce when he moved from Fermoy. And there must have been servants. The new Rose Cottage was a comfortable, respectable environment for a young boy to grow up in.

By now the two Jameses, father and grandfather of John Stanislaus, were in partnership together as 'salt and lime manufacturers and chapmen', or merchants. What survives of their business dealings in the records concerns the buying and selling of land, and their ownership of a brickfield outside Cork. In 1852 the brickfield is noted in Griffith's *Rates Valuation*, the official record of lands in Ireland, their owners and their values. The sale of lands at Ballinasmought on the north side of the city is also recorded in a deed of 1853.

But business, perhaps because of the post-Famine decline in Ireland, was not good. Towards the end of 1852, James Joyce & Son was declared bankrupt. The finalisation of the proceedings involved a trip to the bankruptcy court in Dublin and took place there before Commissioner Macan on 25 February 1853. This was the second and final meeting for audit, proof of debts and payment of a first and final dividend. The company was able to pay 2s.6d. in the pound. John's father is said to have been made bankrupt a second time, but there is no formal trace of this in the Bankruptcy Indices from 1857–72, while there are references to both William O'Connell (No. 1280) and John O'Connell (No. 1293). (Not all the files are indexed, however.)

The 1852 'bankruptcy' may have amounted to very little. For many people it could be a very loose term covering other kinds of insolvency, and often it was a device to avoid debts by businessmen who were soon as active as they had ever been. The Joyces had already divested themselves of the White Street property by transferring it into the trusteeship of Ellen Joyce's brother, William O'Connell, most probably as a temporary measure to avoid losing it. Certainly by 1856 James Joyce senior was established again as a builder, with premises at 61 Douglas Street, just to the south of White Street. Stanislaus Joyce knew of his great-grandfather's reputation as a 'prosperous builder', the final apotheosis of the fierce old fire-eater. He can scarcely have been sixty, but James Joyce the elder seems to have died towards the end of the decade. It is likely that he was buried not in Cork but in the ancestral plot in Fermoy.

Inevitably the O'Connell connection was a dominant one in the child's life. His other grandfather, John O'Connell, would also die in the late 1850s, so that all that John Stanislaus really knew of him came from his mother's stories, like the one about Daniel O'Connell and his knee-breeches. But John O'Connell belonged to a small group of prominent Catholic traders, who included his own grandson, John Daly, and his nephew, Peter Paul McSwiney, influential figures in Cork and, later, nationally.

Possible bankruptcies notwithstanding, these O'Connells still had their drapery business at 15 and 16 Great George's Street. On 29 September 1856 a further lease for 764 years was taken out on the back offices and premises there leading out on to Tobin Street. This would be the imposing warehouse and shop that John Stanislaus was often taken to visit as a young boy. William O'Connell now also had his own linen shop in Castle Street. The family was firmly established in the political life of the city as well. In 1841 William's (and Ellen's) father John, along with other Catholics, had been elected to Cork Corporation and by 1850 he had become an Alderman for the St Patrick's Ward.

It was not only in Cork that the O'Connells and their connections had been thriving. In 1841 Daniel O'Connell had been made Lord Mayor of Dublin – a breakthrough in Catholic politics. And in 1845 he was pulled through the streets of Cork on a triumphal car, a last hurrah before the Famine. He died in May 1847. Then, in 1852, Peter Paul McSwiney moved to Dublin with George Delaney, in anticipation of the International Exhibition of 1853, and soon afterwards opened his New Mart in a prime city-centre position facing the General Post Office in Sackville Street. A millionaire in modern terms, McSwiney was an example of the success that the fortunes of business could now bestow in Ireland on a few far-seeing Catholics. James A. Joyce admired the fortune, but had no desire to emulate the hard work of the O'Connells and McSwineys – nor, indeed, of their successors the Clerys, Lombards, Sullivans and Healys. Still, the phrase 'my cousin Peter Paul McSwiney' would long remain part of the verbal stock-in-trade of his son, John Stanislaus Joyce.

Used to relative prosperity all his life, James A. Joyce was not of the same metal as his late father or grandfather. He was dependent on his wife's people; the couple may even for a while have lived with or near the O'Connells in Sunday's Wells, the attractive suburb on the north-west of the city, as Stanislaus Joyce later hinted. Stanislaus by then had come to resent the 'large, square, low-fronted' O'Connell features found among members of his family and refers to his father's 'O'Connell snout', preferring what he thought of as the fairer features of the Joyce face, even though he did not share them.

After old James Joyce's death, John's father appears to have abandoned the family trade entirely. It was his father-in-law, Alderman John O'Connell, who secured for him a municipal sinecure as Inspector of Hackney Coaches (or 'jingles'), with an office in the City Hall. This post, an ideal position for a worthy gentleman who had failed in business, was overseen by a subcommittee of the Corporation, officially called the 'Jingle Committee'. Ellen Joyce can only have been disappointed by this development, however: she had her own ideas of respectability, as her elegantly posed portrait suggests. The conviction that the world owed the Joyces a living seems to have begun with her husband and would be enthusiastically embraced by her son; her grandson James Joyce, too, would not repudiate this particular family tradition when the time came. All three generations would always believe in the benefit of a word in the right ear.

In about 1856 John Stanislaus made his First Holy Communion at the South Presentation Convent in Douglas Street, where it is likely he also received his early education. He was prepared by his aunt, Alicia O'Connell (now Sister Xavier). She, who had remained at the convent when her sister Ellen had left, was an exceptional personality and, so the Joyces later claimed, would almost single-handedly found another convent of Presentation nuns, incorporating a school, in Crosshaven, a hamlet on the sea, near the city. If we can judge by the man, her young nephew may not have been particularly religious, even though his family connections were.

James A. Joyce was friendly (as John later recalled) with Fr Theobald Mathew, one of the most charismatic figures of the day in Cork or Ireland. One of Fr Mathew's associates in organising the temperance movement was a John O'Connell, a Cork merchant who later moved to Queenstown and was probably yet another relative in the extended web of the O'Connell clan. Having become involved with a temperance society begun by Cork Quakers, the priest was the driving force behind the total abstinence movement that swept Ireland in the years after the Famine, when thousands took the pledge. The sway of drink and religion in Ireland manifested itself for John Stanislaus early in his life. Though his father would have known Fr Mathew through the O'Connell and South Chapel links, given his unsteady nature it may be that James A. Joyce too was for a time a repentant drunkard (much like the one represented in Haverty's famous painting of the day).

In trying to assess the religious culture of John Stanislaus's youth, we should remember that the habits of the Georgian period, including a certain laxity of faith, lingered longer in Ireland than across the water. The controversy over the restoration of the Catholic hierarchy in England (characterised as 'Papal aggression') was less important than the decrees of the 1850 Synod of Thurles and the elevation of Dr Cullen as Archbishop of Dublin and Primate of Ireland. Cullen's views would largely shape the public face of the Catholic Church in Ireland for the rest of John Stanislaus's life. To him would be owed much that came to be accepted as 'traditional Catholicism', while much that had been traditional, especially in rural Ireland, such as patterns and wakes, would be frowned upon and suppressed by the priests. With their drinking and rough lewdness, wakes were especially ill thought of.

The reforms initiated by Cullen marked a new kind of ultramontanism which was inimical to certain Irish habits of mind. Determined that the Church should be the dominant feature of Irish life, Cullen had to contend with the descendants of such anticlericals as old James Joyce, who thought religion all very fine for the women, but that it should not be allowed to interfere with business or politics. The two streams washed around the early years of the infant John Stanislaus.

The public excitements of the period would have been only rumours for the child. The Famine, or its legacy, never seems to have been part of John Stanislaus's imagination. The visit of Queen Victoria to Cork in 1849 was certainly an event and gave rise to the foundation of the Queen's College, Cork. Perhaps he felt the earthquake on 10 November 1852. The Cork Exhibition of 1852 was a provincial imitation of the Great Exhibition but Cork, being then a wealthier city in so many ways than Dublin, had its own importance. Cork's wealth was built on butter and beef exports, army supplies and transatlantic shipping. The Crimean War, stark tragedy as it was for many Irish soldiers, at the Charge of the Light

Brigade, for example, was for Cork an opportunity for enterprise. The transatlantic cable from Valentia Island was opened on 5 August 1858, followed in December by a meeting in Dublin of bankers, merchants and others to plan a transatlantic seaport on the west coast of Ireland to rival Liverpool. That James Joyce would later write about this suggests that the Cork interest must have been involved and likely impinged on the Joyce–O'Connell nexus. In the late portrait of John's father there is in the background a small ship clearing a harbour mouth – a further indication perhaps of those shipping associations which connected the Joyces with the Hearns, another local family involved with maritime trade.

But for young John Stanislaus there was something more important than religion or business, despite their influence on the lives of his relatives. A dominant feature of his early childhood, as of his adult life, was music, whether made at home or encountered in church or, a little later, in the theatre. As he himself recalled while he was growing up there was much gossip-mongering about famous singers of the day. One of these figures was the premier basso cantante Luigi Lablache (1794–1858), who John Stanislaus thought was from Cork – in fact, though his mother was Irish, Lablache was born in France and reared and trained in Italy. As an old man, John Stanislaus spoke of the singer in an interview. (As with all extracts used here from this valuable source, eccentricities of spelling and punctuation have been preserved.)

La Blache? He was from Cork too. There was a man named Jeremiah Blake in Cork. He was a shoemaker and he had a son called John Blake who had a great bass voice. I remember Jerry Blake on one occasion talking about his son John and speaking like this, said: 'My son John was in London the other day and when going along the Strand he met the great La Blache who asked him how he was. My son John said that he was very well' – and the old man added, 'You know my son John is a full octave lower than La Blache.'

Though already well known in Italy, Lablache made his London début only in March 1830, but was an immediate success there. As a child he had sung in the memorial service for Haydn and he sang, too, in Mozart's requiem for Beethoven. He was also one of the thirty-two torch-bearers at Beethoven's funeral and was for a time Queen Victoria's singing master. As Lablache's last years were clouded by illness, this encounter with John Blake must have taken place in 1856, and John Stanislaus would have overheard the story from Jeremiah Blake at about the age of six or seven. Jeremiah Blake (like John Blake's other son, Denis) was a shoemaker – an important enough business in those days – with premises then at 59 George's Street, quite near the new Theatre Royal. His eldest son, Jeremiah Charles, was a prominent Cork attorney-at-law from 1853 onwards, followed in turn by his son Alfred. These legal and mercantile interests were enough to ensure that the O'Connells and Joyces knew the Blakes, and the memory, slight as it is, provides a graphic illustration of the odd mixture of provincialism and sophistication that characterised Cork musical circles. Be that as it may, from his earliest years, music, especially song, became a central and determining feature in the imaginative life of John Stanislaus Joyce.

This undemanding childhood came to an end at the age of nine, when John was sent away to school at Fermoy in the spring of 1859.

CHAPTER 3

At St Colman's

On St Patrick's Day (17 March) 1859, John Stanislaus Joyce was entered at St Colman's College in Fermoy, where his education was supposed to begin in earnest.

He was nine years and eight months old. He would remain, apart from the brief summer vacation, only until 19 February 1860, according to records, now untraceable in Ireland, that were provided to James Joyce's chief biographer, Richard Ellmann, by Rev. D. F. Duggan, President of St Colman's. Herbert Gorman, his first biographer, however, drawing on his subject's own testimony, says that John was there for three years – that is until 1862; the account books for the early years suggest that the average pupil stayed for two and a half years. The missing papers may provide, one day, the truth of the duration of John's stay at the school.

St Colman's was the Diocesan College for the Catholic diocese of Cloyne. It stood on the brow of a hill on the south side of Fermoy, flanked by St Patrick's Church, the Catholic Presbytery (or priest's house), and the Convents of the Presentation and Loreto nuns. The college contained not only a seminary 'for the preparatory education and training of the youth of this diocese aspiring to the ecclesiastical states' (according to the letter to his priests written by the bishop, Dr Keane, the founder), but also a secondary school for the sons of gentlemen. Keane, as the local novelist Canon Sheehan recalled, was at this time the 'most popular and well beloved bishop in Ireland' and had 'the reputation of being a strong, almost an extreme nationalist': he entertained, for example, the Fenian leader James F. X. O'Brien at the college on his release from prison in 1869.

The pupils came from all over Munster, but not all of them slept in the college. Some boys, such as Peter O'Leary, later a noted Gaelic writer and priest, who arrived in May 1859, took lodgings in the town and attended as day students, which was cheaper than boarding. John Stanislaus, who had connections in Fermoy (such as the owner of the pub in King's Square, just below the college), was not to be a boarder. Fr Peter O'Leary (who mentions his experiences at St Colman's in his autobiography) says the fees for boarders were thirty guineas a year; whereas those boarding out paid only six guineas. The surviving records (such as they are) show a payment by Joyce *père* of seven guineas, which covers fees plus extras, such as music. But where exactly John Stanislaus boarded out is not known.

The college, constructed in the fashionable Italianate style with a campanile, was built in the local red sandstone with limestone facings. From the terrace one can look north over Fermoy towards Castlehyde, Acres and in the distance the blue haze of the Ballyhoura Hills. This edifice was new. The college had been proposed at the end of 1857, and was built in a few months under the supervision first of the parish priest and then of the great Dr Croke, still the Catholic curate of Mallow. It opened its gates to receive students in September 1858. Croke, according to his biographer, was to leave his mark on his students, inculcating the 'two great College virtues – humility and obedience'. These were not qualities to be noted in John Stanislaus Joyce.

John Stanislaus was one of the first draft of approximately 109 boys, some of whom were intended for the secular priesthood. From contemporary sources (such as Canon Sheehan, Fr Peter O'Leary and William O'Brien, the maverick nationalist politician whose brother went to St Colman's) it is possible to reconstruct what his first experiences would have been. Probably in an open conveyance, with his parents he would have been driven up the sloping drive to the front door (at that date on the west side) and then ushered through the hall into the

bare, shiny, beeswaxed little reception-parlour, furnished as ascetically as a cell in the Thebaid; a rough table, with a jug of cold water – it looked like ice-water – on the same; an expanse of uncarpeted floor suggestive

of rigid Lenten regulations; whitewashed walls staring you out of countenance with their chastity; and a morsel of fire in the grate barely sufficient
to act as a satiric sting of the flesh to anybody who should apply for
comfort for unmortified appetites in that quarter.

There would also have been other parents there with their boys.
William O'Brien in his novel, *When We Were Boys*, describes in
graphic and typically provocative terms these aspirant gentlefolk:
one boy's parents are 'strong farmers' who have 'emerged from
the Great Famine fat with the spoils of their weaker brethren' and
now appear at the school dressed in finery which ill suits their
social standing. As the President of the College would say, these
were 'excellent Christians, and invaluable to their parish priest,
but they think their boy ought to be made a proper priest cheaper
than their three-year-olds could be fattened for the Shrove Fair'.

This cheerless, beeswaxed room was the one which the President
entered to greet the Joyces: the fabled Dr Croke, 'a strong-built,
massive-headed, precipitous-looking figure, with masses of storm-
cloudy wrinkles piled over his eye-brows'. The President greeted
his parents warmly. There was one point which he always insisted
upon: fees in advance, 'invariably in advance'. For John Stanislaus
piano and singing lessons were an accepted extra. Though there
are no records to confirm or deny it, it is likely that the habit of
music and song that had flourished among the Joyces of the northern hills had been maintained, and that James A. Joyce was hoping
to make another singer of his heir.

It may be that the Joyces were already acquainted with Dr Croke,
but he would have given his usual speech anyway, and pointed out
to young John that he might be a family friend, but that it would
make no difference: he must behave himself. From the President
he would get simple justice, raw and unboiled, just as he earned
it – no less and not a grain more. John would have been taken to
the study hall where the boys in the school 'formed a dumb and
frightened mob around the rostrum of a peevish-looking young
ecclesiastic, with beady yellow eyes and a majestic soutane'. Lies
or peaching on another boy were disapproved of, the one by the
authorities, the other by the boys. John Stanislaus would pass on
in turn to his son James, as he entered his boarding-school, only

34

the useful advice not to peach on a fellow. It was a strange world, and there was much for John to learn. Punishment was often to have to read aloud in the punishment room passages from moral works such the *Meditations of St Alphonsus Liguori.*

Croke, proud of his College and keen to encourage boarders, would also have shown them around the five trim, whitewashed, gas-lit dormitories, the beds in their individual cubicles with blue and white counterpanes, fed with the free air of the hills, and featuring Dr Croke's lauded *calofière,* a patent heating apparatus which did everything, the boys said, but heat the place; the mystic little chapel, steeped in the dim religious light of pink and blue panes of glass; and the library on the second floor, its books still laid out only on painted deal shelves. (An impressive list from a slightly later date contains not only classical and theological works, but original Gaelic manuscripts, still preserved in mahogany splendour at the college.) William O'Brien commented that Croke and his staff, though surrounded by ghostly regiments of the Greek and Latin Fathers, read only the College pass-books and their Breviaries.

Not everyone admired the diocesan colleges. William O'Brien put his opinion into the mouth of one of the boys:

These clerical schools ain't the ticket ... A parcel of damned young bog-trotters, and elderly bog-trotters in soutanes set over 'em with birches to flog 'em to their prayers. It is done cheap and the fellows like it – they are reared up to their stirabout and litanies ... There aren't three clean pairs of gloves in the whole college. And the accent! – well they might teach a fellow either Irish or English, and do the thing above-board. But, no! they must go and muddle the two together, like jam and trotter oil, and turn you out upon the world with such a confusion of tongues, that I verily believe if you found yourself in the Strand, the policeman could not understand what language you spoke when you asked the way to Temple Bar.

Those who were to be priests, the teachers would cram with the Christian classics and catechism right enough; a boy like John Stanislaus with no such ambition was, it was said, fated to go into life knowing his prayers, the whole prayer-book, and nothing but his prayers. The division between the pupils led to a first-night

ritual called 'Baptising the Blacks', in which the clerical students
were given black painted faces. Such attitudes would have appealed
to some earlier Joyces, and the lifelong personal opinion of the
clergy and their works held by John Stanislaus might be traceable
back to some encounter here at St Colman's.

Despite Dr Croke's warning, in the refectory John, the youngest
boy at the school it seems, was a favourite of the President's, who
seated him beside him at dinner, as John himself remembered.
Croke had been in Paris in 1848, and had tales of the barricades
and the wild revolutionary days that must have entranced the boys.
The regime was spartan enough. The Father Minister was said to
have a theory that neck of mutton and vegetable soup 'made the
best brainfood going', and was careful to limit the butcher's bills
in each session. Butter and tea were extras, as was ale, which the
boys were taught to drink. A good diet of butter and porter twice
a day amounted to two shillings and fourpence a week. John Stanislaus's surviving account of his first year records the issue of the
occasional sixpence as pocket money, and he had a few haircuts
at fourpence each.

For sport in winter there was rackets and an alley for handball,
a sort of palm squash still common in Ireland, while there was
cricket in summer. The boys were called to order during games
by the prefect with a trumpet rather than a whistle. A photograph
exists at the college of the boys playing cricket in the summer of
1860, though they are too distant for even wild guesses about
identities.

The President's study gave on to a long corridor that served as
a playground when the weather was wet. There was also the nearby
attraction for maturing boys of other boys' sisters in the convent
garden next door. As yet John Stanislaus was interested only in
working little and playing much, however.

The college was generally well conducted, under the overall
supervision of the Bishop of Cloyne, by the President and a competent staff of secular priests and laymen as professors and tutors.
The boys received a classical education which fitted them either
for entrance to the Theological Seminary in due course, or to the
academic courses that led to the learned professions. Some of the
impressions in Canon Sheehan's novel *Geoffrey Austin* (which drew

partly on the author's experiences at St Colman's) describe the inculcation of the Classics: Greek and Latin, as well as mathematics, music, nature and the mysticism of the German poets. Other subjects were Geometry, Algebra, History, English Composition, Christian Doctrine, French and Elocution. It was too early to make decisions about John's future, but perhaps, like many mothers, Mrs Joyce hoped her son would be a priest, while her husband foresaw a successful doctor or lawyer.

Outside the school, Fermoy had some distractions. In the ballroom of the local hotel (Millard's on the Quay which had an English manager who spoke of his 'pint of bittah') there were performances by a theatrical company from Cork (probably the Holts, with whom both William O'Brien and John Stanislaus would later be associated). Shakespeare bored the local people, but the burlesques were more fun. These presented Irish jigs and Irish comic songs, with local allusions in them, which brought laughter and appreciative showers of sticks from the gallery. One attraction of the group was the lovely young actresses, who, with the pretty girls of the town in the audience, may have encouraged one of John's Fermoy relations to take the boy to a show.

Croke was enthusiastic on the subject of Irish education. He spoke at a public meeting in Mallow early in December 1859 on the National System of Education, which he felt was insufficiently Irish in its approach. His desire was for an education that taught Irish language, history and patriotism, and at the same time emphasised the heritage of the faith.

Already the seeds of Fenianism were being planted in John Stanislaus's subconscious. James O'Brien, the older brother of William O'Brien, seems to have ingested them while a student for the priesthood at St Colman's. The boys were encouraged, for example, to watch from the terrace of the college the funeral cortège of the Fenian Peter O'Neill Crowley as it passed over the bridge and up the hill to the church, during the revolutionary events of March 1867.

At the beginning of July parents were invited to the annual examination of the pupils and distribution of prizes. An English composition was read out, then the Advanced Greek class was examined by Professor Mr Thomas Lloyd Coughlan LLD. The Latin class was taken through Horace by the Rev. Mr Doyle. A demonstration of his pupils' grasp of History, conducted by Dr Croke himself, followed. (Science then consisted of geography and the use of globes, and astronomy – the orrery could with some justice be regarded as a local device.) John's parents, if they attended, must have been relieved when the orchestra under Professor Hutchinson concluded with such old favourites as 'The Harp that Once', 'Let Erin Remember' and 'Dear Harp of My Country'. Music and singing were in fact an important part of the life of the school. A piano was bought in the first term, and accordions were on sale to the boys at thirty shillings each. 'My father', Stanislaus recalls, 'seems to have had a good treble voice, for he sang at concerts at an early age.' The brass band was a noted feature of feasts and picnics. Outings were made to Araglen, Rathcormac and Kilworth on the Ballyhoura slopes, the students walking, the priests going by coach with the food and porter.

The first Dean and Bursar was Fr William Hickie – the model for 'Fr Mulpetre' in *When We Were Boys*. Apart from Croke and Hickie, there were only two other full priests on the staff: Fr Golden and Fr P. J. Doyle (later President of the College), and so the lay professors must have been of great influence on the boy as well, though their names now mean little: D. Tierney, Peter Kavanagh, T. Harding, P. Riordan, T. Hutchinson, John Ryan, Thomas Lloyd Coughlan (a convert) and Signor Silvanti who taught dancing (one source, perhaps, for the enthusiasm John Stanislaus and later his eldest son shared for things Italian).

If the records seen by Ellmann are to be relied upon, John Stanislaus was withdrawn from St Colman's on 19 February 1860, when he returned home to Cork City (though, as noted above, Gorman passes on John's firm conviction that he was there for three years. The suggestion that fees were unpaid when he left also seems odd, as all payments were demanded strictly in advance, and the confusion may have arisen from the fact that Ellmann, who did not visit Fermoy, had to rely on the records he was sent by Fr Duggan). Certainly, John Stanislaus suffered from severe rheumatic fever at school, and had not always been in class, and he later remembered that Dr Croke himself had finally taken him from his bed and bathed him all over in hot water – he never, he said, felt a twinge of rheumatism again. When he was stricken by typhoid fever and came very near death for the second time, his parents took him home. Doting, as they did, on their one son and heir, they were not prepared to accept for him the epidemics and indifferent food that were part of school life in Victorian Ireland.

Whatever kind of education James A. Joyce had received, John Stanislaus's stay at St Colman's, of whatever duration it may have been, was more akin to his mother's at the Ursulines. Though the Joyces, like the O'Connells, had made their money in trade, in common with many moderately prosperous Catholics they were now edging their children a little higher up the social scale. Their son was to be made a gentleman. In his turn John Stanislaus would place his son James in an even more distinguished school when he sent James to Clongowes.

There is no trace of anywhere else that John went to school – if he left St Colman's at the earlier date. A claim by Judge Lennon that John had been at Clongowes's sister school, St Stanislaus's College, Tullabeg, is not confirmed by the records there. Short though it may have been, his time at St Colman's was important to John Stanislaus, and he would retain it in his highly selective memory when other aspects of his schooling were conveniently forgotten. And John Stanislaus's contempt for the Christian Brothers, as revealed in Simon Dedalus's famous denunciation of the teaching order, may well have had its origins in this more prestigious establishment. He had sat as a child at the feet of a great man, for by the end of the century Dr Croke was among the most influential men in Ireland.

CHAPTER 4

Learning to Swear

John Stanislaus returned to Cork from St Colman's with his health undermined. His father was now determined to build up the delicate boy. From this time dates the drill John Stanislaus later boasted about, of cold baths and exercises. (As the uncle, modelled on John Stanislaus, puts it in 'The Sisters': 'Why, when I was a nipper every morning of my life I had a cold bath, winter and summer. And that's what stands to me now. Education is all very fine and large . . .' Leopold Bloom's interest in the body-building exercises of Eugene Sandow may well have been that of the athletically minded John, rather than the scrawny Jim, though some of John's other sons would inherit this discipline from their father.) Rowing and athletics would become John Stanislaus's forte. But first his health had to be regained.

His father's notion was to send John to sea, not on a ship, but with the pilot boats that worked the Cork Harbour navigation. As Stanislaus recalls, he

arranged with the Harbour Master of Cork to allow him to go out on the pilot boats that went to meet the transatlantic liners, for which in those days Queenstown was a port of call. As a result, no crossing of the Irish Sea, however rough, ever upset him. But besides the robust health which he acquired from the briny Atlantic breezes, he learnt from the Queenstown pilots the varied and fluent vocabulary of abuse that in years was the delight of his bar-room cronies. In the pages of *Ulysses* it has shocked most of the censors of polite literature in Europe and America.

In 1861 there were some eighty-six pilots employed about Cork Harbour, resident in several places, though the great majority of them were in Queenstown. (In 1929 there were only twenty-three pilots left.) Paid more, on average, than pilots in other ports in Ireland, they were licensed under the Merchant Shipping Act of 1854, sec. 346, and needed proof of two years' sea service in a square-rigged (that is deep-sea) ship, and six months at least spent as a boat hand in a pilot boat licensed for the pilotage district.

The Pilot area covered the port, harbour and river of Cork, and the high sea within a line drawn from Power Head on the east to Cork Head on the west (with a look-out from the Old Head of Kinsale to Ballycotton for vessels coming in). One or two pilots were also based at Ballinacura, the pier that served Middleton, Ballycotton, Power Head, Cape Clear, Galley Head, with eleven at Kinsale and nine at Crookhaven. There were also thirteen Branched Captains to pilot steam vessels – then a new feature of the shipping scene.

Some ships came up the River Lee through Lough Mahon to berth at the quays just east of the Joyces' home. Others, mainly passenger boats on the emigration business, anchored at Queenstown (now Cobh). But many ocean-going liners passed by, merely pausing to pick up or drop mail between Ireland and America. This was brought from ship to shore by the pilot boats that met all vessels at the entrance to the harbour at the No. 1 buoy off Roche's Point lighthouse.

Up to some time in 1861 there were five pilots based at Carrigaloe, and one at Passage West: these pilots, being less busy, would probably have had more time to take on a lad like John Stanislaus. This was not real work for the boy, but a form of healthy activity in the open air ('a good breath of ozone round the Head', as Mr Dedalus says in the *Portrait*). However, the pilots were a foul-mouthed lot, and just as John Stanislaus had been taught his prayers at St Colman's by his pious teachers, so now he famously learnt other language lessons from the impious seamen.

John Stanislaus's tales of this period lingered in the family memory. Able Bodied Seaman W. B. Murphy (with discharge papers from the SS *Rosevean*), the sailor who intrudes into the cabman's shelter in *Ulysses* with strange, wild tales of foreign parts, is from Carrigaloe, across the channel from Passage West and Glenbrook where the O'Connells had a summer house. Stephen Dedalus is familiar with the area:

—Know where that is?

—Queenstown harbour, Stephen replied.

—That's right, the sailor said. Fort Camden and Fort Carlisle

Murphy the sailor has a wife and an eighteen-year-old son (now in a draper's – a significant point as several of the Joyces' relatives were in the drapery business). Cork was full of sailors of one kind or another, with or without curious postcards from Bolivia. They were easily met with on the pilot boats, the quays or in public houses. But it may just be that the 'original' of AB Murphy was actually the Cork pilot with whom John Stanislaus was placed – there were two Murphys listed in 1861, a John and a Patrick, both at Queenstown (but alas no W. B. Murphy).

The pilot resident at Passage – perhaps, however, the most likely candidate for mentor of John Stanislaus – was a Daniel Gorman (aged sixty-six); those at Carrigaloe were Daniel Butler, Thomas Harris, John O'Neill, Thomas Sweeney and Michael Geary.

The Harbour Master of Cork, with whom James A. Joyce had arranged John's engagement, was a Captain T. C. Clark (with a deputy at Queenstown named O'Brien). These officials were appointed by the Corporation of Cork, with which the Joyces had some influence. To escape from his wife, John's father was accustomed to take the train on the Cork, Blackrock & Passage Railway from the terminus on Albert Quay beside Anglesea Street out to Queenstown, where he would meet, among others, the American captains.

The two forts mentioned by W. B. Murphy command the entrance to Cork Harbour, and date back to the eighteenth century. Named after two viceroys of Ireland, they represented the British occupation of Ireland for many nationalists, as did Spike Island in the harbour, the last British garrison in the Free State to be handed over to its government in 1937. For ships entering the harbour the red and white leading lights marking the forts were crucial navigation aids. Ahead of them were the roadsteads in front of Queenstown, where both naval and merchant ships would anchor. At this date the port was one of the main exit points for Irish emigrants. (Indeed in the 1880s the nearby lodging houses would be the subject of a special inquiry into the sordid conditions that prevailed for emigrants there.)

Ringabella and Crosshaven are again alluded to in *Ulysses*, where Simon Dedalus uses them as a mock Fenian password to his old friend (who is, it seems, a Cork man), Ned Lambert, on entering St Mary's Abbey. Ringabella Bay was a little to the south-west of the entrance to Cork Harbour, where the pilot boats waited to pick up incoming ships. Crosshaven (which had family associations for the O'Connells) may have been where some smaller ships moored and where sailors came ashore to catch a train into Cork City at the local station.

During this period of the pilot boat adventures John Stanislaus heard Italians singing on the quays at Queenstown: opera then represented the latest thing in music and what he heard appealed to his own already formed appreciation of song. This may well have been his first experience of Italian opera. James Joyce would turn his father's recollections of this into a poetic flight in the 'Sirens' episode of *Ulysses*:

It was the only language Mr Dedalus said to Ben. He heard them as a boy in Ringabella, Crosshaven, Ringabella, singing their barcaroles. Queenstown harbour full of Italian ships. Walking, you know, Ben, in the moonlight with those earthquake hats. Blending their voices. God, such music, Ben. Heard as a boy. Cross Ringabella haven mooncarole.

Barcaroles, the songs of the Venetian gondoliers, was a word which had entered the English language only a little earlier. Opera was starting its great heyday in Europe, especially in France and Italy, but it would have been unfamiliar to natives of Cork. The impact of the Italian male voices on the young boy is unsurprising.

Quite why Queenstown should have been full of Italians is a small mystery – perhaps they were emigrants on their way to the United States. At this date the whole of Europe was watching the tortuous progress of Italian unification, begun in 1859 with the war against Austria and continued in 1860 with Garibaldi's invasion of Sicily. In 1861 Victor Emmanuel assumed the title of King of Italy. Many Catholics were dismayed at the attack on the Pope's patrimony, while at the same time they were enthralled by the spectacle of resurgent Italy. There were echoes of the 1848 rising. What the children of Young Italy could do, so could the children of Young Ireland. Nationalism, rather than opera, was the movement of the age.

In the United States Abraham Lincoln had been elected President on 6 November 1860; this was followed on 20 December by the secession of South Carolina. The Civil War began on 12 April 1861 when state troops fired on the federal fortress at Fort Sumter, South Carolina. Once again, though many Irishmen fought in the Union army, others found good business in trading with the Confederacy. Irish officers and men who had served in the American Civil War were to provide the backbone of the Fenian movement that would sweep Cork and Ireland in the late 1860s.

The connection between these colourful tales and the style of grand (and comic) opera is clear enough: John Stanislaus's taste was not penny plain, when he could have tuppence coloured, bravura in preference to chiaroscuro.

CHAPTER 5

His Father's Son

John Stanislaus's adventures at sea cannot have lasted all that long. When he had returned from St Colman's and had recovered his strength, he must have been given schooling somewhere in Cork, but it is mysterious that the family memory seems not to have retained any notion of it. Perhaps it was not thought to be distinguished enough. On 30 March 1861, James A. Joyce took out a mortgage on some of the marriage settlement property; he had, as was customary, to make over an insurance policy at the same time. The significance of this remains obscure. He was an inveterate gambler and had perhaps been losing on the horses. There are allusions to long periods of illness at this time which suggest chronic ill health, or a problem related to alcohol, or both.

One of John's favourite few novels of later years was *Frank Fairlegh* by Frank E. Smedley (1850). Though it will be discussed in more detail later, it may be worth noting here that its subtitle, *Scenes from the Life of a Private Pupil*, was possibly what first attracted John to this author. The book concerns a small group of boys who board with a tutor with a view to entering the army or one of the professions. Though the novel was also filled with exciting incidents involving rowing and horse-riding, John may have had a closer sense of underlying identification with the handsome hero because he too had been a 'Private Pupil'.

But little is certain about John's education at this time. He could have returned to Fermoy, but if so there would have been no secret about it. His ability to quote the Latin tags that littered his conversation and letters to the end of his life, as well as his professional career as an accountant, both certainly suggest that he was not without a good secondary education. But whether this was at a private school (of which there were many in Cork), or at one of the new Catholic schools, or even with the Christian Brothers, is not clear. He laid claim to no school except St Colman's and none has laid claim to him. Nor, indeed, do any school friends appear upon the horizons of his later life.

John Stanislaus may sometimes have spent his holidays at Fermoy. In 1862 the estate of Castlehyde next to Rose Cottage was bought by Sir Henry Becher (Second Baronet) from the infamous John Sadlier. Many years later in Paris James Joyce was conversant enough with this place to be able to discuss it with the Irish writer James Stern, whose brother then lived in the area. He asked Stern if he knew anything of a 'Sir Francis Becher' of Castlehyde who had written a book on big game hunting, and inquired about another family named Cremin who came from the Fermoy area. As there is (as yet) no evidence that James ever went to Fermoy himself, this local lore must have come to him from his father – though they would have been able to visit the town together one day in 1894, at about the time when the bridge there was being rebuilt by Joyce masons.

In November 1862 two of John Stanislaus's uncles, William O'Connell and John Daly senior, with the solicitor Philip O'Connell (another relation), were elected Town Councillors of Cork for the West Ward of the city. Local politics was still a stepping stone to higher things, as they were regularly being reminded by the progress of Peter Paul McSwiney in Dublin. In 1863 McSwiney became a City Councillor for the North Dock Ward and that year received from the Chief Herald a confirmation of arms in preparation for his election on 1 December as Lord Mayor of Dublin. He took up his duties at the beginning of 1865 and one of his achievements while in office was to lay the foundation stone for a city centre monument to his great kinsman, Daniel O'Connell. This, with another International Exhibition in the summer of 1865 and the reopening of St Patrick's Cathedral after its restoration (which was paid for by the Guinnesses, a matter referred to by John Stanislaus in the late Interview), is likely to have attracted some of the Cork Joyces to visit their cousin in Dublin to see what he was making of himself.

A lease on part of the White Street property to a coal merchant in 1864 suggests that James A. Joyce was still less interested in making money than in accepting it. He treated John Stanislaus more like a younger brother than a son – possibly because they were both equally under the disapproving thumb of Ellen Joyce, who seemed to be a generation older than either of them. James Augustine was now beginning to pass on his habits, good and bad, to his heir. One day he caught John smoking at the corner of South Terrace (a scene mentioned in the *Portrait*) and instead of berating the boy offered him one of his own cigars, given to him the night before in Queenstown by an American sea captain (presumably on his way back from Cuba). Apart from drinking and smoking, chief among James A. Joyce's interests was horses, both for gambling purposes and for more active amusements. John was now old enough to be able to begin riding to hounds and probably acquired a hunter of his own. There is a mysterious reference to an animal called the Kerry Boy. Since some of John Stanislaus's experiences and characteristics are given to Leopold Bloom in *Ulysses*, it might be noted that at this age Bloom too joined a pack of harriers, cut and scarred his hand, and in the process angered his father and saddened his mother. In the late Interview John Stanislaus reminisced about his days following the hounds of the local pack, the Southern Harriers (whose meetings were regularly reported in the local newspapers). It seems that John Stanislaus was not always on horseback, sometimes preferring to exercise his skills as a runner instead:

There is not a field in County Cork that I don't know, for I hunted them all and I now go through all these hunts and the jollifications that we used have after them. They were great. I was one of the best men after the harriers. I used hunt with the Southern Harriers. We had a great pack and I was one of the best on foot.

Foreign events too did not pass without notice in Cork, a port busy with shipping and overseas trade. News of the Polish uprising of 1863, when a Catholic nation rose against its imperial oppressors, was followed in Ireland with passion. As John Stanislaus, who after all bore the name of the last Polish king, recalled, when the aria 'When the Fair Land of Poland', from Balfe's opera

The Bohemian Girl was sung (Allegro marziale grandioso) in Cork it was always received with great appreciation:

> When the fair land of Poland
> was ploughed by the hoof of the ruthless invader,
> when might with steel to the bosom,
> and flame to the roof, completed her triumph o'er right;
> in that moment of danger
> when freedom invok'd all the fetterless sons of her pride,
> in a phalanx as dauntless as freedom e'er yok'd,
> I fought and I bled by her side.
> My birth is noble,
> unstain'd my crest as is thine own.

Heady stuff for some young Irishmen and, even though the Poles submitted to superior strength in May 1863, it was an inspiration for Ireland.

In April 1865 General Lee surrendered at Appomattox Courthouse – virtually bringing the American Civil War to an end. The effects of this too would soon be felt in Ireland politically. John Stanislaus's mind may not have been too much distracted by these excitements, however; in October he sat and passed his Matriculation Examination for Queen's College, Cork. However, John did not enter university at once, perhaps because his father was far from well. Cork City was being ravaged by a severe cholera epidemic, with many deaths.

On about 23 September 1866 James A. Joyce fell ill with a high fever and inflammation of the lungs. An involved and confused memory drawn upon by James Joyce for his play, *Exiles*, suggests that John Stanislaus got money from his father at this time to go to hear the legendary Mario sing in *Carmen* and that when he came home his father was dead – but that opera was first performed in 1875 and though Mario (who would retire in 1867) was on his final tour, he did not sing in Cork. It is possible that the boy in fact went to London this year, where he could also have seen Kate Bateman in *Hamlet* at the London Adelphi.

James Augustine died on Sunday, 28 October 1866 at 6 Anglesea Street, after what was called in the death notices 'a long and severe illness'. He was not yet forty. Memories of him surface in the first act of *Exiles*: (*points to the crayon drawing on the wall*) 'Do you see him there smiling and handsome? . . . He will help me, perhaps. My smiling handsome father.' On 30 October a well-attended meeting of the Jingle Committee of the Corporation was held at the office on the South Mall, at which it was unanimously resolved to send a letter of condolence to Mrs Joyce on her bereavement. On the same day a notice appeared in the *Southern Reporter*: 'Owing to the death of Mr James Joyce, which melancholy event is much regretted in the city, the office of Inspector of Hackney Cars has become vacant. The salary attached to the post is £100 a year, but it is rumoured that a reduction in the amount will be moved in Council.' There were already several candidates in the field, some of whose names the paper carried a little later. This was followed soon afterwards by an advertisement on the front page, paid for by a man named Farmer, who claimed that as the late incumbent's deputy, he had already been doing Mr James A. Joyce's work on and off for several years during his superior's frequent long periods of absence from his post, apparently due to recurrent bouts of illness. Mr Farmer humbly suggested to the authorities that he had earned the vacant job.

Ellen Joyce duly registered her husband's death on 13 November, but as his entire estate was already in trust he left no will and no probate was involved. However, her life was devastated, and she may have taken on a companion, Elizabeth Hearn (though this has proved impossible to confirm). From now on, or shortly afterwards, she would withdraw for the summer months at least to Glenbrook, away from the city and by the sea, bringing John Stanislaus (now approaching his late teens) with her. Despite the shock of his father's death, John did not retire completely from life as his mother appears to have done. The Cork Harbour Rowing Club was then based at Glenbrook and rowing soon became one of his favourite sports. In later years he would relate with glee how he 'broke Pennefather's heart' (the sporting term conveying the administration of a life-threatening rowing defeat); his rival Pennefather was perhaps from the family of that name with property close to the Joyces.

Revolutionary politics was in the air again in Ireland. Around the beginning of the decade James Stephens had founded the

Society of the Fenian Brotherhood, or Irish Republican Brotherhood. The aim of the Fenians was to liberate Ireland from the imperial yoke by force of arms and to establish a republic. Many Irish-Americans were involved who had seen service in the American Civil War, and there was a continual traffic of Fenian leaders through Cork and Queenstown to and from the port. Though bound by oaths which made it anathema to the Church, the movement was riddled with spies. However, the plots continued, and on 17 February 1867 the Habeus Corpus Act was suspended in Ireland by the government. In Birmingham the Corkman Colonel Ricard Burke and one of the Casey brothers bought rifles and shipped them to Cork by sea, hidden in bolts of cloth. From Queenstown these were delivered to a Cork City shop, the draper's owned by John Stanislaus's uncle, Councillor John Daly. Here the arms were picked up by Fenian sympathisers and taken to a safe house for distribution.

The Caseys were a family of four brothers from Kilkenny, related to the Fenian leader, James Stephens. They would have long and active careers as messengers and minor terrorists in the cause of a free Ireland. Two of them at least, Joseph and Patrick, came to know John Stanislaus well and, given the link through Daly's drapery, it is reasonable to suppose that they first met him at about this time. Joseph Casey appears in person in *Ulysses* (though in Fenian style under another Fenian's name, Kevin Egan). Colonel Ricard Burke also gets a mention. How closely John Stanislaus was involved with them at this time remains a mystery: his Fenian days were never spoken of.

The smuggled rifles were used when the Fenian Rising went ahead early in March, a hopeless scattering of blown-up railway lines and police barracks shot at through trees. There were failed insurrections in Cork, Dublin and elsewhere, ending with the battle of Tallaght in the snow of the Dublin Mountains on 7 March. (Some of the Dublin rebels were drapers' assistants from McSwiney's New Mart in Sackville Street.) Arrested Fenians were simply put behind bars for their treason. Later that year, in an attempt to rescue some of them, a policeman was killed in Manchester. This time the culprits were hanged and the cause of the Manchester Martyrs was born.

During these years, Cork seethed with exciting plots in the back rooms of public houses, an atmosphere always congenial to John Stanislaus. But his delay in entering college was more likely a result of the lengthy periods of mourning through which people then passed. His admission to the university in October 1867 may have saved him from the gaol that stood beside it on the Western Road (whose superintendent was another Mr Joyce). Whatever uncertainties and ambiguities surround his schooldays and his politics, The Queen's College in Cork was something John Stanislaus Joyce would remain proud of as long as he lived to tell the tale.

CHAPTER 6

The Queen's College, Cork

John Stanislaus's first academic year was 1867–8. Public controversies over the number of Catholics attending The Queen's College had led to an inquiry by Parliament, and a (then rare) census of students, giving their religion and faculty, was taken in 1868. The name of John Stanislaus Joyce therefore first appears in the *University Calendar* for the year 1869, where he is listed as a second-year medical student.

John was very probably following his late father's wishes when he decided on becoming a medical man. John's mother was by now resigned to the blatantly obvious: she would never make a priest out of her son. Crossing the quadrangle on his first day at the university, John was aware that things would be very different now: as a matriculated student he would be required to wear academic dress, and he would have to do some work. At least the three terms annually would leave him a pleasingly long holiday of three months, July to September, every year.

His course was to cover four years in two parts. During the first part he had compulsory lectures in Chemistry, Botany, Anatomy and Physiology, Practical Anatomy, Materia Medica and Pharmacy. He also had to take one modern Continental language for six months (possibly choosing Italian, for his love of opera), and he had to go to more lectures in Practical Chemistry and Natural Philosophy (which was actually Physics). On top of all that there were six months of clinical lectures in a hospital. During the second period of two years there would be further lectures in Anatomy (Practical and Theoretical) and Physiology to look forward to, along with Surgery, Midwifery, Theory and Practice of Medicine, and Medical Jurisprudence. At the same time he would have to pass his First University Examination and finally his Degree Examination. It would all demand a level of work and commitment that would be a challenge.

In John Stanislaus's day there were more Protestants than Catholics at Queen's College, Cork. A later writer commented that the Medical School lacked the class snobbery of the Arts or Engineering faculties. One hundred and forty students were studying medicine in 1868–9, by far the greatest number of any discipline: by comparison there were only fifty-two doing Arts, twenty-seven Civil Engineering students, ten Law students and some seventy occasional or non-matriculated students. The most important members of staff who taught John were Denis C. O'Connor (Professor of Medicine), William K. Tanner (Professor of Surgery), Joshua Halve (Professor of Midwifery) and Purcell G. O'Leary (Professor of Materia Medica). None of these men seems to have made much impression on their young pupil, however.

The books used for these courses were generally the old friends of most Victorian doctors and no doubt John learnt what he learnt from them. However, university life cannot, of course, be entirely given over to academic study and John Stanislaus was above all a social creature. The formalities of college soon lost their appeal, and he was usually to be seen in the company of the more raffish element, with his faithful dog Jack at his heels, eager for what fun the day might bring. The names of these college companions (about whom, unlike the professors, he would later talk a great deal) were to imprint themselves on his eldest son's memory: James Joyce recorded them in a notebook compiled in 1909, which became one of the working documents for his first novel. After their names had been checked off at morning roll-call, John would often disappear with some of these friends through the college gates in the direction of the 'Groceries', a licensed premises nearby. Through Simon Dedalus, he remembers this pub-cum-shop in the *Portrait*:

— Ay, bedad! And there's the Groceries sure enough! cried Mr Dedalus. You often heard me speak of the Groceries, didn't you, Stephen. Many's the time we went down there when our names had been marked, a crowd of us, Harry Peard and little Jack Mountain and Bob Dyas and Maurice

Moriarty, the Frenchman, and Tom O'Grady and Mick Lacy that I told you of this morning and Joey Corbet and poor little goodhearted Johnny Keevers of the Tantiles.

To this list of John's contemporaries may be added Dick Tivy and Ned Lambert from *Ulysses*, and from the late Interview, Stephen Ronan.

The college records cast some light upon several of these people. Lacy ('Poor Mick Lacy! . . . That was the boy who could sing a *come-all-you*, if you like') was M. A. Lacy, who matriculated in 1862 and took a diploma in engineering in 1867. Henry Peard, who matriculated in 1865, the same year as John Stanislaus, never graduated. Nor did John Mountain, though he passed his first medical exam in 1869. Maurice Moriarty achieved his BA in 1867. Also listed in the records is a William J. Tivy, an Arts student. This was a brother or other relative of Richard Tivy, later of 5 Adelaide Villas, Summerhill, Cork. The Tivys, a Presbyterian family originally from Scotland, were well known in Cork for their antiquarian interests. Edward J.('Ned') Lambert was probably later another Cork exile in Dublin. In *Ulysses* Ned Lambert, a grain store owner, has recently returned from the park races in Cork where he has been staying with Dick Tivy; he tells Simon Dedalus the news that their old friend has nothing 'between himself and heaven': 'By the holy Paul! . . . Dick Tivy bald?' Mr Dedalus replies in wonderment.

Several of the professors at Queen's were Catholics and are likely to have been on closer terms with the Catholic minority among the students than their Anglican colleagues. It may be that the 'Joey Corbet' with a taste for drink was in fact old Joseph Henry Corbett, Professor of Anatomy and Physiology. Born in 1813, he had originally taught at the Medical School in Cecilia Street, Dublin, but had moved to Cork with Professor Alcock, whom he succeeded in 1853. He retired due to ill health in 1875 and died, 'of paralysis', in 1878.

Of John's college contemporaries Stephen Ronan would later become one of the most eminent. The Rt Hon. Stephen Ronan (as he was later) took his Matriculation in 1864 and his BA in 1867. He was called to the Irish Bar in 1870, became Queen's Advocate in 1899 and was appointed Lord Chief Justice in 1915.

Ronan was in the last year of his life when John Stanislaus spoke of him in the mid-1920s Interview: 'Lord Justice Ronan was with me in the Queen's College and he must be nearly eighty years of age. He was lop-sided at that time. His feet were paralysed at one side but he was a great fellow for cricket. I had a happy time of it then.'

Though he was a man of only medium height, it was primarily in athletics that John Stanislaus's sporting abilities lay and he seems to have won competitions at college. In after years he would speak with pride of his hop, step and jump, in which according to his son Stanislaus he claimed to have held the college record for years, with an initial hop of eighteen feet. The same source also mentions his 'indefatigable' cross-country running and his shot-putting skills, and that he rowed in college races on the River Lee. But he enjoyed his cricket too (an enthusiasm later shared by James, who spun many of the names of great Irish cricketers into *Finnegans Wake*). John would have watched the future Lord Chief Justice play (and perhaps joined in) on the ground at the Mardyke, a tree-lined promenade leading from the city centre. Such activities provided many a welcome distraction from his studies.

In contrast to John's college set, there was another group, absent from the college records, who may be called his town friends. Of these, little is known apart from a few of their names: Bob Dyas, Keevers and the old man in the *Portrait* called Cashman. In that book Simon Dedalus would reminisce lovingly of times spent with companions such as these:

When I was a young fellow I tell you I enjoyed myself. I mixed with fine decent fellows. Everyone of us could do something. One fellow had a good voice, another was a good actor, another could sing a comic song, another was a good oarsman or a good racket player, another could tell a good story and so on. We kept the ball rolling anyhow and enjoyed ourselves and saw a bit of life and we were none the worse of it either. But we were all gentlemen . . . at least I hope we were – and bloody good honest Irishmen too.

There is no evidence that John Stanislaus ever played rackets after St Colman's, but that apart, Stephen's old man, looking back, was reliving for his son not memories of his companions, but rose-tinted memories of himself.

The Queen's College Dramatic Society was re-established in March 1869 and John Stanislaus joined it at once. On 11 March he first appeared on the boards in a show to raise funds for two Cork infirmaries and the Ophthalmic Hospital, held at the Theatre Royal in the city. Though, as the *Cork Examiner* said the next day, 'considerable interruption prevailed throughout the performance, one of the amateurs having, it is said, made himself politically obnoxious to a portion of the audience', John 'acquitted himself creditably' as Jacques in Tobin's turgid comedy, *The Honeymoon*. In the course of the evening he sang 'Paddy M'Fadden' and 'The Groves of Blackpool' (parodied by Richard Milliken, the quintessential Cork poet). 'The Groves of Blackpool' is a humorous look at Cork 'beauty spots': Blackpool was a less than attractive area in the north part of the city, but the song contrives to extol even its leather workers and its Foundling Hospital:

> Oh, sure, there's no nation in Munster
>   With the Groves of Blackpool can compare,
> Where those heroes were all educated,
>   And the nymphs are so comely and fair.
>
> With the gardens around so entertaining,
>   With sweet pretty posies so full,
> That are worn by those comely young craters
>   That walk in the Groves of Blackpool.
>   Ri fol, &c.
>
> Oh! many's the time, late and early,
>   That I wished I was landed again,
> Where I'd see the sweet Watercourse flowing,
>   Where the skinners their glory maintain.
>
> Likewise that divine habitation,
>   Where those babbies are all sent to school,
> That never had father nor mother,
>   But were found in the Groves of Blackpool.
>   Ri fol, &c.

Whichever version he sang, John proved that he could be, as the

Unionist *Cork Constitution* reported in the morning, 'exceedingly funny and intensely popular' on stage.

For all his love of opera, John Stanislaus always enjoyed singing comic songs of this type, as well as love songs and patriotic ballads, and on occasions he could be prevailed upon to let off the standard Victorian recitations as well, such as Caroline Norton's 'The Arab's Farewell to his Steed'. It was at about this time that another comic Irish song, significant to the Joyces, became popular – certainly it was to be successful at Kilkee the following summer. This was 'Tim Finnegan's Wake'. Curiously enough, the song would be quoted in Canon Sheehan's 1909 novel, *The Blindness of Dr Gray*, which draws on the novelist's experiences as a curate at Queenstown in the 1880s. In the book a character appears on stage playing Hamlet's father's ghost, his name Tim Finnegan. Since James Joyce would be in Dublin in 1909 when it was being reviewed, it is tempting to draw Joycean links between *Finnegans Wake*, Sheehan's novel and *Ulysses*, in which the prevailing paternity theme is explored by viewing the relationship between Hamlet and his father as an expression of William Shakespeare's relationship with his own father, John. The song would remain a favourite with the Joyces for many years.

The Theatre Royal had been built in 1760 and after an interval caused by fire, lasted until 1875, when it was bought as a central sorting office by the GPO. In John Stanislaus's day it was a popular venue for touring singers and *artistes* from London and elsewhere, but The Queen's College Dramatic Society also helped to fill it fairly regularly. After his initial success, John became a leading attraction of the student company and was hailed in the *Southern Reporter* as the group's mainstay for comic roles. In what the *Examiner* called 'the very laughable farce of "THE MUMMY"', performed a month later as part of a benefit for Mrs Holt, widow of the leading light of Cork theatre, he rescued a 'rather stupid' play with his 'excellent acting'. Taking the part of the 'Irish Character' or stage-Irishman Mr John S. Joyce 'displayed a considerable talent for imitation, which tickled the fancy of the audience'. However, perhaps his greatest accolade appeared in the *Southern Reporter* in May after he played the lead in another farce, *The Irish Emigrant*: 'To Mr Joyce's acting in the latter piece it affords us pleasure to be able to refer in terms of unqualified approbation. It was full of quiet humour, genuine and racy of the soil and admirably sustained. Mr Joyce is a young gentleman of considerable dramatic talent and excellent promise.' John would keep all these cuttings among his papers for years, evidence of a career that might have been.

In contrast to these dramatic triumphs, evidence of any academic success on John Stanislaus's part is hard to come by. He would claim when interviewed in the twenties that he had won 'several Exhibitions' while at college, but this cannot (as yet) be confirmed from the *University Calendar* or other records. His story was that the Exhibition Certificates disappeared when he pawned a suitcase for ten shillings with Cunningham, the well-known Dublin pawnbroker ('a very decent fellow') at 85 Marlborough Street beside the Pro-Cathedral. 'There was a set of false teeth in the bag too, but he sold bag, teeth and certificates which were in it.' This must have taken place in the hard times John Stanislaus would pass through during the Great War, since, whatever else was in the bag, the lost teeth suggest the older rather than the younger man. A few weeks after *The Irish Emigrant,* John failed his Second Medical Examination and was forced to repeat the year.

The next year was no more successful. John Stanislaus is again listed in the Calendars for 1870 and 1871, but seems to have been present only until the end of 1870. His name does not appear in the official return of faculty and students for a second college census which was taken for 1870–1: he was never to complete his degree course. However, it was not unusual (as John Murphy, historian of the college writes) for those studying medicine not to graduate: many went on instead to take the exams of the College of Physicians or the College of Surgeons rather than a degree. John may have tried this too, but if he did, he failed.

Though John Stanislaus would remain proud of his Cork connections, none of these early associates seem to have featured much in his subsequent life (though he saw some of them on later visits to Cork). John was growing up: on the fourth of July 1870 he celebrated his twenty-first birthday. He now came into the first tranche of his inheritance under the terms of his parents' marriage settlement of 1848. This money, said to have been £1000, effectively gave him independence (financially at least) from his mother. When in October he did not return to Queen's to continue his studies, he had, in any case, far more interesting things to think about.

All that summer Cork was in a ferment as news came in from the Continent. In July 1870 the Franco-Prussian War had erupted. After the collapse of the Empire following the Battle of Sedan and the capture of Napoleon III, France became a Republic at 4.15 p.m. on 4 September. A little later, on 20 September, Rome fell to the troops of the King of Sardinia and Italy was reunited at last. These were heady and confusing days for a young man. In a report of 20 August, the *Freeman's Journal* gave a taste of the mood of the city:

DEMONSTRATION LAST NIGHT IN CORK

An attempt was made to-night to get up a demonstration in celebration of the French victories. Three tar barrels were brought into Patrick-street by a large crowd, who were proceeding through the streets when they were stopped by a file of police and ordered to put down the tar barrels. After some remonstrance they complied, and the police extinguished the tar barrels. Much excitement prevailed, and the crowd largely increased, but a few charges without bayonets sufficed to clear the streets.

John Stanislaus had no wish to defend the Papal States, but France was another matter. The family story (as related by Stanislaus) was that John, with the help of some of his new money, ran off with two friends to join the fighting in France. There was an Irish company of the French Foreign Legion which was in action near Monteiard in January 1871. An Irish Ambulance Corps of 300 men had also left for France on 8 October 1870. This corps (probably a cover for other activity) had been organised by Peter Paul McSwiney and George Delaney, among others. (They were later awarded the Légion d'honneur for their help to the French Republic.) However, whichever unit John Stanislaus hoped to join, his scheme was frustrated. Highly alarmed, his mother hastily followed him and somehow tracked him down in London before he had set off for Paris. Taking no nonsense, she brought him back to Cork. It was only four years since Ellen Joyce's husband had died: she had no desire to lose her only son, the new focus of her life, as well.

But though she had rescued John from the battlefield, it did not mean that there were not (from Ellen's point of view) unwholesome associations for him in Cork too. The campaign to achieve the release of Fenian prisoners after the 1867 Rising still continued, and on 15 December Gladstone announced the early release of at least some of them. When, in January 1871, the prisoners arrived home in Cork there were huge demonstrations. In the years ahead other political groupings would come more strongly to the fore, as instanced by the great Home Rule Conference held at the Rotunda in Dublin in November 1872, but this was not the end of Fenian (or IRB) activities: plotting, sabotage and the occasional use of arms and explosives would continue as before.

If this was when, as the family believed, John Stanislaus became most closely involved with the Fenian movement, it was a time that he would have particularly enjoyed. Every Sunday, groups of young men from Cork travelled out into the countryside for training and drilling, and it seems probable that John was often among them. It was out of doors, which suited him, and there were rebel songs to sing, which suited him more. There were, too, other attractions. As William O'Brien fondly described (of a little earlier) in his *Recollections*, 'if the mountain road by night often resounded with the measured tramp of men, it was still oftener vocal with the concerts and dances of blooming girls and joyous young rebels on the moonlit summer evenings.' Mr Dedalus in the *Portrait* says of his late father: 'He was the handsomest man in Cork at that time, by God he was! The women used to stand to look after him in the street.' John Stanislaus was no different in this respect from James Augustine and the secret gatherings of the North Cork Militia would have given him many opportunities to practise his own charms on the fairer sex. It must have been at this time that he became briefly engaged to a local girl, Hanna Sullivan, who was 'dark and energetic'. Whatever his increasingly jealous mother knew of these nocturnal activities, it can confidently be stated that she would not have approved: she had almost certainly put an end to a previous alliance that John Stanislaus had made with another girl, very likely a Miss Justice from Youghal. Mrs Ellen Joyce's voice, the voice 'that called [Miss Justice] the black protestant, the pervert's daughter', would be heard again in James Joyce's play, *Exiles*.

CHAPTER 7

Young Man About Town

Inheritance or no inheritance, John Stanislaus had to set about finding himself a place in the adult world. Though he was unacademic in the sense of not having being willing (or able) to pursue a medical career, he had a good head for figures. It must therefore have been now, or soon afterwards, that he became an accountant. This was just before accountancy was established on a professional basis and some who styled themselves accountants were little more than book-keepers. He may initially have worked as an unpaid apprentice on the same basis as his own son, Stanislaus, would later do.

In after years John Stanislaus would run his life through a system of personal contacts with familiar businesses, often in the drinks and accounting trades. One can follow him from year to year along a line of family or personal connections. He had adopted this method of self-advancement from his father, whose job in Cork had, of course, depended on his O'Connell in-laws. Some of the people who would later employ John in Dublin had known his father – men such as Henry Alleyn, John Daly and John Dunbar – and it is among some of this group or their associates in Cork that John Stanislaus was likely to have been found working between the end of 1870 to April 1873, though he almost certainly began with the O'Connells. It was work that would stand him in good stead in the years to come.

As an accountant in Cork he would go from shop to shop or business to business, checking the tots and the receipts and making regular returns of each office's annual figures. This routine was flexible and allowed for a great deal of idle chatter, and the occasional drink in shop, business or bar. This would be his life some years later and the pattern must have been established early. Yet at this stage he evidently displayed some efficiency or personal ability that appealed to employers. Witty charm and the bright word would have worked very well in this area for a smart young man about town with a new moustache and a cigar. As he much later said: 'I remember I used to buy cigars from the father of the present Postmaster General of the Free State. He had a shop in Parliament Street and sold papers and tobacco.' Here the old man seems to be mistaken: certainly a Martin Walsh sold cigars at 8 Parliament Street in Cork, but the father of the future Postmaster General, John Joseph Walsh, lived in Bandon, some distance from Cork, where his eminent son would be born in 1880. (However, this supposed connection with John Stanislaus was enough to earn Walsh an eventual place in *Finnegans Wake*.)

At this time John would still have been a regular follower of hounds. In 'Circe' Simon answers his son's cry of '*Holà!* Hillyho!', by uttering the beagle's call, giving tongue: 'Bulblul! Burblblburblb! Hai, boy!' In a scene that closely echoes an old tale told of Fermoy (to be found in J. R. O'Flanagan's *The Blackwater in Munster*, 1844), this is followed by a mad rush of staghounds through the phantasmal brothel. For the young John Stanislaus the excitements of the hunting field also merged into less healthy pleasures, for certainly after hours there were wine, song – and women.

The mid-century Cork of John Stanislaus's youth contained (so one writer claimed from well-researched local knowledge) some eighty brothels, with 200 known prostitutes and perhaps 100 part-timers. Cork was not only a great seaport awash with sailors of all kinds, it was also a significant military base, with 2500 soldiers. In the Contagious Diseases Act of 1863, which called for compulsory police controls over prostitutes and brothels, and for medical examinations and hospitalisations of the diseased, Cork and Queenstown were specifically addressed. The latter was where the passenger ships berthed, but the city quays where most of the trading ships docked were only a little to the east of Anglesea Street, where the Joyces lived. There is little published information about vice in Cork, yet the diseases with which the act dealt had nevertheless a significant presence.

The 'Holy Ground', as the brothel area of Cork was known, undoubtedly gave men of John's age (and older) sexual outlets not available elsewhere in Ireland. John Stanislaus's recollection from his early teens that the cigar his father had given him had come from an American captain encountered in Queenstown makes one wonder whether this meeting took place in a sleazy hotel or brothel there. (If the mysterious sailor from Carrigaloe, W. B. Murphy, who drifts into *Ulysses* with his strange tales, was not one of the harbour pilots, he may have been another character from one of the dubious drinking dens and knocking-shops around the shores of Cork Harbour.)

Probably already sexually active while at college, it was perhaps inevitable given the times that John Stanislaus should contract a venereal infection. Much has been made by James Joyce's biographers and others of the effects of syphilis among the Joyces, so it is essential to emphasise here that John Stanislaus was not in fact a syphilitic. The suggestion that he was has its origin in a claim that he himself made to a Dr Walsh some thirty years later to the effect that in his youth he had cured himself of a syphilitic chancre on his private parts. This would then have been possible only if the lesion was *not* a syphilitic one (though it would have been contracted, like syphilis, through a breach of the epidermis during sexual connection). The confusion is understandable. The initial lesion of syphilis, or *hard chancre*, appears at an infectious stage of the disease. It is quite distinct from *soft or simple chancre*, a local venereal lesion with an incubation period of under a week. After a long dispute among medical researchers, simple chancre was distinguished from syphilitic chancre by Bassereau in 1852. A little later, in 1858, Rollet explained how the muddle had arisen: people often contracted both sorts at once. But it was not until 1889 that the nature of the soft chancre was established by Ducrey when he discovered the specific streptobacillus that causes what is actually an ulcerative pydermatitis. Unlike true syphilis, this does not give rise to constitutional infection, but a less than assiduous ex-medical student of the period might easily have been unclear about the matter. There was no reason for John Stanislaus to keep up with medical research in later years, so his comments on his condition have to be read in the light of his early knowledge (or lack of it).

In the nineteenth century the best application for a simple chancre was pure carbolic acid, tincture of iodine, or thermocautery, preferably followed by dusting with iodoform powder. John Stanislaus specifically told Dr Walsh in 1920 that he had treated the lesion himself with carbolic, clearing himself of the infection. But he may have left himself with a real fear that he was in fact still carrying the terrible disease in his system, a fear that is likely to have had its consequences upon his subsequent dealings with women.

His sexual and romantic adventures apart, the mainstays of John Stanislaus's life, as for so many other young men, were sport in summer, music and theatre in the winter, and a good deal of drinking all year round. Travel does not seem to have been a consideration, though trips to places like Youghal and Mallow to take the waters with his mother are possible, given the allusions to these towns in his son's writings. After a year or so, he is likely to have improved his position at work, becoming personal assistant to a chief accountant, or even Company Secretary to one of the larger Cork firms. It is probable that he now worked in some capacity for Henry Alleyn, the prominent Cork businessman who had been very friendly with his father. In late 1872 or early 1873 John applied for the post of Secretary of a distilling company, to be based in Dublin, which Alleyn was floating with other Cork businessmen. Though John also offered to take up shares, and the offer was accepted, it is unlikely even in Victorian Cork that a job of such responsibility would have been given to a young man with no experience or references: Alleyn clearly believed in the potential of John Stanislaus.

In April 1873 Mrs Ellen Joyce leased the house, yard and premises of Rose Cottage, the family home on the corner of Cotter Street and Anglesea Street, for 150 years to one John Baggott of Waterloo Buildings, Anglesea Street, a vintner. Part of the premises was to be used as a pub. Later the old front garden would be built over and John Stanislaus's childhood home for ever hidden from view. This lease effectively marks the break for John with Cork. Before he left, his friends organised a gala dinner to wish him farewell, and invited a number of singers from an English opera company currently touring Ireland to join in the festivities. John sang an aria for them afterwards and was rewarded by the enthusiastic praise of the visitors' leading tenor: as Stanislaus reported, undoubtedly echoing his father's words, the Englishman 'said he would willingly have given two hundred pounds there and then to be able to sing that aria as my father had sung it.' Soon, however, Mrs Joyce and her son would take the train north, finally passing through the tunnel on the outskirts of Dublin that symbolically both links and separates the city from the rest of the country. From now on John Stanislaus's life would be committed to the capital.

CHAPTER 8

Something in a Distillery

John Stanislaus's time with the distillery in Chapelizod ('the mill that was still') was one of the passages in his life which his son James wanted him to be specifically asked about in the late Interview. His reply makes a lively introduction to a curious enough episode. Asked for his recollections of the time he spent in Chapelizod, he said:

I knew the place very well for I was Secretary to the Distillery there for 3 or 4 years. It was owned by the Dublin and Chapelizod Distilling Co. You know that the premises were very historic. Formerly the place was used as a Convent, then Begor it became a soldiers' barracks and after that William Dargan got it and set up a Flax Factory. His monument is in Merrion Square. Eventually it became a distillery. It was owned by Corkmen, Henry Alleyn was the Chairman of it and John Dunbar, afterwards MP for New Ross, and a brother-in-law of Alleyn's, was one of the directors. Alleyn knew my father very well. I applied for shares – I had money at the time – and I took £500 worth on condition that they appointed me secretary. At that particular time I had nothing particular to do, and after an interview by Henry Alleyn, Dunbar, George Delaney, another director and a Corkman too, I was appointed secretary. Delaney knew my friend John Paul McSweeney [Peter Paul McSwiney] who was a first cousin of my mother's – he was twice Lord Mayor of Dublin. John Daly who was a first cousin of mine and MP for Cork was also Mayor of that city.

Anyway I was appointed Secretary with a salary of £300 and I stopped there for about three years. Chapelizod was a very quaint old spot. The Earl of Donoughmore's family are buried there in the old church; he lived in the house on the hill, which is now a lunatic asylum.

67

The Dublin and Chapelizod Distillery
(from Barnard's *Distilleries of the United Kingdom*)

(John Joyce's reference to the earl was by that late stage of his life characteristic. The family seat had indeed by then been taken over, by the Stewart Institute for Imbecile Children and Hospital for Mental Diseases.)

Irish whiskey was in this period at the height of its vogue: generally it was drunk in preference to Scotch everywhere, though already the threat from the new-style blended Scotches was evident. To keep up with the demand, capacity was being expanded in Ireland. In July 1872, for instance, work had also begun on a whiskey distillery at Jones's Road on the north side of the city. In this year George Delaney, one of Peter Paul McSwiney's partners in the New Mart in Sackville Street, retired from that firm, which was then converted into a public company with McSwiney as chairman. These moves seem to have released for both of them some surplus capital for Alleyn's new venture in Chapelizod.

Alleyn, already successful in Cork, had established himself as a merchant in Dublin some time in 1870. He had his premises at 30 Bachelor's Walk – beside the Alexandra (later the Carlisle) Hotel, John Stanislaus's favourite house in Dublin – which had a large warehouse to the rear, opening on to Lotts Lane. There he had three companies: two wine importing businesses and the Dublin Distillery Co. This last firm had been marketing whiskey under its own label from 1870 onwards, though the spirit seems to have been made by others. (His registration of the name meant his Jones's Road rivals had to call themselves the Dublin Whiskey Distillery.) With the boom in the export market for the spirit, Alleyn clearly thought it was time to make his own.

The site that Alleyn chose had formerly been the barracks of the Irish Royal Artillery Regiment and was developed as a flax mill by William Dargan (the virtual founder of modern Bray) after the Great Dublin Exhibition of 1853. Dargan's early death led to the mill's eventual demise in May 1873, when most of the machinery was sold off. The property came with forty-eight workers' houses, which alone would provide £250 a year in profits. On 23 June Alleyn leased (for 900 years) the site of nearly ten acres from Charles Hoey, of Belvoir, Stillorgan, when it was put on the market after the death of Robert Hoey, who had run the mill after Dargan. Alleyn by this date had moved from Cork to Brooklawn House at Palmerston, overlooking the site over the River Liffey. He paid Hoey £4500 for the property. The mills had run on water power and the great water-wheels were still in place to be utilised for the distillery. Alleyn then re-leased the premises for a shorter term to William McKenzie and others, and sold the property's ownership to his new company for £25,000 (estimated a little later to be about one third of its real value). Of this he received only £5000 in cash, taking the rest in shares, while retaining the option of retrieving the £20,000 later. On 22 September 1874 the Dublin and Chapelizod Distillery Company (Reg. No. 1748) was incorporated, with offices in Trinity Chambers at 41 Dame Street. The formally stated purpose of the company was to acquire, under an agreement dated 26 July 1873, the lands and premises at Chapelizod, to erect thereon a distillery for whiskey, and to carry on the business of distillers and vendors of whiskey. The nominal capital of the company was £80,000 in 8000 shares, and initially seven partners took one share each. Alleyn held only a quarter of the stock, however.

Such was the position of the company when John Stanislaus became its Secretary. He took fifty shares with his £500 and agreed on a salary of £300 a year. His association with the firm would last from the autumn of 1873 to the summer of 1876 – his '3 or 4 years'. The company issued a prospectus which a later historian of the distillery's successor would describe as 'a romance'. They needed £12,000 to complete the work, but claimed that by early the next year (1874) they could undertake to produce 600,000 gallons of whiskey annually and, with a further investment of £4000, double that. The brochure concluded: 'At the present time, when the demand for Irish whiskey is so enormous & daily increasing, the new company appears to be starting with every advantage in its favour, & among these advantages must be placed the premises which have been secured for its operations.' The role John Stanislaus played in the company prospectus is likely to have been a small one, but its confidently bullish tones would have appealed to his innate appreciation of the 'surefire gamble', a trait that would remain with him all his life.

Soon the company office was moved from Dame Street to Chapelizod. It was there that John Stanislaus established himself. The valuation records for this period note for the mill site that there were 'extensive additions going on to be made into a Distillery but at present unfinished'. On this document, to the words 'Dublin and Chapelizod Distillery Co.' (in red), 'John S. Joyce Secy' has been added in yellow-green ink. The revised Ordnance Survey map (published in 1876) clearly shows the extensive site and its ancillary cottages, with the completed distillery already in place.

The actual production of spirit began at the end of 1873, and by March or April 1874 the distillery was well under way; it was fully at work when, in November, as a final rearrangement, Alleyn and McKenzie leased the buildings formally to the Dublin and Chapelizod Distillery. These complex arrangements were destined to bode ill for all.

Chapelizod had important literary associations. It was the setting for Joseph Sheridan le Fanu's novel, *The House by the Churchyard*

(1861), to which many allusions are made in *Finnegans Wake*. Le Fanu had died in 1874 and the novel was one among the few John Stanislaus owned. But it was not literature that now primarily occupied John's leisure time, as the Interview makes evident: 'There were several inns in Chapelizod and the name of each was over the door on the wall. People used to come out from Dublin at that time and go to these Inns for their jollifications.' When his son was seeking information from John Stanislaus about Chapelizod, the Broadbent family of the village were one of James's interests. John had known them very well but supposed that by then they were all dead and gone:

At all events I don't know any of them. Broadbent and I were very great friends. He had the Mullingar Hotel there, and a fine decent fellow he was. We used have great times then. There was a bowling-green at the back of his hotel and I was considered a celebrated bowler; and I remember winning a prize at the time I was secretary to the Distillery Co. It was a match between ourselves and the Dollymount Club – we were the only two clubs then in Dublin. On one occasion Dollymount challenged us to a game. We won and we stood them food and drink after it. That was followed by a splendid musical evening as we had a lot of musical fellows down with us. I remember Edward Crotty – this was before he went on the stage – he was there. We beat Dollymount and I made a big score; and by God I was carried around the place and such a time we had. I beat my man to love – anyway I gave him a good beating. I was made a lot of and was taken around by the boys on their shoulders; and my God the quantity of whiskey that I drank that night! It must have been something terrible for I had to go to bed. I was not very long in bed when half a dozen of the fellows came up to me and said that they were having a singsong downstairs, adding: 'Come on Jack, don't have them beat us at the singing.' I told them to go to hell that I couldn't come down, Begor I could not walk so I told them to clear out to Blazes ... The Broadbents did not fail in their business. They were very decent respectable people, English people, but Broadbent was born in Dublin – they were Protestants.

The Mullingar Hotel was to be the setting for *Finnegans Wake*, and the novel's main 'character', H. C. Earwicker, who also seems to be a Protestant, may have been suggested by John Stanislaus's old friend, Robert Broadbent. His bowling club was called the Victoria Bowling Club; the green behind the hotel on which John played has now vanished.

James Joyce was to place the abode of Mr Duffy in 'A Painful Case' in the actual 'house by the churchyard', Church House, and this building too was where one of the Murrays, the family into which John would marry, would later live for a time.

A little way upstream along the Liffey were Lucan and Leixlip: 'The Spa at Lucan was a very fashionable place in those days and it is a lovely spot in summer time. The Sarsfields lived there and the Colthursts or some of the family are living there now. A son of Sir George Colthurst, of Blarney Castle, is there now,' John recalled. 'I never did any fishing so I cannot tell you much about the salmon fisheries at Leixlip, but Begor hunting was the game for me.' Asked if he knew anything about the quality of the water of the Liffey, he answered: 'Not a damn bit because I never drank it without whiskey in it.'

Work at the distillery, for there was work, had its own excitements too. Though some of what Stanislaus Joyce records has proved to be wrong, he expands John's version from his memory, mentioning that some of the shareholders were English and that Alleyn was the managing director (both facts that are confirmed by an article in the *Wine Trade Review* in October 1873). Alleyn drove over from Brooklawn every morning, apparently with a 'tiger' (a liveried servant) behind him on his dog-cart, arms folded. 'My father used to describe him as a kind of duodecimo Lord Chesterfield. The workmen hated him, and once tried to kill him by dropping a heavy beam of timber on him from a gallery when he was going his rounds. My father was quick enough to pull him under a shed an instant before the beam crashed just where he had been standing. My father, on the other hand, was a favourite with the men, with whom he used to play bowls.'

In the mind of Stanislaus, the move to Dublin was fixed by the O'Connell Centenary (which actually fell in 1875). Ellen Joyce may have had hopes, he suggests, that her son would become secretary to Peter Paul McSwiney, elected Lord Mayor of Dublin for a second time in December 1874. It was not to be. (His secretary was first a relative, the painter Michelangelo Hayes, and later Fr Edward O'Connell, Parish Priest of St Laurence's in Seville Place, who would afterwards be involved with the Liberal Registration Club.) Stanislaus Joyce wrote of his father and grandmother, 'They lived outside Dublin somewhere down along the bay towards Dalkey. He had a little sailing boat and a boy to look after it, and he sang occasionally at concerts.'

The years of his young adulthood in Dublin were evidently very pleasant ones for this young man-about-town. Trips along the railway line down to Bray, County Wicklow, and through 'Brunel's' tunnel over the sea round Bray Head to the little fishing village of Greystones five miles further on, 'properly' in Wicklow, where there was a country pier and fish and bowling on the lawns of the La Touches' Hotel. Spinning his little yacht along the coast with a friend, and pulling in for a swim or a drink at Bullock Harbour or Sandycove with its Martello Tower and its bathing place, or jostling with other yachts within the two great arms of the piers at Kingstown. And dances in the big hotels, and perhaps even in some of the grand Yacht Clubs.

John Stanislaus probably joined the Dolphin or the Neptune Yacht Club around now, both near the mouth of the Liffey at Ringsend. True to form, he found himself engaged once more, this time to a girl called Annie Lee. But again, it was destined not to last. Of John's early romances, little detail has, alas, remained. His children were to learn not much more than what they were told by their mother – someone not in the best position to know the true facts, nor with the best reasons to impart them. She believed that in each case, the engagements had been broken off 'in a fit of jealousy' by John himself. Whether in fact this 'unreasonable jealousy', as his wife called it, was his own or his mother's must remain a moot point. A powerful woman, Ellen Joyce was quite capable of deterring her son's floozies if she wanted to, not least with her formidable invective (a talent her son would inherit in full), and she was not above acting behind his back if she so wished. All the evidence points to the likelihood that she did so wish.

But there was always singing for John to go back to, and particularly during the winter when outdoor pursuits were uncomfortable, he enjoyed a desultory concert circuit, singing on stage in little halls around town to raise money for a club or a charity, and very likely making appearances at garden fetes as well when the weather improved. He remained an avid concert-goer too, and no doubt spent a good deal of money escorting young ladies to the opera. His (auditory) experiences in the theatre were ones he would never forget.

In old age John Stanislaus was full of reminiscences about singing and eminent singers such as Joseph Maas, Campanini, Sims Reeves and Barton McGuckin. With the last of these he had a curious experience around 1874, very soon after his arrival in Dublin:

McGuckin was a tenor in the Carl Rosa Company; he was the leading tenor. A most extraordinary thing about McGuckin and myself was this. At this time I was a young man about 25 years of age and I had a very good tenor voice. I sang at the concert in the Antient Concert Rooms which was got up for some purpose the object of which I forget now. Anyway as I said, I had a very good tenor voice at the time – a better tenor than when I was in Cork. After this concert when McGuckin used pass me in the street he used watch and look after me. I used wonder why he looked so hard at me and by God I never could make out what it was all about; and it was only after he was dead for some years that I heard the story. It was in one of my favourite houses on Batchelors Walk one evening where a lot of fellows used meet in the evenings for a jollification, and while talking of one thing or the other – of course singing cropped up. John Phelan said to me 'you had the best tenor in Ireland.' 'Yerra my God what put that into your head?' says I, and he said, 'I heard it from the very best authority.' 'Who was that?' says I. 'Well,' says he, 'did you ever hear of a gentleman called Barton McGuckin?' 'I did indeed,' said I, and John said 'that is my authority,' and that accounted for the way he used look so hard at me. When I asked him what McGuckin knew about me he said, 'McGuckin heard you singing at a concert in the Antient Concert Rooms and said that you had the best tenor voice in Ireland; and Begor he ought to be a judge.' Anyway I had a devil of a good tenor in those days – and they were great days, My God! they were!

Once John Stanislaus had been set talking about great singers of the past, like Mr Browne in 'The Dead' he was hard to stop: lying back in bed, he went on: 'I knew Joseph Maas very well. He had a lovely voice and I have never heard a better tenor before or since. Poor fellow, he died very young. It appeared that he went fishing, got a cold and caught consumption. He died very young, poor Joe Maas, I often heard him and he had a beautiful voice.' Joseph Maas was English, born in 1847. He made his London début at one of Leslie's concerts on 26 February 1871, in place of Sims Reeves (another great hero of John's) and was an immediate success. He became the principal tenor of the Carl Rosa Company in 1878 both for London and the provinces. Though an indifferent actor, he was admired for his voice which was said to resemble Giuglini's. He was equally popular in concert and oratorio. He died in London in January 1886, from rheumatic fever, bronchitis and congestion of the lungs, which were indeed brought on by fishing. The *Athenaeum* wrote that his 'greatest triumphs were gained in the concert-room rather than on the stage. For several years he has stood in the very first rank of tenor singers, not only by reason of his magnificent voice, but of his thoroughly finished and artistic style'. And they added the traditional accolade: that by his 'amiable personal character the deceased artist won the esteem and affection of all who had the privilege of his friendship', among whom, it seems, in Dublin, we can count John Stanislaus.

'Campanini was a great Italian singer and came to Dublin a few times. He had a very fine voice; he was a big awkward man.' Another great tenor, he was born in 1846, making his first London appearance in 1872, and was seen as the successor to Mario and Giuglini. He sang at Drury Lane until 1882 and from 1887 at Her Majesty's, as well as making tours. But he never fulfilled his promise, though after retiring for some years he made a comeback with considerable success, before dying in Italy in November 1896.

It was during the 1890s, too, that John Stanislaus heard Sims Reeves sing in Dublin. Reeves was the top singing star of the age, whose brother lived in Dublin as professor of singing at the Vice-regal Court. 'Sims Reeves? Of course I knew him. I used hear him singing here when he was an old man, and at that time he used generally keep the high note for the finish.' Years after this James Joyce remembered his father's interest in Sims Reeves and sent him a copy of his autobiography.

John had also heard Ireland's favourite tenor, John McCormack, and thought him good, but not as good as Joe Maas. His memories of all these singers were not always accurate: he thought of Lablache as a Corkman, and that Foley the bass, or Signor Foli, as he preferred to be known, was from Cloyne, County Cork, when in fact he came from Cahir, County Tipperary: 'My God he had a splendid voice. I heard him in opera and he would delight your heart to hear him.'

But these were only a fraction of the great artists it was possible to hear in Dublin. John Stanislaus also had the opportunity to meet many of them. He became friendly with James and Michael Gunn soon after moving to Dublin. They owned a music store in Grafton Street and had opened the Gaiety Theatre just around the corner in 1871. Often John would slip into the back of the theatre with James Gunn, and listen to such legendary voices as Trebelli and the great Tietjens in rehearsal. Therese Caroline Tietjens had been a great favourite since the 1850s, whose appearances in Dublin were always occasions for raucous celebration. She died in October 1877, having made a final appearance at a benefit in Dublin on 8 January 1877 at the Exhibition Palace.

Barton McGuckin was not alone in thinking John Stanislaus a talented singer: John thought so too. Stanislaus, for one, would take a sourer view of his talents and wrote that if there were a bar near the hall where he was performing, John might delight his friends by singing the second verse of a song before the first. And yet even Stanislaus had to admit that his father had the stage skill and temperament to make an audience friendly towards him: he was perfectly at ease on the boards. In fact he shone in the limelight.

One of John's well-worn anecdotes concerned a professor at the Dublin Academy of Music who was to accompany him at a concert. One song began with a page-long introduction that the professor skipped over, merely playing a few notes and expecting John to start at once. But the singer maintained a dignified silence, until the pianist tried again with another chord or two. 'Bravo! Well done! Good man!' said John Stanislaus heartily when silence fell once more. The professor finally played the music before him and, after the audience had stopped laughing, John sang, unabashed.

The story recorded by Stanislaus Joyce (and hence by Richard Ellmann) that John Stanislaus discovered that the managing director of the distillery was embezzling the funds and challenged him, after which Alleyn decamped and the firm was wound up, simply bears no relation to the actual facts. On 9 March 1876 Alleyn called in his loan or mortgage on the premises, and the company paid him by a bill of exchange on 11 March. This obviously placed an immense burden on the company's resources, but Alleyn was merely collecting the debt agreed to by the directors earlier. On 1 April an Extraordinary General Meeting of the ordinary shareholders agreed that the company would be wound up voluntarily under the terms of the Companies Act of 1862 (as described in the *Wine Trade Review* on 15 September 1876). John Stanislaus later told his sons that the shareholders voted their thanks 'to the young man who had saved them from greater loss' – though the contemporary reports make no reference to this, nor to his claim that he was appointed a trustee for their interests. A judge would later comment on the defective notice of the meeting and wording of the resolution. There may indeed have been certain ambiguities.

As can be imagined, there were heated discussions and complex transactions at the distillery, but on 31 July the mortgage which Alleyn held was executed. The next day another Extraordinary General Meeting of the shareholders was held, and a resolution was passed that Michael Crookes be appointed liquidator. An advertisement in a trade journal two weeks later invited the attention of the English trade to the excellence of the distillery's liquid product. 'It is made from the finest materials, matures rapidly and compares favourably with the leading brands of Dublin whiskey. It is shipped in butts, hogsheads and quarter casks. Quotations and samples on application to the secretary at the company's offices, Chapelizod.'

Yet another meeting on 24 August – a third Extraordinary General Meeting – was called to confirm the previous resolution to wind up the company and ratifying the appointment of Michael Crookes. By now John Dunbar was chairman and James Dempster Company Secretary. In the hurly-burly of the summer of 1876 John Stanislaus had lost his job. The liquidator now began a search for a buyer for the distillery as a going concern, the only way to protect the investments of the shareholders – including John Stanislaus's five hundred pounds.

By this time Irish whiskey, far from selling well, was under extreme pressure from the blended Scotches. A publicity war broke out in 1877, with the Dublin distillers publishing a pamphlet, *Dublin Whiskey, Genuine and Spurious*. This did not make Michael Crookes's job any easier. In October 1877 (over a year after he had been appointed) he issued a circular regarding the debts and assets: not much was left for anyone after the company's obligations to Alleyn were taken care of. In November he sold the distillery and its stock to Scottish interests; and on 1 November the Distillers Company began production again under the direction of William Stein (a connection of the Haigs and the Jamesons). The liquidators had hoped for an (inadequate) £30,000, but in the end got only £26,250. These monies were the only assets of the company and angry shareholders now took action. On 10 December John Rogers, a salesmaster of 25 Smithfield who was one of the creditors, filed a petition in court to wind up the company. This was as a result of a major rift in the shareholders, some of whom had been holding out for a higher price. After a hearing lasting several days the petition was granted on 1 February 1878. And that was the final end of the Chapelizod distillery. The premises were now called the Phoenix Park Distillery, but after selling the stocks, Distillers closed the premises for a time. They were 'disused' at the time of 'A Painful Case' and Mr Duffy's fictional residence in Chapelizod, and though they were reopened again for a while, finally closed in 1923. In Joyce family legend Alleyn had fled the country; actually he retired in dignity to Menton where he died after a painful illness on 10 January 1880. His memorial as an unpleasant and irascible employer was erected by James Joyce, when he used his name in his short story 'Counterparts'.

Stanislaus records that some of the shareholders' funds rescued by his father were lodged in his name in the Bank of Ireland, and that in after years John wondered if he could get at them, 'but a worldly-wise friend advised him to let a sleeping dog lie'. The papers of the firm, as he recalled, were kept until about 1886 in a confused mass in various Joyce attics.

Following the loss of his job and his shareholding – his £500 represented almost half of his original cash capital (so far as we know) and he must have spent most of the rest by now – John Stanislaus had to find himself other work. By the spring of 1878 he was established as an accountant with an office at 13 Westland Row. It is likely that he had moved there at the very end of 1877, after Rogers began his action to wind up the distillery. The house was large and double-fronted, with three storeys over a basement in a terrace backing almost on to the grounds of Trinity College – it was later a hotel. John would have had an office on the first or second floor, for the ground floor was given over to a shop.

Though it is not usually seen as a Joycean district, this street seems to have retained its special significance for James Joyce. Nearly all of the whole of the fifth episode of *Ulysses*, 'Lotus-Eaters', is placed in this area, for a reason which is not entirely clear from the novel. Here, at 49–50 Westland Row, was the post office where Mr Bloom collects the letter from his light of love, Martha Clifford. Opposite, at No. 5, was the then fashionable Grosvenor Hotel (manager Mr George Joyce), outside which he admires the elegant young lady with a gentleman who is either her lover or her new husband. John Stanislaus's offices faced St Andrew's Church ('All Hallows'), at No. 46, where Bloom sits in on the end of the ten o'clock Mass. (A non-fictional Dublin dentist named Bloom then had his rooms at 23 Westland Row. This gentleman is referred to by name in *Ulysses*.) Also in Westland Row was the Royal Irish Academy of Music at No. 36, while the Antient Concert Rooms were conveniently close. At the head of the road was Sweny's Chemist, at 1 Lincoln Place, where Leopold Bloom buys Molly's beauty preparation and his lemon soap. A little way off is Conway's pub, the 'Mosque of the Baths', the back gate to Trinity and its cricket pitch (where the college porter, Hornblower, was on duty), the offices of the *Irish Homestead* which published James Joyce's first stories, and Finn's Hotel itself, where Nora Joyce worked and which (as at least one Joyce commentator thinks) was the initial focus of the book that was to become *Finnegans Wake*. This significant knot of associations clearly owes something to the absorption by his son of John Stanislaus's recollections of his time here. Possibly John Stanislaus may also have lived at No. 13, for no trace of any other address has been found, assuming that he is not the John Joyce listed (for this one year only) at Springmount, Howth. It is more likely that he stayed in the Grosvenor Hotel – where he shared a name, and, putatively, distant kinship with the manager, George Joyce. There is no trace either of an address for Mrs Ellen Joyce, but, wherever she was living at this time, John was probably with her. If this was here he was also well placed to take a train along the coast from Westland Row Station just across the street to Blackrock, Kingstown, or Dalkey, where he had his boat.

But what did John Stanislaus do as an accountant? He walked the city from business to business, getting to know people, at first checking sums and soon suggesting investments, learning the streets, talking. John Stanislaus the Corkman was becoming a Dublin man as well. As his business connections had already been with the drinks industry it is likely that they continued that way. There were many potential clients among the publicans and licensed vintners and spirit grocers with which the city abounded – and other new contacts could easily be made in such congenial surroundings. At a later stage in his life the trade paper of the drinks business was almost the only thing he read. This period of their father's life appears to have been unknown to (or ignored by) the ex-apprentice accountant, Stanislaus, but it was very much alive for James.

On 18 January 1878 Luke Doyle, an impatient creditor, petitioned to have the Dublin Mineral Waters Co. Ltd wound up. This firm had been registered on 7 March 1877 with a nominal capital of £5000. It had bought out the interest of J. J. Murphy, Mineral Waters and Cork Manufacturers, a company already established at 27 and 28 East Arran Street. Who the partners were is unclear, but the company cannot have done much business. After the initial hearing, on 11 February the official order for the winding up was made by the Master of the Rolls; and in March at a morning meeting in his chambers at the Four Courts, the Vice-Chancellor of Ireland appointed Mr J. S. Joyce of 13 Westland Row to be the official liquidator. A legal notice to this effect was inserted in the *Dublin Gazette* by John J. Adams of 73 Dame Street, solicitor for Luke Doyle.

There is an allusion to this affair in a 1923 letter of James Joyce: 'I am so careless in these [money] matters like you with your mineral water papers...' No record has come to light of J. J.

IN THE HIGH COURT OF JUSTICE IN
IRELAND,

CHANCERY DIVISION.

In the Matter of the Companies Act, 1862, and the
Dublin Mineral Waters Company (Limited).

THE Vice-Chancellor of Ireland has, by Order
dated the 21st day of March, 1878, appointed
John S. Joyce, of No. 13, Westland-row, in the
city of Dublin, Accountant, to be Official
Liquidator of the above-named Company.

Dated this 1st day of July, 1878.

A. T. Chatterton, Chief Clerk.

John J. Adams, Solicitor, 73, Dame-street.

Notice of appointment as official liquidator of Mineral Water
Co. from the *Dublin Gazette* 1878

Murphy's ever being officially wound up, despite considerable searching. But it is quite clear what happened: in the course of his travels around the city, John Stanislaus had lost some (or all) of the company papers. Still, unlikely as it may seem, he had in the process made a good friend in the forgiving Luke Doyle, the petitioner, who may have had no return on his shares whatever. Luke Doyle, a building surveyor, and his wife Caroline, appear in *Ulysses* as old friends of the Blooms during the days of their courtship. Their home, to which the Blooms were invited in 1887 to charades, was in Kimmage, just beyond Terenure and Harold's Cross, where the young Joyce couple themselves lived. They gave the Blooms (and perhaps the Joyces) a wedding present: 'a dwarf tree of glacial arborescence under a transparent bellshade ...'

Luke Doyle in point of fact had an office in Anglesea Street. He lived first at Dolphin's Barn (which might carelessly count as Kimmage) and later in a large mansion at Mount Brown, where he died in 1886. His wife, incidentally, was named Mary, not Caroline. He had begun as a builder, but later became a loss adjuster, working with the numerous insurance companies in the business area off Dame Street.

For Leopold Bloom, as probably for John Stanislaus, Luke Doyle

81

is to be counted among his few very closest friends. Even Stanislaus, normally hostile, recognised that it was to be remembered to his credit that though he had 'innumerable acquaintances', Pappie (as John's children would almost invariably call him) 'had a few real friends'. Most of Bloom's best friends have left some trace on history and most of them he would have shared with John. Though no echo remains today of Percy Apjohn, Bloom's childhood play-mate killed in the Boer War at Modder River, of the others, Philip Gilligan was owner of the Oval Bar in Abbey Street and though in *Ulysses* he dies of tuberculosis in Jervis Street Hospital in 1894 in reality he had a stroke that year and died (of heart failure) seven years later; Matthew Kane drowned in Dublin Bay in 1904; Philip Moisel was a Jew from Heytesbury Street near where the Joyces would live, who married the daughter of a Church of Ireland clergyman and died around 1903 also in South Africa; the journal-ist Michael Hart was another who succumbed to TB, but in the Mater Hospital; Matthew Dillon, with useful political associates and relatives, entertained from his house in Rathgar; and the Corkman Alderman John Hooper was editor of the *Evening Telegraph* and father of another editor, Paddy Hooper. The list is a reasonably accurate (though necessarily incomplete) roll-call of John's most treasured Dublin companions until about the turn of the century. His family aside, they are the people in John Stanislaus's life for whom he got up in the morning and who kept him up late at night. They saw the best of him; and none of them, as far as can be known, would ever betray his friendship.

CHAPTER 9

A Shouting Politician

For John Stanislaus the daily work of an accountant may well have proved too strenuous and the legal side of it too exacting. Again through his family connections, a position was found for him as Secretary of the United Liberal Club in Dublin. If the Conservatives represented landed interests, often Protestant, for the most part the Liberals represented new, often Catholic, urban business interests – the sort of people who had been behind the distillery. It was a good move: even the generally ungracious Stanislaus suggests he fulfilled his duties here efficiently.

The Club seems to have come into existence late in 1877. That October, Gladstone had made a month-long visit to Ireland. Since 1874, when his Land Bill for Ireland had led to the defeat of his government, he had been in retirement, busy with various literary writings (including, it should not be forgotten, his pamphlet on *The Vatican Decrees*, which argued that Catholic doctrines were incompatible with loyalty to the Queen). He was speaking all over the country on the Balkan atrocities, a campaign which would eventually lead to his return to Parliament and to the leadership of the Liberal Party three years later. This excursion to Ireland (the only one he ever made) became more of a private visit than was intended, though he did meet many people in Dublin and elsewhere. It was reported that an appeal was made by 'a gentleman of Cork' that some organisation should be established to secure the Liberal vote in Ireland. Gladstone, already aware of the rising importance of the Home Rule party, at first baulked at the idea, but, notwithstanding, the United Liberal Club, welcoming both Liberals and Home Rulers, was started with the aim of boosting the anti-Conservative vote and increasing the number of such voters on the register in the city. By the autumn of 1878 it was well established in rooms on the second floor of 54 Dawson Street (now demolished), with John S. Joyce as Secretary. These were the two main reception rooms of the Georgian building. A nearly contemporary picture shows it to have been an elegant townhouse, with a cast-iron balcony. The whole provided a rather grand background for John Stanislaus's operations. Gorman, who received much of his information from James, suggests that John's appointment came about through Peter Paul McSwiney and, as he was the most influential Catholic Liberal in Dublin and a creature of Cardinal Cullen's, this may well have been so. (Cullen died in October 1878; with him a certain kind of Catholic reaction passed away.) And the Club, like McSwiney, had its other O'Connell connections as well. However, once more it is unlikely that John Stanislaus would have been appointed to this organisational and financial post without some reasonable credentials for the job.

The Liberals at this date were still an important element on the Irish political scene. Or, more accurately, they thought they were. Up to the election of 1868 when it was a choice between Liberals and Conservatives, the Liberals formed a national majority and were particularly strong in the boroughs. However, the emergence of the Home Rulers with the election of 1874 had begun their decline, especially in the country seats. Coming from Cork City, which had been overwhelmingly Liberal since 1832, John Stanislaus may not have sensed this. All the influential political folk he knew there and in Dublin were Liberals. As yet Home Rule was far from being a substantial force. Those closely involved with the Club included Dr Lyons, a Cork Liberal (and perhaps even 'the gentleman from Cork' alluded to above), Maurice Brooks (a Home Ruler), George Delaney (another Corkman, partner of P. P. McSwiney in the Monster Mart and a director of the distillery), Hugh Tarpey, the Lord Mayor (whose name would be given to one of the four old men in *Finnegans Wake*), the printers Alley and O'Reilly (W. J. O'Reilly later printed James Joyce's first publication), the expansive Home Rule lawyer, Valentine Blake Dillon, James McCann, J. G. Swift MacNeill and Thomas W. Begge, a wine-merchant. Fr James Daniel, Parish Priest of Francis Street Catholic Church, sat on the Club's Committee as Hon. Secretary;

while John's job was actively bureaucratic, secretarial skills were not required of Fr Daniel.

The Liberals had won one of the two Dublin seats in 1865 with Jonathan Pim, and again in 1868, when Sir E. A. Guinness came in as a Conservative for the other seat. Guinness was unseated over a little matter of electoral fraud and his seat went in 1870 to Sir Daniel Corrigan, a Conservative Catholic medical man. At the next election Maurice Brooks, a leading builder's merchant in the city, stood as a Home Ruler, and ousted Pim, so that in the election of 1880 it would be a straight fight between the Tories, Guinness and Stirling, against Brooks as a Home Ruler, and Lyons as a Liberal. (At the next election the city would have four members and an enlarged electorate, all of which secured it for the Nationalist interest, with only an occasional win by Liberals or Unionists.)

The Club was an agreeable place to meet, to smoke and drink, and perhaps even to dine – all very much to John Stanislaus's taste. He enjoyed an active social life. Local politics meant events at the Mansion House: 'I had many a damn good night there at dances and suppers, in the good old times.' These Mansion House Balls (though nothing like the splendid levées at Dublin Castle attended by Unionists) were riproarious affairs and often deprecated as a waste of money, mere sprees for well-connected Nationalists.

There was a great revival of the songs of Thomas Moore in 1879, his centenary year. John Stanislaus, like the rest of Ireland, always had a soft spot for Moore's 'Melodies' and often sang them. A 'Grand Musical and Literary Demonstration' of Moore's work was held in May at the Exhibition Palace in Earlsfort Terrace, which John is likely to have attended. It seems that he was also among the party at the June unveiling of a statue (by Farrell) of the late Sir John Gray MP, as mention is made of the ceremony in 'Grace'. A character in the story may be echoing John's opinions when he sums up the family with the succinct comment: 'None of the Grays were any good'. But John Stanislaus's main interest, aside from the political work, was always singing. Indeed it may have been as a singer (rather than in his capacity as accountant or supplier of whiskey) that he first came into contact with the Murray family of the Eagle Tavern in Terenure. Their daughter May, then nineteen, was highly musical and had been trained to sing and play piano by her aunts, the Flynns (well-known teachers in Dublin who had sung in the oratorio performed in celebration of O'Connell's centenary). Their shared enthusiasm provided a link for John Joyce with this pale, delicately pretty young girl. He fell in love again.

John Stanislaus was not approved of by the girl's father, who was annoyed one day to find them together in Grafton Street – possibly visiting Gunn's music shop. John Murray was from Longford, but his wife came of very old Dublin stock who traced themselves back a couple of centuries in business. What his precise objections to John were can only be guessed at, but John put it down to 'just the usual story of the beautiful daughter and the irascible parent'. He pursued her avidly, and she fell for him.

The course of John Stanislaus's courtship during 1879 ran concurrently with his preparations for the election. Parliament was dissolved on 24 March and the election came off in April. Even the fire which destroyed Michael Gunn's first theatre, the Theatre Royal, on 9 February would not have distracted John Stanislaus from the heat of political strife. During the weeks before the poll he had the run of a Townsend Street office of the *Freeman's Journal*, around the corner from the ruins of the theatre. Among the advertising gimmicks of the campaign was an advertisement for Brooks and Lyons, showing (somewhat patronisingly) how the ballot paper should be marked by their supporters. This quite conceivably was

INSTRUCTIONS HOW TO VOTE BY BALLOT.

1	**BROOKS** (MAURICE BROOKS, Sackville-place, Merchant, J.P., T.C.).	✗
2	**GUINNESS** (Sir ARTHUR EDWARD GUINNESS, Leeson-street, Bart).	
3	**LYONS** (ROBERT DYER LYONS, 6 Merrion-square, West).	✗
4	**STIRLING** (JAMES STIRLING, 19 Fitzwilliam-place, Managing Director).	

The above is a facsimile of the Ballot Paper that will be handed you by the Returning Officer Mark it exactly as above.
Any other mark on the Paper but the above invalidates your Vote.
Vote solid BROOKS and LYONS. Split votes neutralise their value.

an idea of the ready-minded John Stanislaus. But winning the election also involved canvassing the electors registered on the electoral roll, which was revised every year from the lists of rate-payers. On the doorstep, or as often as not propped up at a mahogany bar counter, John Stanislaus would have used his charm on many a hesitant voter.

After a hectic fortnight of campaigning, the election was held on 5 April 1880 and counting began as soon as the polls closed. The results were announced by the Returning Officer at the Exhibition Palace in Earlsfort Terrace. This was John Stanislaus's night of nights, as he himself recalled:

The count of the votes took place in the Exhibition Palace in a very big room. All the tables were there and I had four men on each table. I didn't at all expect that we would get the two members in – I would have been satisfied if I got Brooks in but I didn't at all expect that Lyons would get in. In the end towards the end of the count I got the rough figures [from the men at the tables] and I totted them up two or three times and by Gor what was it but I knew the two were returned! This was the hell of a thing for me. Our solicitor, Stephen Sheehan, a tremendous big man, he was over at a table and says I, 'By Gor our men are in, Stephen – not one but the two of them.' Who should be sitting next to me but Sir Arthur Guiness [*recte* Guinness] and his cousin the Hon. David Plunkett, and the two were in evening dress. He lived at the time in Stephens Green; at the north side of it he had a house, his brother Lord Iveagh has it now. Sir Arthur asked me 'Have you got the figures?' 'I have, Sir Arthur,' I replied, and he asked me how did it go. I then had the pleasure of telling Sir Arthur Guiness that he was no longer a member and I said that Maurice Brooks got so much and Lyons so much.

The Conservatives had been trounced. Maurice Brooks of the Home Rule Party had 5763, while Dr Lyons, the Liberal, had 5647. Sir Arthur Edward Guinness had 5446 and Stirling 5059. Never again would Dublin return a Conservative MP. To add to the good results, in Cork, another two-seater constituency, John Daly – John's cousin, of the drapery emporium – headed the poll with 1923 votes to his companion Charles Stewart Parnell's 1505, and both were elected. As long as John Stanislaus lived, he would take credit for this Dublin triumph: 'I won the election in Dublin,' he boasted in the 1920s, 'and I was the man that put in Maurice Brooks and Lyons, and put out Arthur Guiness as he then was, the sitting member, and of course Sterling, who was going up with Guiness, never got in.' And, by his account, the victors' supporters agreed with him. It was time to celebrate:

We went out soon after and had a thanksgiving meeting in the Rotunda bar. I was the cock of the walk that day and I will never forget it; I was complimented by everybody. I got one hundred guineas [£105] from each of the members. When I found that we had the election won, I was going out but there was a great crush at the door. When the people outside heard the news there was the devil's shouting and cheering. I could not stir but I saw my friend the Baby Policeman at the door. He helped me out and I don't know what I would do without him . . . He was only 6 feet 5 inches in height. And he was a damn decent fellow too, and he used be generally on duty at the end of Grafton Street, outside Trinity College and on the night that the poll was declared . . . I met the 'little baby'.

Gallaher of the *Freeman's Journal* got hold of me, when I pushed my way through the door, to get the figures. I went down to the office in Townsend Street where there was a very big crowd and when they heard the news there was more shouting and cheering. I left the *Freeman* office after giving them the correct figures and went up to Abbey Street. The Oval Bar was just at the corner of that street and it was owned by a damn decent fellow [Phil Gilligan] – I knew him well. I had not taken a drink of any kind during the election – a whole fortnight – and I would not have one for God Almighty if he came down especially from the Heavens. A car drove up and all around about there was shouting and cheering for the victors at that hour of the morning. My God it was three o'clock in the morning and the excitement was great and I was the hero of it all because they said that it was I that won the election. I was seized by a fellow who pushed his way up to me: 'Where are you pushing me?' said I – and who in the blazes was this fellow but the poor decent man that owned the Oval Bar. I had to go in with him – he was a brother-in-law of Nugent, that's Michael you know. He was there with two others on the car. We all went in and by God Almighty such drinking of champagne I never saw in my life. We could not wait to draw the corks, we slapped them against the marble-topped counter. The result was we were there drinking for about three hours and when we came out the question was what were we to do with ourselves at that ungodly hour of the morning. The Turkish Baths came into my mind and there I went after having any God's quantity of champagne. Oh dear, dear God, those were great times.

The name of 'Guiness' had been long associated with Dublin, as politicians, generous benefactors and, above all, as brewers. Whatever John Stanislaus might have thought about the family's political role in the city, he had no complaints about the product of their business at St James's Gate: he did not, he admitted, know much about the history of the firm, but, the interviewee said plaintively from his bed, 'I know this much, they make damn good porter – I wish I had a pint of it now.'

Meanwhile the purse from the new members gave John a bonus on which to start the new life he was planning. He could well congratulate himself on the position he had achieved, which was a considerable advance on his father's and grandfather's. The future was still full of possibilities. From limeburners to successful political activist and businessman in three generations was a success of a distinct kind. There was already talk among John's political friends that he might himself run for public office one day, for as Stanislaus remarks, 'he had a glib tongue and had been among the first to greet the rising star of Parnell'. Parnell had first appeared on the political scene in 1874. He had been defeated for Dublin County but had taken a seat in Meath. In 1880, with his election for Cork City, he had become the dominant figure among Irish Nationalists of all kinds. He would dominate John Stanislaus's life for the rest of his days.

John Stanislaus was also becoming prominent in Dublin in other ways. Soon after leaving Cork he had taken formal voice lessons with Madame Daviez-di-Bella in the Abercorn Music College in Harcourt Street or with one of several other Italian ladies who offered instruction in the capital. Though this lady had been so impressed by her pupil's voice that she believed that she had 'found the successor to Campanini', the celebrated Italian tenor, John failed to live up to her expectations of a musical career for him. However, he was still in demand as a singer, and appeared quite often on stage. On the evenings of 27 and 28 April 1880 he took part in two grand concerts at the Antient Concert Rooms, under the patronage of Sir John Gray's son, Edward Dwyer Gray MP, Lord Mayor of Dublin and owner of the *Freeman's Journal*, and a leading light of the United Liberal Club. John was listed at the head of the male singers, above Sydney McNevin, J. R. Keehy, Charles Dollard and a Captain Joyce (whose singing in an opera sponsored by Lady Marlborough in aid of relief in the west of Ireland – currently close to famine again – had been much applauded). The ladies taking part were Miss Bessie Herbert, Miss Croker and Miss Maggie Walsh. Miss Martin was at the pianoforte, Mr N. P. Healy on the violin, and the conductor was none other than the eminent Professor W. G. Goodwin, from Frankfort Avenue. This appearance was obviously a most suitable one for John Stanislaus to shine in, especially as several Members of Parliament had also promised to attend, though in the event it seems they did not. While it was not explicit in the publicity for the concert, the presence of the celebrated Fr Ring, an Oblate priest, who was involved both with the community at Inchcore and the Reformatory which the Oblates ran at Glencree (the setting for one of the significant memories of the far past that echo through *Ulysses*) suggests that the funds were being raised for the Oblate orphanage at Goldenbridge which catered for 170 children, and perhaps for the Glencree Reformatory as well.

By now John Stanislaus was living at 15 Upper Clanbrassil Street, just on the city side of the Grand Canal. May Murray, now officially his fiancée, lived down the road in her father's house at No. 7. It is likely that the house was a convenient short-term lodging taken for the purposes of the impending wedding and not where he had previously been living, since he is not listed there in the street directories. Across the street, directly facing this large house – it had four storeys – stood the smaller one in which James Joyce was to place the birth and childhood of Leopold Bloom. This building, which possibly James Joyce mistook for his father's old one, is currently somewhat eccentrically decorated with a memorial plaque to the fictional voyager of *Ulysses*.

Though John Murray was now more or less resigned to his daughter's engagement to the ebullient John Stanislaus, predictably there was strong opposition closer to home. John's mother Ellen was vehemently hostile to the match. Her son was marrying against her will, into a family she gnomically described as 'troublesome people'. The truth was that Ellen Joyce would have disapproved of anyone who took John away from her. For fifteen years since her husband died she had devoted her life to her rough diamond of a son and now he was deserting her. No doubt she cajoled and threatened John, but after this had failed she took more active measures. Catherine Coffey, a friend of May's, would remember one of these, when Ellen Joyce attempted to turn the young May Murray against her own son.

Catherine Coffey, *née* O'Donnell, was married to John Coffey, later of Bray. They were members of the choir of Rathgar Church, where both John and May also now sang – John's love of music at this stage still outweighed his antipathy to the Church and he may also have felt it advisable to offer lip-service to organised religion in order to win over the woman he loved: May Murray was a particularly devout young lady. May became close friends with Catherine Coffey and afterwards explained to her what had happened.

One day May had been bidden to call on Mrs Joyce, perhaps in the Clanbrassil Street house. Her future mother-in-law frankly advised her against marrying her son and told her to wait until he came home for his midday meal. As Catherine Coffey was told, the house had 'a folding door between the drawing-room and the dining-room and the old lady seated May in the drawing-room with the doors slightly ajar. Soon her son came in to lunch and, sure enough, spoke roughly to his mother using coarse language.' But Ellen Joyce's ploy failed: virginal romance was not to be swayed and May was determined to go ahead. While Catherine Coffey never retracted her high opinion of John's fine singing voice, before many more years had passed she would have seen enough of him to state her own bald opinion: John Stanislaus Joyce was mad.

Some time before (or, just possibly, after) the wedding Ellen Joyce ratified her disgust by leaving Dublin and her son entirely. She returned home to Cork in search of better treatment from relatives there. Her vitriolic reaction left scars on John Stanislaus that were to be visible in his son's later writing: Gabriel in 'The

Dead' remembers his mother's 'sullen opposition' to his marriage and broods on 'some slighting phrases she had used' about his wife. Old Mrs Joyce was an adept of the slighting phrase. It was a family skill that would not be lost as the generations passed.

John's split with his mother was also to find its place in the play, *Exiles*, written more than thirty years after the event. The main character, Richard Rowan, recalls that his mother 'died alone, not having forgiven me, and fortified by the rites of the holy church'. Before she died, she had sent 'a letter of warning, bidding me break with the past, and remember her last words to me ... How can my words hurt her poor body that rots in the grave? Do you think I do not pity her cold blighted love for me? I fought against her spirit while she lived to the bitter end ... I waited, too, not for her death but for some understanding of me, her own son, her own flesh and blood; that never came.' Like Richard Rowan, John Stanislaus may have tried to defy his feelings of guilt about his mother, but in later years he rarely cared to speak of her.

It was from 15 Clanbrassil Street that John and May were married in Rathmines Parish Church (the Church of Our Immaculate Lady of Refuge) on 5 May 1880. The marriage certificate noted that the bride was a minor: she had not yet reached the age of twenty-one; the groom, ten years older, was described simply as 'Gentleman' (and in Dublin's newspaper for gentlemen, *The Irish Times*, the wedding notice duly appeared). The ceremony was conducted by Fr Patrick Gorman and the witnesses were John George Lee (the jilted Annie Lee's brother, perhaps) and Margaretta Lyons. Fittingly, one represented John Stanislaus's outside interests and the other his wife's devotion to her family – Margaretta Lyons was Mary's first cousin. John's and May's married life was beginning with a deep division of interests and loyalties between them, which would remain a permanent feature of their relationship. It did not augur well.

In the outside world of politics, 5 May 1880 was more auspicious. A new and particularly ineffectual Viceroy of Ireland, Lord Cowper, was being sworn in that very morning and, far more significantly to John, his wedding day also happened to be the day upon which the President of the Irish Land League, Charles Stewart Parnell, officially announced his decision to accept his Cork City seat in

Westminster. Then, when the Parliamentary Party (composed of an alliance of Home Rulers and Irish Liberals) assembled in the middle of May after the General Election, Parnell was narrowly elected their leader. His most enthusiastic champion was another Corkman, Timothy M. Healy. Here too was a new beginning.

PART TWO

Father

'. . . his father and two of his cronies drank to
the memory of their past.'
Drawing by Dodie Masterman
(Copyright © Folio Society 1965 from their edition of *A Portrait of the
Artist as a Young Man*)

CHAPTER 10

John and May

Mr and Mrs John Stanislaus Joyce decided on a honeymoon abroad. It was another beacon to the world of John's confident social expectations. As if to spite his mother for dragging him back from there when he was a boy, he took his bride to the capital of the Empire, London, where William Gladstone was currently busy, at the age of seventy-one, forming the Liberal government of 1880. An opportunity to meet Irish members was not to be neglected – to remind some of them of the debt owed to John Stanislaus. But for the time being John's attention was focused on the enjoyment of more personal politics. As well as the usual sightseeing (with perhaps restorative explorations of London's famous hotels), he intended to sample with May the pleasures of evenings at the theatre and the music-hall, something they both appreciated. Between such entertainments John would have called on the O'Connells, relatives of his mother who had settled in the city, to show off his new bride. And he, at least, relished the excitement of shared nights in strange bedrooms.

For imperial good measure they took the train down to Royal Windsor, where Queen Victoria's castle bulked over the Thames. James Joyce called the great river 'liquid history' and indeed the place exuded the pomp of power. As an eager tourist John could indulge his sneaking respect for royalty. They hired a boat. It should have been a romantic occasion: 'Sweete Themmes! runne softly, till I end my Song' is the refrain of the beautiful bridal ode 'Prothalamion' by Edmund Spenser, that other Cork landowner. But when they were 'floating on the Christal Flood', John could not resist showing off his legendary prowess as an oarsman and challenged to a race another boat containing another couple. His mood darkened when May had difficulty with the steering and soon she was being colourfully sworn at by him in public, his training on the Queenstown pilot boats coming to the fore. They won the impromptu contest in the end and John was as proud of his inventive language as he was of the victory. For May, however, the insults could not be forgotten. She had known that she was likely to be growled at sometimes, but it was disheartening to be subjected to foul-mouthed abuse on their first holiday together.

When the Joyces returned to Dublin, John soon found a house to rent. In a row of modest but handsome grey brick houses, 13 Ontario Terrace was set a little back from the Grand Canal at the top of Mount Pleasant Avenue. (In *Ulysses*, Leopold and Molly Bloom occupied the same address at a later date.) A social step up from Clanbrassil Street, there was room for a maid and John probably engaged one. The terrace was conveniently situated: May was still within a short mile's walk of her parents and John was near enough to town to enjoy taking the air on pleasant summer mornings on his way to the Liberal Club, crossing the canal at Portobello Bridge, and strolling down Harcourt Street and through Stephen's Green. (That August the Guinnesses passed the Green over to the public for the first time since 1814 – a move that Dublin cynics ascribed to an attempt to curry popular favour after the recent electoral defeat.)

May had been pregnant when she returned from the honeymoon. She set about turning the new house into a family home, encouraged by her husband 'to do it decently'. James Joyce's notes for *Exiles* give glimpses of his parents' early married life together: they describe the young wife 'putting out the lights in the drawing-room after a social evening in her husband's house, kneeling outside a confessional in the jesuit church', and ordering new carpets from one of the shops in Grafton Street, where even window-shopping was a social statement. Switzer's and Brown Thomas's were much grander than the store north of the Liffey owned by 'my cousin Peter Paul McSwiney', where they might have even got a discount 'for family'. McSwiney's political power was waning in any case, prompting John into other associations.

Observing his wife's family at play gave John material for many a story afterwards. He was included in various Murray family excursions, but though he got on rather well with May's mother Margaret, still in her forties, he had not won over her husband and his relationship with May's brothers was also difficult. But none of this really mattered: he loved May and May loved him. All in all, as Stanislaus sardonically reports, during these early months the couple 'seem to have been what Divorce Court judges call "reasonably happy".'

On 23 November 1880, less than seven months after the wedding, the Joyces' first child was born. To John's delight, it was a boy, like every Joyce child for the previous three generations. The birth took place at home in Ontario Terrace and Margaret Murray was there to help with the delivery. The baby was named John, after his father, and was given his paternal grandfather's second name, Augustine. It was a coincidence, but pleasing for May, that her own father's name was John and that her brother William's second name was Augustine. Little John Augustine Joyce's role in the future of the illustrious family line was doomed. The baby was sickly when he was born and, after only eight hopeless days, he died. Margaret Murray, who had been there at the end, testified that the boy had not survived because he was premature. This may have been true, but any alternative explanation would have admitted that her daughter had been pregnant at her wedding. Given the young bride-to-be's piety, this seems to be unlikely, though her suitor's attentions may have been extremely ardent. He, at least, was experienced in such matters.

Since there are no surviving records of a baptism, there must have been a hasty ceremony at home. This was a matter of extreme urgency: unbaptised children who died were destined for an eternity in Limbo, a noisy region of the Catholic universe reserved for unchristened babies and other heathens. (Some years later, when the family was living in Bray, some of the young Joyces witnessed the effects of Limbo on another mother who tried to fling herself from a first-floor window as her unbaptised child's coffin was being removed for burial. The Catholic Church has since abolished Limbo.)

While the devout May Joyce at least had the limited consolation that her sinless baby was bound for Heaven, John was deeply affected by the loss, and the optimism of his new life was badly shaken.

As *Ulysses* was to acknowledge: Marry in May and repent in December. Years later, after many more tragedies and disappointments, John could still say, as his daughter Eva recalled, that his life was buried with his son. John Augustine Joyce (in the words of the *Wake*) had been his 'firstborn and firstfruit of woe'. With the ghost of Rudy Bloom, the baby's short life would have important echoes in *Ulysses* and also a place in *Finnegans Wake*. For the funeral, John bought a plot in Prospect Cemetery, Glasnevin, where he knew the Superintendent, David Malins. This was the only estate he would manage to hold on to until his own death. Glasnevin was on the northern outskirts of the city; the large graveyard there had the melancholy distinction of being 'the Irish Valhalla', as the burial place of, among other national heroes, Daniel O'Connell, who had helped to create it as an almost exclusively Catholic cemetery. There were very few mourners at the freezing graveside; even the baby's mother was not there – it was not then customary for women to attend funerals.

When it came, the couple's first Christmas together was a gloomier occasion than they had anticipated. What little comfort there was for May would have come mostly from her mother. As for John Stanislaus, it was surely now that he received one last bitter letter, as mentioned in *Exiles*, from his own unforgiving mother in Cork.

The Irish Society of St Cecilia, devoted to the promulgation of church music, held an annual festival in Dublin which united several contingents of singers from the churches in the diocese. On 26 and 27 January 1881 it was held in St Andrew's Church, Westland Row, opposite where John's accountancy practice had been some years before. May Joyce came through the snow to be among the choir of 140 voices that sang a wide selection of sacred music, including an anthem by Pierluigi da Palestrina, 'the prince of church musicians'. On the second day, the feast of St John Chrysostomos, after a choral High Mass the vast congregation was rewarded by a sermon from the celebrated Fr Thomas Burke, 'a born orator'. Many years later, James Joyce would name Palestrina as one of his two favourite composers. The other, Schoenberg, might have appealed to his mother rather less.

New beginnings were in the air, both politically and in the personal lives of the Joyces. At Westminster, Parnell was gathering momentum and his involvement with the semi-revolutionary Land League gave him useful extraparliamentary teeth at home. A leader of the thirty-strong Irish Party in Westminster, he had by now attracted the epithet that summed up John Stanislaus's view of him: 'The Uncrowned King of Ireland'.

When the Annual General Meeting of the United Liberal Club took place on 4 January 1881, despite his triumphs, John Stanislaus had ceased to be its Secretary. The Club was mutating into a Voter Registration Association and it would not be long before the premises lost all connection with politics and became a Whist Club. Many of John's friends were now enrolling in the new Catholic Commercial Club at 42 Upper Sackville Street, which soon had 740 members. Here, as secret police files reveal, the Land League organisers could mix with and influence a wide range of Catholic opinion. It was time to move on, to catch any fresh wind that the recent electoral victories in Dublin might blow. The previous autumn, Gladstone's government had sent the progressive and industrious H. C. E. Childers on an investigative visit to Ireland. While he was in Dublin a convenient centre of operations had been the United Liberal Club and John Stanislaus could hardly have failed to encounter him there; they may have been introduced by a grateful Brooks or Lyons. A far-seeing man – he early advocated the use of telephones in his department – Childers was among the first senior British politicians to sympathise with the concept of Home Rule. When his report came out, it recommended (among other worthwhile reforms) the establishment of a Catholic University.

Through the bush telegraph, John had heard of a possible new career opportunity. It was the responsibility of the Lord Lieutenant (or Viceroy) to appoint one-third of the posts in the Collector-General's Office, the agency for levying and collecting the city's domestic and other rates. One of these posts became vacant in January, just as John finished with the Club. It was partly a political appointment, since, as well as making sure that the monies were collected, the work also involved checking the electoral registration of households according to district. The position was secure and respectable and, though the pay was largely performance related, the successful candidate was likely to earn upwards of £400 a year, with a pension on retirement. This was at a time when that mythic figure, the Dublin Working Man (who was unlikely to live long enough to worry about a pension that never existed), would have been doing extremely well to make £2 a week. The financial appeal of the Civil Service was a long-term fact of Irish life. John Stanislaus thought himself admirably suited for the task: his activities over the previous couple of years had given him a useful knowledge of the government and municipal structure of Dublin, and of the relationship between money and influence. His friends were willing to put his name forward for the job. It is possible that Peter Paul McSwiney, John Daly or Lyons, himself an MP, put in a good word for John. Certainly, the support of the United Liberal Club was assured. The Club's aim was to enfranchise as many Liberal (and Nationalist) households as possible and John Stanislaus would be an ideal 'impartial' operator on the ground. Whoever it was that pulled the strings, on 25 March Lord Cowper sent a letter of nomination to W. E. 'Buckshot' Forster, the Chief Secretary, and the job was formally offered to Mr John Stanislaus Joyce.

While all this was going on, May's mother, who had suffered for years from a complaint of the womb, had died. At about the same time the Joyces left their sad memories behind them in Ontario Terrace, set their faces to the future and moved across the Grand Canal to 30 Emorville Avenue, off the South Circular Road. The new house was an unusual one among the terraces surrounding it, a single storey perched above a basement on the corner with St Vincent Street. With only six rooms in all it was modest enough. May's father, John Murray, lived nearby in Upper Clanbrassil Street, probably still with one or more of his sons, while the father of his daughter-in-law Josephine, James J. Giltrap, owner of the celebrated dog, Garryowen, was a stone's throw away across the South Circular Road. Nearby was Stamer Street, where the Joyces' friend Major Powell lived with his children. May already knew most of their neighbours and all the local shops, and since the sociable John had also been a local resident in the months before his marriage, it must have been a relief that they could both spend a good deal of time with friends. Many of these friends would eventually contribute in large measure to the past of Leopold Bloom.

Although the Joyces were not very far from their first house in Ontario Terrace, they were now in a quite different and distinct area of the city: the network of quiet redbrick streets clustered around Clanbrassil Street and Leonard's Corner was rapidly becoming the heart of Jewish Dublin, as anti-Semitic persecutions drove refugees out of Lithuania and other parts of eastern Europe. It was John's memories of these settlers that enabled James Joyce to construct a convincing background for Bloom's early life. Before long, these streets would have a thriving Jewish population, with names that would be used in *Ulysses*, such as Herzog, Masliansky and Bloom itself. A short step up Emorville Avenue from the Joyces' house the home of another such family, the Citrons, can still be seen, perhaps where Bloom remembers Molly occupying a basket chair during one of the 'pleasant evenings' they spent there. The Citrons had a lodger who nearly caught her washing her pregnant body in front of the window. And it may have been because Reuben J. Dodd, soon to be John's sworn enemy, lived in this area (at one stage almost directly opposite the Giltraps), that everyone assumed that he too was a Jew.

There was just one minor formality before John Stanislaus took up his office of profit under the Crown. A Victorian reform to ensure that a minimum competency should go with the unavoidable patronage meant that he had to pass a simple examination first. At the end of March he paid the entrance fee and in April he failed the examination. Perhaps he was taken up with the move to the new house; perhaps the family tragedies had been too upsetting; perhaps he was overconfident or misled as to the necessary amount of preparation: there were several possible explanations. Whatever the excuses, it was a serious setback. He badly needed the money. As is often the case with only children, John Stanislaus loved babies. He also loved making babies: before the beginning of June his wife was pregnant again. For John the eldest would always be special, but this would be his first real child. He hoped for another son. However, all children were expensive if they were to be brought up properly. It was essential that he should build up a good financial base for the whole family – however large it might one day be. He discovered that the job had still not been filled and tried again. After another round of lobbying, in mid-May the Chief Secretary was somehow persuaded to nominate him a second time for the position, and a date for the next exam was set. John prepared more assiduously for the test this time. Half-way through the year he resat it and, on 18 July, news came that he had passed.

At the end of June, news of a different sort had come from Cork. On 27 June Ellen Joyce had died, without summoning her only son. John had enough loyalty or social responsibility to inform the deaths column of the *Freeman's Journal* – though on this occasion he did not bother with the *Irish Times*. The notice read, in the clipped, unadorned style of the day:

> Joyce – At Sundays Wells, Cork,
> Ellen, relict of the late James
> Augustine Joyce, aged 65 years.

Mrs Joyce had probably been in the home of a relative, John Thomas O'Connell, at 11 South Mall, Rosemount, when she died. How welcome this difficult woman really had been there is doubtful, since no one felt it necessary to announce her death in any of the Cork papers. During her last months, far from softening towards her son, she had talked of altering the terms of the family trust, which left all the family property to John after his mother's death. However, her brother, William O'Connell, the surviving trustee, would not countenance breaking the trust and on 30 July he signed the deed to execute the legacy. John had now become the owner of tenanted houses in six different locations in Cork City, including one property that William himself had been keeping in his own (temporary) possession. In a sad twist, just four days after the deed was signed, William's wife died. She left her widower a little over £600. John could thank his Uncle Bill for a lot more than that.

Virtually overnight, the Joyces found themselves extremely well off. A more expansive life-style now offered itself. John Stanislaus Joyce Esqre relished his new standing: he was now an absentee landlord (albeit in house property, not 'proper land'). He could expect some £500 every year from the Cork rents; this on top of what he would make in his new job (starting in the New Year) would put him well into the top few per cent of earners in Ireland. He had already done immeasurably better than his father ever had and, after the difficulty and tragedy of the previous months, as the summer came to an end his confidence was on the mend.

In August, Gladstone's government, as a forced concession to Parnell and his party, passed the Land Act. This was in fact the beginning of the end of the Land War. As physical force was gradually dying away (until it returned in 1916), parliamentary politics became the primary road taken by Nationalists towards reform in Ireland. Yet for Parnell, it was not enough. The new Act merely gave the tenant some relatively minor rights over his land and brought some rents down a little. He travelled around the country making inflammatory speeches in support of the Land League and linking himself still further with the enemies of the Crown. A great demonstration in Dublin was organised for 25 September, in which John Stanislaus doubtless joined. Then, in October, Parnell was arrested and politely locked up in Kilmainham Gaol, where he was to stay for the next seven months. In prison, the leader's supposedly parlous state of health was attended to by Dr Joseph Kenny, who reported upon it in worried tones to the public. However, it did not stop the prisoner enjoying himself with an airgun he had openly brought with him, nor even deter him from playing vigorous games of handball in the exercise yard. John Stanislaus later knew Joe Kenny, the 'mad Fenian apothecary' (as one cynic called him); his brother Bob would one day be the Joyce family doctor.

In Dublin, the day after the arrests, Friday, 14 October, a 'monster' meeting (the phrase evoked Daniel O'Connell) was held at the Rotunda, with the Lord-Mayor-elect, Charles Dawson, in the chair. Most of those on the platform were immediately afterwards themselves incarcerated and within twenty-four hours an important group of leaders had joined Parnell in Kilmainham. These included the Land League stalwart, John Dillon MP, William O'Brien, Cork-born author of *When We Were Boys* and editor of the Parnellite newspaper *United Irishman,* and the voluble Andrew Kettle ('the Kettle with the spout'), about whom John Stanislaus would speak almost fifty years later. On the eighteenth, in gaol, they all signed the No Rent Manifesto, urging tenants to withhold payment. (As a modest urban landlord John had nothing to fear from the recommendation, which was primarily agrarian in aim.) The Manifesto was to have little effect anyway, as most tenants were quite glad that their rent had come down a little under the new Act, and paid it.

But something more significant came out of Parnell's sojourn in Kilmainham. Now, embedded in the minds of the Irish people, was the picture of 'The Chief' behind bars. There was rioting for several days in the streets of Dublin. In the eyes of many (John Stanislaus included), the quasi-martyrdom of prison raised Parnell to the status of a national Messiah. From now on, John Stanislaus Joyce would be unshakeable in his devotion to this gentleman politician.

The Joyces were soon on the move again. In the summer of 1881 they transferred to a house in Kingstown (now Dún Laoghaire) – conceivably where John's mother had been living immediately before leaving for Cork. Some ten miles south of the city, Kingstown was both port and genteel dormitory town to Dublin. From 47 Northumberland Avenue, off George's Street, the main thoroughfare, they could hear the sirens of the ferries from Britain as they slipped in and out of the harbour. The famous Davy Stevens had already established his pitch by the pier, where he sold newspapers and extended a hundred thousand Irish welcomes to travellers, be they rebels or royalty. He is still selling newspapers in *Ulysses*.

Waiting for his new job to begin in the New Year, John had very little to do in Kingstown except watch his wife incubate his child. He enjoyed taking the train into town to meet friends, to dabble in what was left of his accountancy business and to plan future investments. In the autumn he contacted the insurance company Drimmie's (with which his affairs would be entwined until his death) and had no difficulty in raising a mortgage on some of his Cork property. This mortgage, the first of many, was merely a temporary measure to tide him over until the job began and to give him something to invest should the opportunity arise. It would be paid back after two years. At the same time he signed an insurance bond for the Collector-General, who demanded that all its prospective employees indemnify the Office against any possible future fraud they might commit.

John therefore had the leisure in Kingstown to cultivate new companions. One of the most entertaining was Captain Thomas Cunniam, the owner of a pub on Upper George's Street, conveniently placed half-way between the Joyces' house and the railway station. Cunniam was a publican with a past, a retired American sea captain who would in time prosper and have other wine, spirits and grocery interests in town. His extravagant style of story-telling appealed to John and made him laugh. It was probably in Kingstown, and partly thanks to Captain Cunniam, that John's growing tendency to roll home drunk became firmly established. The friendship between them was to last long enough for Stanislaus to remember Cunniam years later as 'a drunken vulgarian'.

Cut off from her family and friends for the first time as her pregnancy advanced, May Joyce sought solace in prayer and wondered about the future. She did not have long to wait: by Christmas 1881 they had moved again, this time to what she hoped would be a more permanent home. Rathgar was then an up-and-coming suburb of South Dublin that was being colonised by prosperous Dublin professionals, with as many Protestant as Roman Catholic residents. The Joyces' house was 41 Brighton Square, a redbrick development so new that it was uncompleted. (The square was in fact to remain awkwardly – Joyceanly – triangular.) Among their 'toney' neighbours was one Plato Oulton, a Trinity man. Nearby was a Wesleyan Chapel. Within walking distance were the homes of friends such as Mat Dillon with his bevy of decorative daughters, and Luke and Caroline Doyle. May's brother, William Murray, and his wife Josephine were also uncomfortably close by; while John could put up with Josephine, relations between the brothers-in-law were not improving.

In January 1882 the new job began at last. It was not yet entirely secure: there would be a probationary period to be endured before John became a virtually unsackable government official. The position was notionally under the aegis of Dublin Castle, the seat of Irish administration. In practice, however, John had a largely municipal rather than a sub-imperial task and political sensitivities could be dismissed. Besides, he worked not in Dublin Castle itself but at 43 Fleet Street, which ran parallel to the Liffey between Dame Street and the south quays, almost half a mile away in the commercial heart of the city. The office, behind the Bank of Ireland, the building that had housed the last Irish parliament nearly a century before, was roughly where the 'homerule sun' was supposed to rise up from a laneway (as Bloom remembers Arthur Griffith remarking about the device of the *Freeman's Journal*). There was no Nationalist sunburst over No. 43, where Edward Byrne Esq., the Collector-General, controlled an elaborate hierarchy of agents, clerks (of various classes), assistants and other officials.

The Collectors proper numbered a dozen and, of these twelve tax-gathering Apostles, most had responsibility for a ward (sometimes two) of the Corporation area. Initially, John Stanislaus was given the division known as Rural Districts to collect. Though scarcely very rural any more, this was larger, more scattered and less populated than the average Collecting District, taking in townships on the hinterland of the city: to the north, Glasnevin, Knockmaroon and Kilmainham near the Phoenix Park, and to the south, the suburbs of Rathmines and Pembroke, and the seaside towns and villages that lay scattered along the railway line towards Bray, such as Blackrock, Kingstown, Dalkey, Killiney and Ballybrack. It was an enormous area to get to know, but it was the basis of John's eventual expert knowledge of the whole extended city.

The Collector-General's men normally gathered up to eleven different taxes or rates, depending on location and circumstances. These were the Police Tax, Poor Rate, Water Rates, Improvement Rate, District-sewer Rate, Grand Jury Cess, Burial Rate, Bridge Tax, Quay Wall Tax, Vestry Cess and the Borough Rate. Because John Stanislaus's areas were outside the city boundary his districts were not liable for all the urban-specific charges. (This was a continuing cause for argument, as much of the outlying population used inner city services every day.) The Police Tax, however, was levied in all areas and became the principal responsibility of the office's new member. It has been suggested that John Stanislaus was in effect collecting the salaries of the agents of his country's occupation, but the Police Tax was raised solely for the Dublin Metropolitan Police (the DMP), an unarmed domestic force, rather than for the Royal Irish Constabulary which was indeed an agent of the country's imperial masters. There was never any sense among his acquaintances that John Stanislaus was a collaborator.

The job suited him: he had always enjoyed exploring and meeting people. Much of each day was spent out and about in one or other of his areas, where there was nobody to keep an eye on him and plenty of opportunity for gossip. The taxes – and the right to vote in elections – were then limited to the owners of property, some of them well worth getting to know, with substantial estates on the edge of the catchment area or important business and political interests in town. Mr Joyce, dapper in silk hat and spats, the elegance of his dark suit scarcely compromised by the collecting bag, would call to discuss with the master of the house the matter of the electoral register or perhaps to iron out some slight oversight with a Police Tax moiety notice. This new Collector was a beguiling conversationalist: he got the business over quickly and then, in no great hurry to go, he was talking and listening, dispensing stories and collecting new ones. These men would all remember meeting (however fleetingly) John Stanislaus. As he moved from place to place around the outskirts of the city he soon had something pithy to pass on about most of his eminent householders.

Work, which began at the civilised hour of ten a.m., finished at four and John would usually find himself in town. The twelve 'Apostles' formed a vaguely coherent group, set apart from the Chief Clerk and his staff. They would meet back at the office at the end of the day and inevitably most of them would drift off to compare notes over a drink – in and around Fleet Street there was no shortage of decent places to go: they were at the centre of Dublin's pub culture.

John Stanislaus, or 'Jack' as his friends called him, was a good drinker. He had a general air of bonhomie, and his companions enjoyed his spontaneous humour and were soon discovering his talent for conversation. Delivered in a musical Cork voice, his observations and anecdotes were enlivened by shockingly accurate bouts of mimicry, physical as well as verbal, in which no doubt the Collector-General and the Chief Clerk featured. Every evening in the pubs and small hotels around Dame Street and the Liffey quays – the Bodega, O'Neill's or the Scotch House – there were new and old stories to tell and re-enact: and if most of Jack Joyce's tales displayed Jack Joyce as hero, that was more than compensated for by his sharp wit and skilful timing. His delight in the unexpected yet exactly appropriate phrase or word was infectious – many examples would later be purloined by James Joyce. During these first weeks of the job it must sometimes have been difficult to abandon his new audience and catch the Rathgar tram home to his now heavily pregnant wife. Farrington of 'Counterparts' would follow in his footsteps to O'Neill's and Mulligan's, both close to Fleet Street. However, by Farrington's time (about 1904) John Stanislaus would be unable – following Bloom's unspoken challenge – to cross Dublin without encountering a pub.

CHAPTER 11

Another Joyce

On Thursday, 2 February, the Feast of Candlemas, John Stanislaus took a day off work. This was not caused by a hangover or religious devotion: at six o'clock that morning his wife had given birth to their second child. As John had hoped, the new baby was another boy, and this time was pink, chubby-cheeked and vocal. To be on the safe side the child was baptised quickly: when he was three days old a christening service was held in the Chapel of Ease, St Joseph's, not far away in Roundtown. The Rev. Fr John O'Mulloy CC pronounced the names of Saints James and Augustine over the squalling bundle.

Though in some cultures it is often the practice to name a new baby after a dead sibling, the Irish usually do not treat shadow babies in this way. The choice of 'James' was obvious: it was John's father's name – and May must have reflected that John and James were the only two brothers among the biblical Twelve Apostles. As for his second name, Augustine, James would later seem to have believed that it was in fact 'Agustin'. Perhaps this variant had been suggested by his mother: it was redolent of Catholic pride and achievement. Don Antonio Agustin had been Papal Nuncio at the court of 'Bloody' Mary Tudor in 1555 and had studied around Europe from Salamanca to Padua, becoming a doctor of laws and a scholar of philology, numismatics, heraldry and theology. A century ago in Catholic Ireland, Church history was far more vividly alive than it is today. But James Agustin Joyce remains a curious name. It never really 'took', and the significance of 'Agustin' would largely be ignored in favour of Augustine by everyone including its owner, though as late as 1925 he was still suggesting that it be used in a book about him.

John had asked Philip McCann and his wife Helen to be his son's godparents. McCann was a successful ship's chandler and general merchant, originally from Dundalk; they were respectable people and may have had distant family connections with the Joyces through one (or both) of John's grandmothers. The couple lived in a handsome town property at 183 Great Brunswick Street (now Pearse Street) and would move in 1887 to an even more imposing house called Fairfield, in the leafier purlieus of Sandymount. Helen McCann was to die soon afterwards and would be forgotten about by her godson, who told Herbert Gorman that his godmother had been one of his mother's aunts, Mrs Callanan. However, Philip was a good choice: he was to keep in close touch with the family until the end of his life and would occasionally even give the lad presents – he presented him with two snuff-boxes on his way to boarding-school at the age of six, which were much appreciated though under the circumstances scarcely very practical. Philip McCann was to have a (somewhat enigmatic) presence in *Finnegans Wake*, though he would be long dead by the time the book was written.

From the start, John took a keen interest in his son's welfare and enjoyed spending time with him. Sometimes he would sing to him and on sunny days they went out to the grass in the middle of Brighton Square, where he liked to tell the child some of the stories and folk-tales that he had learned at his own father's knee. Though James would have no memory of his time in Rathgar, for John these months would never be forgotten: when he saw photographs of his grandson Giorgio in 1906, he told James that they brought back to him 'all the happiest moments of my life'.

In almost his last letter to James, less than a year before he died, John Stanislaus remembered being out in Brighton Square with him and telling the tale of a fairy cow who 'took little boys across' – that is, spirited them away. *A Portrait of the Artist as a Young Man* opens to the voice of Stephen Dedalus's father telling him the same old family story: 'His father told him that story: his father looked at him through a glass: he had a hairy face.' There seems to be only one father, but really the fathers stretched back through the generations, each telling of the moocow and the boy. Did another Joyce boy long before imagine that the moocow had come down the long steep road from the Ballyhoura Hills where the ancestors lived, an emissary from the family past, plodding towards Fermoy with her burden of stories, until she stopped at Rose Cottage where the mountain road met the Blackwater? Now Stephen has met the moocow himself, and he can join in his father's song:

> O the wild rose blossoms
> On the little green place.

And in a field in north Cork, beside a wild rose-covered cottage near the river, a moocow still crops the grass, her journey over.

This 'nicens' little boy in the *Portrait* was called 'baby tuckoo', or in babytalk, 'baby cuckoo'. In the secret back of his father's mind, Jim, as he was usually called at home, had usurped the cot of his dead elder brother. John Stanislaus was the last of his proud and unusual family line of first-born male succession. He had failed to do what his father, his grandfather and his grandfather's father had done: to replace himself exactly, magically, miraculously. The sequence had been broken.

The feeling that his new son was a substitute was never to be admitted. John refused to feel guilty for disappointing his forefathers. He intended to make James into a Joyce worthy to receive the family stories. This child was not some sort of changeling: his father would prove it by loving him more than his predecessors had ever loved their only sons. John's later children would be less favoured, but until the last day of his life his combative love for James was never to wane: he had more than a little of his possessive old mother in him.

At the age of six and a half weeks, James Joyce became an official citizen of the United Kingdom of Great Britain and Ireland when on 20 March his mother registered his birth with the State Clerk, who wrote his second name down as 'Agusta' – perhaps prompting James later to give Leopold Bloom the middle name of 'Paula'. His father, when he heard about the error, may have reflected upon why he himself was not called after his father and whether a family story he had been told, that the drunken parish clerk had got his name wrong, was in fact reliable. Was there some other reason? Could it be that he too was really a second son, that his elder brother had also died? It could never be known now. Such a coincidence might go some way towards explaining Ellen Joyce's exclusive love for John, which was itself to be matched by John's similar emotional dependence on James.

On these and many other linked matters, there can only ever be questions, but they are questions of a sort that would be repeatedly asked by James in his fiction, where the whole subject of the meaning of fatherhood, sonhood and inheritance is subjected to intense scrutiny – notably in Stephen's discussion of Hamlet, whose father's crown (and life) have been taken by his younger brother. In notes for *Ulysses*, written after he had left the family nest to become an artist, an intriguing scrap of verse may sum up baby tuckoo's view of the matter:

> the cuckoo's a fine bird
> he sings as he flies.

Back at work, the ebullient new father toasted the health of his son and heir with his colleagues. Several of these men were to find their way into James's work, either as themselves (a questionable concept most certainly) or in varying degrees down to the purloining of their names. Edward Cotter of Drumcondra, who is an old friend of the narrator's father, Jack, in 'The Sisters', was one of the 'Twelve Apostles'. So too were Messrs Henchy and Crofton, whose names appear in 'Ivy Day in the Committee Room'. In fact John Stanislaus may even first have heard about his new job from J. T. A. Crofton: Crofton had been living in Stamer Street when the Joyces had been nearby. Though there were two Croftons working at different times in the Collector-General's Office, that the one in 'Ivy Day' was a Unionist does not in any way rule out a cordial friendship with John, for whom politics (and religion) were usually a subject for heated discussion rather than enmity. Another Collector also came from the 'Jewish' district of Dublin, Mr H. Hughes of Lombard Street West (off Emorville Avenue). Hughes's family may be the one commemorated by the macabre song in the 'Ithaca' chapter of *Ulysses*, in which Little Harry Hughes drove his ball 'o'er the jew's garden wall' and 'broke the jew's windows all' before having his head cut off with a penknife as punishment.

Of the other Collectors little more is known beyond what has survived through John Stanislaus's stories. A 'weird shadow' in *Ulysses* by the name of Wetherup was a Tory Castle Nominee to the Collector-General's Office, a Freeman and Orangeman. He was said by John to be an ex-waiter and someone who might rob you on a walk in the country. Stuart Gilbert, with whom James Joyce collaborated on a book about *Ulysses*, refers to Wetherup as a 'disreputable friend of John Joyce' and identifies him inconclusively as the mysterious 'Man in the macintosh' who haunts the novel. About the real man all that is known is that he lived at 37 Gloucester Street Upper and was in fact a Mr W. Weatherup. There were also Mr W. E. Wilkinson of Rathgar, whose collecting areas were the Mansion House and Royal Exchange Wards, and Mr Frederick A. Buckley, a raconteur whose off-colour story of how he shot a Russian general in the Crimea (while the officer squatted at stool) appealed to two generations of Joyces and duly made its way into the *Wake*. The one of the Twelve Apostles whom John Stanislaus seemed most actively to dislike was Hugh M'Intyre, from Clonliffe. M'Intyre was to use what he had learned of property under the Collector-General to good effect by later becoming a north Dublin house agent. In this potentially useful capacity, however, he would do no favours for his old colleague.

The first week of May 1882 was a time of high excitement in Ireland. On an understanding informally known as the Treaty of Kilmainham, Parnell was released from gaol and was soon followed by the other political prisoners. (The go-betweens of the 'Treaty' had been the then obscure MPs, Willie O'Shea and Joe Chamberlain, representing the Irish Party and the Liberal Party respectively. That O'Shea's wife Katharine – 'Kitty' – had given birth in February 1882 to Parnell's child was not yet public knowledge.) The same day the Chief Secretary of Ireland, W. E. Forster – who had signed John's job nomination and was by now known in Dublin Castle circles as 'The Pendulum' for his indecisiveness – decided on something and resigned. He was immediately replaced by Lord Frederick Cavendish. Two days later Lord Cowper left his post as Viceroy. To celebrate the releases and the promises of change that the 'Treaty' was said to have won, Dublin took to the streets on the evening of Friday, 5 May. John Stanislaus's presence among the vast procession that wended through the city by torchlight can be taken for granted. Though Parnell himself was not on the platform, having already gone to address Parliament at Westminster, the multitude cheered as though he were among them. It seemed certain now that The Chief would lead the country safely to Home Rule before the year was out, without another drop of blood being spilt.

For Forster, resignation had not come a moment too soon. The next day, while the new Viceroy, Lord Spencer, was unpacking in his official residence in the Phoenix Park, he heard frenzied screams outside. Within a matter of yards from the Viceregal Lodge, Forster's successor, Lord Frederick Cavendish, and his Under-Secretary, Thomas Burke, were being bloodily put to death with long surgeon's knives. The Invincibles, a Fenian splinter group, had struck. Though they had missed the hated 'Buckshot' Forster, they were pleased enough with their kill: Cavendish was an English grandee and Burke a 'Castle Catholic' *in excelsis.*

The Phoenix Park Murders caused a sensation. The news broke in the Gaiety Theatre at about half-past nine, where the popular Carl Rosa Opera Company was performing Wallace and Fitzball's *Maritana.* A friend of John Stanislaus's, J. B. Hall, a canny Dublin reporter then on the *Evening Telegraph,* was in the audience. Barton McGuckin – that admirer of John Stanislaus's tenor voice – was playing the part of Don Caesar de Bazan and during the first act he raced round to Hall's box with the theatre's proprietor, Michael Gunn (another old friend), and told him what had happened. To avoid panic it was decided to continue with the opera in shortened form while the news percolated around the auditorium. It was already all over the city.

Though the Invincibles' deed was greeted with delight by Irish-Americans in New York, Parnell and other leaders hastily distanced themselves from the assassinations by signing a formal statement of abhorrence. Rumours were rife. Almost everyone in Dublin was in some way touched by the event, including both John and May Joyce. The following spring, when the trial was held, it emerged that the plotters had in fact intended to kidnap and kill Forster, 'the dirty old impostor'. The main witness for the prosecution was one of the Invincibles, James Carey, who had been a Town Councillor and was, as J. B. Hall was to write, 'a citizen of repute

... with a reputation for ostentatious piety'. John Stanislaus and all the Collector-General's team would have known him through their work.

While the murders were generally condemned in Ireland, the turncoat Carey had committed the much more heinous sin of informing on his fellow conspirators in exchange for his freedom. He was seen as the living embodiment of the tradition of betrayal that had dogged all political action in the country for a century and more. On his evidence five of the Invincibles were hanged for the crime in 1883 and, though in Unionist circles a threepenny glass of whiskey-and-water became gleefully known as 'three cold Irish', very few people mourned when the informer was shot dead on board ship as he fled for Africa. Carey's killer was afterwards himself convicted and executed for the deed, and a monument honouring his memory was reverently erected in Glasnevin Cemetery. There is a more cryptic memorial to the Invincibles in *Ulysses*, when a man thought to be James 'Skin-the-Goat' Fitzharris (the getaway driver for the assassins) appears as the keeper of the cabman's shelter in 'Eumaeus'.

The 'sad comedy' of Ireland's responses to her own violent tradition would be noted by James Joyce in an essay on 'Fenianism', written in 1907. Giving as examples the Fenian bombing of Clerkenwell Prison and the Phoenix Park Murders, he commented upon how, after an atrocity, the British would always propose a new reform. The supporters of physical force and the constitutionalists would then both claim the credit for the reform and 'revile each other with the greatest scorn'. In truth, for many Irishmen the ambiguity was internal. In John Stanislaus's case, his old Fenianism and his continuing friendship with such men as the gun-running and bombing Caseys coexisted easily with his devotion to Parnell and his secret respect for monarchy. The real enemy was betrayal. However mutually exclusive his allegiances might seem, John would not have betrayed any of them. But, like his son after him, he would always keep his best eye peeled for a traitor.

The fortunes of the Joyces were gratifyingly buoyant, but for some other members of the clan things were not going so well. In the summer of 1882, McSwiney & Company failed to declare a dividend for the second year in succession, and it would not be long before the store passed from McSwiney's hands. Down in Cork, Uncle Bill O'Connell was also now in trouble. On 9 August 1882, at the Extraordinary General Meeting held at 4 Market Street, the wine business he had become involved with was wound up and a liquidator appointed. Quite a concern, it had been registered in 1877 with a nominal capital of £13,000 in ten-shilling shares, but now, after only five years, there was nothing to be salvaged. Having lost his wife the year before, he had now lost almost all his money. However, O'Connell was still a name to reckon with in Ireland. Less than a week later, the elaborate Memorial to Daniel O'Connell, of which the foundation stone had been laid in 1864 by McSwiney when Lord Mayor of the city, was unveiled in Dublin. It was designed by Ireland's greatest sculptor, John Henry Foley, and its grandeur and location by O'Connell Bridge (which in 1880 had superseded Carlisle Bridge) made it a Nationalist riposte to Admiral Nelson on his Pillar further up Sackville Street. It was also significantly positioned within sight of the former (and perhaps future) Parliament House. To pay for it, funds had been collected for more than twenty years, with subscriptions from as far away as Buenos Ayres (as it was then spelt), British Kaffiraria in the Dark Continent and County Mayo, whence another John Joyce had sent £1. Attendance at the ceremony was *de rigueur* for the John Joyce of Dublin: anyone related to 'The Liberator' had almost a duty to mention the fact to the Memorial Committee, and he knew several of its members. The notes to *Exiles* suggest that he even got seats on the crowded platform for himself and May. Young Jim no doubt stayed at home with the maid.

People travelled from all over the country to attend the spectacle. The contingent from Cork assuredly included a good number of O'Connells and it may be that Uncle Bill was among them, happy to forget for a day the collapse of his company. Whether or no, it was around this time that John Stanislaus, aware of the plight his uncle was in and grateful to him for foiling his mother's attempted disinheritance, invited the widower to come and stay with his family whenever he liked. Uncle Bill probably did not accept immediately, but the seed was sown. He was a gentle soul and would be no trouble at all.

While her husband was getting used to a life in gainful employment, May Joyce was busy with her own activities. Dotted around the city there were many aunts, cousins and friends to visit, and little Jim was shown off to them all. She had always depended on the Church and as the years went by her religion was to assume even greater importance in her life, in part because it gave her some degree of independence from her husband. Both now and later she spent far more time on Church matters than her husband, always suspicious of priests, ever would. But John was still going with her on Sundays to the sparkling new Church of the Three Patrons nearby on Rathgar Road, where they both sang in Dr Smith's choir, already one of Dublin's finest. They were very probably present to add their voices to the celebrations when the lavish Romanesque building was formally dedicated to the three principal saints of Ireland: Patrick, Brigid and Colmcille. At this stage, John was still happy to join in tunefully with the rituals of religion, but it was a little more than that: for it to be known that he did not attend Mass regularly would have been social suicide in certain circles. In any case he enjoyed the singing.

He was even happier performing at some of Dublin's many secular concerts, which he quite often did. Richard Vincent O'Brien, composer and teacher of music, was a friend of the family; he had invited John to appear at the Antient Concert Rooms in Great Brunswick Street. On the night, John sang Gounod's 'Fairer than the Morning', while a friend and fellow-chorister from the Three Patrons, Mr Coffey of Bray, sang 'The Cruiskeen Lawn'. O'Brien's son Vincent (who would later become conductor of the Palestrina Choir in the Pro-Cathedral, and was to teach singing to James – and to Ireland's greatest tenor, John McCormack) also appeared with 'Tell me, Mary, how to woo thee', one of Gerty McDowell's favourite songs in *Ulysses*.

May's devotions may have been of particular comfort to her around this time for, before Jim was a year old, it seems likely that a third pregnancy ended with either a miscarriage or a stillbirth. John Stanislaus's O'Connell fertility was not to let him down, however: by the end of the following April Mrs Joyce would be pregnant again.

As if to reassure themselves of the fact of his son's continued survival, some time around the beginning of 1883 John had a

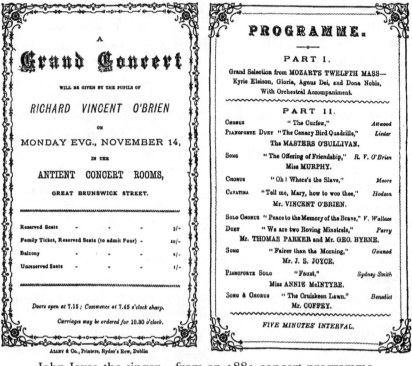

John Joyce the singer – from an 1881 concert programme

photograph taken of him, most likely at William Lawrence's modern Sackville Street studio near Nelson's Pillar. The ritual may have marked either Jim's first Christmas or his first birthday. The photograph, the earliest known of James Joyce, still survives. Draped in a rudimentary toga, he is seated bolt upright, playing with his fingers and peering earnestly out from under a tumble of hair that as yet shows no sign of the scissors. By today's standards he is rather podgy, with a deep dimple on his chin, evidence of a good rich diet – what might now be considered overfeeding. (It is the only picture of a plump James Joyce.) The photographer has not managed to get him to smile, possibly because he was not at this stage the most cheerful of toddlers: his cheek shows the redness caused by the uncomfortable arrival of teeth. But, however difficult he may at times have been, when the photograph was developed there was no doubting that the little boy was a handsome, alert and sturdy fellow, a son worthy to bear the Joyce name.

The previous August, the name of Joyce had appeared in all the newspapers. In the wild Irish west beyond Cong, yet another John Joyce and his wife, mother, son and daughter had all been shot dead in their cabin. John Joyce, a poor tenant farmer, was found stark naked and face down on his earthen floor. The repercussions of the Maamtrasna Murders, as they were known, soon became politically contentious. Several people were arrested, but two of the suspects were freed when they agreed to testify against members of the Joyce and Casey families. After a trial conducted in English, a language not all of them could understand, three of the accused were hanged by the ghoulish English executioner, William Marwood. One of the condemned, Myles Joyce, made a personal statement in Irish from the scaffold, which was jotted down by a reporter. A translation reads:

I am going. Why put me to death? I am not guilty. I had neither hand or foot in the killing. I don't know anything at all about it. God forgive the people who swore against me. It's a poor thing to die on the scaffold for what I never did. I never did it and it's a poor case to die. God help my wife and her five orphans. I hadn't hand or part in it. But I have my priest with me. I am as innocent as the child in the cradle.

The execution, which took place in February 1883, was botched and the man's last minutes were a horrible spectacle. Blatant Crown complicity in rewarding the actual murderers caused unease in the legal profession, and documents left lying around Dublin's Green Street Courthouse revealed that the Crown had suppressed evidence from the defence. The lawyer (and MP for County Westmeath) Timothy Harrington, whose friendship with John Stanislaus would last for almost thirty years, was involved in seeking redress and even wrote a pamphlet about the case. Though he believed that the episode was essentially a murderous feud, the case epitomised for Irish Nationalists the arbitrary nature of British justice. James Joyce, still turning the affair into copy decades later in Trieste, would emphasise (perhaps not entirely accurately) in a 1907 article that the accused had all belonged 'to the ancient tribe of the Joyces', a point that would not have escaped his father. In *Finnegans Wake* there was to be further literary use made of the

Maamtrasna scandal in the account of the trial of Festy King, another 'child of Maam ... in the heart of a foulfamed potheen district', who is described as 'deposing for his exution with all the fluors of sparse [flowers of speech] in the royal Irish vocabulary'. It was not often that the ancient Gaelic roots of their tribe came to the attention of the Dublin Joyces; John could reflect with relief that his family's Irish-speaking peasant origins were far behind him. He was not going to be one of the victims.

In 1883, a new face, already familiar to John, appeared at work when Edward Atherton Malins, son of the Superintendent of Glasnevin Cemetery, David Malins, and his wife Elizabeth, became a Clerk in the Rates Office. The Malinses were also friendly with May's musical aunts. Though Edward (or 'Teddy', as he was known) would die in 1894, he was to have a ghostly presence in 'The Dead', James's story based on the Christmas parties at the Flynns' Academy – a tradition even in the 1880s. Indeed, Edward is positively identified when a tipsy Mr Browne addresses the gentle but even more intoxicated Freddie Malins as 'Teddy'. Typically, Mr Browne was himself based on another family friend, Mervyn Archdall Browne, professor of music, organist, dance pianist, businessman and bankrupt. Teddy Malins's aunt (or possibly his sister) had married into the Brownes in what may have been a 'mixed' marriage, since Teddy was a Catholic and the Brownes were Protestants. However, there is some evidence that a branch of the Malinses had converted to Catholicism some time after the family had come from Britain in the 1850s, possibly because Teddy's father, David Malins, would not have got his Superintendent's job in the Cemetery if he had been a Protestant.

John Stanislaus was still collecting the Rural Districts, but the enormous area he covered was evidently too much for one man and in 1883 the Collector-General appointed a Mr J. J. Fleming to bear some of the load. John still did a great deal of travelling, however, much of it on foot. When north of the river, he would occasionally visit his old haunts in Chapelizod, perhaps taking time out for a stroll in the Phoenix Park afterwards. One afternoon, when he was still just about on speaking terms with his brother-in-law, John Murray, both Johns were crossing one of the Park's huge open spaces, then used by the Army for training and manoeuvres.

A company of cavalry came charging towards Messrs Joyce and Murray, and the latter took to his heels in a hopeless attempt to reach a tree to hide behind. Unruffled, John Stanislaus caught up with him and made him turn to face the onslaught. The galloping horses were divided around the two men and, according to the self-styled hero of the day, the commanding officer paid a tribute to his cool head by giving the order that sabres be drawn to salute him as the troop thundered past. The incident soon became part of John's repertoire and was to acquire embellishments over the years. Eventually, this evidence of his brother-in-law's cowardice would lead him to refer to both the Murray brothers, John and William, as 'highly respectable Gondoliers', an allusion to the lines from the Gilbert and Sullivan opera:

> In enterprise of martial kind,
> When there was any fighting,
> He led his regiment from behind
> – He found it less exciting!
>
> . . . In the first and foremost flight, ha ha!
> You always found that knight, ha, ha . . . !
>
> When, to evade Destruction's hand,
> To hide they all proceeded,
> No soldier in that gallant band
> Hid half as well as he did.

Of the two Murray brothers who stayed in Dublin, John became a clerk in the accounts department of the *Freeman's Journal* and William took on similar work in the solicitor's firm of Collis and Ward in Dame Street. John Murray was also derided for some lost reason as 'the cornet player'. Almost undisguised, they are the Red Murray and Richie Goulding of *Ulysses*. A third and youngest brother, Joseph, emigrated to London and stayed there. As time passed by, John Stanislaus grew to despise the whole family with what James called a 'medieval intensity'. 'Weeping God, the things I married into,' he would exclaim bitterly.

Their father, John Murray the elder, also incurred the contempt of his son-in-law, who called him the 'Old Fornicator' because he had remarried within a few months of his wife Margaret's death in 1881. The new wife, Christine, also marrying for the second time, did not find favour with John Stanislaus either. Not only had she stepped into the shoes of almost the only one of the family that he had liked, but she was actually Margaret Murray's niece. In truth, almost anything was enough to supply John with material for picturesque insults: that old John Murray, after leaving the Eagle House in Roundtown, became a commercial traveller for John Power's Whiskey Distillery and later for Thomas Begge, the wine and tea importer on Bachelor's Walk, was excuse enough for another sneer: 'a bottle-washer in a paper hat'. As Stanislaus writes in *My Brother's Keeper*, his father's hatred of the Murrays was unrelenting and 'amounted to an obsession'. However, May Joyce kept in touch with her father, who was fond of his little grandson and liked to sing to him: James's favourite song in later life came from his ex-publican grandfather: 'The Brown and the Yellow Ale'.

Away from the family, when he could be, John Stanislaus continued mixing with the great. On 11 December 1883, at Morrison's Hotel, he attended a dinner given in honour of Parnell. The occasion was to celebrate the success of the 'Parnell Testimonial', an international campaign to raise money for the leader, whose Wicklow estates were endangered by an inherited mortgage on the property. The Lord Mayor had just begun a florid speech when Parnell said abruptly, 'I believe you have got a cheque for me.' The frustrated orator agreed that he had and continued with his encomium, only to be stopped in his tracks for a second time with the words: 'Is it made payable to order and crossed?' It was, so Parnell put out his hand, took the cheque (for some £37,500) and indicated that the Lord Mayor should resume his seat. While many were scandalised by this behaviour and others took it as a joke, John Stanislaus appreciated Parnell's brusqueness and understood the duress of any mortgage. The gesture was a world away from the florid conventions of Victorian rhetoric and Irish sentimentality, and for John it was a living example of the almost regal detachment that he so admired in The Chief.

However, there was soon a development at home that could not be entirely ignored. On 18 January 1884, May Joyce gave birth to her second healthy child, this time a girl. Since her mother was dead, May had been assisted in the birth by a professional midwife,

Mary Thornton, sometime of Denzille Street (opposite Holles Street Lying-in Hospital). Mrs Thornton registered baby Margaret's birth a few days later, baldly defining the child's father on the official form as a 'Collector of Rates'; by contrast May, after James's birth, had called John 'Government Clerk'. In *Ulysses* Bloom thinks of her: 'Old Mrs Thornton was a jolly old soul. All my babies, she said. The spoon of pap in her mouth before she fed them. O, that's nyumnyum.' The whole Joyce family would become very fond of her.

John made no objection when his wife asked one of the 'highly respectable gondoliers', John Murray, to be the baby's godfather and Josephine Murray, the wife of the other one, to be godmother. Margaret Alice Joyce was baptised, like James, in St Joseph's by Fr O'Mulloy, her first name in memory of May's late mother. Josephine Murray for some reason missed the ceremony, and so the Joyces' maid, Catherine O'Donnell, had to stand in for her. In the years ahead, Aunt Josephine was to make up for her absence and would become an important figure in the lives of the Joyces, old and young, for the rest of her life. Oddly, she gets only a single brief mention in *Ulysses*, Bloom remembering her spineless husband's backache and his wife 'ironing it for him'. She had first met William Murray when he was an accountant under her father, James J. Giltrap, in his law agency at 2 Morgan Place beside the Four Courts. Able and intelligent, and a Murray only by marriage, Josephine was at this stage tolerated by John, particularly as she could play piano trios with him and May. In time, he would dub her 'the seal' and 'Aunt Hobblesides'.

Margaret, being only a girl, was not in the eyes of her father a particularly important addition to the hallowed Joyce line. Though John's attitude was indicative of the patriarchal age in which he lived, in his case it was stoutly reinforced by the fact that for generations no true-born Joyce had been female. It was probably this fact that allowed May to choose the two Murrays for the baptism. As it turned out, the name given to her that day would be very rarely used: among family and friends she would always be known as Poppie.

CHAPTER 12

Being a Gentleman

With their new baby, the house in Brighton Square was becoming cramped, so the Joyces decided to move. The previous December, probably with this in view, John had taken out a second mortgage on his Cork properties and now, in March 1884, he added a third. In the spring they took a house in Rathmines, 23 Castlewood Avenue. This was only a mile or so from Brighton Square and May could keep up her usual church services and choir rehearsals in the area without too much difficulty. For John the move was welcome too. The Leinster Cricket Club's grounds were around the corner alongside Mount Pleasant Avenue – near their Ontario Terrace house of four years before – and on summer days he could wander down to watch: cricket was still an enthusiasm which he would pass on to his favourite son, though there are no reports of John ever actually playing. (Molly Bloom remembers Simon Dedalus in his tall hat watching a game through glasses – 'such a criticizer . . . and a great big hole in his sock'.)

Joe Gallaher, a journalist with the *Freeman's Journal*, lived up the road at 13 Castlewood Avenue. The son of a ventriloquist, his wife Louise was one of the Powells, who were already friends of the Joyces: Louise's father, the choleric Captain Malachy Powell (or 'Major Powell', as he liked to be known), was also on the *Freeman* as 'Military Correspondent' and would contribute characteristics to Molly Bloom's father, Major Tweedy. It was Joe Gallaher (or perhaps his brother Fred, another newspaperman – accounts vary) who had been the first to convey news of the Phoenix Park Murders to an American newspaper, using an ingenious code to baffle rivals. Joe was a good companion with, like John, a zest for enjoying himself – in *Ulysses* he dances with 'Red' Murray in Stamer Street, wearing two lady's hats on his head. Living close to the Gallahers gave John another inside track to the world of the Dublin press.

Rathmines was more gentrified than Rathgar. The avenue itself was a generous, tree-lined thoroughfare linking Rathmines Road with the rather grand family houses of Belgrave Square. The Joyces' neighbours were mainly Protestants: old money rather than new. Next door lived a Mr Jones, Secretary of the Church of Ireland Temperance Society. Up the road at No. 5 was Walter Osborne, said to be the only true Irish Impressionist painter. His reputation was growing: in 1884 twenty of his paintings of Breton peasant life were hung in the Royal Hibernian Academy. Once again it was evident to all that the family had gone up in the world.

But the main advantage of the new house was its space. John wanted to entertain on a scale more befitting a settled professional with modest political ambitions than was possible at Brighton Square. Number 23 was ideal: a solid, double-fronted building of three storeys, with a dozen wide steps up to the unusual double-pilastered and fanlighted front door, and a good garden. They now had spare rooms for guests and before long William O'Connell, with his beard and his evil-smelling pipe, finally exchanged will for deed and came up from Cork for the first of many extended visits. On and off, Uncle Bill was to stay with the family for years, dividing his time between Cork and Dublin, where, as well as the Joyces, he had a son, William Desmond. For May, even with the help of Catherine, running a house of this scale was too much; and about now the Joyces engaged a second domestic servant, whose duties included being nursemaid to Jim.

Even with this extra help, with Jim at the unruly age of two and Poppie still a babe in arms, when May discovered in April or May that another was on the way she realised that she could do with yet more assistance with the children. It may have been Uncle Bill who suggested a solution. Mrs Elizabeth Conway, from the respectable Cork family of Hearn, was looking for somewhere to live. Mrs Conway was a strict and devout Catholic: she had once almost become a nun, though, after inheriting a fortune from her brother, she had married instead. After two years, still unblessed by children, her husband had left and was now said to be in Buenos Ayres with all her money. Through her sister's marriage to one of the Justices of Cork, Mrs Conway was linked to the family that John had known in Youghal in the old days, and she may have had other lost connections with Cork Joyces as well. Since John never liked her, it may be that her arrival in the household was tolerated for reasons of some degree of moral hold that she had over him – perhaps, as has been surmised, because she had been the companion of his mother after the death of his father. For the Joyces, giving her a home would be seen as an act of good Christian charity, and she could show her gratitude by helping with the children. The idea appealed. One more mouth to feed could not make much difference. And so it was that the fat and formidable Mrs Conway joined the family, unwittingly taking her first weighty step towards immortality in the pages of the *Portrait*, where she is Dante (as little Jim was probably soon calling 'the auntie').

Finances were beginning to give John Stanislaus some cause for concern. Any move is expensive and, though he was making a great deal of money each year, he was spending more. It was a relief when in September he was released from his initial mortgage, but he was still servicing two others. Household expenses had shot up, though Uncle Bill contributed what little he could. Castlewood Avenue had been decorated lavishly, the family portraits conspicuous in the largest reception room. John urgently needed more income: he had plans for parties and dinners, where he could welcome his friends and allies to share in his prosperity and perhaps even to make things happen in the world. It was important to keep one's contacts well watered. His home could become a centre for political discussion: what if The Chief were to drop by?

It was remarkable how often political and financial power coincided in Dublin. The name of John Stanislaus Joyce was by now familiar to a large number of city financial agents and bankers. He had never been silent about his 'Cork fortune' and found himself being approached about exciting investment opportunities. Some of these schemes, which often involved the growth potential of places such as Argentina, were so attractive that it was obviously worth raising further temporary mortgages to take advantage of them. But this was the age of the Robber Barons and swindles abounded. Precisely what John's dubious business

ventures were is unknown, but it is certain that they did not succeed. If any of them had, James, and later his readers, would
certainly have heard about another of John Stanislaus's triumphant
coups.

But there was really nothing to worry about. All in all, things
were going very well, and one or other of his speculations was
bound to strike gold before too long. His job was lucrative and
the Cork freeholds would provide almost limitless collateral (and
rent) for ever; there was no reason why his easy rise towards the
higher echelons of Irish life should not continue. He looked forward to a golden future as the universally beloved paterfamilias of
a handsome and intelligent brood. He would send his sons to good
schools and to university, encouraging them to take their deserved
places in the life of Dublin as barristers, doctors or even city fathers.
At the elegant weddings of his beautiful daughters his speeches
would be proverbial for their wit as for their wisdom.

There was one thing to do before the family flag could be said
to have been properly hoisted. John investigated the heraldic
potential of the family, and in Burke's *General Armory* (1884)
(which he may have consulted in the new Capel Street library,
where his friend Patrick Grogan was librarian) he found a Joyce
coat of arms: 'argent an eagle displayed gules charged on the breast
with a bar gemel ermine'. The design was not quite the family
tradition he claimed, but a misprinted version of the Galway Joyces'
escutcheon, whose eagle has two heads. Through this corrupt piece
of Victorian heraldry he could now call himself 'a gentleman of
coat-armour', but since the arms had not been officially granted,
he would in fact be displaying arms without authority. In Irish
practice the need for such authority was widely ignored anyway,
so display them he did: a crimson (one-headed) bird spreadeagled
on its shield of silver was duly engraved and framed, and took its
proper place on the wall at home, setting off the family portraits
nicely. Now John Stanislaus Joyce Esquire could say, as Giraldus
Cambrensis had done about them centuries before, that the Joyces
were '*pernobilis et pervetusta familia*'. Unfortunately the bogus Victorian heraldry advertised pretension rather than ancient accomplishments. Pappie was a forger.

Peter Paul McSwiney died in August 1884, and the funeral was a social event not to be missed by his Joyce cousin. In best silk top hat and sombre but immaculate suiting, John looked impressive. He enjoyed dressing up, tending towards a certain flamboyance of style, waxed moustache and all. It may have been around now that he took to wearing a monocle ('in one eye', as Herbert Gorman felt it necessary to make clear). One evening, invited to a grand masquerade ball in Dublin Castle, he emphasised his sense of chivalry by appearing in the colourful uniform of a guardsman. The cabman who drove him to the gates was fooled until offered a notably mean tip: 'Holy Jaysus – I thought I had a real officer,' he muttered. 'You have,' replied the chocolate soldier with his usual effrontery. 'I have', said the jarvey, 'a cottonball one.' The incident, with its strange word, soon became part of the expanding treasury of John's stories.

On 17 December 1884 Mrs Thornton delivered the latest addition to the family and John was presented with another boy. This time he endowed the baby with both of his own names. (In time, however, the 'John' was dropped by the ungrateful recipient, who preferred for his own reasons to be known as Stanislaus, or Stannie.) At the baptism after Christmas, conducted in Rathmines Church by Fr John Morris, none of May Joyce's side of the family was asked to be godparents. Instead, the fontside promises were made by Uncle Bill and Dante Conway, representing the family's glorious Cork roots. Being a boy, John Stanislaus Joyce Jr had emphatically to be a Joyce.

Having spent his youth in a family of no more than three, John now found himself at the head of quite a substantial household: four adults, three children and two servants. Jim was very much the favoured child. Stanislaus, though he had no recollection himself of Castlewood Avenue, passes on a memory of his brother at about the age of three coming out of the nursery at the top of the house and yelling 'Here's me!' all the way to the dining-room where the grown-ups were indulgently finishing their dinner. After evening meals his mother or father might go to the piano and they would sing: John's repertoire embraced many of Moore's Melodies – 'The Last Rose of Summer' was a favourite at this time – and his sweet tenor could draw tears with 'M'appari tutt' amor' from Flotow's *Martha* or with a host of other arias, never forgetting

Dublin's 'dear old Balfe'. May would accompany him and would usually sing as well. Even Uncle Bill, despite a paralysed tongue and a stammer, sang too; he had a curious way of speaking that always amused the Joyces, though in fact his old man's singing voice was 'not unpleasant' for parlour ballads – Stannie mentions 'Oh! Twine me a bower all of woodbine and roses' and 'In happy moments day by day'. The master of the house, sitting in a happy haze of Victorian respectability, with a glass of special whiskey in front of him, listened contentedly.

Though never a great reader, John Stanislaus knew what he liked and was enthusiastic about his small collection of favourite books. One of these was Sir Jonah Barrington's *Personal Sketches of His Own Times*, an insider's view of Irish politics at the beginning of the century, winningly combined with a rackety account of society and high spirits – the roistering of the nobility in gaunt spectral mansions, as his son would put it in *Dubliners*. Barrington's account of the gradations of the gentry naturally appealed to John: there were:

1. *Half-mounted* gentlemen.
2. Gentlemen every *inch of them*.
3. Gentlemen to the *backbone*.

The book was full of recyclable punchlines and stories. John liked the one about the orator, John Philpot Curran, who complained after a particularly bug-ridden night in Carlow that if the fleas 'had been *unanimous*, and all pulled one way, they must have dragged me out of bed entirely!' John's most striking appearance in *Ulysses* is in 'Circe' as 'His Eminence Simon Stephen cardinal Dedalus'. Wearing a red soutane, a rosary of corks with corkscrew cross and a 'battered silk hat sideways on his head', he scratches himself and announces: 'I'm suffering the agony of the damned. By the hoky fiddle, thanks be to Jesus those funny little creatures are not unanimous. If they were they'd walk me off the face of the bloody globe.'

Another chapter in Barrington told of the metamorphosis of Patrick Joyce from Kilkenny into Dr Achmet Borumborad and back again. This stately, plump, exotic figure, reputedly 'the first *Turk* who had ever walked the streets of Dublin in his native costume', had lost his social cachet when more than a dozen drunken MPs of the Irish House of Commons contrived to fall into his Turkish bath after dinner. This appears in the *Wake*. But Barrington was more than a repository of stories: he was a man to identify with, a man from the genial, racy world of the late Georgians, whose spirit lingered on into Victorian times in Ireland.

However, perhaps John's favourite books were two novels set in England. Written by the crippled Frank E. Smedley, *Frank Fairlegh: or, Scenes from the Life of a Private Pupil* and *Harry Coverdale's Courtship and all that came of it* were published in the 1850s. *Frank Fairlegh* is a portrait of the author as a young man. In the course of the book, the hero is bullied, witnesses a young man being savagely and graphically flogged (illustrated), rescues a friend from drowning, successfully fights a duel and rides a great many horses. The novel opens with the parting words of the boy's father as he is packed off to be educated at an establishment with private tutors: 'Never forget, under any circumstances, to think and act like a gentleman, and don't exceed your allowance.' Something much like this may have happened to John in Cork, when he was being prepared for his Matriculation Examination for Queen's; he would echo the parental advice when the time came with Jim.

The second novel, *Harry Coverdale*, is almost a continuation of the first, the tale of a young blade, crack shot, expert horseman and reader of Byron. Both books contain a good sprinkling of Latin tags of the sort John Stanislaus used and some quite tolerable jokes – the Rev. B. A. A. Lambkin, for example. The somewhat sickly romantic sub-plot in *Harry Coverdale* has a streak of misogyny running through it: two engravings by Dickens's illustrator Phiz are prophetically captioned: 'Wife-breaking! – (Theory)' and 'Wifebreaking! – (Practice)'. But for John the primary attraction of the novels was how they recaptured rosy memories of his own past. Harry Coverdale is a man of action, happiest out hunting, until he reveals a 'rich, powerful voice' to his future wife and sings with her the duet 'Là ci darem' from Mozart's *Don Giovanni*, which John no doubt had sung with May. The same song would become an important motif in *Ulysses*, appearing eleven times.

The Parnellites now had control of Dublin City Council and were flexing their muscles. In the spring of 1885 they denied an official address of welcome to the Prince of Wales when he laid the foundation stone for the new Museum of Science and Art. This was reputedly not the only laying he was to do – it was common knowledge (even if untrue) that the welcome he received from the ladies of Dublin more than made up for the rudeness of the City Fathers. Personally, John had no objection to Prince Edward whatever: Eddie too had suffered from an overbearing mother and deserved his bit of fun.

John Stanislaus now numbered among his friends several local politicians, such as the solicitor, John Henry Menton, a municipal wheeler-dealer based at 27 Batchelor's Walk, and Valentine Blake Dillon, another legal man close to Parnell, who was famous for the generosity of his hospitality and his waistband alike. In Castlewood Avenue these and other associates began to mingle with his musical friends. Too often for his liking the teetotal Mr Jones next door had to put up with 'outsider' cars noisily taking away inebriated town councillors in the small hours of the morning. Begrudging remarks from neighbours were only to be expected, but John's guests could sometimes not refrain from making them too. A malicious story would be spread about that he had got so far above himself as to engage a footman in uniform for the evening and it was even whispered that the family portraits were actually 'readymade' ancestors he had picked up from some junk-shop on the quays. Most people knew that John Stanislaus from the Rates Office was trying a little too hard to impress, but that was no reason not to enjoy his exuberant hospitality.

There was still occasional talk among John's political friends that he should run for public office. This would not necessarily have been in Dublin. In *Ulysses* the notion that Bloom might stand for parliament is connected with John Hooper (who in that book gave the Blooms 'an embalmed owl' for their wedding). In 1885, however, Hooper was still based in Cork where he was Alderman for the South Ward and editor of the *Cork Daily Herald*. Given the Hooper link, the plan is more likely to have been for John to contest a seat in Cork. In February 1884 his relation John Daly had accepted the Chiltern Hundreds (resigned from Parliament), leaving one of the Cork City seats vacant, but it had been won by John Deasy, the son of a Cork civil engineer. With his property interests and family connections there, this seat would have been ideal for John, and the thought of sharing the city's double constituency with Charles Stewart Parnell was irresistible.

A General Election was called in 1885 and Deasy announced that he was going to run for Mayo West. Because Alderman Hooper was already committed to the South East Division of the County of Cork, a new Nationalist candidate was needed for the vacant Cork City seat. In the run-up to the election John may have hoped that Hooper would try to get him adopted; indeed, Hooper may well have campaigned on his behalf. But whatever moves in this direction were made, John Stanislaus was not selected. Possibly it was felt that his financial base was not strong enough: MPs were unpaid and a reserve of private money was required for such a career; more likely it was recognised that, as Stanislaus later thought, John 'had neither the patience nor the docility that elder politicians expect to find in their juniors in the party'. His links with the collapsing Irish Liberals may not have helped either: their time was almost over, and they would take less than seven per cent of the votes in the 1884 poll and only one per cent the following year. When Parnell's secretary, Henry Campbell, announced to the election committee that the leader had endorsed both Joe Horgan and Maurice Healy for the single nomination, the committee decided that the latter should be offered it.

Maurice Healy, a solicitor from Bantry, was almost ten years younger than John and was not in Parnell's view an ideal candidate. He was a shy and modest man, but he was a brother of the fiery Tim Healy, Campbell's predecessor as Parnell's secretary and once his closest associate, whose relationship with The Chief was already under strain. Before the decision Tim Healy (who like John had gone to school in Fermoy, though to the Christian Brothers rather than the more patrician St Colman's) had told Maurice that Parnell would accept him as a colleague only 'when he fails, as fail he will, to get anybody suitable whom the Cork people would adopt'. Though John Stanislaus was clearly unaware of what the Healys were saying to each other, his suspicion that between them they had thwarted his political ambitions was the origin of a deep hatred of the brothers, a hatred that would only intensify through the rest of his life.

Though Lord Salisbury's Conservatives gained power in Britain, his government lasted only a few months. John campaigned for his friends in Dublin at the ensuing election in December 1885. This time the Liberals were returned in Britain and Gladstone had the conditional support of the Irish Party to copperbottom his majority. In the early months of 1886 a plan was formulated between the two leaders to repeal the Union and give Ireland a parliament of her own. Though this legislature would be under the Crown and subordinate to Westminster in several respects, the idea was vehemently opposed by the Conservatives in Britain and by the Protestant majority in Ulster. It was also opposed by the still militant heirs of the Fenians. Even so, most thought it the best hope for a solution to the Irish question that had been seen in nearly a century. Parnell's skill in converting Gladstone to Home Rule deserved John Stanislaus's admiration, and got it.

John was as active in bed as he was out of it. May had borne two children in 1884. She managed to get through the whole of the next year without giving birth, though, given the number of failed pregnancies for which there is evidence, she may have lost a baby some time in the summer. In October 1885 she realised that she was pregnant again. The Joyce seed was making up for lost time.

Though his hopes of practising his oratory at Westminster might have been quashed, John Stanislaus had no intention of being trapped in the Rates Office for ever. He had backed the right political horse and he worked hard at election times: it could not be long before he reaped some rewards. Some thirty new magistrates had been appointed for the County of Dublin under Lord Salisbury's government. Perhaps it would be his turn next time around. He could go for a safe seat in the coming Irish Parliament: the new Bill was the wave of the future and could hardly fail. Opponents of the Gladstone–Parnell plan could do their worst, but it was votes in Westminster that counted now. Dublin buzzed with excitement. Before the year was out, after more than eight decades, it seemed that the old Parliament Building on College Green would once again echo with voices raised in triumph: an Irish Parliament for an Irish people.

Stanislaus interpreted Gabriel's speech in 'The Dead' as a heightened version of his father's 'after-dinner oratory'. At the Flynns' party in the New Year of 1886 John doubtless polished up his public speaking and led the festive choir in rousing choruses of 'For they are jolly gay fellows', which nobody could deny 'Unless he tells a lie, Unless he tells a lie.'

But lies were being told. When the crucial Government of Ireland (or 'Home Rule') Bill came to the vote in June 1886, it was defeated by 343 votes to 313. Gladstone had been betrayed by rebels in his own party. Unable to hold the Liberals together, he went to the Queen and there was yet another election in July. In Dublin, Robert D. Lyons MP had no further need of John Stanislaus's campaigning skills as he did not stand again: he was to die within six months. Salisbury's Conservatives took office again. They were to remain there for some six years. A new Viceroy of Ireland, ironically named Charles Stewart, Marquess of Londonderry, moved into the Phoenix Park. Gladstone, the Grand Old Man at seventy-seven, seemed to have shot his bolt and, though the Liberals still promised support for the principle, the prospect of Home Rule had for the time being suddenly melted away.

In July 1886 May's pregnancy came to term, and on the twenty-fourth, again through the good offices of Mrs Thornton, a fourth child joined the family. The third boy to survive, he was christened Charles Patrick and, being male, John's choice of godparents again bore witness to his loyalties. Charlie's godmother was Emma Tarpey, from the Parnellite family that lived in the Stamer Street area near the canal. One of the Tarpeys, Hugh, had twice been Lord Mayor of Dublin in the late 1870s. The godfather was an uncle of John's, Charles Patrick O'Connell, who probably was happy to think that the boy was named after him (though undoubtedly Charles Stewart Parnell also had an influence on the baby's name). Though the family knew him as Uncle Charles, he had used the name Patrick in his religious career since 1872. The confusing change of name has led some to suspect that he was no longer a practising priest, perhaps having been for some mysterious reason debarred, but the reality is less picturesque. Ordained in 1868, Fr O'Connell had served as a curate in several respectable Cork

136

parishes such as Passage and Glanmire, but for eighteen years he was one of the priests in the Bishop's own Parish of St Mary's. He had some reputation as a preacher and was said to have conducted the funeral of Francis Mahony, the famous 'Fr Prout', in May 1866. It was while he was at Glanmire that he had for some reason ceased to call himself Charles and become Patrick. He would die on 13 September 1934 at the age of ninety-one, as Canon O'Connell, parish priest of Ovens. John was no friend of the clergy and like his grandfather preferred not to let any of them 'put his two feet under his mahogany', but Fr O'Connell represented the blood that the family shared with the 'Great Dan'. May Joyce might have preferred a godfather from her side of the family, but she could not veto Fr O'Connell. For John, even a priest was better than any more of those Murrays.

When she was not otherwise occupied with giving birth, May Joyce enjoyed visiting the theatre with her husband. The Gaiety Theatre, though still Dublin's finest, had been losing audiences to Dan Lowrey's more populist Star of Erin Music Hall. To win them back, Michael Gunn built another venue on his site on the corner of Hawkins and Great Brunswick Streets, empty since the Theatre Royal had burnt down in 1880. The Gaiety would put on the touring operatic companies like the Carl Rosa and D'Oyly Carte's Opera Bouffe, and of course its pantomimes and its plays (which often presented such stars as Sarah Bernhardt, Henry Irving and the Terrys). Meanwhile the new outlet would stage concerts, boxing displays, lectures, oratorios, circuses and the like. Called the Leinster Hall, it opened on 2 November 1886, and Gunn would have sent John and May an invitation. Leaving Dante, Uncle Bill and the servants to look after the children, they often went back. Their first love still remained the opera, but Leinster Hall events could be memorably spectacular: one night John took May to see the Christy Minstrels perform there in their black-face and 'golly-shoes' and in 1887 John L. Sullivan, the greatest heavyweight boxer in the world, gave a moving speech after an exhibition bout, expressing his sympathy with the native struggle for Home Rule. The rousing words of the Irish-American 'pucker' set the city buzzing.

That the names of John Henry Menton and Valentine Blake

Dillon (and that of John Hooper) are among the list of Molly Bloom's 'lovers' (really those whom Mr Bloom suspects of leering at her) suggests that the delicately alluring May Joyce may have been the object of similar attentions. These were not encouraged by her jealous husband. The couple went to a good many parties, at which John always kept an eye on her and what she was up to. At one dance the hostess light-heartedly mentioned that an optimistic guest, spotting May across the room, had begged an introduction to 'that pretty young lady' and had to be informed that the lady in question was the mother of four children. (It was not yet apparent to anyone that she was already carrying another.) While John could hardly have claimed that it was May's fault that strangers found her attractive, he complained anyway, grumbling and muttering at home to her about the incident. A respectable gentleman should not be made a mockery of, especially by his wife.

CHAPTER 13

Bray

Barry O'Brien, friend and biographer of Parnell, recounts how on the evening of 18 April 1887 The Chief walked into the House of Commons to be buttonholed by Tim Harrington with a copy of that morning's *Times*. Harrington was in a state of extreme agitation, for the paper contained a facsimile of a letter signed by the Irish leader which showed that, far from condemning the Phoenix Park Murders (as he had publicly done), Parnell actually felt that Burke 'got no more than his deserts' and that Cavendish's death was an 'accident'. Harrington, who repeated the story to Barry O'Brien (and also no doubt to John Stanislaus), was astonished by the leader's reaction: merely glancing at the paper, he pointed to the 'S' in the signature, and coolly commented that he had not made 'an S like that since 1878'.

This letter, the first of a series, linked Parnell with the Invincibles and the violent 'hillside men' of Fenian tradition – at a time, conveniently, when the Tories were introducing a Coercion Bill to quash Irish political agitation. When the letters were eventually found to be forgeries, even in Britain Parnell grew in public esteem. Having seen off the conspirators and *The Times* with dignity, The Chief seemed in Ireland to be invincible. However, forces close to him were already mustering to bring him down.

One spring day a large horse-drawn removals van appeared outside 23 Castlewood Avenue. After three years in Rathmines, John Stanislaus had decided to move. On 21 April 1887 he raised some money from the National Bank (using the Cork property as usual) and relocated the family to Bray, on the borders of Counties Dublin and Wicklow. The move may have been more expensive than he had envisaged because, when they got there, almost his first action was to take out another secured loan (this time from a Dublin money-lender named Morragh). At this time, he was calling on his collateral in Cork whenever he needed a boost to his regular income: though three previous loans were paid off during 1887, interest repayments continued to deplete his ready cash.

The family's time in Bray coincides with Stanislaus's earliest memories and is already too fully covered by him (and hence by all subsequent biographers) to merit repeating in great detail. However, John Stanislaus's perspective was not that of a boy of four. The supposed reason for the move to Bray is a case in point: John said, no doubt frequently, that he could avoid the Murrays there as they were too poor to afford the fare from Dublin. But the fact that John's remark is a prime example of his sardonic and dangerous wit does not guarantee that it is true. The real motive for the move was twofold: No. 1 Martello Terrace was cheaper and it was beside the sea, and the Joyces may very well have already taken holidays there or in Greystones, a little further down the coast.

Known as the 'Irish Brighton', Bray was a town of six and a half thousand people (out of season), easily accessible from the capital – if Dublin was a real capital: the matter seemed problematical. It was served by frequent trains on the Dublin, Wicklow and Wexford line and the sea air was universally popular. From the city it could be reached either from Westland Row Station (the coastal route, through Kingstown) or from Harcourt Street Station (the inland route, through Ranelagh and Stillorgan). There was an Annual Regatta, an Aquatic Sports and Horticultural Exhibition, and Horse and Dog Shows. The area was also noted for its 'many fine private demesnes' and it had several thriving hotels. The largest of these was owned by Edward Breslin, a self-made tycoon who had continued William Dargan's good work and done much to develop the town as a tourist resort: as an active Town Councillor he had a finger in every pie, officiating, for example, at the annual Bray Races. Breslin had organised the building of the mile-long esplanade (using stone from Parnell's Avondale quarries) where, during the season, military bands played and where Dante Conway once swatted an unlucky old man on the head with her umbrella for standing to attention during 'God Save the Queen'. (Mrs Conway was an enthusiastic Home Ruler and almost as fond of Parnell as John Stanislaus was – even though she did not normally approve of Protestants.)

Living not far from the railway station, John was now in very easy reach of his south Dublin collection areas. No doubt his colleague J. J. Fleming was encouraged to concentrate on the northern ones. A gentle daily journey along the coast (popularly 'like the Bay of Naples'), stopping off at Sandycove or Dalkey to deliver a rates demand or two, perhaps lunch-time in Kingstown at Captain Cunniam's 'Shrine' (as Stanislaus called it) and then into town. This was John's plan. It was a pleasant prospect, but it was not to be. The Collector-General had other ideas for John Stanislaus. Something was amiss.

The office had heard a sad story from John of a misadventure that had befallen him in the Phoenix Park, near Chapelizod. Apparently, crossing it one evening he had a strange meeting with a 'cad with a pipe', some sort of ne'er-do-well, who relieved him of his satchel with the municipal rates in it. It was unfortunate that he still had the money with him after the day's work. A more heroic version of the incident – probably the one told to the family – claims that John saved the day by valiantly fighting off no fewer than two vicious assailants with only the aid of his trusty shillelagh. Whatever it was that happened to him in the Park, if anything did at all, the business later became for James Joyce a farcical rerun of the Phoenix Park Murders and an elemental anticipation of the *Wake*. In 1937 Joyce remarked to Frank Budgen that 'the encounter between my father and a tramp (the basis of my book) actually took place at that part of the Park'.

James and the others may have believed his father, but the Rates Office surely suspected that the incident had been invented (or even staged) by the victim. They knew perfectly well that in the evenings John Stanislaus was far more likely to be waylaid in a pub by friends than in a park by robbers; but awful things did happen in the park and the tale could just be true. We can never know for certain now, but when John found himself penniless and in need of another drink, the temptation must have been great to help himself to something from the satchel. He could always pay back the money before handing it in for counting at the end of the week. But a little loaning is a dangerous thing. Once the borrowing became a habit, it was inevitable that one Friday the shortfall would fail to materialise. There were sudden expenses, mortgages took time to arrange and for some people credit is always scarce.

John's formal borrowings were also becoming more frequent. It is remarkable how many different lenders he cultivated: public and private banks, various insurance companies and, increasingly, private (and high-speed) money-lenders whose rates were fixed in accordance with the desperation of their client. That he rarely used the same source more than a couple of times may say something about his reliability, but it may also suggest how skilled he was at being 'difficult': he was a past master at picking holes in contracts and generally obfuscating the issue, while his delaying tactics were often as effective as Parnell's at Westminster, where 'obstruction' (the simple device of making speeches that lasted all day and long into the night) had become both an art form and a highly effective parliamentary tool. If John Stanislaus knew anything, he knew how to talk.

For whatever reason – none was necessary – the Collector-General now suddenly removed John Stanislaus from the Rural Districts and reassigned him to cover Inns-Quay and Rotundo Wards, in the centre of Dublin. This could be seen as promotion to a more onerous area, extending north from the Liffey to the Royal Canal and containing, as one might expect, both the Rotunda on Rutland Square and the legal swathe that included the Four Courts and the King's Inns. The move was, in fact, nothing to complain about: John was now closer to the life of the streets, which he liked, and it also suited him to be closer to the money-men in Dame Street and along the quays. That it was now easier for his superiors in the Rates Office to keep an eye on him suited him less. He was now sometimes accompanied by an Inspector Manly. His duties, too, had changed radically. As well as the Police Tax he also had to collect the other rates and charges that were applicable only to the city proper. John disliked paperwork and soon fell behind. He began to farm out the form-filling to others: when deadlines for final notices approached, 'he would have a couple of unemployed old clerks scribbling in his house from

Rose Cottage (now Grange Cottage) outside Fermoy where
John Stanislaus's grandfather James was born in 1827
(Photo: Peter Costello)

The bridge over the Blackwater River at Fermoy (built by Joyce
masons)
(Photo: Peter Costello)

James Joyce, unsigned portrait
painting, circa 1845
(Poetry Library, State University of New York
at Buffalo)

Anne Joyce, unsigned portrait painting,
circa 1845
(Poetry Library, State University of New York
at Buffalo)

Hunting waistcoat belonging to John
Stanislaus, embroidered with heads of
hounds and stags by Anne Joyce – a
family heirloom
(Joyce Tower Sandycove, Photo: Robert
Allen)

James A. Joyce as a youth, unsigned
portrait painting, circa 1845
(Poetry Library, State University of New York
at Buffalo)

Joyce's Court, White Street Cork – the key element in the family property John Stanislaus inherited
(Courtesy Arethusa Greacan)

'The handsomest man in Cork': James A. Joyce, John Stanislaus's father, as a mature man
(Poetry Library, State University of New York at Buffalo)

Ellen O'Connell Joyce, unsigned portrait painting, circa 1848
(Poetry Library, State University of New York at Buffalo)

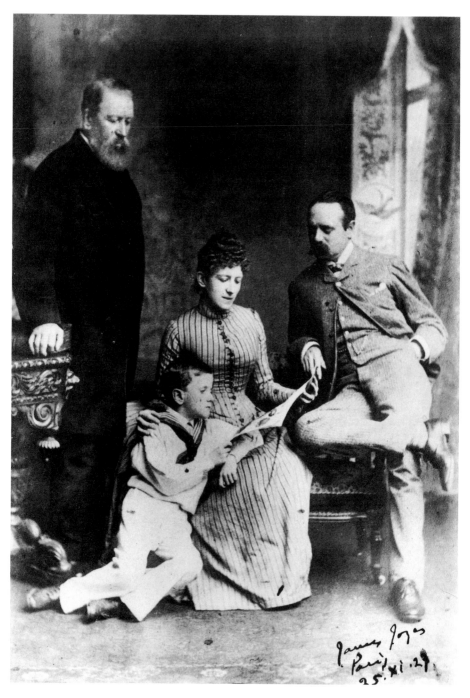

John Stanislaus and May Joyce and their son James with John
Murray before James entered Clongowes in September 1888
(Poetry Library, State University of New York at Buffalo)

An important event in John Stanislaus's youth: the
rebel Fenians are scattered by the police at the
Battle of Tallaght, March 1867

John Kelly, former Fenian and Land
League organiser, the model for 'Mr
Casey' in Joyce's fiction
(Courtesy National Archives of Ireland)

T.C. Harrington, John Kelly's patron and
friend of John and James Joyce, in his
robes as Lord Mayor of Dublin, 1902
(Courtesy Central Catholic Library Dublin)

The registered label for the whisky of the Dublin Distillery Company in John Stanislaus's time
(Courtesy Patent Office Dublin. Photo: Damien Maddock)

The church of the Three Patrons, Rathgar, where John Stanislaus and May Murray sang in the choir
(Courtesy Peter Costello)

Rathmines Church, another musical church, where John Stanislaus and May Murray were married
(Photo: Peter Costello)

Barton McGuckin, the famous Dublin singer of the day, who thought John Stanislaus one of the finest tenors in Ireland
(Courtesy Peter Costello)

13 Ontario Terrace, where the Joyces'
first son, John Augustine, was born and
died
(Photo: Peter Costello)

May Joyce in her early married life
(Courtesy National Library of Ireland)

26 Castlewood Avenue, off Belgrave Square,
Rathmines, the finest house the Joyces lived in
(Photo: Peter Costello)

St Colman's College, Fermoy (as it is today), where John Stanislaus
was at school
(Photo: Peter Costello)

Robert Dwyer Joyce
(Courtesy John Wyse Jackson)

Dr Croke, President of St Colman's, who
befriended John Stanislaus
(Courtesy Central Catholic Library Dublin)

morning to midnight'. Though the clerks were another drain on his resources, they got the job done and gave John time to live. But the authorities were on the watch and by February 1888 the Collector-General was considering 'The Case of Mr Joyce'. His personnel file was growing thicker.

Most mornings John Stanislaus caught the train into town, but there were days off to be enjoyed too. For a few days in June 1887 Dublin was lit up and all public offices closed for the Golden Jubilee of Queen Victoria – half a century on the throne. The extra holiday was most welcome. John liked living in Bray. The house (which he rented from a Mrs Kelly) had thirteen rooms and a view out to sea. This was delightful on warm summer days, but the water was so close that when there were storms the whole terrace was lashed violently by spray. James may have contracted his lifelong fear of thunderstorms here, cowering under a table while lightning flashed over raging breakers beyond the nursery window and the wind howled. To calm him down his mother would tuck him up in bed and give him a kiss. The next day, Dante graphically explained how his terrors were nothing compared with the eternal torments of Hell, where bold boys who told lies would go. Dante's scare tactics apart, the worst punishments at this time were meted out by May, who is said sometimes to have pushed Jim's head down the lavatory and flushed. The children found that Pappie took little part in either comforting or disciplining them when he was at home. He preferred to go out swimming or drinking.

There were also the new people to get to know. Jim and Poppie hung round outside Betty Byrne's shop at 46 Main Street – though in the *Portrait* she purveys sweets in Rathgar. Further up the street at No. 92 was the local 'Medical Hall' of W. & J. Vance ('Established 1864'). James Vance, owner and chief chemist, lived with his family beside the Joyces in another of the Martello Terrace houses. Also a failed medical student from Cork, he was soon on the best of terms with John Stanislaus and they went out together fishing for plaice and flounders. Both men were also keen on bathing, which they did from Bray beach – one of Stannie's earliest memories was of paddling at the water's edge while his father, 'swimming a long way out, was lost in the dazzling reflection of the sun on the level sea'. Stanislaus uncharacteristically leaves to the reader's imagination his thoughts about his father's chances of drowning. In fact John was a good swimmer and always swam back.

May Joyce got on well with Mrs Vance and James quickly made friends with Eileen, one of her daughters. Though the young couple's proposed marriage was no more than a childhood fantasy, Dante made evident her disapproval of the Vances' Church of Ireland Huguenot background – she still embodied much of the anti-Protestant bigotry of her Cork forefathers, who had surely imbibed Pastorini's prophecies of exclusive Catholic salvation on the Last Day – the same millenarian atmosphere that had impinged on the Joyces living in the Ballyhoura Hills in the early years of the century. Neither John nor May saw anything wrong with cross-faith fraternisation. Some of John's good friends were what were then called 'Swaddlers' or 'Soupers'. While Catholic–Protestant friendships and even marriages were not unusual in Ireland, in general social relations were often more civil than cordial. The gains and losses of the Reformation and subsequent Irish history were a live issue for very many, but (as in the *Portrait*) John Stanislaus could be amusing or relaxed about such matters:

> O, come all you Roman Catholics
> That never went to mass.

James Vance was, like John, a reasonably accomplished oarsman and it was probably he who introduced John to the Bray Boat Club, where he became a member. The Club's boathouse was conveniently at the end of Martello Terrace and was the centre for a good deal of socialising: an annual Smoking Concert was held (to raise money for the August Regatta) at which, as the local paper reported, 'the friendly glass was circulated freely, though without excess'. In 1887 they had had a particular success, with two 'Amateur Ethiopian Performances' featuring 'Bones and Tambo', Christie Minstrels in black-face who stole the show with songs both humorous and sentimental. Here John got to know such local worthies as James Coffey and James Lacy, a Town Commissioner. Lacy's Hotel on Bray Head also offered musical evenings and May, too, was soon making friends among these families. But the Boat

Club was not exclusively for smoking and drinking in, and John was soon avidly rowing stroke again.

Living so far out had to some extent cut off the family from their relations in Dublin, but if John imagined that he would never have to see much of the Murrays again he was being too optimistic. In 1887 another Joyce baby, a boy, appeared on his father's birthday, 4 July. Pleased with the coincidence, John at last allowed May to choose the godparents for one of her sons. (Perhaps none of John's important friends could 'afford' to come all the way out to Bray for the ceremony.) May's brother John and one of her Flynn cousins, Mary Ellen Callanan, were present as the boy was christened George Alfred – his first name in honour of his great-great-grandfather, the earliest Joyce to move to Cork City. This time it was May who registered the baby's father simply as 'Rate Collector'.

The ceremony was held at the local parish church, the Holy Redeemer, where the Parish Priest was Dean Lee. But Dean Lee's were not the only sermons the Joyces heard while they were in Bray. Just south of the town across the Dargle river was the connected village of Little Bray. The incumbent there, Fr James Healy, was a national celebrity. An indefatigable bon vivant, he was lionised for his sharp repartee and even wrote occasionally for *Punch*. Healy, being the snob he was, was a regular tuft-hunter at Lord Londonderry's levées in Dublin Castle, where he exchanged barbed remarks with John Pentland Mahaffy of Trinity and his ilk. Visitors to the famous presbytery at Little Bray were given an excellent dinner of real Wicklow mutton, liberally spiced with the priest's practised witticisms. His guests included Archbishop William Walsh, Lord Randolph Churchill, Lord Powerscourt, 'Honest' John Morley MP, Prince Edward of Saxe-Weimar and John's old beneficiary, Maurice Brooks MP. Fr Healy had once made Gladstone laugh over breakfast. In April 1885, when the Lord Mayor of Dublin tore down a royal flag in front of the Prince of Wales, the priest had commented, cigar in hand, 'Instead of pulling down flags, it's putting down flags he ought to be' – that is, laying paving stones in the street. The Protestant grandees of public life, like the Guinnesses – Sir Edward Cecil Guinness was another close friend – were much cultivated by Healy, who was inclined to sneer at their *arriviste* Catholic successors. But he could be forgiven, being a highly entertaining man (and no relation to the Cork brothers), and he appealed to John Stanislaus.

Dean Lee of the Holy Redeemer was a cleric of the old school, who believed in the dignity of his calling and whose cordial dislike of Fr Healy was well known. Nationalist in outlook and a stickler for morality, in 1885 he had barred a play from the parish hall simply for its title, *A Kiss in the Dark*. In 1887, to annoy him, someone put a forged report into the *Freeman's Journal* announcing that Dean Lee was retiring in favour of Fr Healy. Perhaps disappointed when the truth emerged, the Joyces began to attend St Peter's in Little Bray and May was soon singing for Fr Healy in the choir. Part of the attraction was the church's reputation for music, but just as important to John was that its incumbent was a true gentleman. It was of no account whatever that Dean Lee would soon be the Right Reverend Monsignor Lee, one of the Vicars-General of the Diocese of Dublin.

It was while they were in Bray that the Joyces went to the party nostalgically described in *Ulysses*, which took place at Matthew Dillon's house in Brighton Road, off Brighton Square. Mat had eight daughters (including Tiny, Attie, Floey, Sara, Nannie and Mamie) and 'a solid silver coffee service ... on the mahogany sideboard'. When John and May lived nearby they had met Valentine Blake Dillon and other eminent Dubliners there, and (like Molly and her Poldy) no doubt played musical chairs with the sprightly maidens. The last such occasion in the novel is set in May 1887, and while Mrs Dedalus and Stephen, 'a lad of four or five in linsey-woolsey', are both present, the part of John Stanislaus is played by Leopold Bloom. John Henry Menton dances with Molly ('a good armful') and is beaten at bowls by Bloom, while the other guests look on in amusement from the shade of the garden lilacs. Bloom modestly puts his victory down to a fluke, but John Stanislaus, as he boasted forty years later, 'was considered a celebrated bowler'. If he beat Menton that evening, it would have been no fluke, in his opinion.

Both Joyces liked to keep in touch with old friends living nearer town. To this end, May often left the children with their nurse (to be remembered variously as 'Sarah' and 'Cranly' in the later writings of James and Stanislaus) and journeyed back to the Rathgar area for church events. On 1 February 1888 she was one of the principal singers in a large choir assembled to expedite the repose of the charitable soul of a Mrs Murphy of Harcourt Street. The Mass took place at the new monastery church of St Paul of the Cross, Mount Argus. A report of the service shows that Mrs Joyce's soprano was heard in a highly 'Joycean' setting: also in the choir were two of Mat Dillon's daughters, two Misses Bloom (probably daughters of the dentist confusingly mentioned in *Ulysses*) who sang contralto, and someone suspiciously like the Mrs Kearney of 'A Mother'. The Rev. Frs Gabriel and Constantine (names given to the Conroy brothers in 'The Dead') were two of the three officiating clergy. Names from James Joyce's Dublin tend to appear both in his work and in *Thom's Directory*, and it is often difficult to assign definite connections between them. But the factual reality of his sources mattered to him – even as *Ulysses* went to press he was desperately asking Aunt Josephine what she knew about Mamie Dillon, so that he could quickly insert a detail or two about her into the proofs.

May Joyce's interest in Mount Argus and its Passionist community may have owed something to the presence there of the unworldly but accident-prone Fr Charles, a monk celebrated throughout Ireland as a miraculous healer. Up to 300 people a day visited this timid but somewhat eccentric old priest for blessings and it would be odd if she had not fallen to some extent under his spell. Today, his fervour might seem pathological to some: sometimes, terrified of an unfavourable Last Judgement he would cry out piteously to the Virgin Mary during mealtimes, 'until called back to himself by the voice of the Superior: "Father Charles, Father Charles, you are disturbing the Community"'. He need not have worried: more than a century later he is well on his way towards a comforting canonisation.

John Stanislaus may not have much appreciated his wife's bringing all this piety home with her. When asked about him in the late Interview, his only comments were: 'Father Charles of Mount Argus – he was a Priest out there. What in the name of God does [Jim] want to know these things for? I am afraid that his head is not all right. The only thing I ever saw Father Charles doing was taking snuff. He was a very fine tall man, I think he was a Dutchman.'

John was partly right: Fr Charles was originally from Holland, but by the time John would have come across him he was a prematurely aged and feeble old monk with an incipient stoop and a bad limp. However, his snuff-boxes are still treasured at Mount Argus.

The same day that May Joyce was singing for the benefit of the monks, Nationalists were welcoming a pair of English politicians to town, the Marquess of Ripon and 'Honest' John Morley MP, both supporters of the Liberal Home Rule position. (Morley was credited with converting Gladstone, though it was Childers who had led the way.) Their torchlit progress from the Kingstown ferry was cheered by large crowds all the way to Dublin. It was the eve of James's sixth birthday, and since Bloom remembers watching the cavalcade (though on the wrong day) from 'a secure position amid the ramifications of a tree on Northumberland road', perhaps John Stanislaus as a treat took the boy to Ballsbridge by train to soak up the excitement. Certainly, by now he was already teaching his son the politically correct responses.

The 1888 concert in aid of the Bray Boat Club was held on 26 June at Breslin's Hotel on the Esplanade and the Joyces appeared eagerly on stage. The *Wicklow Newsletter* reported on 30 June that 'a large number of distinguished amateurs lent their services for the occasion with the result that the concert was a pronounced success'. As the programme records, Mrs Joyce and Mrs Vance performed a duet by 'Kucan' (actually F. W. Kücken) called 'The Fisher's Evening Song'. John Stanislaus was in sentimental mood and sang 'My Sweetheart when a Boy' by Wilford Morgan and Frederick Enoch. The song's strangely ambiguous title conceals a lament for a past love. It ends:

> Still on my heart the beams remain
> In gay uncloudy joy,
> When I remember her again
> My sweetheart – when a boy!

As the last note faded away, May could reflect thoughtfully on her husband's first lost sweethearts. If John had anyone in mind while he sang, it is impossible to say who; her name, if it was not Justice, is probably long forgotten. But neither of them would have dwelt on the matter for long, since Jim, whom his mother had dressed for the occasion in a Little Lord Fauntleroy suit, was about to make his first formal public appearance. He had learnt the old music-hall song, 'Houlihan's Cake', which was quite an ambitious piece containing some of those big words that can make people so unhappy, but Jim was a bright boy and had a good memory. (He was never to forget the song: the first two lines are used in *Finnegans Wake*.) For the audience, as for the proud parents, the six-year-old's rendition was surely splendid:

> There was plums and prunes and cherries
> And citrons and raisins and cinnamon too,
> There was nutmegs, cloves and berries
> And the crust it was nailed on with glue.
> There was carraway seeds in abundance –
> 'Twould build up a fine stomach-ache –
> You would kill a man twice after eating a slice
> Of Houlihan's Christmas Cake.

Some of the audience noticed that the boy was embarrassed by the word 'stomach', which might have been rather rude, and mumbled the word as 'Smmm . . . mmm'. Dante's puritanical attitudes were having their effect; it was not to last.

Bray was a good starting place for explorations of County Wicklow where, at Avondale, Parnell had his estate. The family went on several expeditions, sometimes even with members of the Murray clan. For one trip May invited her father and his second wife, Christine, to picnic with them at Powerscourt Waterfall, one of the great natural wonders of Ireland. Nobody had remembered to bring a tablecloth to spread on the grass and Christine joked that if one of the ladies took off her petticoat they could use that instead. John Stanislaus said nothing at the time, but later at home he exploded, saying that he had been shocked and disgusted by the immoral suggestion – to think that the incestuous wife of the 'Old Fornicator' imagined that his own May would even consider such an action. For years afterwards his stepmother-in-law's flippant sally was evidence of the moral turpitude of the whole lot of them.

Eccles Street, where the Blooms would live in 1904, was in John Stanislaus's new collecting patch. On one occasion, late as usual in sending out notices to pay, he sent Eccles Street residents summonses instead. It would save work and get the rates money in more quickly. When the list of 'defaulters' came up in court, George Keys LLD, Divisional Police Magistrate, who lived at No. 61, was on it. He also happened to be the magistrate in charge of the case. He was fortunately unaware that he had never been sent the bill in the first place, so his first move was to square it with John Stanislaus. Fulsome assurances of good faith were made in private by both sides and Mr Keys's name was hurriedly removed from the list. At the hearing one angry ratepayer waved his receipt in front of the court to prove that he had already paid, but to no avail: the magistrate swiftly declared, 'We all know that Mr Joyce is a most capable and conscientious officer. Decree granted.' Similar stories about John were beginning to circulate through Dublin: how true they were was always a matter for conjecture and remains so, but his laziness – and a reputation for fancy financial footwork – were rapidly becoming common knowledge.

The Collector-General decided to move John Stanislaus again. In the winter of 1888 he was given an area to the east of Sackville Street to collect. This was the North Dock Ward, extending north from the Liffey to the city boundary with Clontarf at the Tolka. (The appointment may be one reason for George Moore's later sneer to the effect that James Joyce was a denizen of the Dublin docks.) In the ward most of the money was concentrated around the shipping companies downriver of the city centre. The other great industry was sex.

The streets around Montgomery Street (Purdon Street, Mecklenburgh Street, Mabbot Street, Bella Place, Faithful Place etc.) formed the brothel quarter. Every so often the authorities tried to clean it up, but nothing radical was ever done: the previous year Mecklenburgh Street had been renamed Tyrone Street in the vain hope that it would smell less sweet. With Dublin's numerous garrisons, there were plenty of frustrated 'swaddies' about, and many other exiles from the holiness of Ireland supported it as the biggest red-light district in Europe. To Dubliners in general it was known as 'Monto'. To Oliver Gogarty and his medical student pals it would be 'the Kips'. To James Joyce, it would be 'Nighttown' – originally the press nickname for the late shift on the *Freeman's Journal.*

Among John's ratepayers were the madams Mrs Cohen and Mrs

Mack, both to be found plying their trade in 'Circe'. Whether he accepted payment in kind is unknown, but it is perhaps remarkable that of all the (often bad) press that he would later receive from his voluble and frequently hostile children, none of them ever hints that their father was at any stage of his life unfaithful to their mother. But after all, May took her conjugal duties seriously, and their consequences. The children just kept on coming.

The education of his eldest son was a matter of no little importance to John Stanislaus Joyce. Mrs Conway had taught Jim the 'three Rs' and in Bray he had been going to a local private dame-school. This was probably where it was noticed that he had inherited his father's weak sight as well as his blue eyes. A pair of glasses was bought and it was through these that he would soon see his first proper school.

Before Jim set out for his new life as a boarder at Clongowes Wood College, William Lawrence's were instructed to take a family portrait. The photograph shows John and May Joyce with James reclining at his mother's knee. Standing to one side is the stern but distant figure of Jim's grandfather, the 'Old Fornicator', looking the model of bearded Victorian propriety he no doubt was. The photograph is the only one of John Stanislaus known to have survived – unlike his son he was no Flashbulb Jaysus, as Gogarty might have put it. Caught just as he enters middle age – he was thirty-nine – John Stanislaus perches slightly awkwardly on an armrest looking down at his sailor-suited son. His hair and walrus moustache are dark and raffishly well groomed; his jacket done up by the top button only, revealing waistcoat and watch chain. Over his left knee his right ankle jauntily lies crossed. His right hand nearly – but not quite – touches his wife's left hand, which is holding up a large sheet of photographs for Jim (devoid of spectacles) to look at. And just over John's left shoulder a decorative bird painted on a panel behind him seems to hover, poised for flight. (As *Ulysses* would put it: 'Lapwing. Icarus. *Pater, ait.*')

Jim was very young to be flying away – even to somewhere as near as County Kildare, where Clongowes was. As he said after he arrived there, he was only 'half-past-six'. It was a younger age than his father had been when he was sent off to Fermoy: Jim too would be the youngest in his school. Clongowes was one of Ireland's top

schools, a college for gentlemen. Run by the Jesuits in the castel-
lated seat of an old Catholic family, it was where Daniel O'Connell
had educated his (legitimate) sons. An O'Connell great-uncle of
John's, when a pupil there in the 1840s, once gave an address of
welcome to the Liberator. It was probably this family memory that
decided John that it would be worth paying the fees for Jim, which
were £25 per annum, though even this amount felt like a considerable sacrifice.

The clothes were bought in town and the trunk packed, and on
1 September 1888 John and May Joyce set off to deliver their son
into the hands of the priests. The train journey and arrival are
described in detail in the *Portrait*, as is the rector, Fr John Conmee,
who welcomed the Joyces to the college. In the gloomy entrance
hall the father gives his son two crowns (altogether ten shillings).
Like Frank Fairlegh in Smedley's novel, the new pupil is also given
some important advice: 'Never peach on a fellow.' For John, to
betray one's fellows was the worst failing. He probably did not
know that the sons of Richard Pigott, the man who forged the
'Parnell' letters in *The Times*, were also at Clongowes. Before long
their father would shoot himself in a Madrid hotel to avoid arrest.
Respectability being the internalised force it is, Pigott had been
selling his forged 'Parnell' letters to help pay the fees. Betrayal was
the price of their becoming Irish gentlemen, and it was more than
John Stanislaus would have been prepared to pay. May, missing
Jim desperately, paid her fee of tears.

CHAPTER 14

At Bay

While James was away at Clongowes, the Special Commission in London began to take evidence on the Pigott letters and to examine Parnell's links, if any, to the Land Leaguer's agrarian violence. Reports of the hearings were published daily in the papers and gave John Stanislaus a topic for discussion during the Christmas holidays. The festival was enlivened by a visit from one of his best friends, John Kelly ('of Tralee'), who was on good terms with The Chief himself. Kelly was in fact a Corkman from Bantry, but had moved to Kerry. He had a draper's shop there which went bankrupt in 1879. He and his brother had been arrested as Fenians in the 1860s and he retained his radical views. An associate of Harrington, he became known as an inspiring speaker at meetings of the Land League. Then he was imprisoned for holding 'illegal courts' and, as an obituary would put it, 'the government took good care that his business as a draper in Tralee was ruined'. To compensate, Kelly had been appointed National Organiser of the Land League and was given £500 after a collection among his admirers. It was through intermediaries like Kelly that Parnell could communicate with the physical force men: the Commission would have been interested indeed to eavesdrop on some of the conversations in Martello Terrace or in the Commercial Club. Kelly had spent several spells of up to six months behind bars in Armagh, Dundalk, Clonmel, Derry and Tullamore, generally for fomenting sedition from the backs of carts in country towns. When not in prison he lived at the National Club in Rutland Square. He had great charm and occasionally would accompany John and May to the opera, once telling John: 'If you got three months in jail, you'd sing any of those fellows off the stage.' In Bray he enjoyed the food, the children and the admiration of his host, who hung on his words. John Stanislaus knew that his friend, a true patriot, would never compromise either politically or personally. His eyes and his lungs had been affected by his prison term, his fingers from picking oakum – 'making a treat for the queen', as he put it to the children.

So, most of the talk was of Parnell and some of the songs they sang – Mr Kelly's mellow bass complementing John's tenor – were no doubt of old Ireland free. But Parnell was not the only good man under investigation. The Collector-General was now taking seriously various complaints that had reached his ears about John Stanislaus. He made an official accusation of malpractice against him (and against E. C. Cotter, who collected for the Mountjoy Ward). It was a nasty moment, but, in the end, nothing too incriminating could be pinned on John. In January 1889 he was given a formal warning and put on probation for a year, during which he would have to submit monthly certificates of good behaviour. In fact it was a reprieve. As for Parnell, when the Commission finished hearing all 450 witnesses in the autumn, it too would report that there were no firm grounds for action against him either. Both men were living dangerously.

Soon after Jim had been sent back to Clongowes at the beginning of 1889, Mrs Thornton appeared again and May gave birth to yet another daughter. When the child was baptised in the Holy Redeemer, her name must have startled the latest pair of May's relatives to be godparents, Patrick Murray and Julia Lyons: the child was christened Eileen Isabella Mary Xavier Bridget Joyce.

That year, on 4 July, Georgie celebrated his second birthday and his father his fortieth. John at this time was strong and fit: the walking he did for his work ensured that. His rowing was still good enough to put him in a winning boat at the Bray Regatta that summer, or so he would later claim: in fact, as far as can be ascertained, none of the newspaper reports of the event mentions his name, though James Vance appears in 1888 as stroke in a boat that won second prize. But there were also more relaxed – and boisterous – nautical occasions. Stannie, who was about seven, was brought by his father on boat trips out into the bay, accompanied by Mr Vance and some local fishermen. The object of these odysseys was supposed to be 'fishing and swimming', but the memories the little boy retained were of his own boredom, his Pappie's hairy chest and the general popularity of 'the contents of the stone-jar in the stern-sheets of the boat'.

According to Stanislaus, his father's drinking was already damaging the family. He was, unknown to his friends, a street angel and house devil. Still able to consume large quantities and remain conscious, he was often seen about town very much the worse for wear, but usually in festive mood. When he got home from the pub, however, he sometimes refused to eat or even talk; he just sat and glared at May, grinding his teeth and frightening her with *sotto voce* growls and threats to 'end it now'. Finally, she could stand it no longer. One day in the confession box she plucked up courage to 'peach' on John and told her confessor what she was going through at home. Whispering in the dark, she pleaded with him to help her get away to a life without her husband. But it was no use. The priest reminded her that her marriage was a true and consummated one and told her that there was no possibility of a separation. She was to go home and pray. May had no choice but to obey and so matters went on much as before.

It is unlikely that her husband ever realised how close his life had come to collapse – or that for his rescue he had the priesthood to thank. Stanislaus suggests that any separation would probably have been temporary. However, the void left by the lack of a female controlling influence (for the first time since leaving St Colman's) would surely have been overwhelming – particularly in view of his stalling career and what was about to happen to that other anchor in his life, Charles Stewart Parnell. If May and the children had left him, John could very well have lost everything, including, perhaps, the will to live: his family (meaning primarily May and Jim) was all-important to him. Some thirteen years would pass before he would learn what it meant to be without a wife.

John, as has become evident, usually had various schemes on the go that were intended either to raise immediate cash or to increase his assets generally. It is impossible now to trace the precise nature of these balancing acts, but official records provide a few hints. His interests in Cork, for instance, were not just confined to rents and mortgages. On 13 October 1889 he acquired from Elizabeth Sutton and John and Simon O'Connor (merchants of

South Terrace, Cork) the freehold of some property in the city to
add to his existing portfolio. How and why this was done is lost in
the mists of time, but the release papers suggest that he may not
have been acting alone: the address given on the documentation
was the home of an agent of the Royal Bank of Ireland, Charles
Graham Brown of Sandford Road, Ranelagh, from whom he may
have borrowed money for the purpose. Whatever else, the Ranelagh connection is a sign that John Stanislaus's finances were
becoming ever more tangled.

John's money worries and complications were already having
their effect on his children. When Jim was seven and Poppie five,
both of them already knew that it was good to have large quantities
of money. Now or a little later, having seen their father signing
important pieces of paper, they sat down and laboriously inscribed
a document stating that each of them would have more money
than the other one by the time they were twenty-one. When it was
finished, they went out into the garden, dug a hole and buried it.
Then they solemnly swore to each other that when they reached
twenty-one they would come back and dig it up again and see who
was right. That they would not reach twenty-one at the same time
did not seem to have occurred to them. No doubt Jim was confident
of victory, but it would be a close-run thing in the end.

The Bray Christmas dinner in 1889 passed off amicably. Everyone was in a cheerful mood about the way things were going for
the leader, Parnell: he had been negotiating hard with Gladstone
in anticipation of the Liberals' return to power and, even better,
in November he had been cleared by the Parnell Commission
of all accusations of violent sympathies. After the verdict Parnell
accepted with cold contempt *The Times*'s invitation to sue it for
libel and won. There may have been disturbing new rumours being
whispered about him, but there are always rumours and these were
probably as fraudulent as the forged letters. The uncrowned king's
reputation was reaching new heights in Ireland and John Stanislaus
could see the future beckoning.

Two days after John Stanislaus had carved the Christmas turkey
(no doubt keeping the 'pope's nose' for himself), the rumours
proved to be true. On 27 December 1889 *The Times* first carried

the news that Captain William O'Shea was going to sue his wife for divorce on the grounds of adultery and had cited Mr Parnell as co-respondent. The revelation that so prominent a figure in public life was a seducer and a cuckolder caused a sensation in both Great Britain and Ireland, and its effects on the prospects of Home Rule were catastrophic. Gladstone's hopes depended on the support of the Liberal Nonconformists, whose conscience he had described as the 'backbone' of his party: but it was a conscience that would not easily forgive a fornicator. The Irish Catholic bishops saw an opportunity to reassert their authority: they had already been uneasy with Parnell's popularity – he was, after all, a Protestant. They were also alarmed by the rhetoric being used about him: such figures as the ex-Fenian Michael Davitt had referred to him as another Moses, while some even called him the 'Risen Christ'. As for many of his colleagues in the Irish Party itself, who might have offered Parnell their loyalty for his achievement in transforming them into the spearhead of a mass movement, it did not help that he had tended to be aloof and was hard to control: his attitude towards them was almost Bonapartist in its appeal to the public.

The scandal therefore provided powerful ammunition for attacks from various sides. However, it would take almost a year before matters came to a head. In the meantime, the people of Ireland made up their minds, some for Parnell and some against. Given that the heir to the British throne was a notorious womaniser (hence the 'Pox Britannica' joke in 'Cyclops'), many Home Rulers did not feel inclined to sacrifice their exceptional (and monogamous) leader on the altar of selective English sensitivities. As an old Fenian, an old fornicator and a priest-hater himself, John Stanislaus's loyalty to The Chief, if possible, increased.

In January 1890, the family was enlarged yet again by a daughter, Mary Cathleen. Another two from May's clan did the baptismal honours, William Murray and the sister of old John Murray's scandalous second wife, Maria O'Donohoe – Maria would be the model for the lonely spinster in 'Clay' who always sees everything as 'nice'. John Stanislaus had no such illusions: it was probably from necessity that he entered into another mortgage in April. (The lender, Margaret Bridgeman, earned the dubious distinction of a cryptic mention in *Ulysses*.)

There was still fun to be had, however. May and John sometimes had days out at the races at Crosstown or Leopardstown, which had been opened two years earlier. On these occasions the couple had the chance to gossip with other enthusiastic race-goers like Major Powell's daughters, Mrs Clinch and Mrs Gallaher, Alderman Robert O'Reilly (very likely the man called 'Maggot' O'Reilly in *Ulysses*) or Christopher Friery, the Rutland Square solicitor. Bloom in 'Circe' speaks of that day, when 'Molly won seven shillings on a three year old named Nevertell and [was] coming home along by Foxrock in that old fiveseater shanderan of a waggonette . . . eating a sandwich of spiced beef out of Mrs Joe Gallaher's lunch basket [and] laughing because Rogers and Maggot O'Reilly were mimicking a cock as [they] passed a farmhouse. . . .' Occasional jaunts of this sort apart, however, 1890 was a miserable year for the Joyces and it is probable that in the autumn May had another miscarriage, her third. (While there are naturally no records of May's failed pregnancies, the frequency with which John fathered successful children on her, and the fact that the number of her spontaneous abortions *is* fairly reliably recorded, means that there are very few gaps in her childbearing life when she was not pregnant with a child that lived, for a time at least. Into these four (or, just possibly, five) gaps, four miscarriages have to be fitted.)

John was beginning to lose his patience with Dante Conway. As the year advanced, the bishops became more vocal in their anti-Parnellism and she was following their lead. This political divide at home, coupled with her religiosity and her endless complaints about a bad back, were tedious enough, but now she had started interfering in John's personal life. On the piano in the parlour John had mischievously arranged a number of framed photographs of his old girl-friends, Annie Lee, Hannah Sullivan and perhaps Miss Justice. To her credit, May Joyce did not herself object to this salon of *fiancées refusées*, even claiming to like them there – they were, she said in the famous phrase, 'all nice-looking girls'. Dante was less tolerant and convinced May that she should burn them in case the children asked awkward questions about why the pretty young ladies were on display. When John came home in the evening and found out about the holocaust, he was less than pleased. May tried to take the blame, but he knew at once that the real culprit was 'that old bitch upstairs'. (Dante, perhaps wisely, always went to bed early.)

What Dante and others saw as the worst side of Parnell was exposed by the O'Shea divorce trial in November 1890. Slapstick details of the subterfuges the couple had used to conceal their liaison became the matter of gossip and speculation in two countries. Among Joyce's unused notes for *Ulysses* is a song from this time, entitled 'Charlie Parnell', with its derisive refrain: 'You want Home Rule for Ireland / And you can't Home Rule yourself!' Nobody knew whether he could continue to rule the party.

John Stanislaus bought a ticket for the public meeting at the Leinster Hall held on 20 November 1890. It was supposed to discuss the plight of evicted tenant farmers, but, as he no doubt anticipated, rapidly turned into a forum for the examination of Parnell's future. The Chief was not there, but on the platform were several members of his Irish Party, the star being Timothy Healy (who, though he claimed to be ill, had spent the day in court on behalf of some ratepayers who were challenging, as it happened, a decision of the Collector-General's Office). Tim Healy, as brilliant a barrister as he was Machiavellian a politician, had been Parnell's secretary and his right-hand man in Westminster, though always something of a maverick. The *Evening Telegraph* reported the next day: 'When Mr T. M. Healy MP appeared, there arose a storm of cheers which lasted for some minutes.' John Stanislaus would not have joined in.

Tim Healy was the most prominent of the 'Bantry Gang' (known to themselves as the 'Bantry Band') with such other MPs from Cork as James Gilhooly and the plutocrat William Martin Murphy, who now owned half of the McSwiney store. Another member of the Bantry Gang was also on the platform, Healy's uncle and father-in-law, T. D. Sullivan, who lived on the South Circular Road near Portobello. The owner of *The Nation*, a newspaper that had been moulding Irish opinion through polemic and poetry since the days of the Young Irelanders in the mid-century, Sullivan was already privately urging Parnell's resignation.

After an animated discussion, the Leinster Hall meeting finally endorsed Parnell's leadership. Though Tim Healy was given much of the credit for swaying the assembly in this direction, his speech was a masterpiece of sophistry: in effect, it placed Parnell into the paradoxical position that to be worthy to remain as Party leader he would have to resign from the post. While few present seemed to notice (or object to) the implications of Healy's pronouncements, John Stanislaus recognised double-talk when he heard it. In a fury, he got to his feet in the body of the hall and bellowed, 'You're an impostor! You're only waiting for the moment to betray him!' Healy's reaction was skilfully obtuse. Affecting to believe that his heckler was calling for Parnell to stand down, he responded, 'Already . . . in one quarter, where the least we might have expected was silence (hisses), I observe a recommendation of retirement (No! No!)'. This wilful misrepresentation of his objections enraged the 'shouting politician' even more and, after a contretemps, in the end officials were forced to drag John Stanislaus from the auditorium, still protesting loudly. The dramatic interruption arguably marked the high point of his political impact – years later several people, including W. B. Yeats's painter brother, Jack, remembered witnessing the incident. And before very many days had passed, John's instincts were to be proved correct and Parnell too would soon be abusing Healy, as 'the chimney sweep' and worse.

Tim Healy was still in Dublin recovering from his 'illness' when the rest of the Irish Parliamentary Party met in London to decide on whether to re-elect Parnell for the next parliamentary session. On 25 November, without any real discussion, they did just that. Most people, including many of his supporters, expected that after this endorsement had proved the Party's loyalty to him, Parnell would gracefully resign and that his resignation would be reluctantly accepted. It seemed the honourable course to take. Even the chief London correspondent of the still firmly Parnellite *Freeman's Journal*, J. M. Tuohy (yet another close friend of John's), had recommended this outcome soon after the Leinster Hall meeting. When everything blew over, The Chief should be able to take up the reins again. But Parnell, not for the first time, confounded the prophets and, once he had been re-elected, remained defiantly at the helm. His insistence on retaining the leadership would tear Irish politics apart.

On 1 December, in Committee Room 15 of the Palace of Westminster, the Irish Party met again. The only official record of the dramatic deliberations over the next few days was that printed in the *Freeman's Journal*, by a team of reporters under the direction of Tuohy. John Stanislaus would much later be gently teased by James for claiming influence with 'Jimmy' Tuohy, but in fact he knew the journalist well through his other pals on the newspaper, Gallaher, Jack Hall and the rest. Some of the more interesting aspects of the meetings (their electric atmosphere, the demeanour of Parnell, Healy's caustic asides and so forth) were inevitably omitted from the paper's published version, but before too long, John Stanislaus would be able to hear a detailed personal narrative of everything that happened in Committee Room 15 from Jimmy Tuohy himself. What he heard would confirm his convictions.

For the Parnell loyalists, the battle of the Committee Room was disastrous. In what Healy called 'the stench of the divorce-court', Parnell's alliance with the Liberals had fallen apart. At the same time, Healy's public advocacy of The Chief magically evaporated and during the acrimonious meetings over the next five days the Corkman's sharp tongue became one of the factors that turned the Party against its leader. His triumphant inquiry, 'Who is to be the mistress of the party?', might have been a rhetorical question, but it was an unforgettable one. On the last day, Healy cried out, 'Allow us to depose you!' and the party irrevocably split, a majority announcing that Parnell was no longer their leader. Parnell immediately refused to accept the verdict: ultimately he had always answered to the Irish people and not to his colleagues. While without Tim Healy's contributions the outcome would probably have been much the same, John Stanislaus's prophetic outburst in the Leinster Hall had been confirmed. For him, the old Fermoy Christian Brothers' boy was from now on the quintessential Irish traitor.

Parnell firmly believed that the people of Ireland were still behind him and most of Dublin at least agreed. On 10 December 1890 he travelled back to marshal his support. Healy was on the same boat and after he arrived was assaulted in the street. Probably John Stanislaus was at Kingstown to give them both a good welcome. With a large following at his heels, when he reached the city Parnell went straight to the Abbey Street offices of *United*

Ireland, which had been taken over by the Anti-Parnellites (or APs as they were being called). There, his supporters 'made pie' of the beds of type while Parnell confronted the turncoat acting editor, Matthias Bodkin, and had him thrown out, 'with some violence', as Bodkin later complained. (A Dublin wag commented, quoting *Acts* I.26, 'The lot fell upon Matthias'.) Later that evening there was a march through the city and at half-past eight a combative Parnell appeared apotheosised before a packed Rotunda, while outside at the top of O'Connell Street, to the light of thousands of torches and the accompaniment of brass bands, a vast multitude of cheering Dubliners testified to their continued faith in The Chief.

The National Club on Rutland Square was close to the Rotunda and became the Dublin headquarters of the Parnellites. There Parnell surrounded himself with an enthusiastic and militant band of stalwarts, made up of his loyal Parliamentary rump and a group of Old Fenians and Landleaguers (like the Club resident, John Kelly). These were all people with whom John Stanislaus could feel comfortable in these exciting times. Daniel J. ('Jack') Hishon, who would for a long time remain one of his closest friends, was busy mustering all the support he could as Assistant Secretary of the Parnellite National League's Organising Committee, recently established nearby at 43 O'Connell Street (Upper) beside the Catholic Commercial Club, another bastion of loyalty. John Stanislaus undoubtedly spent as much time as he could in the thick of things.

Before Parnell set off for Cork on 11 December, news came that the *United Ireland* building had been recaptured by the APs. With Dr Joe Kenny, he jumped into a carriage and, followed by Henry Campbell, William Redmond and others, raced round to Abbey Street to find a throng of waiting supporters and a firmly locked door. Someone suggested trying to get in through the basement and a healthy contingent leapt (Bloomlike) into the area below street level. Restrained from following them and too impatient to wait, Parnell seized a crowbar and levered open the front door himself. Behind the door an apparently hostile band of men were charging towards him in the gloom of the hall. The Chief put up his fists and managed to land a blow. He hit Jack Hishon, who had broken in through a basement window at the rere. In the ensuing confused mêlée Parnell's hat was knocked off. Some minutes later the new editor, Henry Campbell, appeared at an upstairs window to introduce a flushed and bareheaded Parnell, who rousingly addressed the mob in the street below. The few APs in the building had sensibly crept out a back way and made their way round to the front to join the throng of goggle-eyed spectators, which by now had swollen to over two thousand.

In *Ulysses*, Leopold Bloom recollects being present at this 'historic fracas', where he picked up and returned Parnell's silk hat. Parnell, 'being a gentleman . . . turned round to the donor and thanked him with perfect *aplomb*, saying: *Thank you, sir*'. It is natural to think that this honour fell to the writer's father, John Stanislaus, an excited witness to the affray. In later years Jack Hishon would be able to remember Parnell's physical assault upon him with as much modest pride as Bloom does his own small service to The Chief.

But the real test of the mood of the rest of the country was at the Kilkenny by-election a few days later. There, Parnell spoke fiercely about how he had been betrayed by the party: he was becoming increasingly bitter and desperate. His aristocratic detachment gone, he attacked his old colleagues – and Tim Healy in particular – with intemperate venom. Among the minority of MPs who stood by him was Timothy Harrington, who had been in America during the split. Harrington realised that in Ireland as a whole it would now be a battle between the wounded leader and the Catholic Church. He was disgusted to observe that at the hustings the clergy instructed the people 'to declare they could not read and the voters came in bodies with the priests [at] their heads declaring they were Catholics and would vote with their clergy'. Parnell's candidate lost the election, but not before quicklime had been thrown into the leader's eyes while he was haranguing the crowd in the village of Castlecomer. Neither John Stanislaus nor, after him, James would ever forgive the priests or the people for what they had done.

Back from Clongowes for Christmas, Jim showed the family what he had learnt at the school from the piano teacher, Edward Haughton, a friend of his mother's from choir days. John Kelly was there again for a good dinner and to hear the Joyce children sing their traditional Christmas hymn in front of the tree. Though Jim's lessons had cost Pappie the sum of eleven shillings and sixpence the previous term, there were more important things to think about: he had a great deal to discuss with his friend. The pair may have had a skirmish with Dante – as a very old lady Jim's erstwhile childhood 'fiancée', Eileen Vance, remembered hearing raised voices coming from No. 1 Martello Terrace that Christmas. As it happened, Kelly was not to enjoy John's hospitality for very long. Stanislaus corroborates the *Portrait*'s account that a couple of nights after Christmas the house was visited by an enormous policeman from Galway. The officer, who was also named Joyce and as proud of the clan as John, brought news that yet another warrant for the arrest of John Kelly had been issued. Kelly gratefully made off into the night, heading for Dublin by road, and the next morning Sergeant Joyce reappeared, impassively bearing the necessary papers, and looked disappointed to discover that the bird had flown.

In these tense times, life had to go on. In February 1891 John Stanislaus paid the term's fees for Clongowes as usual and soon afterwards had the reward of seeing his son appear on stage at the college; though pupils did not go home for Easter, parents were encouraged to attend the occasional open day. Jim, still one of the smallest and youngest boys in the school, was adorned in a curly fair wig, smock and tights to play one of the 'Courtiers, Attendants, Imps, &c' in a burlesque version of *Aladdin, or The Wonderful Scamp*. John and May Joyce most probably took the train down to Kildare to see their white-headed boy perform. Stannie came to Clongowes with them once or twice as well and they may all have turned up for the Sports Day later in the term.

On 1 June 1891, a savage article headlined 'Stop, Thief' appeared in the *National Press*, an anti-Parnellite newspaper set up the previous March by Tim Healy and his allies. The article, almost certainly written by Healy himself, alleged that Parnell had been embezzling party funds. It was only one of many personal attacks now being mounted upon him by the APs. When Mr Charles Stewart Parnell married Mrs Katharine O'Shea (*née* Wood) in a register office near Brighton at the end of the month, a renewed bout of ridicule against the couple began. Another by-election took place in Carlow and Andrew Kettle was persuaded to run for the cause, but with so little optimism that he demanded beforehand that his expenses be paid. He was duly defeated. At the end of July the *Freeman's Journal* (now owned by Edmund Dwyer Gray) finally switched sides and came out against the doomed leader. There was nothing anyone could do to stem the tide of opinion – though Tudor McDermott, Parnell's nephew, would spread some satisfaction by ambushing Tim Healy in the Four Courts and publicly horsewhipping him. (A meeting of Parnellites later voted to reward the assailant with a gold-handled whip.)

After his summer holidays, Jim travelled down to Clongowes for the last time. He would be back in Bray by the middle of the term. This was perhaps because he had an illness, like Stephen in the *Portrait*, and he may not even have returned to the school when he had recovered. It is very probable that his father was now seriously worried about the fees: money was increasingly tight and John was aware that his job might not survive after the new Dublin Corporation Act came into effect. His son was already beginning to realise that his home was not the bastion of middle-class prosperity that his fellow Clongownians enjoyed: Stephen feels let down that his father is 'not a magistrate like the other boys' fathers' and even dreams of his being 'a marshal now: higher than a magistrate'. It was evidently also financial pressure that decided John that he was soon going to have to move house: in any case the noise and dust of Bray had become unpleasant on account of the new harbour pier under construction behind Martello Terrace. Then, on 7 October, domestic difficulties suddenly dwindled into insignificance: the shattering news arrived from England that Parnell was dead.

A few days before, a drained and ailing Chief, after three days' rest at the home of Dr Joe Kenny, had ignored his host's advice and set off for England from Westland Row Station. He happened to spot John Kelly and J. J. Clancy MP at the station and asked them to accompany him on the short train journey to the Kingstown ferry. There, they helped him aboard with his rug and bag, and Clancy said his farewells and went ashore. Alone on deck,

John Kelly and Parnell stood for a while together, watching the crowds that had come to see off their stricken leader. Then Parnell clapped Kelly on the back and promised that he would be back in Dublin the following weekend. John Kelly was later mentioned in the *Freeman's Journal* as probably the last man in Ireland to have shaken hands with The Chief.

Four days later, the mailboat bearing Parnell's body came into Kingstown. He had kept his promise. In the *Portrait*, Stephen, still at Clongowes, is there in his imagination: 'A tiny light twinkled at the pierhead where the ship was entering: and he saw a multitude of people gathered by the waters' edge to see the ship that was entering their harbour.' John Stanislaus, who by now had spoken to John Kelly, was among this crowd and would have told his son how a 'wail of sorrow went up from the people' as the heavy oak coffin started on its final journey to Dublin.

Festooned with ivy (Parnell's emblem), the coffin was placed in the City Hall, where more than 30,000 Dubliners, Parnellites and APs alike, filed past it, some of them plucking a leaf as a memento. On the evening of Sunday, 11 October, The Chief's remains were taken in a great procession through the wet city to Glasnevin Cemetery. There had never been an occasion anything like it in Ireland – not even the funeral of the great Liberator came close for national pathos – and recent divisions were temporarily forgotten: 'No man is good in Ireland until he is dead, and unable to do anything more for his country,' The Chief had said prophetically in Wexford ten years before. The poet Thomas Stanislaus Clery (author of *Twitterings at Twilight*) distributed hastily printed copies of his 'Elegy on the Death of Parnell' along the route. At the cemetery, where John Stanislaus was among those standing silent in the rain, mourners saw a shooting star flash across the dark sky as the body was being lowered into the grave: Standish O'Grady, who was there, impressively told W. B. Yeats that 'the sky was bright with strange lights and flames'. Though James may not have been with his father at the graveside, in *Ulysses* he would one day pay his own tribute to their lost leader by marking the birth of Leopold Bloom with a comparable astral phenomenon.

CHAPTER 15

Crossing the Liffey

Less than a fortnight after Parnell's funeral, May Joyce gave birth to her ninth child, Eva Mary. Aunt Josephine was in attendance and she and young Jim stood as godparents at a christening performed the same day. The haste was either because the baby was delicate, or, just as likely, because the family was leaving Bray the next day. John had rented a substantial house called 'Leoville' on Carysfort Avenue in the town of Blackrock, along the coastal railway line between Kingstown and Dublin. However he managed it, it was a bigger and better dwelling than the one they were vacating, with a rateable valuation of £30. Situated on a quiet, even select, road between the Anglican church and the home of the Raynolds, whose son Aubrey Jim would befriend and mention in the *Portrait*, it had the distinction of a handsome Doric portico surtopped by a stone lion, with the poet Dante and his muse Beatrice illuminated in stained glass at the front door.

It was all a great upheaval. At Blackrock, John or May persuaded the Prioress of St Catherine's Dominican Convent nearby at Sion Hill, Mount Merrion Avenue, to take in Poppie, Stannie and perhaps Charlie as day pupils. As for Jim, during the time they were to live in Leoville, John would not send him to school at all. He had brought his schoolbooks home from Clongowes and, already a keen autodidact, had begun to teach himself, with a little help from his mother and Dante (Conway). He had begun writing religious verses, no doubt encouraged by his 'aunt' (whose idea of an instructive outing for her pupil was a visit to the National Gallery to see Francis Danby's terrifying painting, *The Opening of the Seventh Seal*). She was currently working on the family's morals, as, enthroned on cushions, she held readings of the Rosary and the Litany of the Blessed Virgin every evening in the conservatory.

It can be assumed that John was never present at these devotions: his diatribes against the perfidious bishops were now a heartfelt cabaret, to be echoed by Simon Dedalus; 'Billy with the lip' was one contemptuous sobriquet for His Grace, Archbishop William Walsh of Dublin, who though a Nationalist had been among the first to speak out against Parnell. Paul, Cardinal Cullen was, with savage sarcasm, 'an apple of God's eye' and the Primate of All Ireland, Cardinal Logue, a supporter of Tim Healy, became 'that tub of guts up in Armagh'. The priests and the priests' pawns were attacked as 'Sons of bitches'. This sort of talk was horrific to Dante and horrible to May. As the emotion generated by Parnell's death died away, the divisions in Leoville were those of the country in miniature.

Just before the end of 1890, the Dublin Corporation Act had become law. It would enable the 'Corpo' to collect the rates. The end was in sight for the Collector-General's regime. While he was at Bray, John had liked to bring one or other of his sons with him as he went about his business in villages on his patch such as Stillorgan, Goatstown and Dundrum, and Jim or Stannie now often went with him into town for the day. The company of a son did not mean that John stayed off the drink: most pubs were not the mere drinking establishments that they are today and John could imbibe at the bar while his son waited for him across the room in the part of the shop that sold groceries. With a skinful, Pappie could be alarmingly boisterous: on one such expedition he grabbed Jim as they were crossing Capel Street Bridge over the Liffey and suspended him by the feet over the dirty water swirling far below. It is to be hoped that John took the precaution of removing the boy's spectacles.

Returning with their father by train could also be an ordeal. Once, his semi-drunken mutterings in a third-class carriage almost caused a fight with a soldier. When the soldier turned out to be the lad who had looked after John's sailing boat in Dalkey in the 1870s, the chance meeting naturally called for a drink. On reaching Blackrock the red-coated serviceman and the tipsy rates-collector went off to a pub together, abandoning Stannie to find his own way home along Carysfort Avenue. On another occasion John embarrassed the children by commandeering an Italian barrel-organ in the main street of Blackrock and accompanying himself to general acclaim in a rendition of 'The Boys of Wexford', a song of 1898 by his distant relative, Robert Dwyer Joyce. William Field's butcher's shop was in the same street at No. 6, its canopy extended over the pavement. Field's business would soon expand until he controlled several shops around Dublin, becoming known as one of the city's 'merchant princes'. A Nationalist politician, he had been among the official party that had met Parnell's coffin off the ferry, and later became an MP. Whether or not he saw John's performance, Field must have got to know him at about this time. John called him 'Hamlet' (conceivably because he sold ham) and James would eventually use the butcher and his family as the basis for a story, 'After the Race'. It does not appear, however, that Field and John Stanislaus ever particularly warmed to each other.

In Leoville, the tension came to a head on Christmas Day. By now old enough to be fêted by his father and dine with the grown-ups (the others were still fed in the nursery), James was, with his mother and Uncle Bill, a witness to what took place between Dante, John Kelly and his father over the dinner-table, and would later reconstruct the scene for the first chapter of the *Portrait*. Artistic skill apart, the writer's detailed verisimilitude is evident: John Casey's (John Kelly's) Kerry phrase, 'Were they, faith?' is just one example. The explosive scene gives a good picture of John Stanis-laus as he was at this time, at first trying to spread Yuletide bon-homie, and finally failing even to keep his temper. As Casey, Kelly enrages Dante by recounting how he once spat a gob of tobacco juice into the face of an old woman who was screeching anti-Parnellite insults at him – a tale reported in a newspaper of the day, though with a priest as victim.

Siding with his friend against the priests, Simon Dedalus invokes the revolutionary fervour of his anticlerical grandfather, whose portrait hangs above them: 'He was a good Irishman when there was no money in the job. He was condemned to death as a Whiteboy.' If this was a claim of John Stanislaus's, it is another indication of his exaggerated pride in his rebellious forebear – no records have been traced of any such James Joyce having been either sentenced to death or reprieved. It is, however, very likely, as we have seen, that George Joyce's son was involved with the ragged band of rural guerrillas that operated around Fermoy and may have been briefly arrested. Such an incident would have given his descendant quite enough material for his story.

The bitterness unleashed by the argument drove Dante Conway out of the house for good. Though she was not much missed (Stanislaus later called her 'the most bigoted person I ever had the misfortune to encounter'), she could view her departure as a principled victory of a sort. When she left, she took Poppie away with her. In Dante's care, the eight-year-old would continue with her religious instruction, paying for her keep by acting as an unpaid housemaid. That John was willing to surrender a daughter, apparently without protest, may be an indication of his view of daughters in general; though in later years Poppie always irritated him most and he may not have been sorry to see her go.

John celebrated the double holy exodus by encouraging Jim to turn from devotional to political verse. He undoubtedly got a hand on Jim's elegy to Parnell, apparently Jim's precocious imitation of Byron, which was composed 'on the back of one of his father's second moiety notices'. This famous lost effusion was probably inspired by Clery's poem that had been given out at the funeral. According to James much later, when his father was drunk he was liable to make up 'verses containing the word *perchance*'. The surviving fragment of Jim's poem does not feature the word, alas, but the elegiac mood of the half-dozen disconnected lines that have been remembered is somewhat compromised by the supposed title, '*Et Tu, Healy*', which is likely to have been John's. James Joyce himself later referred to the poem as 'Parnell'. The more pointed title sounds like a later anecdotal embroidery by John, but perhaps it was added by him when he took the verses to the printers, Alley and O'Reilly of 9 Ryder's Row, a firm he had used before for Liberal Club election literature, music programmes and the like. Of the 'thirty or forty' copies he had run off on yellow paper, none now survives (unless possibly filed away unnoticed in some library under the title of 'Parnell'). John Stanislaus is said to have sent one to the Pope, but inquiries in Rome have failed to find it. If he did, the verses would have meant as little to the then Pope, Leo XIII (though he was a poet himself), as *Ulysses* did to the pontiff who was tricked in later years into blessing a wrapped-up copy of the novel. (After James Joyce's death, the *Irish Press* would refer to Jim's little publication as 'a short life of Parnell' – but it also said that *Finnegans Wake* was unfinished, though the book had come out almost two years earlier.)

In the cruel Cork City by-election in November 1891 following the death of Parnell, despite tireless campaigning by Tim Harrington, John Redmond for the Parnellites had been defeated by a candidate called Martin Flavin, who had the support of Tim Healy and the assembled priesthood. Lord Salisbury's Conservative government resigned a few months later and a general election was called for July 1892. It was the cue for a last effort from the few faithful disciples of the dead Chief and John offered his electioneering services to the Parnellite side in Cork. As he was not due any time off work, he pleaded illness (a ploy he had used before), then caught the train down to the city. Cork was now split almost equally north and south between the Redmondites and the followers of William O'Brien, currently an AP, and John was there to witness the brawling between the factions that took place whenever rival parades met. He made his own contribution to the cause by showing Jim's lament for Parnell to his friends. Despite these efforts, O'Brien was elected. Unfortunately somebody spotted the 'invalid' John Stanislaus at the hustings and informed the Collector-General that he seemed to be thriving. This was no minor matter: the office had paid a temporary collector to do the job while the incumbent was 'recovering'. On his return to the office John was admonished and his file was taken down again from the shelf. Though he may never have discovered the informer's identity, John was becoming more and more convinced that there was a conspiracy against him. There had, after all, been one against Parnell.

Like Mrs Conway, Uncle Bill now left the Joyces for the last time, though on more cordial terms. On 31 August he died of pneumonia, three days after getting back to Cork. John is unlikely to have been able to convince his superiors to let him make a second trip down to his native city, however much he would have wanted to be there for the funeral of the old man.

He did not have to look hard to find evidence for his conspiracy theory. People were beginning to suspect that John Stanislaus's days of employment might be numbered and lenders, getting cold feet, were pressing to get their money back before it was too late. At the same time, and for the same reason, John was less keen than ever to repay them. He ignored what demands he could and, when confronted, argued forcefully about it. The result was a series of court judgments against him, the first of which forced him to pay back £22.15s.0d that he owed to a Parnellite solicitor and costs drawer (or insurance assessor) who had lived on the South Circular Road opposite the Giltraps. This was the 'tall blackbearded' Reuben J. Dodd, agent for the Patriotic Insurance Company. John would have reason to remember the name. There were court costs of £5.6s.0d on top. He may have had to raise the amount through a second very short-term loan from a Bolton Street merchant in potatoes and corn, Richard Dawson, for in October the Queen's Bench Division forced John Stanislaus to repay Dawson £30 (with another £5.11s.0d costs). With several different skeins of financial dealing all going on at once, it is impossible to work out today what was happening to John's Cork rents (or to his wages, in 1892 almost £400). It was probably impossible to work out then.

Meanwhile, negotiations had been going on to decide the fate of the Collector-General's Office itself. On 9 May, after digesting a committee report on the matter, the Corporation had determined to become the sole collector of rates from the beginning of 1893. Another inquiry by Messrs Holmes and Soady into the running of the office made its report at the end of August. It was followed by the protests of staff, who finally realised the imminent danger of the sack.

John was still confident of his accountancy skills and even at this stage probably planned to fall back on them if the worst came to the worst and he were retired on the changeover in the New Year. It was a reasonable plan, in theory. He knew everyone. He could write an impressive and official-looking letter to instil confidence in his bona fides. The market couldn't go on falling. And he would have a generous pension from the Collector-General's Office when he left. However, everything seemed somehow to be going wrong at once: he was borrowing from his collecting bag, he was taking out short loans at high interest, he was investing in 'get-rich-quick' schemes of various sorts (like Bloom's Royal Hungarian Lottery) and he was drinking too much. He was also still trying to keep up appearances. On one appearance he made in Grafton Street he was heard loudly keeping up a tirade against an impatient bank manager: 'If I get another impertinent letter like this I'll remove my overdraft to another bank'.

It really had not been a good year. Earlier, driven to desperate measures, John had risked the family furniture as collateral against another loan for a very large sum, £130.10s.0d. The amount is an indication of the considerable value of the contents of the house: he had bought a good number of expensive and showy things for Castlewood Avenue and there were also any pieces that his mother had left behind of inherited Joyce furniture, the family heirlooms. No doubt the £130 was intended to double in a matter of months, but it disappeared without trace. On 2 November the angry creditor, John Lawler, a city centre financial agent, took out a court order for his money. This caused the name of John S. Joyce to be published in *Stubbs' Gazette* and *Perry's Weekly*, periodicals that printed blacklists of debtors as well as bankrupts. If Lawler thought that this would have the effect of making him pay, he was disappointed: John's available funds promptly shrank, as not only was publication a warning to John's other creditors to redouble their efforts, but the Collector-General saw his name and immediately suspended him from duties. Under such personal financial pressure, John S. Joyce could hardly be trusted with public money.

Both James and Stannie later thought that their father had officially been declared a bankrupt, though in 1893 Stannie loyally attacked a boy from Blackrock who dared to say as much. In fact, John never actually was bankrupted, though he easily might have been: if an opportunity to double-mortgage any of his Cork properties, for example, had somehow presented itself at this juncture, he would have leapt at it. But in practice the only thing he could now do was to move house immediately, leaving the rent unpaid and taking the furniture with him if he were quick enough.

May made John a father again less than a week after his name had been in the gazettes. On 8 November 1892 Florence Elizabeth Joyce came to see what her father's world had to offer her.

*   *   *

The family was leaving the genteel and airy southern suburbs for ever. Much of Dublin north of the river was already beginning to crumble. Its great squares and elegant streets were now increasingly occupied not by the prosperous aristocrats and professional men for whom they had been built at the other end of the century and earlier but by a shifting population of the more or less impoverished. Large families were being brought up in single rooms in these houses, hungry and cold beneath magnificent plasterwork ceilings. While some areas, like Rutland Square at the top of Sackville Street, still maintained something of their former selves, these were islands in a rising sea of shabbiness and squalor. Crossing the Liffey was a symbolic act in Dublin, no matter the direction of travel. The Joyces were going the wrong way. It was a traumatic move for another reason too. Despite their hurry to get out, they were beaten by Lawler's bailiffs, who carried off all (or nearly all) the furniture from the house, mercifully sparing the ancestral portraits. By now, too, the silver that had graced the sideboard in Blackrock had gone, most likely to the pawnbroker. This included the cups awarded years before to John for rowing and the triple jump. (Stanislaus thought for some reason that his brother had won them at Clongowes – but Jim was always far too young there for athletic distinctions.)

The remaining yellow sheets of the Parnell poem were left behind on the floor, glimpsed by Stannie on his way out of Leoville for the last time. In the *Portrait*, the bailiffs' vans, bulging with what was once the family furniture, 'lumber . . . along the Merrion Road', watched by Stephen and his tearful mother from the train that is taking them to the north side of Dublin. That evening, the boy's father would tell him fiercely: 'There's a crack of the whip left in me yet, Stephen. We're not dead yet, sonny. No, by the Lord Jesus (God forgive me) nor half dead.' But John's whole family had seen the signs and knew that their lives were going to be very different.

Since they had left Leoville so precipitously, John may not yet have found anywhere for them all to live and it seems that the Joyces had to squeeze for some weeks into a rooming house in Hardwicke Street. Details of this uncomfortable stay remain speculative, but James would put some of his memories of 'The Boarding

House' into *Dubliners*. Two establishments, one run by a Mrs Doyle and the other by a Mrs Lloyd, fit the story. They both overlooked St George's Church, whose frequent 'loud dark iron' bells just opposite boomed an unwelcome lullaby for the new-born Florrie.

May had not yet put down religious roots on the north side, or Florrie's baptism had already been arranged for St John the Baptist's Church on Newtown Avenue, for on 2 December the family of eleven – Poppie was with them again – slipped back on the train to Blackrock for the ceremony. They brought with them to be the sponsors the baby's aunt, Elizabeth Flynn, and John Kelly (still at the National Club just around the corner from Hardwicke Street). From now on, the south of the city would be only a place to visit.

Christmas should be the high point of any Victorian child's year, but it was hopeless trying to celebrate. Even the Flynns' annual dance may not have been held this year as Aunt Anne was ill. At least James was invited to a Christmas party thrown by Mat Dillon for his daughter at his home in Rathgar. Jim was not yet quite eleven, but he could already view this as a chance to meet girls, and wrote a poem about one of the Dillons while his father was pleased enough to see him mixing again with the old crowd. After Christmas, John and May took the older children to the pantomime at the Gaiety. This year it was *Sindbad the Sailor*, presented 'under the personal supervision of Mrs Michael Gunn'. In keeping with panto tradition, Sindbad was Miss Violet Evelyn, Mrs Sindbad was Mr T. W. Volt and, intriguingly, the Old Man of the Sea was played by Little Katie Wallace. The seven voyages of the hero included ones that matched the *Odyssey* and later *Ulysses*: there was cannibalism, a living-and-dead burial and the blinding of a malignant giant. Among the less heroic characters on stage were Tindbad the Tailor and Whinbad the Whaler, word play appreciated by Jim. Though he did not know it, he was already amassing a vast amount of material to draw upon in his adult writings: the Dillons' party, for instance, is in the *Portrait* and the *Sindbad* theatre programme, or a cutting from the newspaper about it, may have survived long enough to be used in *Ulysses*. May Joyce would have enjoyed the evening too: Captain M'Turco was played by Edward Royce, whom she had warm memories of seeing as far back as 1873 in *Turco the*

Terrible, a production that Jack Hall of the *Freeman* called the best pantomime ever produced at the theatre.

As it transpired, almost all of John's former colleagues in the Rates Office lost their jobs on 1 January 1893. They were awarded three-quarters of their average wage as annual pension, no matter how long they had served. This generous arrangement did not, however, apply to John Stanislaus. A glance at his file made it clear that the man deserved nothing at all: to add to the long list of his misdemeanours, his collecting records for the North Dock Ward were chaotic and the whole division was going to require detailed reassessment. John Stanislaus argued his case fiercely. A fortnight into the New Year, after agonising negotiations (in which May is said desperately to have pleaded her husband's cause), it was decided that he would be granted £132.2s.10d per annum, less than half of what his colleagues were getting, and only about a third of his former wage. It was no fortune, but it was a pension. The very next day a vindictive official unearthed two further serious discrepancies in John's papers: not only did a cheque appear to have gone missing, but it looked as though he had also doctored a receipt. The pittance was promptly stopped, pending further investigations.

Meanwhile, the family had left Hardwicke Street for a tall terrace in Fitzgibbon Street, which ran east off Mountjoy Square. This was a little to the north of the North Dock Ward, in a declining area of 'auld decency'; around the corner the tenements were taking over. They were in No. 14, while at No. 13 was Mrs Callanan, a relation of the Usher's Island Flynns, and hence of May Joyce. John agreed to pay rent of £25 a year for this 'bare cheerless house' of four storeys over a basement. It was unfurnished, uncarpeted and, with the usual high Georgian ceilings, almost impossible to heat: it was the family's biggest ever dwelling. That winter the weather was particularly foggy and cold and the canals froze over, as Leopold Bloom remembers. There were more than a dozen large rooms to fill and with practically no furniture left, John had to buy second-hand on the quays, using another injection of money borrowed from his old friend and sparring partner in the courts, Reuben J. Dodd. This loan, which had been arranged just before Christmas, was a considerable one, for £400. Once again, the Cork properties were used as security, Reuben J. holding the title deeds in his Ormond Quay office safe. Why Dodd agreed to deal with John Stanislaus again is a mystery, after the bother only six months before for a much smaller amount. In January he insisted that the new loan be converted to a proper mortgage, giving him regular interest (and perhaps capital) payments from John. John would take out several further minor loans from other money-lenders over the next months, most likely to pay Dodd's charges. Another two court judgments for smallish debts went against him in the same period, both of them in favour of a Francis H. Caulfield, bill broker and agent for the Edinburgh Life Assurance Company.

On 8 February there was another occasion when John might have got for himself and May 'a seat on the platform at the unveiling of a statue'. A ceremony was held to launch a statue of Fr Theobald Mathew near McSwiney's old shop in Sackville Street. Back in Cork the first monument to the great campaigner (by Foley who had gone on to do the O'Connell Monument) had been unveiled in 1864 to a crowd of 100,000, which had probably included the temperance apostle's friend, James Augustine Joyce. But now for John times had changed since the glory days, and Fr Mathew most likely preached his first Dublin sermon in stone without the assistance of the Joyces.

While John was juggling with money, his children needed an education. Swallowing his pride, he sent Jim and Stannie to a local free school for boys, apparently the O'Connell School in North Richmond Street off the North Circular Road; others must have been bustled off to a local national school, one of which was run by the Jesuits nearby. The O'Connell School was a Christian Brothers establishment, but for John it at least had the advantage of a family connection: the foundation stone had been laid in 1828 by the Liberator himself, the Great Dan. Jim's time there (if he was there – Stanislaus remembers it, though oddly there is no record of either boy at the school) was never to be confirmed by him.

In any case, the brothers were to change schools before long, for one day in early spring their father bumped into Fr Conmee, whom he already knew as Jim's rector at Clongowes. After leaving Clongowes, Fr Conmee had for a year been prefect of studies at the school's urban non-boarding equivalent, Belvedere College, before ill health forced him to rest and, literally, take the waters. Nominally, he was now merely a teacher (and the director of the religious sodality, a College association of the holiest boys), but he was still an important figure in the school. In 1905 he would be appointed head ('Provincial') of the Irish Jesuits. He was also currently attached to the Church of St Francis Xavier's in Gardiner Street, where some of the Joyces had begun to worship. Belvedere, like Clongowes a school for the sons of gentlemen, looked down over North Great George's Street from Great Denmark Street, five minutes' walk from the new house. It would be perfect for Jim and he would be back with the Jesuits where he belonged. John had no need to paint a rosy picture of his son's abilities, for Conmee was already convinced that Jim would be an asset to the school, but he probably did so anyway. At the time academic ability was a powerful argument, as educational funding was directly linked to results: through government incentives clever pupils could win for their school far more than the cost of their fees and were educated free in return. Fr Conmee told John that Jim and Stannie would be enrolled forthwith and could start after Easter. It was a little bit of good news at last.

By the end of May, John had finally succeeded in talking his way out of the various accusations of the Rates Office, and his meagre pension was reinstated. It was more than welcome. He was in dire need of money: a recent fall in prices had shrunk the income from his tenants, which was already being consumed greedily by the repayments to Dodd. Mary, the family maid, was still with them and had to be paid her £4 a year, and her food alone cost as much again. Nobody could be expected to feed and clothe eleven dependants on a pension of just over £2.10s.0d a week. John cast around for jobs: perhaps someone in the Corporation might find him something. But the Dublin civic world was a small one and his reputation went ahead of him. It was little use his approaching old friends like Valentine Blake Dillon, who, despite the increased bitterness of the split following the death of Parnell, had found a Parnellite past to be no hindrance to his ambitions in Dublin politics: he would be elected Lord Mayor in 1894 and again in 1895. The days were gone when John might have wished to share in Dillon's glory, but Val might have found him a cushy sinecure. He never did.

At this point John formulated an inventive scheme to get his hands on the large lump sum he needed to pay back Reuben J. He went to see him on Ormond Quay and asked if he could have the Cork title deeds. The request was probably put forward as a temporary measure, perhaps just a quick borrow to prove his liquidity for a different, cast-iron transaction to raise the cash. He understood perfectly that the mortgage was still outstanding. But however convincing his reasons, it was no good. Dodd, once bitten, refused him point blank, suspecting that he would never see either the deeds or his money again. John could only counter by refusing to pay the interest on his mortgage, not perhaps the wisest of moves.

Reuben J. Dodd was never to be forgiven by John Stanislaus. A former supporter of Parnell – who claimed that The Chief had once actually visited him at home – the money-grubbing usurer had now failed a fellow-Parnellite in his hour of greatest need. John began a long campaign of vilification against him, which eventually was to be preserved, as in amber, between the covers of *Ulysses*. When Simon Dedalus sees Dodd's stooped figure in the street he curses him with the words: 'The devil break the hasp of your back!' Elsewhere Dodd is called Judas Iscariot and he even makes an appearance in the book as 'Reuben J. Antichrist, wandering jew', clutching at his loins a 'pilgrim's wallet from which protrude promissory notes and dishonoured bills'. Though the Dodds were English in origin, Reuben's name and reputation were Jewish enough for John to heap upon him all the usual calumnies about usury and miserliness. At Belvedere, Reuben Dodd Jr knew Jim and late in life would still remember James Joyce as 'a disagreeable type' who had brought the family vendetta against the Dodds to school with him. At least John Stanislaus had one ally.

The summer trip by train to Cork that is described in the *Portrait* was based on a visit that Jim made there with his father in 1893. Frantic about the hold that Dodd had over him, John needed to discuss the legal situation of his Cork holdings with his long-term agents and rent-collectors there, Scanlan and Son, in the hope that they could suggest a way out. But there was no advice they could offer except to sell up, and John took the opportunity to show off the city to his son, conducting him around the streets, familiar but changed, and calling on former watering holes in search of traces of his youth. The novel has a heightened account of real life, but it is probable that most of the incidents in Cork are factual. If they are, John afforded a room for them at the Victoria Hotel, which Parnell had patronised when in Cork, and they went to the university, where in the Medical School John located his initials carved on a desk, while Jim was shocked by the word 'foetus' that he found on another. In one of the pubs they drifted into, 'Johnny Cashman' told the boy that his father had been 'the boldest flirt in the city of Cork in his day'. The old man was the 'town' friend of John's who could remember as far back as the 'fierce old fire-eater'. John Stanislaus's day had begun with a hangover, as would the next.

The following morning the pair travelled through the sunshine down to his late Aunt Alicia, Sister Xavier's, convent, the Presentation at Crosshaven. There John upset a young cousin (to become Sister Mary Ita of the South Presentation Covent, Cork) who was a pupil there. She had been ordered to sing 'The Fisherman's Goodnight' for them, accompanying herself 'in that stilted hyper-human fashion of most school-children' and would never forget John's comment to Jim afterwards: 'That song does not suit her – and the range is much too low'. It was not only family piety that brought John to Crosshaven: he was hoping to persuade the Superior, Mother Teresa, to take in some of his daughters, or at least Poppie, for nothing. When he suggested as much the nun peremptorily refused.

It seems that John's Cork kin were far from impressed by their long-lost relatives, having doubtless endured a good deal of the late Ellen Joyce's handwringing about her callous son in Dublin. He and Jim may have had a better reception from the Justices in the seaside resort of Youghal: James in later years would remember the town with affection. His notes for *Stephen Hero* suggest that on the train home they met his godfather, Philip McCann, coming back from one of his trips down to Ireland's main port on ship chandlery business. Letters that Jim wrote to Stannie on the trip to Cork showed that he hugely enjoyed being there with his father. When the episode was written up by Herbert Gorman for his biography, Joyce, then battling for publication throughout the English-speaking world, promptly censored it, saying that it was based too closely on the *Portrait*'s fictional treatment of the trip. Even after John Stanislaus was dead his son's combative affection for him would survive. Though John's primary objective in going to Cork had not been fulfilled, the few days that they spent together there were good days for both of them.

Life in Fitzgibbon Street was not easy for the exhausted May Joyce. On 27 November 1893 she produced yet another daughter, her fifth in succession. Christened Mabel Josephine Anne, she would be known all her life as 'Baby'. Her godparents were the still ailing Aunt Anne Flynn and Richard John Thornton, 'an amusing, robust, florid little elderly man' known to May as 'the dicky bird', who tasted tea for a living and whiskey for a pastime. (James Joyce is said to have based the nameless narrator of the 'Cyclops' episode of *Ulysses* upon one or other of these Thorntons.) Some time after the birth, and far more debilitating than another baby, both May and her youngest son Georgie, now aged six, came down with scarlet fever, an uncomfortable, highly contagious and, then, dangerous disease. John had to put them into isolation for weeks in a room near the top of the echoing house. The illness apart, May must have missed both the spiritual sustenance and the human contact that she got from the local churches: though Baby's christening had been held in the Pro-Cathedral in Marlborough Street, which was technically also the Joyces' parish church, May was already singing in the choir at St Francis Xavier's in Gardiner Street. Her hair, always pale, was imperceptibly fading to white.

John's debt to Dodd was growing rapidly. This was no doubt encouraged by Dodd, who had a good idea of the value of the title deeds in his possession. It was essential for John to get the man off his back quickly. On 6 September he had written in his best legalese to the Under-Secretary at Dublin Castle with an ingenious (if ungrammatical) suggestion: 'I am now desirous for the purpose of clearing off charges on a small property I have in the City of Cork, of commuting said pension so granted to me . . .' This unusual request for a lump sum in exchange for a perpetual stipend was passed all the way up to the Solicitor-General, and it was not until the end of the year that an official reply came back, giving the anticipated answer that the scheme was legally impossible. By then it would have been too late anyway.

There was no escape for John from the net in which Reuben J. had entangled him. By the autumn of 1893 it was clear that the Cork houses would have to be got rid of, and on 2 December the first advertisement for the auction was placed in the *Cork Examiner* by Scanlan's, who were auctioneers as well as agents. Less than a fortnight later, at one o'clock on Thursday, 14 December, in the Property Sale Room on South Mall, Cork, the last remnant of John's inheritance ('one of the best paying properties which has been placed on the market for a considerable time', as the encomium in the paper put it) was disposed of. The three lots, the very last of the family's material assets, represented the labours, ambitions and sorrows of uncounted generations of Joyces, remembered and forgotten. John Stanislaus Joyce, their sole heir, was not present to see the end.

CHAPTER 16

Halcyon Days

Over the winter of 1893–4 there was a spate of deaths. Joe Gallaher of the *Freeman* had died in October and John Stanislaus brought his eldest son to the funeral. As well as the Gallaher family and his in-laws, the Powells, Clinches and Russells, practically the whole Dublin press fraternity turned up to bid farewell to his lively soul. John and William Murray were there too. In a way it was the end of an era, and for John and his friends Joe Gallaher would soon become part of the mythology of Dublin in the old days, when times were better and the people you met in the streets were pleased to see you. Poor Joe was well out of it all.

Soon John would have to meet the Murray brothers again at another Glasnevin graveside, for in March their father and May's, 'old' John Murray, passed away after a paralysing stroke. Already a widower for the second time, he had been living with his eldest son John and family in Dargle Road, Drumcondra, where he had been since before his far younger wife, Christine, had died in 1891 while with the Flynns at Usher's Island. It was scarcely a surprise to the Joyces when the old bottlewasher left them nothing in his will.

Yet another body was taken that winter to the cemetery. It was John's young pal from the Collector-General's Office, E. A. Malins, who died at Glasnevin Lodge, his father David's home as cemetery caretaker. Teddy Malins was only thirty-one, but he had been a very heavy drinker and had even once gone for a 'cure' to the monastery of Mount Melleray. Even so, he had been more provident than John: after his few years in the Fleet Street office he left more than £1200 in his will. But not, of course, to John Stanislaus.

In early February the monies from two of the three sold Cork holdings reached Reuben J. Dodd, who as creditor had made it his responsibility to organise all the legal side of the transaction. The buyers, Mullins and Murphy, had come up to Dublin to sign the contracts and between them paid £1875 to Dodd, who appears to have kept it to pay off what John owed him. Since the initial loan of £400 had been taken out little more than a year before, this was not bad going and, when John Stanislaus pondered the figures, it can only have added fuel to the fire of his resentment. In the meantime, however, Dodd must have paid off some of John's other debts in advance of this money coming through: the Bridgeman loan, for example, was cancelled in January. On 14 February Dodd at last put his signature to the formal papers releasing John from his debt to him. A few days later the money from the auction of the third and final lot arrived from the purchaser, a William McMullen of Clontymon House, Cork. This lot, the group of buildings known as 'Joyce's Court' in White Street, was the very last of the Joyce properties. It had been the first of them in the city too, bought by John's great-grandfather in 1830. What McMullen paid for it is not recorded, but this money at least John should have been able to keep.

On the register of Baby's birth a few months earlier, John Stanislaus Joyce described himself again as an accountant. He had in fact been doing some desultory work as a jobbing financial clerk, auditor and scrivener for a man called Thomas Aylward of 53 Sandymount Road, himself an accountant with an office near the Four Courts. But this was far from being a permanent occupation for John. Over the next few years he would half-heartedly sample a variety of different jobs, most of which James Joyce would later bestow upon Leopold Bloom. Stanislaus recalls his father at about this time making (when sober) 'optimistic calculations of how much he could earn "between hopping and trotting"'. But for now, his old trade of accountancy kept a little cash flowing in, and it may even be that he managed to invest part of the lump sum from Joyce's Court wisely: over the next few years there is no evidence of his having taken out any more formal loans. That he no longer had any collateral to put against borrowings may equally explain this apparent prudence, however.

John was now quite out of the running in the political life of the city, although he still often spent time with old associates. Gladstone's Second Home Rule Bill had scraped through the Commons the previous September, but its subsequent rejection by the House of Lords appears not to have bothered John one way or the other: with Parnell gone, he did not much care what happened. He still, after all, had his friends. Jack Hishon and his wife Nora were not far away at 16 Belvedere Road and John Kelly was also about, though he was anything but well (the Joyces always blamed his years picking oakum in prison for destroying his health). Kelly was planning a sea trip to America in an attempt to recuperate and to relax from the constant surveillance he was still attracting from the secret police. And there were other cronies too, like Tom Devin and George Lidwell – decent chaps who liked a drink.

In May 1894 a charity fundraiser styled as the 'Araby Bazaar' was held in Ballsbridge, and Jim, now twelve, may have made an expedition to it, though from Fitzgibbon Street rather than the North Richmond Street address in *Dubliners*. In the story, 'Araby', the schoolboy narrator is given a two-shilling piece to spend by his uncle, who, having gone out earlier in smart suit and brushed hat, returns late, not drunk but with drink taken. The thumb-nail sketch of John Stanislaus is all too recognisable.

In June news came that Jim had vindicated his father's boasts about him to Fr Conmee and had been awarded £22 for himself and £12.4s.0d for the College in the 1894 Preparatory Grade Intermediate Examination. The money was paid to John but he passed it on to Jim, who promptly began to spend it, even taking his parents out to dinner at an expensive restaurant. It was probably this windfall and the goodwill it engendered between them that prompted John to invite Jim to accompany him on a summer trip to Scotland (perhaps, as 'The Dead' seems to hint, for the wedding or funeral of one of the Malinses). John did not have to pay for the sea crossing: as a seafaring man who knew the language since his Queenstown days, he had made friends with some of the personnel of the shipping companies when he was a Collector in the North Dock Ward and persuaded the captain of one of the Duke Line steamers to allow them an unused berth up the Irish Sea. Jim with his winnings could help to subsidise food, entertainment and somewhere to stay.

As Stanislaus remembered, they went first to Glasgow, then a city with a greater claim than Dublin to be the Second City of the Empire: its industrial vigour – in shipbuilding and locomotives – was quite unlike anything to be found in Dublin. James Joyce's notes for *Stephen Hero*, however, strongly suggest that their final destination was beyond Glasgow and that a visit to Edinburgh featured in the lost chapters of that book – the existing parts of which are firmly rooted in fact. Depressingly, it poured with rain, which likely forced them to spend much of their time sheltering in city gin palaces. In delineating the development of the father–son relationship on this jaunt, another *Stephen Hero* note on the same page states darkly: 'We cannot educate our fathers.' On the return voyage to Ireland the kindly captain was severely provoked by his inebriated friend who insisted on arguing vehemently and tediously with him about his favourite subject – Parnell. Afterwards, as he acted out an entertaining version of the story for the family, John reflected wryly that he was lucky not to have been seized bodily and thrown into the Irish Sea. Jim may not have been able to educate his father, but he was certainly learning a good deal from him and about him.

By October or November 1894 it had become a pressing necessity to transfer to a cheaper and easier abode – while there was still some money for removal costs and advance rent. To return to the south side was impossible, but John found a nice enough house near the River Tolka, 2 Holywell Villas, Millbourne Avenue (then really just a lane off the Drumcondra Road), whose rateable valuation was listed in *Thom's* as £17, compared to Fitzgibbon Street's £25. This handsome semi-detached villa, which was quite new, had been built on the edge of the city as a speculation that had faltered after only two houses. It gave the Joyces three bright bedrooms, another small (maid's) room and an indoor lavatory upstairs, while behind the front parlour on the ground floor there was another room where some of them could sleep. (By now, most of the children were already used to sharing beds with a brother or sister. Jim and Stannie would sleep together for almost another decade.) At the end of a passage to the back of the house a spacious kitchen led out through scullery and pantry to a very long secluded garden with young apple trees, good for cricket.

The whole family approved of the move. All around the two houses there were woods and green fields for the children to kick about a ball and generally run wild. (Family tradition has it that Jim would come out to watch the football, loitering on the sidelines where the only thing he deigned to kick were his heels.) Pappie had a referee's whistle and when May told him it was time for the children to come in he would blow it from an upstairs window and let off a mock aria in his best tenor: 'Your tea is served!' For all of them, the villa in Millbourne Avenue was by no means the worst place to be and definitely an improvement upon the bleak Georgian barrack they had just left. Here (as soon as he got himself a decent job) John would be able to feel he was at the head of a good, respectable (if somewhat cramped) household, with nothing to be ashamed of.

The redoubtable Captain Tom Cunniam had moved into town and was now a short distance away from the Joyces at 72 Drumcondra Road. He still had his pub at Kingstown, but had also just opened a 'Family Grocer, Retail Wine and Spirit Merchant' at No. 1 Werburgh Street, opposite Christ Church Cathedral, where one of his employees was a James Cassidy. It may have been Cassidy's mother whose passing was reported in the morning paper at about this time. John spotted the death notice and read it out to May, who had been fond of Mrs Cassidy. When May, shocked, responded: 'Oh! don't tell me that Mrs Cassidy is dead,' John answered her mordantly, 'Well, I don't quite know about that, but someone has taken the liberty of burying her.' The brief exchange became one of the stories about his father that Jim used to tell his friends. Later he put it into *Ulysses.*

Entertaining guests as he once had was quite out of the question, though this did not stop John and May from socialising on occasions as a couple. It was probably during this winter that they travelled with some others in a horse-drawn car out beyond Bray to the fund-raising banquet described in *Ulysses.* Held in St Kevin's Reformatory at Glencree, County Wicklow, apart from, perhaps, Fr Ring and the Oblate Fathers who organised the event, the meal was an exceedingly cordial and unbuttoned affair, with many old friends from the south side for the Joyces to catch up with. In the book, which can be relied on here to imitate the actuality,

Alderman Robert O'Reilly was there, 'maggotty', while Molly Bloom remembers Valentine Blake Dillon, now Lord Mayor, looking at her 'with his dirty eyes'. On the starlit journey home across the Featherbed Mountain, the inebriated journalist, Lenehan 'of *Sport*', ogles her embonpoint shamelessly. The racing tipster from Clonliffe Road, Drumcondra, whose trade marks were bad puns and the cadging of drinks, was a man to make the most of whatever contact with the opposite sex came his way. Whether both Val Dillon and Lenehan's real-life original cast lusty glances at Mrs Joyce that evening is an imponderable. It is quite possible, for May was still only thirty-four, but for all her quiet charm she lacked the glamour, effervescence and ample curvature of Molly Bloom, except perhaps in the mind of her jealous husband.

By now May was pregnant again. If Bloom's occupation at this time is an indication, John had taken some sort of work by Christmas with Hely's, the stationers and printers on the quays. He needed to: the last traces of the Cork money were long gone. His friendly and informed manner with the shopkeepers would have helped to get the merchandise distributed, and the commission was useful – especially if he didn't drink all of it. Perhaps things might be returning to normal. He was not dead yet, by Christ.

Soon after 1895 began, John Kelly came back from his trip to the States. His friends were disturbed to see that the sea air had not improved his health – indeed, he looked far worse. He decided not to return to the National Club, which was now overrun by APs who, with an eye to the mantle, claimed to have been Parnellites all the time. Instead, he accepted an invitation from Jack Hishon to live at his house in Belvedere Road, off the Drumcondra Road a little way beyond the Cunniam residence. Hishon, a solicitor, had retained his vitality – and a relative degree of prosperity – since the fall of The Chief. Some unjustly suspected him of spying for Dublin Castle, but he was very close to Tim Harrington and both men would be active in municipal politics for many years, without ever losing too much of their Parnellite lustre. It was a rare feat. These days, John always found a warm welcome at Belvedere Road and had the leisure to spend many a liquid evening there with Hishon and Kelly in song and reminiscence.

As Jim tried to concentrate on his homework amid the chaos of the Joyce household, Pappie, if he had been drinking, would ask him repeatedly, 'Are you going to win? Eh? Are you going to win?' Usually he did: he was rewarded even more handsomely at the 1895 examinations (£23 for three years – though the year after he would not be paid, being considered too young at fourteen to take the qualifying Middle Grade examinations). Having heard of the boy's ability, one day a posse of head-hunting Dominicans appeared, offering to educate him at one of their own establishments. John left the decision to Jim, 'to make a man of him'. He was pleased when Jim turned them down in favour of the Jesuits he knew. So were the Jesuits: towards the end of his school career he would win further sums both for himself and for his school.

John was even more pleased when, on 18 July, May bore him another son, Frederick William, and four days later the birth was announced in the *Freeman's Journal*. After five daughters in a row, Freddie was John's first male child since Georgie, eight years before. He was baptised by Fr Caffrey at Fairview Church on the twenty-eighth, but despite the attentions of a local medical man, Dr Tuohy (son of the *Freeman*'s London correspondent), Freddie was dead within a few days. The baby's birth was never officially registered with the state, but his burial in the family grave is noted in the Glasnevin records. Tuohy's failure to save John's son would not be resented (nor, perhaps, even remembered) by John when the doctor's son painted the celebrated portrait of him almost thirty years later.

The death hit John Stanislaus hard; and his family was made to suffer even more as a result. Alcohol has different effects on different people: John, when he was very drunk, was one of those who could become somebody else entirely. One evening May and Poppie were forced to run out of the house to get away from him. Carrying Florrie and Baby with them, they found sanctuary with the McKernans who lived in the adjoining house. They told them what had happened: John had come back in a foul mood from his day's drinking and had suddenly grabbed his wife viciously around the neck, bellowing 'Now, by God, is the time to finish it!' Fortunately Jim was there and managed to knock his father to the floor before he could carry out the threat. The Dublin Metropolitan Police were informed (probably by the McKernans) and shortly afterwards a sergeant called and interviewed the couple at length in the front room, to the lasting shame of the older children. But the police warning, or his own shame, meant that John would never again attack his wife physically. Savage verbal onslaughts were quite another matter.

John was still looking for a job. One of the problems was that he greatly disliked being tied down to the regular hours of an office and he was certainly not prepared to do menial, much less manual, work of any kind. However, his old supporter and fellow Corkman 'Alderman' John Hooper (who had left the paper he edited in Cork to become a parliamentary correspondent on the *Freeman* and was now the editor of the Dublin *Evening Telegraph*) was still in contact with him. He currently lived at 22 Belvedere Place, off Fitzgibbon Street, and had become the butt of an obscure family joke relating to Shelley's poem 'The Sensitive Plant'. Though Hooper was a highly professional newspaperman, under his control the *Evening Telegraph* was, like most Dublin newspaper offices, a companionable and somewhat informal concern. It shared premises and management with the *Freeman's Journal* and *Sport* in the city centre block between Prince's Street and Middle Abbey Street. There, people could drop in simply to pass the time of day or to find someone to go for a drink with. Two of John's preferred establishments were Phil Gilligan's Oval Bar almost next door and the Ship on Lower Abbey Street, both favourite haunts of the press. There was always room for another freelance advertising canvasser to drum up revenue for the papers: John persuaded Hooper to let him have a try. The work suited him well: it had an element of creativity, which he enjoyed, and it entailed travelling around the city from one business acquaintance to another, and convincing them, if possible over a drink or two, that the publicity would be a good investment whether business was good or bad. The disadvantage was that there was no salary: commission was paid only on publication.

There are no records of how many ads John succeeded in attracting. From Bray and Blackrock days, he may have thought of canvassing the hotelier Edward Breslin or William Field, MP and butcher. An easier port of call for him was Captain Tom Cunniam, with his Werburgh Street shop. Accordingly, every Saturday in the first three months of 1896, there was published in the *Evening Telegraph* the following advertisement, a masterpiece of the publicist's art, with its deathless dialogue:

HUSBAND AND WIFE

HUSBAND: My dear, try a drop of Cunniam's malt; it is really delicious.

WIFE: No, thank you, my dear. I am charmed with this cup of his unrivalled tea.

THOMAS CUNNIAM
FAMILY GROCER,
RETAIL WINE AND SPIRIT MERCHANT
1 WERBURGH STREET
(Opposite Christ Church)

This advertisement very soon spawned another that has interesting echoes in *Ulysses*. In the spring of 1896, James Cassidy left Tom Cunniam's employ and took over Alexander Keyes's licensed premises in Capel Street when the latter opened a 'luncheon bar' at Ballsbridge. Cassidy was also invited to place an advertisement for his new venture in the paper and on 21 March it appeared on the same page as Cunniam's (see overleaf).

When Bloom in 'Aeolus' brings his incomplete Alexander Keyes advertisement to the *Evening Telegraph* office, he explains to the foreman, Councillor Nannetti, that the crossed-keys design has to be lifted from a previous ad. It can be seen from its details and its layout that the Cassidy ad has been somewhat clumsily recycled from an earlier Alexander Keyes one. (In fact the 'foreman' must have been Joseph Nannetti Jr, son of the 'Councillor' often known as J. P. Nannetti JP, who would in his time be both Lord Mayor and MP. The honorific may, of course, be a jocular prefix for the unfamous son of a famous father.) Nannetti agrees to publish Bloom's ad and also offers, if a 'three months' renewal' is forthcoming, to run a little 'news' paragraph calling attention to it. On page 2 of the actual *Evening Telegraph* of 21 March 1896 there appears just such a paragraph. It not only mentions Keyes's new Ballsbridge emporium, but James Cassidy's shop and, for good measure, Cunniam's. Two of the sections of 'Aeolus' that describe Leopold Bloom's negotiations bear the headlines 'WE SEE THE CANVASSER AT WORK' and 'HOUSE OF KEY(E)S': James Joyce

JAMES CASSIDY
SUCCESSOR

SELLS NOTHING
LIKE HARDWARE,
BUT CHOICE SELECTIONS OF
JJ & S, JOHN POWER AND SON
WHISKIES
GUINNESS'S STOUT
BASS'S ALE, HOPS
AND
WINES OF THE FINEST QUALITIES.

JAMES CASSIDY
128 CAPEL STREET

was precisely recycling his father's activities of 1896. It is likely that his mother suffered, like Molly Bloom, from having to be 'always listening to him and Billy Prescotts ad and Keyess ad and Tom the Devils ad'. Although Prescott's is easily recognised as a cleaners and dyeworks that advertised often in the *Freeman* and *Evening Telegraph*, 'Tom the Devil' has never been identified: given how often the boisterous American sea captain had led John Stanislaus astray, it can be reckoned that this was a family nickname for Thomas Cunniam, a man whose demeanour (and whose American accent) Stannie was clearly not the only one in the family to despise. It is tempting to think that 'Tom the Devil' is a rare surviving spark of May Joyce's wit.·

As a vestige of their middle-class status, the Joyces still retained a servant. One day, John heard that a scurrilous rumour about Jim was going around Belvedere and indignantly took himself to the Rector to find out what it was all about. Fr Henry clearly knew something damning about Jim's morals. However, possibly because he was unable to act on information received in the confessional (though Jim himself for his own reasons went to confession else-where, his brothers did not), Fr Henry confined himself to hints, telling the baffled parent only that his son was a bad lot and would give him trouble. Quite in the dark, John Stanislaus asserted his parental prerogative: 'No, he won't, because I won't let him.'

May Joyce knew her son, and with a mother's intuition had a good idea of the truth about the scandal. The 'hoydenish' slavey had been seen at home indulging in rough-and-tumble spanking matches with Jim, but May suspected that there was more to it than that: after all, Jim was palpably his father's son. She was right. One windy day, while Jim and the servant girl were out for a walk near the woods close to the house, she had stopped for a piss, telling him not to look. This was too much for a boy who had recently passed puberty and he had 'jiggled furiously' in response, as he admitted in a letter in 1917. Much later, he even blamed all his subsequent eye trouble on the experience, which he remembered as 'the sight of his life *et une autre chose encore que je n'ose pas dire*'. May insisted that John sack the unfortunate maid. The Joyces would never employ another.

The school's memory of John Stanislaus Joyce was to endure.

More than fifty years later, the then Rector of Belvedere would describe him as a 'bounder' and even suggested that it might have been better if he had sent his sons to an establishment whose standards were less at odds with the family's cultural and religious background, preferably away from the temptations of the city. He added that James Joyce 'had great ability – genius; he might have done much in the Church'. By September 1896, whatever it was that the boy might have been doing outside the school did not disbar him from being appointed inside it as Praeceps of the Sodality of Our Lady: perhaps he was already walking the streets with his rosary, as a sister remembered.

These days, John could still muster his air of gentlemanly insouciance for a riotous evening with 'fine decent fellows able to do something'. The seventeenth of March 1896 was exceptionally wet and the weekly meeting of the Bohemian Club at the Dolphin Hotel on Essex Street (a continuation of Fleet Street) was ill attended: being St Patrick's Day, which traditionally was the only respite from the thirsty rigours of Lent, there were several other special events in town. (Eight years later that would change, when the Gaelic League pressurised the Corporation to close all bars in honour of the National Patron's Day.) John Stanislaus had written a song called 'Erin's Heroes' and he sang it to the beshamrocked company. Among them happened to be Joseph Holloway, Dublin's incurable chronicler of decades of the city's theatrical and musical life. Holloway reported to his diary that night that John Stanislaus was 'a great man to swear. He gets off a string of swear words then prays to be forgiven.' As for his song, it was 'a tiresome never-ending topical rigmarole'. No doubt the Bohemians enjoyed it, however: John still could and did transform a social gathering.

On Thursday, 16 April John Kelly finally died of tuberculosis at the Mater Misericordiae Hospital in Eccles Street. He was not yet fifty. John Stanislaus was not the only one to notice his passing: Hooper's *Evening Telegraph* was effusive two days later, describing him as 'the devoted and genial friend of all nationalists', while the *United Irishman* commented lyrically in a leader: 'No matter where you met him, at home or abroad, in joy or in sorrow, he was the same good and genial soul, whose kindly heart shone out of his eyes, let the wind blow where it listeth.' John Stanislaus followed the large funeral cortège from the hospital. It went on a short circular lap of honour through the centre of the city, before heading north to Glasnevin for the noon burial. The grave was placed as close to Parnell's burial mound in its great grass circle as propriety (and Euclid) allowed: to reach it John had to pass his own family plot, not far away in the same section of the cemetery. The size of the funeral and the extensive newspaper coverage it received were moving proof of the affection and esteem that his old Fenian friend had earned: among the mass of municipal and newspaper worthies at the graveside there were three ex-MPs, as well as John Wyse Power, D. J. Hishon, Councillor Sherlock, Dr Bob Kenny, John Henry Menton and 'Long' John Clancy, the city's Subsheriff (the 'Long John Fanning' of *Ulysses*). For some reason Tim Harrington was not there, though he, and the town of Tralee, County Kerry, where the Harringtons came from and Kelly had worked, were represented by his brother.

There was also someone present whose name appeared that day in the *Evening Telegraph* as 'J. Hopper'. This may have been James Hopper, a gentleman tailor from the south side, but it seems unlikely, given John Kelly's almost proverbial disregard for his clothes – as a very young man he had nearly become a priest but had changed his mind when he failed to muster a pair of trousers respectable enough for his first day at the seminary. If the mystery mourner was not the tailor, it was the editor John Hooper himself, misprinted, like many another man before and since, in his own paper. The press reporter also garbled another name on the list (it would happen to 'Leopold Boom' at another funeral): in the *Evening Telegraph* Mr John G. Joyce is there in the company of John Lenehan of *Sport* and the 'prosperous bulk' of another friend (though not relation) of John Stanislaus, John O'Connell, who was now superintendent of the cemetery after old David Malins.

When the burial was over, the gentlemen assembled in the waiting room of the cemetery where J. J. Clancy, MP and solicitor (and not to be confused with 'Long' John Clancy, the Subsheriff), took the chair and said a few words. He had known the deceased for twenty years and had always found him to be true and loyal: John Kelly had lived for Ireland and it was equally true to say he had died for Ireland. To general acclamation the MP proposed that a committee be formed to raise a subscription for a memorial over his grave. John Stanislaus was appointed, though he was not made one of the treasurers, that onerous duty being reserved for such as Hishon and Dr Joe Kenny, now an ex-MP. On the day after the funeral an ode to Kelly's memory by John McGrath was published in the *United Irishman*:

> You did not know him? Then you know not all
>   That nature in a happy mood can plan,
> He was as brave a soul, and yet withal
>   As simple as the world e'er called a man.
>
> He gave his life *to Ireland*. But no thought
>   That Ireland was his debtor spoiled the smile
> That that true heart, unbuyable and unbought,
>   Had aye for every man of his dear isle.
>
> For well nigh twenty years in North and South
>   His voice was known, his genial face was seen,
> From East to West, from Clare right on to Louth –
>   To bring the Red to earth – to raise the Green.
>
> Full many a man in all that time became
>   The patriot of a period, then dropped out –
> But never was there roll-call that his name
>   Was not heard ringing in the answering shout.
>
> True, genial, kindly soul, I wave *adieu*
>   As thy barque droppeth down the unknown sea;
> The wind is fair as ever wind that blew –
>   He steers for port, John Kelly of Tralee.

In their unassuming simplicity, the verses suited their subject perfectly and drew many a tear. With the death of John Kelly, John's closest link with the memory of Parnell was gone.

A year later, on the first anniversary of Kelly's death, John Stanislaus went to another ceremony at Glasnevin. With the money they had raised, the Kelly Memorial Committee had erected over the grave an imposing high cross of grey Irish limestone, handsomely carved with interlocking Celtic designs, 'as solid and flawless as his own true Irish heart'. After listening to prayers and an address beside the new memorial, John and his friends would have crossed the path and paid their tribute to The Chief. A little further along the same path, on the way towards Daniel O'Connell's circle, was the grave of an Owen Patrick Farrelly of Middle Gardiner Street, marked by a large statue of Jesus that had been erected by his widow. Though Farrelly's name was not used in *Ulysses*, this statue was probably the inspiration for the famous story there that Simon Dedalus hears from John O'Connell the caretaker, in which a drunken friend of the deceased, squinting up at the sacred figure, protests to his companion: *'Not a bloody bit like the man*, says he. *That's not Mulcahy, whoever done it.'* The joke, if it was told on this occasion, may also have amused the secret police who were monitoring the event: an undercover man was present to identify mourners and to listen in to conversations. Mr John 'G.' Joyce, however, aroused no suspicions and his name does not appear in the report of the ceremony that was made for Dublin Castle (unlike those of Dr Joe Kenny and John Wyse Power, which do). John Stanislaus, like the others, was at Glasnevin for no other reason than to remember this closest of friends: he was not the only one who would miss John Kelly, but he would miss him more than most.

Soon after John Kelly had been laid to rest the Joyces were taking down their family portraits from the parlour wall once again. After almost eighteen months in Holywell Villas John was probably under pressure to pay arrears of rent: sometimes simply leaving could solve the problem, the landlord being relieved enough to get the defaulting family out of his property, even if he was still owed for a month or two. When, in the spring of 1896, the Joyces moved from Holywell Villas there was nobody much for them to say good-bye to except the McKernans next door. The other neighbours were just cottagers on the lane and the Joyces were mildly surprised when a Mr Duffy, whose son Pisser was a sworn enemy of the boys, turned up practically cap-in-hand on the doorstep to make peace and to bid the family godspeed on behalf of the rough tribes from the cottages. He shambled in and John gave the man a bottle of stout in the stripped parlour.

On one side of North Richmond Street off the North Circular Road was the O'Connell School that Jim and Stannie are said to have attended before Belvedere. On the other was an empty house, No. 13, where a Fr Edward Quaid had succumbed to pneumonia the previous March. This neat three-storey property above a basement was in an early Victorian brick terrace and, with a higher rateable valuation than their last house, should have attracted more rent, normally no recommendation to John. Perhaps the lease offered was cheap because it was short. A cursory glance at the Dublin street directories gives the impression that the family remained here for several years, but confusingly another quite unrelated John Joyce (whose grave can be found at Glasnevin) also lived in the street, at No. 17. John Stanislaus Joyce's stay would be so brief that *Thom's* does not mention him there at all.

The new house was much closer to Belvedere and there were several local convents for the other children who were old enough to go to school. They settled in quickly, already knowing the district well. The area is also familiar to readers of James Joyce, for 'Araby' is set in North Richmond Street, where the young narrator imagines that from behind their spiked railings the houses, 'conscious of decent lives within them, gazed at one another with brown imperturbable faces'. Beyond the ashpit at the end of the Joyces' garden was a door that led into a maze of lanes lined with little two-roomed cottages and stables in which the children liked to watch the horses being groomed and harnessed. Poppie later remembered, probably from this time, that a man she thought might be Russian occasionally came round with a dancing bear and that Jim, who always loved to hear foreigners talk, held long conversations with him while all the local children gathered round in awe. Sometimes, after their evening meal, while the boys were out playing in the twilight, they noticed their homeward father ('uncle' in the story) turning off the North Circular Road into the quiet cul-de-sac: 'we hid in the shadow until we had seen him safely housed.'

'Long' John Clancy lived at No. 7, a useful man to know indeed, for as Subsheriff he had a good deal of influence in the city, being called the 'mayormaker' on account of his power in municipal politics. (He would one day even get himself elected Lord Mayor, though he was to die before he could take office.) Stanislaus, who later came to despise Clancy, would recall his father boasting about his close relationship with him: 'O John Clancy had a wish for me! He'd do a fellow a good turn.' Whether he ever actually did one for John is uncertain, however. Stannie suspected that his father also secretly disliked this gangling Jack-in-office.

Less exaltedly, the Boardmans occupied No. 1 in the street. The young Joyces were envious of Eddie Boardman who had a bicycle with the wonderful new pneumatic tyres. A little further up were Baby's and poor Freddie's godparents, the Thorntons. Thornton, more red-faced than before but as birdlike as ever, used to tell John Stanislaus how he had seen as a child that 'God of Song', the great Giuglini, flying a big kite on Sandymount Strand. Thornton's tea-tasting job at Pulbrook, Robertson & Co. in Dame Street (for whom he worked until 1907) would be given by James Joyce to Mr Kernan in 'Grace' and *Ulysses*, though the writer's father supplied most of this character's other activities. Most notable among these was a nasty accident that happened one night in John Nolan's Public House in Harry Street, when John, excessively drunk, missed his footing on the way down to the lavatory in the basement and landed in a heap at the bottom, damaging, if 'Grace' is to be believed, his tongue, his silk hat and his dignity. When a policeman from the B Division arrived on the scene the injured party would have been arrested for being drunk and disorderly if a friend had not rescued him and taken him home. The good Samaritan was Tom Devin (Jack Power in the story), an official in the Dublin Corporation Cleansing Department on Wood Quay (where, according to *Ulysses*, the River Poddle, like a 'tongue of liquid sewage', flowed beneath his office into the Liffey). Devin's wife, his first of two, sometimes sang as Madame de Vere with the Moody Manners Opera Company. He would remain a good friend to John and his family until the end of his long life, and his rescue of John was not the last favour he would do for the Joyces.

As he was now in his late forties, John's sporting days were over, but he was still an indefatigable walker. On working days he might appear anywhere in town. Sometimes he dropped in to the public library in Capel Street for a chat with old Paddy Grogan, afterwards mimicking the librarian's vain warnings about the sort of books that Jim was borrowing – John never minded what they were and told a prissy John Murray that Jim could read what he liked, even Zola. Sometimes he might walk as far as Thomas Street for an advertisement, calling on 'Tom the Devil' Cunniam near Christ Church for a quick drink on the way back. On Sundays and Holy Days of Obligation John frequently led more rigorous exploratory expeditions further afield, away from the city streets with their muddy cobbles and slimy wooden setts. On these outings he was usually accompanied by one or more of his sons and a friend or two, men such as Charles A. Chance, a pleasant fellow whose periods of employment were almost as variable as John's: in his time Charlie Chance had sold coal (probably for Flower and M'Donald's or one of the firms along the quays towards Ringsend), worked for a railway company and done advertising canvassing for the *Freeman*; in a few years' time, after a spell pen-pushing for 'Long' John Clancy in the Subsheriff's Ormond Quay Office, Charlie would rise to the heights of City Coroner's secretary. Leopold Bloom's existence is thought to owe something to Chance, not least because the Joyces knew Charlie's wife as a piano teacher and amateur singer in the Molly Bloom mould – Mrs Chance used her maiden name on stage: Madame Marie Tallon.

John Stanislaus 'had more talk, more stories, more reminiscences than the rest of the group', Stannie fair-mindedly recalled. His father was an encyclopaedia of Dublin lore and legend. As they strolled along, he brought to life for his fellow-pilgrims the landmarks along the route. With eloquent wit he might discuss the grand home of a wealthy Dame Street solicitor, or point out somewhere Joseph Addison had stayed, a supposed residence of Dean Swift, or the whereabouts of the traitorous 'Sham Squire', Francis Higgins (an early owner of the *Freeman*). Such places, which were named by Stanislaus, can be easily identified. Addison (whose literary 'twin' Steele was a native Dubliner) visited a friend in what is now the lodge of the Botanic Garden in Glasnevin when he was working for the Lord Lieutenant. Swift often stayed with the Delaneys at Delville in Raheny and the Sham Squire, though he died at his house on Stephen's Green, is buried in Kilbarrack graveyard. All are on the north side of the city and are remembered from walks made and itineraries devised by John Stanislaus.

Through his work John by now had an exceptional knowledge of the physical Dublin. But, though an ardent gossip, he was not a bookish man: it is hard to imagine him conning tomes in libraries for too long. However, from 1887 on, Weston St John Joyce (once in the Dublin Metropolitan Police and the son of Patrick Weston Joyce) wrote for the *Evening Telegraph* a number of lengthy but lively articles describing 'rambles' in and around the city. The series was continued by the antiquarian, W. F. Wakeman FRSHAI, who contributed others on 'Old Dublin'. They were all soon afterwards published as pamphlets. Given John's links with the paper, these pieces cannot have escaped his attention and are the likely source of much of his local historical knowledge. Most of the curiosities mentioned by Stanislaus are alluded to in Weston Joyce's *The Neighbourhood of Dublin*, which was published in 1912, too late to have contributed to John's expertise in local history. But since this book merely collected and expanded the *Telegraph* series it could be said that John Stanislaus's neighbourhood of Dublin was, to an extent, his distant Joyce cousin's *Neighbourhood of Dublin.*

These long walks led to James's own habit of walking the streets, either alone or with a friend or one of his brothers. He had discovered (thanks to his father) that the activity of a *flâneur* could be both cheap and stimulating. These pedestrian whorls laid down the foundations for his re-creation of the city in his work. At the same time he was hearing from his father about the buildings, the characters and their histories: stories of public executions, private revenges, and musical and literary greatness achieved in an improbably turbulent history. Jim was thus developing an intimate, microscopic appreciation of what now tends to be called the 'Dublin Experience'. His father once said of him: 'If that fellow was dropped in the middle of the Sahara he'd sit, begod, and make a map of it.' In conversation some twenty-five years later, James Joyce treated the composer Otto Luening to an extempore 'word-painting of Dublin', a feat of memory and observation that astonished the musician. Luening wrote of the performance:

As Joyce described a street, he began with the kinds of cobblestones . . . He made vivid the sounds of horses' hooves, and the sound of footsteps on the cobblestones, and their different echoes; and then the smells –

musty sometimes, sometimes of dirt and sometimes of the fresh, or dried, horse-manure that he called 'horseapples'. He illuminated this street of the mind by describing how it looked at different times of the day, in different kinds of light. He talked about the shops with their particular stoops, entrances, and colours, and why some looked like poor, and some like rich, shops.

John Stanislaus might not have been born a Dubliner, but he applied the enthusiasm of a convert to his adopted city, and passed it on to his eldest son. It was in many ways the most valuable bequest that James Joyce would ever receive.

During the family's months in North Richmond Street May Joyce renewed her musical connection with St Francis Xavier's in Gardiner Street. She was also happy to be seeing more of her sister-in-law, Josephine Murray, these days and the children of both families got on well together with, occasionally, even a touch of cousinly romance in the air. During the summer holidays the Murrays invited the Joyces to come on some of their elaborate family picnics, when they loaded up a donkey-cart and headed west along the river towards Chapelizod and the Phoenix Park, or the Strawberry Beds. There they would pitch a tent, light a bonfire and sit around on the grass singing songs after a good feed of sandwiches and tea. Once, the two families almost filled a tram when they went off on an expedition to the Bull Wall. Uncle William Murray was still on no better terms with John, and one or both of the men would often give such trips a miss. John's own favourite picnic spot was the Hill of Howth (from one angle the image of the Rock of Gibraltar, according to Weston Joyce) and in the summer the Joyces might be found picnicking among the rhododendrons there. Eveline, in *Dubliners*, remembers her father, another of John Stanislaus's *doppelgängers*, making the children laugh on a Howth picnic by putting on his wife's bonnet: 'Sometimes he could be very nice.' Even Stannie agreed that when Pappie was sober he could be an amusing and genial companion. He later summed up these times, with his father 'temporarily, though not bigotedly, "on the water wagon"', as 'halcyon days'.

CHAPTER 17

A Little Learning

Dante Conway left the wicked world behind her in November 1896, dying in the hands of the Sisters of Charity at Our Lady's Hospice for the Dying at Harold's Cross close to Mount Argus, where the saintly Fr Charles had died three years before. On her demise, her long-lost husband reappeared to claim whatever money remained to be claimed; he had been living in Dublin after all, not Buenos Ayres, or so he provocatively said. He would have got very little: the Hospice advertised itself as 'intended for the poor'. John Stanislaus had little inclination to mourn Dante and, indeed, little time: as the lease must have expired the Joyces had to leave North Richmond Street. They moved to 29 Windsor Avenue (also known as Windsor Terrace) off Fairview Strand, the beginning of the coast road to Clontarf and, further on, Howth. Euphemistically named, Fairview was just outside the old city boundary, overlooking the sloblands (mudflats) of Dublin Bay. The house was quite recent, but it was the smallest that the children had ever inhabited: two storeys, no basement and just a single bay window on the ground floor. There was nothing at the front, a yard at the back and no garden. The family was not impressed: James, in *Finnegans Wake*, would refer to the address as '92 Windsewer Ave'.

The owner of this property was a Mrs Mary Love, a widow who had bought it (and the two houses on either side) as an investment and source of income. Her son Hugh, a clerk in the National Education Department of the Civil Service, had the unenviable task of collecting the rents. At first he was paid monthly by John Stanislaus, but soon after the New Year of 1897 it became impossible to get the new tenant to pay any more. John had compiled a rich store of excuses from his own days with a collecting bag and he could add to it: he discovered that the lease was flawed in some way and claimed that until it was sorted out it would be inadvisable to act under its terms. He was to milk this technicality for all it was worth over the next two full years of occupation and contrived never to pay another penny to the Loves. It seemed to be a gift from heaven.

Scarcely surprisingly, since Love must have spent a good deal of time trying to evict John Stanislaus and his brood from their house, he was not popular with the incumbent family. He would get his come-uppance in *Ulysses*. There, Hugh C. Love appears under his own name as a priggish Church of Ireland clergyman with a 'refined accent'. He, too, is owed rent for 29 Windsor Avenue, though his tenant is not Simon Dedalus but the rather hopeless 'Father' Bob Cowley, a spoiled priest. Ingeniously, Reuben J. Dodd is brought into the equation as well: in discussion it emerges that the greedy Mr Dodd is demanding that Cowley pay back a loan, but quite legally Cowley cannot do so because his landlord, Love, has first claim on his money (not that he has any money). As a result Reuben J. 'can put that writ where Jacko put the nuts'. 'Filberts I believe they were,' Mr Dedalus comments drily, ending the conversation on a surreal note. Like Dodd, 'the Reverend' Hugh C. Love figures in the dreamlike 'Circe' chapter, where, officiating at a Black Mass with his head on backwards, he is heard chanting the words: 'To the devil which hath made glad my young days' over the naked body of a pregnant woman. It is difficult now to concede that poor Mr Love deserved such treatment merely for trying to collect his mother's rent. It may be that, as long as the anomalous situation with the lease lasted, John Stanislaus himself benefited from being in Cowley's position, with rent arrears (that are never actually paid) taking legal precedence over other debts.

In a bedroom of 29 Windsor Avenue, some time during the spring of 1897, another pregnant woman was giving birth. Downstairs, her husband had been dragged home from town with a skinful to be there. John Stanislaus was in defiant mood, asserting again that though life might be hard, by God he was not dead yet. The baby was, however. May Joyce was thirty-eight and there would be no more children. As John fulminated below, the body of his last son lay lifeless upstairs. Stanislaus, remembering his mother's lost children, was to comment sourly that 'at least, these infants may be supposed not to have suffered' (unlike the rest of them). The family was, despite everything, psychologically still resilient and could survive such episodes, though they would not be forgotten. When the summer came things were more buoyant. There was an outing to a regatta in Clontarf, where they watched Tommy Joyce, the man whom James later called a 'remote cousin' of his father's. He looked slightly like John – presumably, like the Weston Joyces, he stemmed from the Joyces of the Ballyhoura Mountains. Tommy resembled his cousin in another way too: Jim noticed that he was walking 'with a gait which suggested that he would progress equally well on shipboard in rough weather'. Although this long-lost relative ran the Dublin Loan Bank in St Stephen's Green, and was a yachtsman (later a vice-president of the Clontarf Yacht Club), it does not seem that John made anything of the meeting. Tommy Joyce was not of the true line, which was 'a very considerable cut above buttermilk', as one of John's grandsons would later remark, destined to carry O'Connell blood in its veins. James later imagined that the youth who tried to visit him in Paris was Tommy's son: 'one of the breed is more than enough'.

When the weather warmed up in the early summer of 1897 the Joyces had a visitor. It was young Eileen Vance, still with her father at Loretto Villas in Sidmonton Road, Bray, where they had moved after leaving Martello Terrace; Mrs Vance had died three years before. Eileen was shocked by the pall of poverty that hung over the house in Windsor Avenue: her old friends' home was 'a horrible place', all 'bare boards and scrubbed planks', and a saddening contrast to No. 1 Martello Terrace. She invited Poppie (the nearest to her in age of John's daughters) to come and stay for the summer holidays. Poppie was delighted and leapt at the chance to get away from Fairview and to take the train south to recapture her golden childhood memories. Soon she was telling her friend what had happened in the intervening years and how Pappie had brought the Joyce family to such a pass: as an old lady, Eileen Vance would remember that it was only then that she realised the scale of John's drinking and the damage it had caused.

One afternoon while Poppie was away enjoying the fresh sea air of Bray, her father used her as an excuse to take a trip there

himself. For company he brought Jim along (who may have found
Eileen, his childhood 'fiancée', as alluring as ever). John was
pleased to see the sights again and to chat about past triumphs
with his old companion and rowing rival, James Vance. The chemist, who had always had a high opinion of Jim's brain, must have
been pleased to hear how well he was doing at Belvedere. As they
picked up the threads, John would have noticed that his friend
was obviously seriously ailing: in fact he had not long to live. This
visit was the last time that any of the Vances were actually to meet
John Stanislaus: and when, a few years later, Eileen happened to
see John in an extremely intoxicated condition being steered by
Jim along Grafton Street she decided to 'hide in the shadow'.

John had good reason to boast of his son's progress and was
particularly proud of Jim's school essays, which were read out at
home in Windsor Avenue. At first these were conventional enough:
'Trust Not Appearances', written when he was fourteen, ends with
the sentiment, not entirely applicable to his father, that the man
with 'no ambition, no wealth, no luxury save contentment cannot
hide the joy of happiness that flows from a clear conscience and
an easy mind'. Recently Jim had been having some fun with the
subjects that his English teacher, Mr Dempsey, set him, even baiting
the master (without quite appearing to do so). One particular
composition reduced the family to 'shrieks of laughter' when Jim
read it to them, as Poppie remembered: paragraph after paragraph
of monitory examples, each concluding with the increasingly ironic
moral refrain, plonkingly delivered: 'A little learning is a dangerous
thing!' Dempsey had set it in order to 'humiliate' his star pupil
for his cockiness. Some of the essays, which are the earliest works
of the Joycean canon to survive, were kept in the school and shown
off as models of good writing, and an unused note for *Ulysses* hints
that his father may even once have had a scheme to get them
published by the Dublin firm, Maunsel's, for use in other, less
privileged, schools. John Stanislaus would have smiled to hear that
today some of them have been published for the universities.

John and May still occasionally got out to the theatre. Though
they no longer had a maid, Poppie, at thirteen, was old enough
to keep an eye on the young ones at home, particularly if a brother
was around. Even Baby, now four, was less of a handful than she

had been. Occasionally, some of the older children would come with them if the show was suitable. This year at the Gaiety there was one that wasn't: *The Wife of Scarli*, an English version of the Italian play, *Tristi Amori* by Giuseppe Giacosa. Molly Bloom remembers seeing it, and probably John was keen to go, as it was supposed to be 'fast', but how he might have reacted to the portrayal of the hero's father, Count Arcieri, an uncontrollable spendthrift who has to be disciplined by his son, is not recorded. Also at the Gaiety in November was W. W. Kelly's Evergreen Touring Company's production of W. G. Wills's *A Royal Divorce*, starring Mrs Kendal and her husband. The Blooms were given a box by Michael Gunn to see it and there is every reason to suppose that the Joyces were too. It was the week that Gunn retired and he signed and gave John and May a copy of the 'Souvenir of the Twenty-Fifth Anniversary of the Opening of the Gaiety Theatre' to mark the occasion. Perhaps Jim went with his parents, as the play, about the love life of Napoleon, crops up in the *Wake* as 'the problem passion play of the millentury'; the novel also mentions that in the interval the band played the usual medley from Balfe's *The Bohemian Girl* and Benedict's *The Lily of Killarney*, still the most popular Dublin operas.

Whether John was still getting canvassing work from the *Evening Telegraph* is not known. The job may very well have come to an end in the autumn of 1897, when the editor, 'Alderman' Hooper (lately of 15 Royal Terrace), suddenly died in November, aged fifty-one. The newspaper went into mourning, putting black borders around every column of the evening's issue and three days later there was another great Dublin funeral to Glasnevin. John Stanislaus turned up in the company of 'Long' John Clancy and yet another journalist in the *Freeman* stable, Chris Callinan, legendary in Dublin for his slips of the pen and dropped bricks – just possibly it was he who was behind the unconfirmed story that on Queen Victoria's visit to the city one Dublin paper stated that crowds cheered as Her Majesty 'pissed' over O'Connell Bridge. (Callinan is in *Ulysses* as yet another of Molly Bloom's admirers at the Drumcree Reformatory banquet.) Like John Kelly's, John Hooper's early death was blamed on a stay years before in Tullamore Gaol – two months' incarceration for publishing news of the suppressed Land League. Like Kelly, also, the Corkman was mourned as one of the truest and most genial of Parnellites. Tim Harrington and Dan Tallon organised a fund to help Hooper's widow and many children. Though John Stanislaus's name predictably does not appear among the printed list of subscribers, his friend's passing cut him off even more from his own past, particularly from his early years in Cork, which had always been a link between them. These days John encountered very few people who knew any more about the world of his youth than he cared to tell them. There were, no doubt, advantages to this, but it took the savour from reminiscence, always more enjoyable with two. Then, just after 1898 began, old Hugh Tarpey slipped away after twenty-five years in Corporation politics, an influential man as ex-Lord Mayor of Dublin in the decade before John's marriage and one more relic of times gone by.

John was still not paying any rent, but how he supported himself and his family over the next year or two is a matter for conjecture. There is a strong tradition that at some stage he did accountancy work for Laurence Cuffe & Sons, cattle salesmen and auctioneers, of No. 5, Smithfield. John would still have maintained at least a nodding acquaintance with William Field MP, now indisputably the doyen of Dublin butchers, who as a leading light of the Irish Cattle Traders and Stockowners' Association Field could have put in a well-placed word for him. The livestock auctions were held at the Dublin Cattle Market. With the noise, excrement and stench of the animals, this was an unpleasant place, especially on a Friday which – incongruously in a country that hardly ate meat on Friday – was 'killing day' in the City Abattoir nearby. Most of the business was done in cash and each dealer had someone on the spot to be in charge of the money. The City Arms Hotel at 54 Prussia Street, alongside the Market, was the centre of operations for these accountants, of whom John, it seems, became one. There they would tally sales, work out commissions and fees, and lodge takings with one of the banks who had 'offices', or at least cashiers, on the premises. The day began in the middle of the night and for a moneyman to take a room once a week was common practice. John's experiences surely helped to set the Blooms' sojourn there in *Ulysses*, where even the vagaries of the plumbing in the City Arms

Hotel are knowingly mentioned. The normally most conscientious Bloom once worked for Cuffe's as a clerk, eventually being dismissed for most unBloomlike insolence to a grazier. Being dismissed was an occurrence more frequent in John Stanislaus's life. Simultaneous proximity to card-playing colleagues, alcohol and large sums of money was not perhaps the ideal recipe for a permanent post for him.

Jim, now coming towards the end of his school career, was given the plum role in the annual Whitsuntide play, held at Belvedere on Saturday, 28 March 1898. Stannie also had a small part and John was there with some of the family to watch the boys perform. The play was a dramatised version of Anstey's 1882 novel, *Vice Versa*, about a merchant and his schoolboy son who somehow manage to swap bodies (or brains). Jim was the boy playing the headmaster, and his father must have appreciated his cheeky mimicry of the 'pedantic bass' of the Belvedere Rector: Jim's seniority meant that he could get away with a good deal. Ever since the warning about his son's morals, John had had little respect for Fr Henry, but if the Jesuit was less than amused, he had the good sense not to show it. Poppie enjoyed her evening too. More than sixty years later, as an old nun far away, when a friend reminded her of the play, her 'eyes sparkled, she beamed, and out it all came, with her all aglow: "I was with Pappie that night. I remember it well." ' For James, too, it was a memorable night.

Soon afterwards Jim sat the final public exams of his school career. He did tolerably well by his standards. His mother, though not his father, may have been upset that, though still Praeceps of the Sodality, he had boycotted the 'Bishops' Religious Examination' set by Belvedere. This had no practical use, serving only to reassure the hierarchy that the Jesuits were still influencing their pupils theologically as well as academically. John's son was now old enough to be set to work and it seems that John (or perhaps one of the Murrays) managed to get him into a solicitor's firm off Dame Street for the summer. Any contribution to the family purse helped, though Jim would not have earned very much as an office boy. An acquaintance later recalled that one day the senior partner had given him money and sent him out to get lunch. Jim, surprised by how much he had been given, treated himself to a slap-up meal nearby at Hynes's Restaurant of 55 Dame Street, and he even had enough change left over for cigarettes. When he sauntered back to the office an hour later, the ravenous solicitor furiously demanded to know where his lunch was and on being told that it was inside his employee, fined him sixpence a week until the money was repaid. The incident must have appealed greatly to John Stanislaus – it proved that Jim was a chip off the old block – and it was a story that would have lent itself to embellishments of all sorts as he related it to his friends. John's ability to take the bones of a simple anecdote and make it live in the telling by adding his own ornaments of parody, mimicry and digression was a skill that was being inherited by his son. This process of expansion would later become an essential part of James Joyce's writing method: even *Ulysses* was originally conceived as merely a short story.

Some of Jim's contemporaries liked to spend time with Joyce the elder almost as much as they did with Joyce the younger. Though most of John's friends were about his own age, he could be an attractive figure to the next generation too. He had retained a certain exotic style, cutting an unusual dash with his spats, his monocle and his cane, and the stream of songs and stories that issued from beneath his quasi-military waxed moustache seemed inexhaustible. John always appreciated a new audience. One such 'listener' was a brother-in-law of the solicitor James Brady, Alfred Bergan, then a clerk in the sheriff's office. Described in *Ulysses* as a 'leprechaun', little Alfie Bergan was an impish foxy figure with a reputation for smutty stories, who had been in the habit of accompanying the younger Jim on his Dublin walks. John liked Alfie's company on his own perambulations too. During the second week of August 1898 the unlikely pair went together to *Sweet Briar*, a play in the Gaiety. The association was to last: Bergan would play an important part in John Stanislaus's later life.

A few days later, on 15 August, a slab of granite was carried in state on a meandering route through the streets of Dublin, accompanied by no fewer than eighty brass bands and troops of costumed horsemen from the Irish National Foresters. It was inscribed with the message: '1798. Tribute to Theobald Wolfe Tone, Patriot. Belfast Nationalists '98 Centenary Association. 1898'. Sixteen years before to the day, the memorial to Daniel O'Connell had been unveiled. This equally symbolic occasion was part of a continuing campaign to reunite the strands of Irish Nationalism that had been divided by the Parnellite split. What lingered in the common folk-memory of all Nationalists was the British suppression of Tone and his movement, which had led on to the Act of Union in 1801 that abolished Ireland's last parliament. John Stanislaus and Jim were among the massive crowds who followed the stone on its three-mile progress to the Grafton Street corner of St Stephen's Green, where it was laid in place as a foundation for a memorial to the architect of the 1798 rebellion. The great veteran of both the Young Irelanders of 1848 and the later Fenians, John O'Leary (the man who was to share a grave with Romantic Ireland in Yeats's poem), made a romantic speech over the stone, tapping it six times with his ceremonial trowel (once for each of Ireland's provinces and once for each of her imagined allies, America and France). Then he led the multitudes in song with the emotive words of John Kells Ingram's 'The Memory of the Dead': 'Who fears to speak of '98?' As John Stanislaus joined in, it must have brought back to him both the 'monster meetings' of Parnell's last months and the wilder agitations in Cork during the years before he left. But he knew enough Irish history to be aware that the Wolfe Tone on offer in 1898 was not the anticlerical French Revolutionary of a century before, but a carefully canonised version, acceptable to the churchmen on the platform, who had co-operated in this use of their Holy Day of Obligation.

For many, after the speechifying and the singing, the rest of 'Wolfe Tone Day', as it was called, was spent in the teeming pubs, half of them owned by Aldermen and Town Councillors and all doing a roaring trade. Although the City Fathers – as well as the 100,000 or so Dubliners at the parade – may have hoped ardently for a free Irish future, much of their enthusiasm seemed to melt away when there was real work to be done. Everyone had enjoyed their bit of pageantry, but that was all it was: no memorial to Tone would ever be built on that corner. But John Stanislaus could have predicted that; it was all that was to be expected these days. By now, the world of idealistic politics had all but passed him by, leaving a residue of cynicism behind it, while his genuine early commitment was gradually transmuting into sentiment. To the son standing beside him, his father's emotion was perhaps an equally valuable commodity.

John Stanislaus had no intention of seeing his eldest son working as an office boy for long: he had always intended him to have a proper professional career. The priests at Belvedere thought that a job in Guinness's might suit, but John urged him either to go into the Corporation or to read law. To be a good Dublin barrister was to be solid, well paid and respected, and it was an occupation that could lead on to other opportunities for advancement and success, as men like Tim Harrington had shown. As before (when John had hoped that he would take up Greek at school but his son had chosen Italian) the final decision was left up to Jim. He would have nothing to do with either career idea; he intended to study languages at the Jesuit College on Stephen's Green, now part of the Royal University. The course was then followed almost exclusively by women, but John, once the choice had been made after much discussion at home, exercised no veto, though he made his own investigations into the plan. Almost thirty years later John would claim still to regret his son's decision, telling an interviewer: 'I often told Jim to go for the bar, for he had a great flow of language and he speaks better than he writes. However,' he conceded, 'he has done very well.' James Joyce was by then one of the most famous writers in the world.

On Wednesday, 12 January 1898 Jim's godfather, Philip McCann, had died of tuberculosis aged fifty-one, having left his Sandymount house, Fairfield, some time before. He had been living in the Regent Hotel in D'Olier Street, close to his ship's chandler's business at 2 Burgh Quay; he also had owned other premises further downriver at 13 City Quay. According to the notice in the *Evening Telegraph* the next day, it had been a short illness (and he had died 'fortified by the rites of Holy Church'). The funeral took place on Friday morning at Glasnevin after a nine o'clock Requiem Mass in Westland Row Chapel. It was attended by relatives from Dundalk, various business associates, the seafaring men who had been his customers and, of course, by John and James Joyce. Afterwards, as the mourners reminisced together about their friend, they would have recalled Fairfield's illustrious past: before the McCanns had occupied it, the house had become briefly famous as where the 'Head Centre' of the Fenians, James Stephens, was captured in 1865 after a long police hunt. For all their affection for the late Philip, who had no children of his own, both John Stanislaus and his son awaited the reading of his will with interest and it is wellnigh certain that Jim was left a legacy. This money, however much it was (the will does not survive), became available to help Philip McCann's godson to complete a proper education. Jim would still have to earn something in the holidays, but the McCann windfall meant that he could go to college.

Stephen Dedalus's godfather similarly subsidises the youth in the *Portrait*: it may be that McCann (of the 'reproachful eyes', as Joyce once described him), knowing the Joyces' way with ready money, had organised that his executors should hold a small fund in James's name that could be drawn upon only for this purpose. McCann's was a lucky death: the Jesuits of the college could not waive the fees of the Royal and John would not have been able to afford them, with examination expenses on top, himself: these days he was scraping around for money just to feed and clothe the family. Though in *Stephen Hero* James Joyce was to substitute for his beneficent godfather's name that of another Dublin ship's chandler, Philip McCann would be obliquely memorialised there by the punning line from Sir Walter Scott's song 'Bonny Dundee': 'Come fill up my cup, come fill up my can.'

Jim told a friend, Eugene Sheehy, that on his application form for the college under 'occupation of father' he had filled in 'Going in for competitions'. Though the records show that this supposed entry of Jim's was merely a good story, John was now indeed attempting to win the cash prizes offered in *Answers* and 'that *Tit-Bits* paper'. *Tit-Bits* would be mentioned by Stanislaus as being 'the only one my father used to read for general culture'. The penny magazine, published monthly in London, was made up of quirky snippets of news or historical fact, advice columns, short stories and the like. It enlisted its readers to help fill its pages by offering them a golden guinea per column for material and it had a highly innovative line in competitions. These might involve simple cyphers or rebuses, or perhaps a 'Vigilance Competition' offering 'a crisp Bank of England note for five pounds to the competitor who succeeds in pointing out the greatest number of spelling mistakes in this issue'. Some of the more elaborate competitions were visual, with prizes of up to £50 – though the money tended to be split between several entrants – but it was not entirely unknown for winners to receive a house. Perhaps the best way to get real money out of the paper would have been to join its macabre 'Insurance Scheme': members who were killed in a railway accident would be sent no less than £100 – provided, naturally, that they had an issue of *Tit-Bits* on their person at the time. Although the 'original, complete stories' in the magazine were also theoretically open to all readers, in practice there was a stable of dependable writers who 'won' on a fairly regular basis. One of these was 'Philip Beaufoy, Playgoers' Club, Clement's Inn', the man whom Bloom thinks of emulating in *Ulysses* after reading his 'Matcham's Masterstroke' in the periodical. In the issue of 6 August 1896, a 'Romance of Russia' by John K. Leys entitled 'The Black Terror' may have prompted Jim to write a story about Russian intrigue himself, but if he did, as Stanislaus says, and it was posted, it was James Joyce's first rejection, for it was never published.

A year or two later, in *The Leader*, an influential newspaper-cum-propaganda sheet for the Irish-Ireland movement that would feed into Sinn Féin, founded and largely written by David Patrick Moran, *Tit-Bits* was singled out as one of the worst manifestations of the flood of foreign (i.e. English) cultural values that was swamping Ireland. Moran sneered at the Irishman who, like John Stanislaus, knew no Irish:

> ... the bank clerk in his knickers and brown boots stroking his mustachios ... might learn much about his country in the English tongue if he cared to but he prefers to read *Tit-Bits* and discover how many times one issue, if stretched, would go around the world and that sort of thing.

Admittedly, Moran was fanatical on most subjects. He condemned W. B. Yeats and his ilk (who thought that they were helping to restore the country's pride in its native heritage) for aping British ways, and accused them of cynically injecting what he dubbed the 'Celtic note' into their literary effusions merely to achieve celebrity in England. He called their revival movement 'one of the most glaring frauds that the credulous Irish people ever swallowed'. Even Daniel O'Connell was one of Moran's targets: he had done 'more than any other man ... to kill the Gaelic language and distinctive nature of the people'. In his way as inventive as John Stanislaus with his insulting epithets, he wrote of Protestant 'sour-faces', called the career publicans of Dublin 'Mr Bung' and sneered at the Irish Party at Westminster. Unsurprisingly, none of this suc-ceeded in putting John Stanislaus off his favourite reading. How-ever, there is no evidence that he ever won a penny piece from *Tit-Bits*, much less a house or a hundred pounds.

It may have been after Philip McCann's funeral that John brought home with him from the pub an old sailor with a beard, whom the family understood to be the hero who had 'got James Stephens away'. This man was Captain Weldon of Clontarf. Wel-don's story surfaces in *Ulysses* and, though he is not mentioned there, his name appears in James Joyce's notes for the novel. In 1865 the Fenian leader had been helped to escape from Richmond Prison and it was aboard the Captain's fishing-boat that he was smuggled out of Ireland. Legend had it that when the plotters were stopped by a police launch in Dublin Bay Stephens, wearing a dainty long dress and a veil wreathed with orange-blossom, put the officer off the scent by embracing Captain Weldon and flutter-ing his eyelashes. Tonight, the old salt's position was reversed, for by the end of the evening he was sitting on John Stanislaus's knee as they both delivered a poignant rendition of 'I dream of thee, sweet Madoline', at intervals his host plucking spiritedly at the Captain's pointy whiskers and shouting his usual war-cry, 'Hoop!'. The sudden collapse of the chair supplied an inevitable climax to the evening and to the tale.

CHAPTER 18

A Travelling Man

It is likely that it was during this time that John Stanislaus found employment with *Thom's Directory*, published in Middle Abbey Street almost next door to the *Evening Telegraph* and *Freeman*. The work, updating the annual Dublin Street Directory, would again have been peripatetic: occupancy details for each property would have to be checked against the voters and valuation register by going from door to door. The list for the forthcoming *Thom's* (for 1900) had to be completed by October 1899 so that changes could be inserted into the print-beds, which were let stand from year to year. The job was not well paid, but John may sometimes have been able to boost his income by also supplying his data to the authorities for use in compiling the national and municipal voters' lists, then undergoing one of their sporadic bursts of expansion. The passing of the Local Government Act in 1898 had more than quadrupled the number of electors in the city, though they were still less than one seventh of the population. Spice was added to John's task by the fact that the next city election would be the first in which any women had a vote. Work on the electoral roll naturally kept him in touch with such figures as 'Long' John Clancy, to whom the likely division of votes was a matter of extreme interest. With the wider franchise, as the majority of the population were loosely Nationalist and strictly Catholic, Dublin Corporation looked certain to be dominated by anti-Unionists. Nearly all the seats were up for grabs and anyone could be unseated. There had been a time when John Stanislaus might have hoped to see his name on a ballot paper; there was no question of it now.

However, John's continued connection with Clancy and his colleagues in turn led on to his involvement in the municipal elections themselves. Each year one third of the City Councillors came to the end of their three-year tenure; elections to replace them were held every January, followed by one for the Lord Mayor (which in 1899 Dan Tallon won for the second year in succession). At these elections there were always several 'jobs for the boys' on offer, which ranged from physically organising the polling booths and ballot boxes to acting as Personation Officer to deter would-be multiple voters. This year on polling day John was probably made Presiding Officer in one or other of the wards, a grandiose though not stressful portfolio that involved checking that the correct procedures were followed and looking officious during the count. As predicted, the 1899 election was a landslide. Even Reuben J. Dodd was elected as a Nationalist for Wood Quay, one ward where it can be assumed that Presiding Officer Joyce was not in charge.

In May, the combined efforts of Mrs Love, her son and their solicitor at last succeeded in overcoming the flaw in the lease for 29 Windsor Avenue. After more than two years of relative stability (and rent-free accommodation) the Joyces were going to have to move on. *Stephen Hero* describes how a tip-off from 'a friend in the Sheriff's office' (presumably Alfie Bergan) gave the family five days' unofficial notice of the arrival of 'His Lordship' the bailiff, as John Stanislaus called him. Mr Daedalus warned that they would all be out on the street within the week. Then, 'humming derisively', he set out with polished monocle and well-brushed hat in search of a landlord to impress.

As he always did, John found somewhere. The new place was an old house less than half a mile away on Convent Avenue, at the corner of Richmond Road. The avenue was little more than a glorified approach road to the entrance of Richmond Castle, then occupied by a Sisters of Charity lunatic asylum, St Vincent's. These days, to transfer the Joyce possessions from one house to the next took just a single trip in a low-bodied drayman's cart: by now, almost everything they owned had been turned into cash, even some of the cheap household furniture that John had bought after leaving Blackrock. *Stephen Hero* mentions that whenever the local tradesmen heard that another article of furniture had been carried out on its way to the pawnbroker they hammered on the door for payment of their outstanding accounts, hoping that there might now be some money in the house. There rarely was.

The move was the first of a series of disappearing tricks that John would perform over the next few years. These flits through the streets were usually made after dark to evade the bailiffs, and they would engrave themselves on the memories of the children, who found them rather exciting. Even Pappie could be in cheerful spirits, relieved at having avoided both eviction and homelessness, and sometimes he would be heard singing a love-song at the head of the family crocodile, his voice carrying 'like a muffled flute' in the night air. One of his favourites was the song that Simon Dedalus sings to Stephen in the Victoria Hotel in Cork, a lilting, haunting lament about the dying of love. It ends:

> My love she's handsome,
> My love she's bony:
> She's like good whisky
> When it is new;
> But when 'tis old
> And growing cold
> It fades and dies like
> The mountain dew.

May Joyce would sometimes shush the children and stop to listen to him. Perhaps she also needed a rest. John, May and the older children always carried the heavy ancestral portraits themselves from house to house, not trusting them to the dray: by now, with the Joyce crest, they had assumed an overwhelming importance to John as the only visible symbols of his rightful place in society. Despite having done time in pawn, they had always been redeemed, but with every move the gloomy pictures in their ugly frames were becoming, like their owner, less and less presentable.

In contrast to his father, James 'Agustine' Joyce (as he put on his Matriculation Examination entrance form) was noticed at the university for his 'studied' attire. Though failing to win an exhibition, to mark him out from the common run of students he carried an ashplant, or rowan stick. John now saw less of him at home, even in the evenings: if Jim was not in the National Library he might be at a meeting of the College Library Conference or the Thomas Aquinas Society, and he went to the weekly debates of the Literary and Historical Society (the 'L & H'). He also took up Irish for a while, learning the rudiments and meeting girls (notably Mary Clery) at Patrick Pearse's evening classes at the Gaelic League, where he also met the fanatical Michael Cusack, promoter of Gaelic sports, who would become the 'Citizen' of *Ulysses*. Every second Sunday there was a visit to the daughters of David Sheehy MP for charades, songs and recitations. Though Jim once or twice brought Poppie and his mother to these soirées at Belvedere Place, escorting May Joyce formally to the piano when her turn came to perform, his father was never encouraged to attend. Perhaps the prospect of his getting out of hand in such company was too much to contemplate. But Jim was still happy to be taken to the theatre on occasion by his father and mother. In March 1898 he had accompanied them to see Mrs Patrick Campbell in the somewhat daring play *Magda*, an adaptation of *Heimat* by Hermann Sudermann (a sort of poor man's Ibsen). He told his parents afterwards that the evening had been wasted: they would soon be able to see *Magda*'s subject, 'genius breaking out in the home and against the home', enacted in front of them – by him. John's reaction is not known, but he may have found this claim hard to believe in the light of his son's undistinguished university results so far – a decline that he knew followed his own college career. But James Joyce was doing more than singing and telling stories: he was beginning to write.

James Clarence Mangan's poem, 'The Nameless One', a remarkable personal lament for the wasted genius of the poet himself, 'betrayed in friendship, befooled in love' but still with a soul 'mated' to song, was more than once recited at the Sheehys' by Jim. The artist in the young man was more ambitious to succeed in the world than Mangan had been, and was already determined to do so through art. He showed some delicate verses he had written to his friends and was currently collecting together a sheaf of short vignettes in prose called *Silhouettes*. Within five years he would have begun his first extended narrative work, *Stephen Hero*. This would be almost openly autobiographical: he was either unwilling or unable to invent very much. As the chapters covering his childhood have been lost or destroyed, the existing text begins early in the author's university career. Though there are changes of names, compressions that affect matters of chronology and alterations of certain sensitive facts – the most radical being that James's brother Georgie appears as a sister – the manuscript rings true in its characterisation of the family members (though each is viewed primarily in relation to the narrator). It contains several discussions of Jim's father as he was at about this time.

Mr Daedalus (the spelling adopted in *Stephen Hero*) is first seen hoping that Stephen will 'follow the path of remunerative respectability'. That he has allowed the lad to go to university does not stop him complaining about it. To Stephen, his father's whinges are worth suffering as the price of freedom from wage-slavery. His mother remarks that she has had 'more or less a happy life' with his father, though sometimes she would like to 'leave this actual life and enter another – for a time'. Once, she used to read books, but no longer, as her husband 'takes no interest in that sort of thing', preferring to talk about his athletic past in Cork. She urges him to read a play by her son's hero, Ibsen. Partly to humour her he tries *The League of Youth*, hoping from the title for a dramatic plot of the Frank Smedley type. After two acts he gives it up, commenting that the playwright's photograph looks like an acquaintance of his in a Dame Street office. The remark, if John Stanislaus made it, was precisely calculated to annoy Jim.

On 1 September 1899, Aunt Josephine's father, 'Papa' (James J.) Giltrap, died at his home in Bengal Terrace, a row of five small houses beside Glasnevin Cemetery. The very next day, while Mrs Giltrap (no doubt with her daughter's assistance) was preparing for the funeral, a seventy-six-year-old neighbour, Thomas Childs, was murdered at No. 5, just beside them. The dead man's brother Samuel, the only other person to have a key to the house, was arrested and tried for fratricide. On the jury was Alexander Keyes (of the Ballsbridge 'Luncheon Bar'), who knew John Stanislaus from his advertising days. The case was the talk of the town and the Joyces were fascinated to be close to such a sensation. Jim even sat in the public gallery taking notes that he would draw on in *Ulysses*, and saw Tim Healy and the eminent barrister, Seymour Bushe QC, secure an acquittal for lack of evidence.

May's beloved Josephine Murray had not only lost her father, but her husband had lost his job in his father-in-law's office. As John Stanislaus once had, William turned to freelance accountancy, but he too failed to earn enough to support himself and his family of six children. Finally, a firm of solicitors, Collis and Ward, took him on as a cost accountant. John Stanislaus's continued dislike of the Murrays is made evident in *Stephen Hero* (and elsewhere). Mrs Daedalus's maiden name stinks in her husband's nostrils: marrying into her family is 'the only sin of which . . . he could accuse himself'. As if in revenge, he spends many an evening making everyone miserable at home as he 'pondered, muttered, growled and execrated' about his in-laws. The more John Stanislaus acted like this, the more May and the children took refuge with 'Aunt Jo', where they were always made welcome.

John Stanislaus seemed to be trying to live in every house in north Dublin: Convent Avenue lasted for only about six months. Presumably the reason they had to leave was the usual one: that the rent was not being paid. John may have persuaded the landlord (who was, it seems, a Frenchman named Bosinnet) to issue receipts, however. One way or another, he secured 13 Richmond Avenue, around the corner. In the autumn, the drayman was called upon to shift the family goods and chattels once again. The Joyces shared this new house (and the rent bill) with the family of a hard-drinking one-eyed commercial traveller in hardware, Richard Hughes, portrayed as 'Mr Wilkinson' in *Stephen Hero*. If the account in the novel is taken from life, the house was in bad repair (it has since been demolished), but it had some fifteen rooms to contain the twelve Joyces and three or four Hugheses. They were delighted to find that a piano had been abandoned by the previous tenant in the large and otherwise empty oak-lined drawing-room, at one end of which Hughes dumped his ironmongery samples. John's co-tenant was a Protestant from Belfast, but, as with James Vance, this fact seemed only to add zest to the friendship that quickly sprang up between the two men: every day they would set out for town together from the 'dilapidated mansion', often returning in high spirits to sit in front of the fire and abuse each other amicably about history and politics until the small hours.

It was not only matters Irish that they would have discussed. When, in the autumn of 1899, Britain's invasion of the Transvaal began the Boer War, the politics of the British Empire again become a live issue among Irish Nationalists of all persuasions, prompting the Irish MPs in Westminster at last to come together in an uneasy coalition as the United Irish League. To many Home Rulers the war was just another example of England's rapaciousness, and Irish sympathy with the Afrikaners was all the stronger because there was now another excellent reason to protest against the Crown. Some, including John MacBride (later Maud Gonne's husband) and Colonel Arthur Lynch, who knew both James Stephens and John O'Leary, joined the 'Irish Brigade' or 'Wreckers Corps' to harass the British in Southern Africa – and briefly captured a slippery young war correspondent called Winston Churchill. At home, backed by a vociferous claque in the Council Chamber, 'Long' John Clancy as Subsheriff proposed that Paul Kruger, the President of the Transvaal, be given the Freedom of the City of Dublin. But by then, as the papers were carrying long daily lists of Irishmen killed while serving with the British Forces in South Africa, allegiances were mixed, and the motion was overruled as out of order. John Stanislaus's unmixed allegiance was vehemently with Kruger, and he did not mind who knew it.

On 6 October, the anniversary of Parnell's death, John wore his sprig of ivy as usual. Emotions in Dublin were running particularly high among the pro-Boers, and people spoke of parallels between Parnell and the Boer general, de Wet. A story even went the rounds that de Wet was actually The Chief undead and that all they had buried in Glasnevin was a coffin full of stones. Nevertheless, John would not have missed the ceremonial laying of the foundation stone for the Parnell monument, held two days after Ivy Day that year. The chosen site was near the Rotunda at the top of Sackville Street (or, as everyone was now calling it, O'Connell Street). When Parnell was unveiled in 1911, he would form with Daniel O'Connell at the far end of the street a most satisfactory Nationalist pincer movement on Admiral Nelson. But though the siting was symbolically pleasing, the memorial impeded the flow of traffic and the *Irish Times* wondered if it was entirely necessary to commemorate Parnell's obstructionist skills quite so literally.

*   *   *

On the evening of 20 January 1900, John took Stannie to the Physics Theatre in University College to hear Jim deliver to the Literary and Historical Society a polemical paper called 'Drama & Life', part of his campaign to spread the word about Ibsen. In the ensuing discussion the speaker was attacked by, among others, Arthur Clery (who would become D. P. Moran's right-hand man on the *Leader*) and Hugh Kennedy, soon to beat Jim for Auditor of the Society. Another member, Seamus Clandillon, clapped the speaker heartily on the back afterwards, crowing ambiguously: 'Joyce, that was magnificent but you're raving mad!' John Stanislaus, his eyeglass glittering from his place in the rows of seats looking down on the speaker, was inordinately proud of his son's achievement. The lad had held the whole place spellbound, whatever he was talking about. Having developed an instant dislike of Jim's detractors, John remarked later to Stannie that after Jim had hit back at him in his reply to the criticisms, Hugh Kennedy with his round cheeks and high colour had 'a face like a child's bottom, well-whipped'.

In April Queen Victoria spent three weeks passing over bridges in the city. *Modern Society*, an English magazine filled with royal gossip that formed another large part of John's reading at this time, reported the warm reception that 'Dublin's Darlin'' received. Partly to get away from the loyal tributes and partly to help spend some of the twelve guineas (£12.12s.od) that he had received from London for his precocious article on Ibsen in the *Fortnightly Review*, Jim decided to take a trip to London. He invited his father to share the treat – reciprocity for their jaunt to Scotland six years earlier. Leaving May Joyce with £1 to feed the rest of the family while they were away, they caught the ferry to Holyhead. On the train to the capital John was in a boisterous mood. He picked on an unfortunate fellow-passenger as representative of the English oppressors of the Boers and made inflammatory remarks to him about the South African War. Just a couple of months before, the sieges of Kimberley and Ladysmith had been lifted or 'relieved', and John probably came out with his joke (later borrowed for *Ulysses*) that if it was relief the British wanted, they could have done the job just as well by sending out supplies of the Wonderworker – 'the world's greatest remedy for rectal complaints'; 'insert long round end'. As Con Curran wrote later, John Stanislaus 'could fascinate indefinitely with stories told with consummate art, one neatly fitting into another. And these stories would be of a perfectly drawing-room character till suddenly, as if taken unawares, he would slip into the coarse vein and another side of his nature and vocabulary be revealed.' The sudden switch was always likely to provoke extreme reactions, particularly from strangers taken unawares by his rich expletives – the most celebrated of which is perhaps 'Shite and Onions!'. On this occasion, according to Stanislaus, it was only Jim's mollifying words to both parties that prevented an outbreak of fisticuffs.

When they reached London, the pair stayed in a boarding-house, probably in Kennington, where John gave the monocular landlady the name of 'Cyclopia'. The district was necessarily a cheap part of the city, strongly reminiscent of dirty Georgian Dublin. Locally, an Irish family called Hooligan were pugnaciously giving their name to the language. More importantly for James, it was where William Blake had walked his 'charter'd streets', and he would set one of his own short prose pieces here. The 'Epiphany' speaks of incest between the brother and sister of a certain Maudie Leslie. If this was the Maud Leslie who taught singing in South London (as an Associate of the London Academy of Music), the Joyces very likely knew her though the Gunns – the Gaiety *Sindbad* programme of 1892–3 had advertised Leslie's Opera Voice Lozenges. That most of the 'Epiphanies' were unaltered snatches of real conversations gives some credence to the actual existence of this resourceful family. As for the incest, it is evident that when Eva Leslie said laconically that her brother Fred was 'a whoite-arsed bugger' who once 'went with me ten toimes one noight', it was an example of plain-speaking cockney humour rather than the revelation of a crime.

Jim had never been to London before and John was proud to be able to show him around. They visited the music-hall and very likely the theatre. They also went to see the Houses of Parliament. Standing in the shadow of Oliver Cromwell's new statue outside Westminster Hall, John was drawn into conversation with an old Londoner who remarked that it was a shame that there was nobody like Cromwell left. John, who like all Irishmen remembered only

Cromwell's massacres in Ireland, agreed with him and added with firm logic, 'except perhaps Paul Kruger . . . The Bible in one hand and the sword in the other, you know.' Disgusted by the comparison, the Englishman stalked silently away.

William Desmond O'Connell, son of old Uncle Bill, had for some years been living in the city with his family, and the Joyces paid them a visit to talk about old times. They discovered that William's son, Gilbert, after a hero's send-off at the Honourable Artillery Company Headquarters in City Road, had embarked for South Africa on 11 January aboard the SS *Briton*. Sergeant Gilbert O'Connell, who was not much older than Jim, had enlisted with the City Imperial Volunteers, a force of some 1000 men recruited and funded by the City of London. (Another volunteer was Erskine Childers, nephew of H. C. E. Childers and Clerk of the House of Commons, who would later write *The Riddle of the Sands*, run rebel guns into Howth and father a future President of Ireland.) South Africa was a dangerous posting: the CIV had already come under fire at Klip river. Perhaps thinking of his own attempt to experience the excitements of battle on his first trip to London thirty years before, John admired Gilbert's gallantry – despite his being on the wrong side – and was much impressed to be shown a War Office pamphlet with a photograph of the tall and handsome Sergeant O'Connell on the cover. The London O'Connells, unlike their Cork relatives, found the Joyces to be good company and were pleased to take them on expeditions around the metropolis.

The official excuse for the trip, however, was for Jim to meet people who might be of help to his writing career. As well as calling on W. L. Courtney at the *Fortnightly* to thank him for publishing the Ibsen essay and to ask for more work, Jim was brought by John to the offices of the periodical *M. A. P.* (*Mainly About People*) to meet the famous journalist and MP for Liverpool (Exchange), T. P. ('Tay Pay') O'Connor, an old Parnellite friend of Jack Hall the theatre critic. O'Connor was already at the planning stage of *T P's Weekly*, a popular literary magazine, which when it was launched in 1902 would become hugely successful. An evening or two would also have been spent drinking with Jimmy Tuohy, who lived in Kensington and was still the *Freeman*'s London stringer, and the old friends must have talked of The Chief. There were probably others to see as well who could have been useful, such as John's dear friend Carrol O'Sullivan in the Mile End Road. For all John's efforts, however, not a single literary commission was offered to Jim through these impressive contacts.

When after about a week away the travellers returned from their expedition among the English (whom Jim would later call 'a reptile people'), Jim had only twopence left and John was penniless. John had enjoyed himself hugely in London, though while he was there he had missed another great funeral. Parnell's doctor, Joe Kenny, lately the City Coroner and a founding director of the Independent Newspapers Company, had died on 9 April. His burial near Parnell had been attended by everyone else: most of the City Fathers, Jack Hishon, Tom Cunniam, Fr Conmee and even Reuben J. Dodd and his son. While John would have liked to be there he did not grieve: at home he entertained his family with approximations of music-hall songs he had heard in London, and tried out a new stock of pungently Joycean travellers' tales. As something to show to his friends, he had held on to the War Office booklet with his brave young O'Connell cousin on the cover.

On 22 April an optimistic Clongowes Wood College had reissued its ten-year-old bill for £27.10s.6d covering Jim's interrupted last term there. The envelope was sent to the Collector-General's Office in Fleet Street, but as the CGO had been entirely disbanded in 1898 it was returned. Two days later the College tried again and sent the bill to Martello Terrace, Bray. Again it was returned.

Clongowes was far from being John Stanislaus's major creditor. According to Stephen's father, charging for food was perfectly reasonable, but 'to expect people to pay for shelter the exorbitant sums which are demanded annually by houseowners in Dublin seemed to him unjust'. Tracking him down in Dublin was not always easy. John fled the landlord of 13 Richmond Avenue and his bailiffs in May, but it seems that he managed to hang on to the piano that they had found in the house. Hughes and his family had to leave too and between them the men hit upon an artful method of obtaining somewhere else to live. Mr Joyce (or Mr Hughes) presented to the owner of a nearby vacant rental property a glowing reference written by Mr Hughes (or Mr Joyce), one posing as the other's landlord. By this device they soon gained possession of 8 Royal Terrace, Fairview (close to where John Hooper had lived). Both families were secure again until the next time.

The house was the fourth the Joyces had occupied in two years. It backed on to the grounds of St Vincent's Lunatic Asylum, around which the family seemed to be circling: the screams of deranged nuns could apparently be heard from the lane behind. But though it was reasonably roomy, with two storeys and a basement, rooms were about all they had, as actual possessions were few and far between. When a volume of the Four Gospels and a compendium of parlour songs were discovered falling to bits in the ashpit at the end of the garden they were brought in and lovingly read: in such a musical family the songbook, full of humorous as well as traditional and classical songs, found a wide audience. John probably pored over it with Mervyn Archdall Brown, the old friend of the Flynns, who lived close to the new house. The splendour of the trove may have been the origin of another of John Stanislaus's sardonic catchphrases, used when anything was in short supply: '*Have you tried the ashpit?*' Stannie, who like Jim before him enjoyed the privileges that went with being Head of the Sodality in Belvedere, tackled the Gospels – Bibles were a rare enough commodity in Irish Catholic homes. When he had finished he at once rejected his religion, upsetting his mother by declaring that he would neither take Communion nor confess his sins. Though his father no longer went to Mass himself if he could possibly avoid it, he had enough sympathy with his wife to threaten Stannie with public exposure by informing the College in writing of his son's precocious loss of faith. However, for one reason or another, John never wrote the letter to Belvedere and Jim tore up an essay by Stannie in which he exposed himself anyway. Neither father nor eldest son welcomed another rebel in the family.

In late June or early July 1900 John went to Mullingar in County Westmeath. There was a job on the horizon for Joyce *père*. Tim Harrington had been M P there nearly twenty years before and may have recommended him for work that had to be done on the revision of the electoral roll in the area. Some fifty miles west of Dublin, Mullingar was a large county town in good farming and hunting land dotted with lakes. Despite its good communications

– it was served by the main railway westwards from Dublin as well as by the Royal Canal that linked the capital with the River Shannon at Athlone – the town retained its old reputation of being the stupidest place in Ireland. Decades before, in need of a comic stage-Irishman for his music-hall, Dan Lowrey had devised his own 'Pat of Mullingar'. As well as the town's celebrated bovine qualities there was also its political mulishness, seen in an absurd wrangle that had been going on over the water supply and in the disputes that the local Catholic prelate, Dr Nulty, carried on with his flock. Mullingar was currently being criticised for its sheeplike apathy: only 175 of the 570 registered voters had bothered to turn up at a polling station to vote at the last election; hundreds more should have been registered. It was John's job to get them on the list as assets to the Irish Parliamentary Party.

John brought Jim and Stannie with him to copy lists and the like, and probably contrived to get them paid a pittance as well. With his expertise in patterns of ratepaying, it was simple enough work to investigate the baptismal and marriage registers at Dr Nulty's cathedral. He reported his findings to officials of the Westmeath County Council, whose Secretary, the Unionist Councillor W. C. Levinge, occupied Levington Park, a gracious country house on the southern shore of Lough Owel a little to the north of the town. The Joyces may have lodged for a time with a photographer called Philip Shaw above the Post Office in Earl Street (where Milly Bloom works in *Ulysses*). Phil Shaw was often away touring around the province taking photographs for a publisher, so for company John gravitated towards the local newspaper offices, drinking and exchanging gossip with journalists in establishments like the Greville Arms Family and Commercial Hotel.

One 'Epiphany' shows that the Joyces were on good terms with a Mr Tobin who worked on the *Westmeath Examiner* (the reading of which Bishop Nulty had in 1894 declared to be 'sinful'). This was Michael Tobin, a fiercely nationalistic reporter who wrote for the newspaper on the many political meetings, election rallies and Land League events that took place in the surrounding towns. A Corkman whose fondness for crubeens (pigs' trotters) attracted the town dogs, he had been brought up not far from Fermoy, in Canon Sheehan's Doneraile, and had married a local girl whose father was on the *Westmeath Examiner*. He would later move on, like so many of John Stanislaus's friends, to the *Freeman's Journal*. Normally, agrarian oratory apart, there was little local news for Michael Tobin to report, but on the afternoon of 19 July the whole of Mullingar was set chattering when the body of a woman, Matilda Pender, was found floating in the canal between Scanlan's and Moran's Bridges, on the north-east edge of the town. She was soon identified as an inmate of the Mullingar District Lunatic Asylum, about a mile to the east, who had climbed out of a lavatory window the night before. Though foul play was at first suspected, Constable Brandon who took charge of the corpse was able to report that there were no signs of bruising on the body, coyly explaining to the inquest that he knew this because the woman's night chemise had ridden up around her neck by the time she had been laid on the towpath. An inquiry afterwards recommended an investigation into the asylum, which had already been accused of severe over-crowding. The incident made a deep impression on Jim, who later wrote it up for *Stephen Hero*, where Tobin also appears (as 'Garvey').

But genius was already breaking out in Mullingar. Jim spent much of his time that summer writing *A Brilliant Career*, a play about a young doctor and his first lost sweetheart, 'the first true work of my life'. The play owed more to the influence of Ibsen than to anything else. After it was completed he took the manuscript into his father's bedroom to show it to him. When his recumbent parent saw that it was prefaced with the words 'To my own Soul', he gave the startled response, 'Holy Paul!', before subsiding back on to his pillows. John Stanislaus probably never got all the way through the play, having already had a go at Ibsen. No copy of it now exists, though Stanislaus read and liked it, and gave a resumé of the plot (as far as he could remember it) in *My Brother's Keeper*. He thought that the teeming characters of the play were all modelled on his brother's acquaintances, but Jim told him that the story had come from his imagination. If it had, it was almost the only time he ever devised a plot from scratch. While his stories usually came ready made from life, sometimes in his early writings James Joyce used the 'what if' approach – much of *Dubliners* seems to explore what his own fate might have been if he had not left Dublin. Perhaps, almost unconsciously, he may have founded the central character of *A Brilliant Career* on the man his father might have become if he had stayed in Cork (and passed his medical examinations). And Jim could draw on the now obscure story of John's split from the girl (perhaps Miss Justice) whom he had first wished to marry, followed by his abortive engagements. Had John read the whole play, he might have found it more interesting than he had expected.

Shortly before the Joyces left Mullingar the county of Westmeath was discussing a second sensational fatality. In Dublin, towards the end of August, the semi-naked body of another woman, that of a Baggot Street maidservant, had been fished out of the River Dodder at Irishtown, near Sandymount. This time it *was* murder and a member of the DMP, Constable Henry Flower, was charged with the crime. Flower, and his father before him, were Westmeath men, and the *Examiner* even carried a drawing of the accused wearing a bowler hat. Though the case against him was eventually thrown out for lack of concrete evidence, Flower was widely believed to have been responsible and immediately after his release fled the country.

As Harrington was leading the constable's legal defence, when John got back from Mullingar shortly afterwards he would have learnt more details of the case from him, or more likely from his associate Jack Hishon. The 'Dodder Mystery' intrigued the Joyces, who may thus have discovered matters that never became general knowledge, and James was twice to draw upon it in his fiction. 'Two Gallants' in *Dubliners* is a loose adaptation of many points of the case, while in *Ulysses* Leopold Bloom uses the useful pseudonym 'Henry Flower' to preserve his anonymity when writing amorous letters to a woman he has never met, Martha Clifford. Realistically, in 1904 Dublin, less than four years after such a notorious murder, this was the last name that anyone in search of romance would choose. The image of the drowned woman would impinge again on the mind of Stephen Dedalus in the novel when one of his sisters unsuccessfully tries to beg money from him on the quays of the River Liffey.

John Stanislaus seems to have been unaffected. Back in town, he picked up his life where he had left it, meeting friends and, when he had the money, drinking with them in city centre bars.

He was now in his early fifties and more than three decades of whiskey, pipe tobacco and cigars were taking their toll on his voice. He was no longer in public demand as a singer. But, as Mr Dedalus remarks, music remained 'the only language' for him; John would play the piano (when he had access to one) for many years more, and was even known to scrape out a tune on the violin in bed. Vocally, however, he could still perform well enough for an occasion, and he sang a great deal informally when drinking and often at home. The children were brought up to the sound of his voice: when it was not coming petulantly at them from upstairs, it was very often raised in song. John's choice of songs was not universally appreciated: Stannie saw his father's repertoire as a symptom of his growing sentimentality. (He, after Meredith, defined a sentimentalist as 'he who would enjoy without incurring the immense debtorship for a thing done' and applied it to his father.) Stannie particularly detested that anthem of Cork by the reprobate Old Clongownian, Fr Prout, 'The Bells of Shandon', which made tears roll down his father's cheeks every time he sang it:

> With deep affection and recollection
> I often think of the Shandon bells,
> Whose sound so wild would, in days of childhood,
> Fling round my cradle their magic spells.
> On this I ponder, where'er I wander,
> And thus grow fonder, sweet Cork, of thee;
> With thy bells of Shandon,
> That sound so grand on
> The pleasant waters of the River Lee.

There was a sense in which John was still an unwilling exile from Cork, but it was a Cork of the past: his vain hope of becoming one of its MPs and his later canvassing in the city were attempts to have the best of both worlds, but Cork had changed, as cities do, and there was nothing there for him any more. It was some comfort that, at the General Election in the autumn, Maurice Healy was roundly defeated there by William O'Brien (now *éminence grise* behind the United Irish League), though his bloody brother Tim got back into Parliament for the constituency of North Meath.

CHAPTER 19

The Boer Constructor

On 8 January 1901 Jim appeared on the stage. Margaret Sheehy had graduated from organising the Sunday night entertainments in her father's back parlour, and her play, *Cupid's Confidant*, which had already been staged the previous March in the rere of a Grafton Street café, was allowed one performance in what was almost a real theatre, the Antient Concert Rooms. Jim was the villain, Geoffrey Fortescue, in both productions. No doubt his father was there to watch him on the Great Brunswick Street stage and it was probably he who persuaded Jack Hall to review it in the *Freeman's Journal*. Though Jim told Stannie that 'even the virgin cheeks of his [own] arse blushed for his part in it', Hall's appreciative notice (published in the paper the next morning, 9 January) singled him out as a 'revelation', and praised the young Mr Joyce's 'extraordinary skill'. While John's son would never match the success that he himself had enjoyed as a comic actor in Cork, his pride in seeing Jim in action on the boards was assured.

Technically the new century had just begun (though predictably and proleptically this had been celebrated the year before). That 1901 was the correct year to celebrate was emphasised by the death, three weeks into the new century, of Queen Victoria. Two days later Edward VII was proclaimed in Dublin Castle. As if to reassure the monarch about how many subjects he had in Ireland, the ten-yearly census of the country was held on 31 March. Dublin's population was now 290,638, a sharp rise due partly to the recent incorporation into the city of some inner suburbs, including Clontarf, Drumcondra and Glasnevin. John, with his municipal contacts, was in a strong position to get some welcome work distributing, collecting and collating the census forms.

At home, silencing the children as he always did when there was something important to be written, he filled out his own form in his meticulous and ornate copperplate, a laborious task in a household of twelve. He marked Jim and Stannie down as Irish speakers, though this was a considerable exaggeration. John's own knowledge of Irish was slight, though like everyone else he occasionally uttered a species of 'dog-Erse', with remarks like 'Ditto Macanaspey', a catchphrase used by Simon Dedalus that simply means 'ditto' (though literally it is 'ditto the son of the bishop', a dubious concept certainly in Catholic Ireland). Otherwise, though like Simon in *Stephen Hero* he did not mind his son learning Irish 'so long as it did not keep him from his legitimate work', he himself had no interest in the language that had been so rapidly abandoned by his forefathers.

In the summer there was a second trip to Mullingar for more work on the lists there. Though almost no records have come to light of their presence in the town apart from what has been gleaned from the Joyces themselves, at least one old townsperson still blames John Stanislaus for 'leading her grandfather astray' that summer, with disastrous and tragic consequences for his whole family. What the details of this mysterious episode are remains unclear – it may be that John entangled a Mullingar acquaintance in some financial deal that failed, or it may be simply a case of the evils of drink, but it is a measure of John's delinquent capacity that almost a century later the bitterness remains.

It seems certain that on this visit John, James and perhaps Stanislaus stayed with friends in a house on the shores of Lough Owel. This would not have been the mansion of the Unionist grandee W. C. Levinge, as has sometimes been suggested. But through his work John knew the District Councillor, Mr A. E. Bannon, the head of an extended clan who lived at Portloman, on the western edge of the lough beyond the County Hospital. In earlier days Awley Bannon DC had been something of a firebrand, once breaking into the Mullingar Courthouse, local symbol of British justice and injustice, and hanging the green flag out of one of the windows. If he was the model for Mr Fulham in *Stephen Hero*, he had moderated somewhat in his views in the intervening years. His family also comes into *Ulysses* under its own name, where a love-struck Alec Bannon carries a signed photograph of Milly Bloom (though he describes her in the Mullingar way as 'a skittish heifer, big of her age and beef to the heel'). The Joyces also must have known another lakeside family, the Howards, who were Baptists. As on the previous visit, Jim got some writing done: the manuscript of his translation from German of Hauptmann's play, *Before Sunrise*, bears the inscription 'Mullingar, 23 July 1901'. They were all back in Dublin again by the early autumn.

Though John dismissed the Irish language as barbaric or irrelevant, the Gaelic League, set on reviving it as the country's main tongue, was rapidly growing in popularity. Soon enough, the League would become the core around which the future of Irish politics would coalesce. But the time was not quite yet and at the General Election at the end of September the old guard, in the shape of the United Irish League, did well. Tim Harrington, now an extremely popular politician (though not with Unionists – he was pelted with fruit by Trinity undergraduates the previous year), was returned unopposed and Councillor Nannetti, whose son John also knew from the composing-room of the *Evening Telegraph*, was elected for the College Green constituency. Although John naturally supported the Irish Party in the Commons, he did so with little enthusiasm, and his main interest in the election would have been the casual work it generated and the jovial celebrations afterwards. There would be more cause for carousing at the beginning of 1901, when Tim Harrington was elected Lord Mayor of Dublin as well. Harrington would be re-elected again in 1902 and 1903, making him the only one ever to be so honoured. His mayoral salary of over £3000 a year was second only to that of London. Perhaps Dublin really was the Second City of the Empire after all.

While John was able to lose himself from time to time in the social activity of the city, life for May and the children was becoming ever bleaker. Whatever threadbare dignity they had left was succumbing to recurrent bouts of extreme poverty and each time they moved house things seemed worse. At about this time, in Chapter IV of the *Portrait*, Stephen comes home to Royal Terrace while his parents are out house hunting:

He pushed open the latchless door of the porch and passed through the naked hallway into the kitchen. A group of his brothers and sisters was sitting round the table. Tea was nearly over and only the last of the second watered tea remained in the bottoms of the small glass jars and jampots which did service for teacups. Discarded crusts and lumps of sugared bread, turned brown by the tea which had been poured over them, lay scattered on the table. Little wells of tea lay here and there on the board, and a knife with a broken ivory handle was stuck through the pith of a ravaged turnover.

At least they still had food on the table and tea in the pot – though one of John's daughters later indignantly denied that the family had ever descended to drinking it from jam jars or to burning the wooden banisters from the stairs. But the struggle was wearing their mother out.

That Stephen's parents were looking for another house was one further detail taken from life: in the autumn of 1901, John spirited the family away again. Leaving the relatively pleasant purlieus of Fairview behind them at last, they moved back towards town to 32 Glengariff Parade, between the North Circular Road and the Royal Canal. It was a gloomy neighbourhood, with the great grey bulk of Mountjoy Prison behind the terrace. The mean redbrick house had only two bedrooms to hold them all and they were now so cramped that it was even more difficult for May to keep her children clean and healthy. Jim, for one, had in any case an aversion to washing – he claimed that, as a result, the lice refused to live on his flesh. Across the North Circular Road at the bottom of the street was the Mater Hospital, where John Kelly had died. One of the girls believed it was called that because you went there if 'something was the matter with you'. That they all seemed to be in no need of its services was perhaps more a result of their mother's prayers than of their father's husbandry.

The cause of the family's debilitated state was easy to diagnose. No records survive suggesting that John Stanislaus at this time had any income apart from his small pension and what little cash he could pick up at election times or from friends in the legal world. The children needed food and clothes. Equally, John needed to drink. He therefore divided his financial assets more or less in two between himself and his wife. However, he left out of the calculation anything he might spend during the customary binge at the beginning of the month when the pension cheque came in and at any post-election jollifications. Unfortunately, these blow-outs could last some time and often there was very little money left to divide. Pappie was impossible to control.

On 1 February 1902, the day before his twentieth birthday, Jim read another paper, 'James Clarence Mangan', to the L & H. Once again John Stanislaus was there to listen and applaud. The paper, which was even more difficult to understand than the previous one, was partly a defence of the admired Irish poet against those who spoke more about his vices than they did about his verses. Joyce quoted from Mangan's short unfinished *Autobiography*, just published by Duffy's in a new edition of his translations from the Irish, *The Poets and Poetry of Munster*. In the fragment, 'Ireland's National Poet' had written of his father, a man, as he said, of 'Milesian' fierceness:

... Me, my two brothers, and my sister, he treated habitually as a hunts-man would treat refractory hounds. It was his boast, uttered in pure glee of heart, that 'we would run into a mouse-hole' to shun him. While my mother lived, he made her miserable; he led my only sister such a life that she was obliged to leave our house; he kept up a succession of continual hostilities with my brothers; and, if he spared me more than others, it was perhaps because I displayed a greater contempt of life and everything connected with it than he thought was shown by the other members of the family. If anyone can imagine such an idea as a human boa-constrictor, without his alimentive propensities, he will be able to form some notion of the character of my father. May GOD assoil [absolve] his great and mistaken soul, and grant him eternal peace and forgiveness! But I have an inward feeling that to him I owe all my misfortunes.

My father's grand worldly fault was *improvidence.*

And so it continues. For Jim, the parallels between Mangan's 'iras-cible' parent and his own were striking. The coincidence would be remembered again in a *Finnegans Wake* sentence which yokes together the fathers of both literary Jameses in a double pun on John Stanislaus's support of the Boers and the old Joyce family business: 'Mynfadher was a boer constructor'.

After the paper was finished, Hugh Kennedy again attacked Jim, jealously defending the sublime Romantic bard from the praise of this modern infidel. A quarter of a century later John could still remember with relish the evening and his son's reaction to Kennedy:

Of course I knew Hugh Kennedy, now Chief Justice of the Free State. He was a schoolfellow of Jim's . . . I don't know much about him except his ugliness. By the Holy God he would frighten the horses off their feet. Oh yes! I saw him making a holy show of himself in the College. Jim was reading a paper on some subject – you know Jim had a great flow of language. There was a debate and Kennedy if you please took exception to something Jim said. The cool calm and calculating Jim putting his hand on the table took a note of what Kennedy said. At last Jim stood up and my God he spoke for half an hour and he left Kennedy in a condition that he was not fit to be washed.

As John was for ever reminding Jim, he might have done very well as a barrister. Stannie was no fool, but he was a patient plodder in comparison. As for Charlie, for his father he was hopeless. Always considered the ignoramus of the family, he had never been thought much of by his father and as a defence against mockery had become the family clown, a pose reinforced by a slight squint. Now fifteen, Charlie tried to keep up with his brothers, but he was lazy. Though he could be as shrewd as any of them on occasions, he tended to hide a low opinion of himself and his abilities behind a boisterously loud manner and an erratic religiosity. Yet he too was persuaded to appear in a concert (in the Queen's Theatre) and was delighted by the high praise his performance received in the newspapers.

Georgie, on the other hand, though a year younger, was 'a regular young pagan'. He already showed signs of exceptional qualities that were comparable to Jim's. Buoyant with life, he was popular with the whole family and Charlie in particular was inseparable from him, following his younger brother's lead in most things. As the last of John's sons, Georgie cheerfully occupied his position in the hierarchy as the 'cadet' and presided benevolently over the string of five younger sisters who adored him. Both his parents had high hopes for his future.

On 14 March he went down with a temperature. Enteric or

typhoid fever, spread round Dublin by infected milk, was diagnosed. Both John and May were fearful he would be carried away to the Fever Hospital and consulted a local doctor instead. During the illness the family drew closer together as they watched his sufferings – he never complained, hugging his mother when the pain became too much to bear alone. After school, Stannie, or 'Brother John' as Georgie teasingly called him for his staidness, read Robert Louis Stevenson's story 'The Bottle Imp' to his fragile but still bright-eyed brother. One of the girls later remembered that Jim played his own compositions on the piano and sang for hours, 'while our brother George was dying upstairs'. Pappie even cut down on his drinking and in the evenings entertained 'the Nipper' (as he called him) with animated readings of comic stories, such as 'Mickey Free's Father and the Ghost'. After these loving attentions, by late April Georgie seemed to be over the worst and the doctor, 'a big countrified blockhead' according to Stannie, allowed his mother to give him a little solid food. Though May disliked the man, who often seemed to be drunk when he called to see his patient, he was the only doctor they had, and her son was almost a skeleton. She tried him with some soup and a few small pieces of meat. Shortly afterwards she was horrified to discover foul matter oozing from Georgie's body. Whether or not it was a direct result of the food, he had suffered a perforated intestine. Rushing to the parlour she told Jim, who ran upstairs to try to help his brother. There was nothing he could do. Though Georgie lasted another eight agonising days, he died on Saturday, 3 May of peritonitis, surrounded by John and his family, who put pennies on his eyes. His last reported words had been: 'I am very young to die.' By then, Jim had already gone into town to put his name down for the medical school in Cecilia Street linked to the university: he would become a doctor.

Many years later, John Stanislaus was still being blamed by some of his children for Georgie's death. He should have ensured that they did not have to live in such unhealthy and cramped conditions. He should have insisted that so serious a disease be treated in hospital. He should have called in a better doctor. Above all, he should have insisted on an operation during the last week. (However, even the best Swiss medical care would also fail to save

James Joyce from the fatal consequences of peritonitis after a perforated intestine in 1941.) Stanislaus believed that his mother never recovered from the tragedy, as she blamed herself for giving Georgie the food. He also said that, in contrast, his father 'did not feel his son's death very deeply'. But Stannie, in particular, was never privy to John's deepest feelings. The Rector of Belvedere insisted on giving Georgie, a popular pupil, a rare public funeral at the College, before he went to join his brothers, John Augustine and Frederick, in the family grave. On the way home from Glasnevin the mourners stopped at the Brian Boru pub, where Jim asked his uncle William Murray for a pint of porter. His father was shocked, expostulating: 'Who taught you to drink stout?' Jim was already twenty, but stout was not a drink of which John always approved: in *Stephen Hero* only the drivers of the funeral carriages also choose Guinness, which young Stephen finds savours of 'the bitter clay of the graveyard'.

Georgie would never grow up, but Jim was rapidly doing so. He might often appear callous – during Georgie's illness he had deeply upset his mother by announcing that he was rejecting Catholicism – but the fact that he was very much affected by his brother's death would soon be seen in his writings. How his father also felt about the loss of his youngest son is suggested by the demeanour of Simon Daedalus in a reworking of Georgie's death for *Stephen Hero*:

Her father who was not quite sober walked about the room on tiptoe, cried in little fits every time his daughter showed a change and kept on saying 'That's right, duckey: take that now' whenever her mother forced her to swallow a little champagne and then nodded his head until he began to cry afresh. He kept telling everyone to keep her spirits up.

Though Jim would not take his final exams until after the summer, he finished college in June 1902. Poppie and Stannie had by now left school and were casting around for something to do. Eileen, May, Eva, Florrie and Baby were among the 900 pupils attending the Convent National School attached to St Mary's Industrial Training School and Orphanage, which was run by the Sisters of Charity in Stanhope Street, about a mile away. Charlie gave up Belvedere (early) at the end of the term and enrolled to train for the priesthood in Clonliffe Seminary. The sight of one of his Jesuit teachers weeping over Georgie's body may have convinced him, 'in his dumb sorrow and loneliness', that he had a vocation, and his mother was keen on the plan. Since he would be sleeping and eating at the College, the move was also guardedly welcomed by the others as it meant one less mouth in the house. John thought the premium he paid the priests for taking his son off his hands to be money well spent. Now, on Sundays, a soutane-clad Charlie was occasionally sighted solemnly processing to the Pro-Cathedral, breviary in hand. When one of his superiors informed his father that young Charles Joyce was 'a parti-cularly stupid boy', the priest's remark was passed on to the rest of the family, who brought it up every time their unfortunate brother was mentioned.

In September, John wrote to Carrol O'Sullivan, his friend in London's Mile End Road, about Jim's plans to become a doctor. With his reply O'Sullivan enclosed a recommendation for Jim to pass on to an influential doctor by the name of Birmingham, who might be able to help him in his intended career. However, no action was taken, and on 2 October, after his final university examinations were over, Jim began at the Cecilia Street Medical School. How the initial charges for the course were paid is a mystery, for his godfather's legacy had come to an end. Possibly John or May managed to borrow something from a friend for the purpose – it was, after all, an eminently good cause. Privately, Jim was telling friends that he intended to make a quick fortune as a doctor and then give it up and become a writer.

In the early autumn John took the radical step of buying a house. As he had no money and nothing to use as collateral, this required a certain ingenuity. He instructed David Drimmie, the insurance agent at 41 Lower O'Connell Street, to insure his life for £650 with the Eagle Star Insurance Company. From now on his pension cheque would go directly to the insurers, who, when they had removed their monthly premium from it, forwarded the balance to John through Drimmie's. Since the £650 would be paid out whenever he died, John now had something to borrow against and persuaded the same firm to lend him a lump sum of £550, the interest on which would also be taken from his monthly cheque. This money paid for the new house. At last John could feel that he and his family were immune from the threat of eviction. Although his monthly allowance would be less than before, the arrangement, planned in sobriety, meant that even if he squandered his cash, his wife and children would have somewhere permanent to live. While the decision would not bring back Georgie, it might stop them all resenting John Stanislaus for the sad accident of his death.

On 24 October 1902, therefore, John took possession of a small two-storey property, 7 St Peter's Terrace, Cabra. It was just west of the main road to Glasnevin, in another street of redbrick houses. A considerable improvement on Glengariff Parade, it had five rooms, a reasonable kitchen and a little back garden. The move did little to cheer up his grieving wife, however, and her children would often find her sitting alone, weeping over her sewing. As well as missing Georgie, May must have seen that there was a fatal flaw in her husband's scheme, for it depended on his thrift. John might believe that with nothing to pay for accommodation they were really no worse off than when he got the whole pension into his hand. However, since he had usually defaulted on the rent, there was now actually considerably less income each month and, for all his good intentions, May knew that in practice he would simply spend a higher proportion of what there was on his binges. In any case, the moment they moved in they were already hideously broke. What was the use of owning a house if everyone in it was starving? Her husband, however, ever inventive in such matters, had yet another plan. He was aware that, as a man of property once more, he could use his title deeds as security on a loan, just to tide them over until a decent job came his way. On the same day that he received the deeds he took out a mortgage for £100 from a man called Sheridan. With this he paid the agent's and solicitor's fees and, when business had been taken care of, he had enough 'gold', as he called it, for a gala night on the town.

The story of John Stanislaus Joyce's exploits that night would go the rounds in Dublin for years afterwards. He met up with friends in the Scotch House, the Ship or some such place, where he repaid them some of the casual borrowings that these days he always owed. They no doubt expressed their gratitude in the usual manner and when the time came for John to catch the last tram home he was almost paralytic. It was lucky that little Alfie Bergan and a companion, Jim Tully, spotted him staggering around O'Connell Street. It would have been luckier if the pair had not thought that John lived out towards Dollymount, beyond Fairview and Clontarf. Ignoring his incoherent protestations they shoved him on to a Clontarf tram and warned the conductor not to let him out until he got there. When John came to, he found himself stranded far from home in the middle of the night, and sat down and wept for a while on the sea wall looking out over the Bull Island. His new house in Cabra was more than a five-mile journey away – even for someone walking in a straight line. It was 'blue o'clock in the morning' when Mrs Joyce opened the door of No. 7 to her husband, who by his own account fainted into her arms. He had a blister on his foot 'as big as a pigeon's egg'. May was right: the new house would make no difference. The pattern was beginning again.

A week after the family had settled in there was a refreshing expedition for Jim's parents when, bringing Poppie with them, they went to the imposing premises of the Royal University to see him conferred with his degree. A 'Mrs McBride' (probably Maud Gonne) told the proud mother, 'Mrs Joyce, your son is the most distinguished candidate' and the proud father insisted that an official photographer take a photograph of his son. The plate survives, showing the new Bachelor of Arts with hair slicked down and parted in the middle, suitably solemn and imposing in his graduation robe with fur collar. For the ceremony Jim did not sit with his parents. In fact, he was one of the ringleaders of a near riot, orchestrating from the back of the Aula Maxima a barrage of shouting and booing that reached a crescendo during the singing of 'God Save the King'. After the police had been called Jim, emulating John Kelly, even harangued his fellow-hooligans outside from the back of a cart and demanded passionately that they should be allowed to behave as they liked on such an occasion. The Irish equivalents to *Modern Society*, the magazines *Irish Society* and *Figaro*, which routinely covered the conferring, failed to see the joke, though John Stanislaus would certainly have enjoyed his day.

Not long afterwards, on 1 December, Jim left Dublin. He had quickly given up his lectures in medicine, perhaps because of difficulties with the fees. The new idea was to restart his medical studies at the École de Médecine in Paris, where he imagined he could pay his way by teaching English. The night before he sailed, John had invited a few friends to St Peter's Terrace and May laid on a farewell supper. The occasion was a reprise of his own coming-of-age dinner. Among the guests were Patrick Hoey from the library in Charleville Mall that Jim had used since its opening a few years before, the clubbable Tom Devin and, no doubt, little Alfie Bergan. Decades later James reminisced to Bergan about such evenings, remembering 'all the pleasant nights we used to have singing', when Devin entertained them with 'O boys, keep away from the girls I say', idiosyncratic extracts from *Cavalleria Rusticana* on the piano (and often, his 'cackling hen' routine). John sent his son away with a letter of recommendation, to whom it might concern, that he had persuaded Mayor Tim Harrington to write. The letter, of which Jim would make great use, read:

> Mansion House
> Dublin.
>
> I know the bearer Mr. Joyce since his childhood, and I am also well acquainted with his family. He is a young man of excellent character and whose career as a student has been distinguished by industry and talent.
>
> He goes abroad to have an opportunity of further pursuing his studies and I look forward with very great hopes to his having the same brilliant success that he has had at home.
>
> T. C. Harrington
> Lord Mayor
>
> 29th Nov. 1902.

Harrington had recently been acclaimed by Nationalist Dublin for boycotting the celebration of the coronation of King Edward VII in the summer. His estimate of the young Joyce's abilities was undoubtedly derived from information supplied by his father – in fact, Jim's university results had been less than good. Such petty details were of little account to John Stanislaus, who, with reason, had full confidence in his son's intellectual powers.

On 18 December, John increased his mortgage by £50. He posted a little of the money to his son at the Hotel Corneille in Paris (where, as Jim's friend Con Curran would put it, the writer

Stephen McKenna would soon be living 'on what he borrowed from Synge, while Synge lived on what he got back from McKenna'). Both parents were worried by his letters from Paris: the boy seemed to be starving. John sent him a telegram asking him to come home for Christmas and an unshaven Jim arrived on Christmas Eve, staying until half-way through January. All indications are of a successful visit. The fire might not have been as banked and red as it had been during the 1880s, but there was no shortage of Christmas spirit. Jim thought Pappie 'brown and healthy and neat': in fact both his parents never looked better. At midnight on New Year's Eve Jim threw a loaf of bread in through the door of the house, a custom intended to ensure prosperity and plenty in the coming year. The family would need all the good luck it could get.

CHAPTER 20

A Loving Pair of Sons

As 1903 began, John Stanislaus could feel hopeful that his eldest son had finally been launched in the world, however uncertainly. Although the idea of a medical career for Jim seemed to be evaporating, his father was pleased that he was making some progress in the world of journalism: he was already writing reviews for the Dublin *Daily Express*. On the way back to Paris, Jim, networking hard, dropped in on various London editors, sometimes productively; he also left a note for Jimmy Tuohy of the *Freeman* in the hope that Pappie's old friend could help in some way, but there was no response. John had offered to approach Matthew O'Hara, an acquaintance of his on the *Irish Times*, to see whether the paper might take some pieces from his son, who was hoping to become its French Correspondent. But John seemed to have done nothing and no commissions had come from O'Hara either. In a letter of 8 February (written ostensibly to his mother) Jim complained that it was strange that he himself had 'been able to do more with strangers tha[n] you can do with friends'. Presumably this hurtful remark was actually directed towards his father, but May Joyce was piqued enough to chase O'Hara herself. She wrote to Matthew F. Kane, one of John's chums since Kingstown days and now in Dublin Castle as Chief Clerk in the office of Sir Patrick Coll, the Crown Solicitor, asking if Kane could intercede with the *Irish Times* journalist. This approach had more success and, after a couple of false starts, a somewhat half-hearted interview by Jim with a French racing driver appeared in the paper in April.

In January the annual Municipal Elections had taken place. The absence of any powerful enemy to the United Irish League Nationalists in the Council Chamber was leading to splits and in many constituencies the danger was that the vote might be divided and allow a Unionist, or, even worse, a socialist candidate to win the seat. Although compromise candidates were quite often agreed upon, there was usually a great deal of jockeying between the two main UIL factions, the 'Castle Catholics' or 'flunkeys' (also known as 'loyal-addressers'), who voted for the Corporation to extend official welcomes to visiting royalty from Britain, and those who advocated a less servile attitude to British rule. The roots of the division lay in the Parnellite split a decade before, but as usual both sides claimed The Chief as their inspiration.

Although the man in the street was apathetic about local elections and polls were low, feelings ran high among those involved. Intensive canvassing was needed to see off intrusive challenges to the *status quo* from both the Unionist and the anti-Unionist sides, so this year John exchanged his usual official role in the elections for a more partisan one and became election agent for one of the candidates. As incentive there were official and unofficial payments for canvassing and tactical work, and for providing good information. There were other attractive perks as well in the form of drink and gossip, and there was the prospect of more work in the future, if his candidate won.

Less than three years later, James Joyce was to write a *Dubliners* story entitled 'Ivy Day in the Committee Room'. He drew his details from four elections: the January Council elections held in 1903, 1904 and 1905, and the election in 1904 for Lord Mayor. The story took as its setting a dingy upstairs room in a commercial or solicitors' building in Wicklow Street that had been hired or borrowed as a temporary election office. The date was deliberately left ambiguous, but the electoral division was identified as the Royal Exchange Ward, a salamander-shaped area of elegant streets lying between Dublin Castle, Trinity College and Stephen's Green. South of the Liffey, this was a prosperous part of the city, full of family solicitors, gentlemen's clubs, banks, hotels and good quality shops. Here, in 1903, John worked for the Nationalist candidate, a Mr Cummins.

Cummins was typical of a relatively new breed of Dublin politician: like over a third of those who ran for office in this election, he was by profession a publican, by religion a Catholic and he was a loyal-addresser. For John Stanislaus he had the advantage of a reputation for over-generosity to voter and canvasser alike. The *United Irishman*, Arthur Griffith's anti-flunkey paper, accused Cummins just before the election of having been 'kicked out of Arranquay Ward' (where he had lost his seat in 1902) for bribing the electorate with free drink, in direct contravention of the Corrupt Practices Act of 1883. The accusation did nothing to deter John from offering Cummins his services, but he would have conceded that this publican on the make was certainly no Charles Stewart Parnell.

Cummins's opponent, one J. Cahill, might have been a Nationalist, but he was also a socialist. James Connolly, the trades union organiser (later shot as one of the signatories of the 1916 Proclamation), had for some time been struggling to establish a viable Irish Republican Socialist Party in Ireland. Although his efforts were blighted by vitriolic in-fighting and the inevitable splits, at least there were now representatives of the labour interest running for election and, very occasionally, one of them actually won a seat. (Later in the year, Jim would dabble with socialism himself, even attending a few of Connolly's party meetings.) John Stanislaus Joyce, however, never dreamed of identifying with the working man: his upbringing and the aristocratic memory of Parnell saw to that. But Parnell, like the family fortune, was a thing of the past.

Stannie acted as his father's clerk during the election and wrote to Jim in Paris about the experience. In *My Brother's Keeper* he states that John Henchy, the election agent in his brother's story, was modelled on Pappie, 'toned down to his surroundings'. Henchy is a bossy little man with an inflated sense of his own importance. His official job is to ensure that all possible voters have been doorstepped in support of 'Tricky Dicky' Tierney, a professional local politician and publican in the Cummins mould. John Stanislaus's methods may be glimpsed when Henchy tells the company how he persuaded an old Conservative, a 'regular old toff', to vote the right way. The candidate might be a Nationalist, but he is also a respectable man who pays a large amount of money to the rate-collector. Henchy says to the old Unionist:

'He has extensive house property in the city and three places of business and isn't it to his own advantage to keep down the rates? He's a prominent and respected citizen ... and a Poor Law Guardian, and he doesn't belong to any party, good, bad or indifferent.'

It would be easy to condemn John Stanislaus for deserting his old political loyalties by accepting work from the likes of Cummins, and perhaps his son was doing just that when he described the squalid amorality of the canvassers in 'Ivy Day', but in fact there were now few other jobs that John could do. He had no hope of regaining a salaried position in the Corporation, his compromised financial situation ruled out accountancy and at his age he could scarcely embark on training for an entirely new career. Besides, not only Cummins was no longer a Parnellite; practically nobody was. Parnellism was a fading nebula, a state of mind for obituarists and their safely dead subjects. John Stanislaus was still a useful election worker, with a vast knowledge of Dublin and Dubliners to draw upon, and his loquacious charm made him an excellent canvasser. All his efforts this year, however, proved to be in vain: Cahill, the labour man, beat John's Mr Cummins, who would not regain a seat on the Corporation until elected for the Glasnevin Ward in 1908. It may have been some compensation to John that Reuben J. Dodd also failed to be elected to the Wood Quay Ward and in the attempt earned a denunciation by a priest in the *Irish Times*: 'He had sought the support of Jews and Loyalists and that was quite enough to urge them [the voters] to see that he got as few votes as possible.' Even Dodd narrowly outpolled James Connolly, however, who dourly commented that the ward was 'priest-ridden'. That Mr Cummins ever again called upon John Stanislaus's services is unlikely, but there would be a good deal more temporary election work for John during the next few years. He enjoyed it, but he was quite aware that it was no way for a gentleman of principle to earn a living.

On the last day of January John conscientiously wrote a three-page letter to Paris to congratulate his eldest son on the occasion of his twenty-first birthday. Deeply affected by the family significance of the occasion, Pappie regretted his inability to settle money on the *dauphin* of the Joyces: '. . . but, circumstances alter cases, and as my cases are circumcised, I must ask you to forgive me, Jim, for the "might have been".' He continued in a paean to the values of primogeniture: '. . . Jim you are my eldest Son I have always looked up to your being a fitting representative of *our* family one that my father would be proud of. I now only hope that you may carry out *his* ideas throughout your life and if you do, you may be sure you will not do anything unbecoming a gentleman . . .' The 'might have been' was of course that whereas John had inherited £1000 at the same age, all he could pass on to his son was a cottonball patrimony of rich songs and funny stories. For James Joyce, in time, it was to be enough. In the meantime Jim had to content himself with a 'budget' of birthday cards from the family and a cigarette case from Aunt Josephine.

After the elections, John found a job of sorts in Mountjoy Square, very likely copying documents for a solicitor called James J. Henry, Assistant Town Clerk under Parnell's trusted secretary Henry Campbell (who had been rewarded with the post of Town Clerk for his services to The Chief). It was the sort of drudgery that John had once employed retired clerks to do for him. Though this work was not to last for long, it helped a little. John was still the only member of the family earning anything worth counting. Stannie had finished his schooling and now went every day to an accountant's office, where as an apprentice he was not usually being paid anything at all. Even this had been interrupted by a worrying chest infection. Charlie had lost his vocation for the priesthood and left the seminary, and his mother was seriously concerned about his state of mind. Though it sometimes seemed that his time with the priests had 'improved his demeanour', now he just hung around indoors all day, trying to learn French and muttering bitterly about his father's drinking. Probably at May's behest, John did not bully him to go out looking for work and offered instead to pay his fees if he enrolled in M'Guire's Academy, a private college that prepared its students for the Civil Service Entrance Examination. However, even this Charlie refused to do, daring his parents to throw him out of the house; if they did so he would sing in the streets for money like a tinker. Poppie was no better off than her brothers and at the age of nineteen was unable to buy herself as much as a pair of gloves. She could find neither employment nor a course of study and, as her mother told Jim in a letter at the beginning of March, was 'beginning to cry out about herself'. And though Jim might be far away he was still an expense: in the same letter May enclosed £1.12s.od from John for Jim's Paris landlady (whom he called 'Blackface'). He must have raised a sceptical eyebrow when his mother told him that not only did she and the children 'pray constantly for your spiritual and temporal welfare' but that Pappie did so as well. To his credit, Jim was worried that she had sold a carpet from the house to support him, though an earlier offer to buy her new false teeth from his first earnings was not repeated.

Though Jim was sorry to hear of the death of 'poor old Thornton' the tea-taster, Baby's godfather from North Richmond Street and like John an admirer of the voice of Sims Reeves, he told his mother that nobody who had brought up a family had entirely failed, adding pointedly, 'You understand this, I think.' But while one old friend of his father's was being buried in Dublin, Jim was getting to know another in Paris. John had given him the address of Joseph Theobald Casey, an unrepentant Fenian from the Kilkenny family related to James Stephens, one of whom, with Rickard Burke, had sent arms to Daly's drapery in Cork long before. John Stanislaus had kept in touch with another of the brothers, Patrick, since his own Fenian days in the city, but had not met Joe for many years. Unlike John, all four of them had successfully gone on to see action in the Franco-Prussian War. Of the two survivors, Pat was back in Dublin, while Joe, in Parisian exile with his family, had spent more than two decades working as a type-setter, at first on *Intransigeant* and latterly on the *New York Herald*. The old man was well known for his involvement in 1867 in the Fenian bombing of Clerkenwell Prison, part of a failed escape attempt that had cost the lives of a dozen passers-by, though he, imprisoned there at the time, had been technically acquitted of a charge of complicity in the plot. Pat was now a neighbour in Cabra.

Michael Davitt, originally a Fenian himself but currently a prime mover in the peace-loving and toothless United Irish League, once described his former comrade Joe Casey as 'a blatant "refugee" who lived in Paris with a leaning towards dynamite and absinthe'.

James had no reservations whatever about meeting such a man, viewing the ex-revolutionary as an interestingly romantic figure from his father's past. They spent St Patrick's Day together and Casey gave him a sprig of shamrock to wear in his coat (though Jim turned down the offer of a ticket to that night's Irish Ball at the Salle Hoche on the very Joycean grounds that he had nothing to wear). In *Ulysses*, Joe Casey is confusingly disguised under the name of another Paris Fenian, Kevin Egan. As he rolls his own cigarettes over a glass of 'green fairy's fang' (absinthe) in a Right Bank café, the old man talks of the past and sings 'The Boys of Kilkenny'. He is much moved to notice that the young Dubliner has inherited his father's voice. As if further to prove that he was his father's son, Jim borrowed seven francs from him on the strength of the old connection (though Joe Casey afterwards claimed it was ten).

Back in Dublin in the week before Holy Week, which in 1903 fell at the beginning of April, John's friend, the black-bearded Mat Kane, with the help of Charlie Chance and a Mr Boyd, somehow managed to cajole him to accompany them on a three-day retreat in the Jesuit Church, St Francis Xavier's in Gardiner Street. (May no longer sang there – the Pope had recently barred female singers from church choirs.) The triduum had been advertised as a 'Mission' to businessmen and attracted many of John's old comrades from Dublin's political and financial circles – a number of whom had been avoiding him since his star had begun to wane. John had not been to Sunday Mass for years, so Mat Kane must have been very persuasive; but his genuine friends were important to him and he may have sensed their concern about him. He tried to conceal his reservations behind a bluff façade of explorative curiosity and was assured that, in any case, it would not be undiluted penance: after the day's services they could all have a few drinks in Patrick Butler's of Moore Street or some other convenient snug. On the third evening, Stannie followed the small party to the church to observe the fun. He was rewarded by seeing Pappie 'fumbling shamefacedly' with the lighted devotional candle that they were expected to hold. Stannie's amusement was particularly ripe since the night before he had written down an overheard conversation between Charlie Chance, his mother and his father about the next day's activities, when John was going to see the inside of a confession box for the first time in many years. The account of this conversation survived (and Jim would draw upon it for a short story, 'Grace'), as Stannie enjoyed it enough to transfer it to his later diary:

CHANCE   Holy Communion on Sunday morning and then at half five go to renew baptismal vows. They'll give you candles – and then all together we'll –

PAPPIE (*very drunk*)   Oh, I bar the candles, I bar the candles! I'll do the other job all right, but I bar the candles.

CHANCE   Oh, that'll do all right – only a formality – but what hour'll we call for you tomorrow night to go to Confession? Matt Kane and Boyd and myself are going at half seven.

PAPPIE   Oh, I don't know, I don't know –. I'll –. Well, call at half seven then. Will that suit you?

CHANCE   Splendidly. And you'll come then?

PAPPIE   Oh yes! Oh yes! Old fellow, I'll go, never you fear, I'll go –. Can you go to whoever you like?

CHANCE   Oh yes! They've all equal power, all the same.

PAPPIE   I don't mind, you know. I don't mind, you know. I don't care. I'd go to the first felleh that's open. I haven't got much to tell him, you know. D'you think I have much to tell him?

MOTHER   I do. God forbid I had as much.

CHANCE   Oh, that's not the point.

MOTHER   Oh no! That's not the point of course.

CHANCE   It doesn't matter how much you have to tell him, it'll be all wiped off; you'll have a clean sheet.

PAPPIE   I don't mind, you know. I'd go in to the first bloody felleh that's open and have a little chat with him.

Pappie need not have worried about confessing his sins. In a precarious state of grace the next day he told his family over a celebration breakfast that according to a priest whom he has spoken to afterwards he was 'not such a bad fellow after all'. That same evening, when May stopped him taking some money she had been saving up to buy a suit for Jim, he swore at her in front of Charlie Chance and stormed out of the house in a rage.

Mrs Joyce had not been feeling well for some time, though she tried to hide the fact from her family. A week after her husband's brief flirtation with religion she fell seriously ill and John called in old Dr Bob Kenny, the late Joe's brother, to examine her. Bob Kenny was now a neighbour of the Gogartys among the élite of Rutland Square East. He was a good doctor, still respected for his battle against typhoid in the city. Though he served the North Dublin Union, which treated the poor for free, as householders the Joyces did not qualify, but it is more than likely that the Parnellite credentials that he shared with John meant that he did not charge him for visits. His report on May's condition was not optimistic and John immediately dispatched a telegram to his son in Paris. It was garbled on the way: NOTHER DYING COME HOME FATHER. Jim, alarmed and baffled by the unexpected news, borrowed the fare from Joseph Douce, a young champagne merchant who was taking English lessons from him, and set off at once for Ireland. He was met at the boat by his father, who, unusually, took his hand; Jim noticed a 'new warmth' in his voice. John Stanislaus was badly shaken: he needed all the support he could get.

Dr Kenny's diagnosis was cancer of the liver, though some of the Joyces would later think he had said cirrhosis: it may be that the latter term was used to conceal the fact that their mother was indeed dying – she was no drinker. In order to pay for her medicines and other expenses, on 24 April John took out a third mortgage (for £50) on the house, bringing his debt to Sheridan up to £200. Out of this he repaid Monsieur Douce on Jim's behalf, enclosing with the money what James later called a 'florid letter of thanks which was an expression of his Irish Francophile sentiments'. Some of the money also went to pay for a second opinion from an expert, Dr James Little, the Regius Professor of Physic in Trinity College (where he would soon be celebrated as 'Honorary Physician to His Majesty'). But Professor Little agreed that there was nothing to do but sit back and hope that Bob Kenny's treatment would work.

For the next month or two, May tried to keep cheerful, joking that the dapper Bob Kenny looked like Sir Peter Teazle from *The School for Scandal* (by another Dublin Sheridan). She even seemed to be recovering a little, but gradually it became obvious that the end was approaching. As he had for Georgie, Jim played the piano and sang for her. Aunt Josephine, deserting Uncle Willie and her children in North Strand where they now lived, spent every day with her sister-in-law, nursing her and helping Poppie to run the household. Priests and relatives came and went, and the front room of St Peter's Terrace became overrun with visitors for whom there was no significant news. John Murray, whom John still loathed, had to be let in to see his sister. There was grumbling about 'Murray vultures'. Even sympathisers barely expecting a cup of tea became a drain on the physical and moral resources of John Stanislaus and his whole unhappy brood. In these circumstances family friction rapidly escalated.

By the summer, when the rest of Dublin was following the first visit to Ireland as King of Edward VII and his Danish Queen, Alexandra, John was watching his wife deteriorate before his eyes. A white china bowl was kept permanently by the bed to hold vomited bile. She became extremely difficult, picking bitter arguments with John and the children, particularly Poppie, and once lost her temper with Aunt Josephine when she did not know who Sir Peter Teazle was. In her wracked body May's mind was confused. If Jim's fictional versions of his mother's last months are not exaggerated, and they had no need to be, she sometimes picked imaginary buttercups off the quilt and babbled in gibberish. In one of her spells of lucidity, terrified not of the death she knew was coming but of the life she was leaving, she called Poppie in and asked her to solemnly swear not to desert the children. Poppie had no choice but to acquiesce to what might be her mother's last request.

Tension in the house was rising to a peak. John, unable to stand it, drank more heavily than ever. In *My Brother's Keeper* one night is described when John came back from the pub in a state of alcoholic misery and resentment to find his wife awake, with Josephine, Jim and Stannie by her bedside. This is Stanislaus's version of how the scene continued:

He walked about the room muttering and then, coming to the foot of the bed, he blurted out:

– I'm finished. I can't do any more. If you can't get well, die. Die and be damned to you!

Forgetting everything, I shouted 'You swine!' and made a swift movement towards him. Then to my horror I saw that my mother was struggling
to get out of the bed. I hurried to her at once, while Jim led my father
out of the room.

– You mustn't do that, my mother panted. You must promise me never
to do that, you know that when he is that way he doesn't know what he
is saying.

Almost fifty years later, Eva Joyce told an interviewer that Jim had
locked John in another room upstairs, but that he had escaped
through the window. Her sister May, however, would deny that the
horrific incident actually took place at all and said that Stanislaus
had mixed it up with the occasion in Holywell Villas when John
had attacked her mother. Whatever the truth, it was a grim time
for them all.

In a coma, May Joyce died at last on 13 August 1903. She was only
forty-four. In accordance with custom, the next evening friends and
neighbours, Mat Kane and Tom Devin among them, called to the
house to express their sorrow. The visitors tiptoed one by one into
the parlour to look at Mrs Joyce in her coffin. She was wearing
the brown funeral habit of her lay order, probably that of the
Franciscans of Adam and Eve's Church on Merchant's Quay, where
her aunts the Flynns had worshipped since her girlhood. In the
next room, John Stanislaus accepted condolences and dispensed
drinks.

A dismal service in the mortuary chapel at Glasnevin was held
a few days later. Afterwards, in the downpour, the coffin containing
the earthly remains of Mary Jane Joyce was borne on a trolley along
the gravel path to the still unmarked family plot, where it was
consigned to the ground. Pappie wept, saying (as in *Ulysses*), 'I'll
soon be stretched beside her. Let Him take me whenever He likes.'
In the emotionally intense atmosphere of the special day, he made
an effort to be civil to the Murrays and was even briefly reconciled
to John Murray (though normal hostilities would soon be
resumed). Once the funeral was over, however, it was Uncle Willie
who came home with the Joyces and the brothers-in-law went out
for a stroll with Jim and Stannie in the countryside on the edge
of the city. They stopped in a convenient pub to shelter from the

weather. When Jim saw that this was likely to turn into a drinking bout he insisted that it was time for them to go home again.

That evening John was left sitting miserable and alone in the front parlour, with not even Nigger, the family dog, to comfort him. Stannie found him there and, enraged at the sight of what he took to be self-pity, savagely unleashed on his father all his carefully nurtured resentments. If John had failed to break his wife's heart, as in anger he had often threatened to do in their twenty-three years of marriage, he had broken her body by almost two decades of unnecessary poverty and the sixteen or seventeen pregnancies he had put her through. John heard his son out and when the tirade had finally come to an end said quietly, 'You don't understand, boy.' This time he knew precisely what he was saying.

The next months were harrowing ones for John and his family. In the little terrace house in Cabra there were now living ten souls: John, Jim, Poppie, Stannie, Charlie, Eileen, May, Eva, Florrie and Baby. John was fifty-four, Jim twenty-one, Poppie nineteen and Baby nine. Poppie did her best to keep things going domestically, but it was almost too much for her. She had a terrible job squeezing anything out of her father to feed them all. Everything was different now and the veneer of domestic civilisation once maintained by her mother and more recently by the saintly but down-to-earth Aunt Josephine quickly wore away.

During this period the pace and confidence of Jim's prose writing began to increase. He had already written parts of what would become the unfinished thousand-page manuscript of *Stephen Hero* (which finally became the *Portrait*). He may have begun it as early as his second trip with his father to Mullingar: his sister May remembered hiding under the sofa in St Peter's Terrace in 1902 to listen to him reading chapters of it to their mother. Further sections of the novel and the earliest *Dubliners* stories were now being written. Stannie too had been writing up his diary for at least the past two years. After his brother's death he would claim that this inspired Jim's first autobiographical fiction. (He would also say that he had suggested the title of Jim's autobiographical essay, 'Portrait of the Artist', which was written around now, and that he had chosen the names of both *Chamber Music* and *Stephen*

Hero as well.) Jim always read Stannie's 'Bile Beans', as he mockingly named the journal, and always dismissed it with a laugh or a sneer, but it may indeed have prompted Jim to realise that his subject was all around him and that he, and his father, were part of it.

The room where May Joyce had died was soon back in use and her meagre legacy of personal effects cleared away. Stephen, in *Ulysses*, recalls finding his mother's 'secrets' after her death: 'old featherfans, tasselled dancecards, powdered with musk, a gaud of amber beads in her locked drawer'. Jim found another secret in the drawer, a bundle of letters written to her by his father, which had been kept safe since before their marriage – John may not even have been aware of their survival. Jim took them into the patch of garden at the back of No. 7 and settled himself down to read. As the family anatomist, he hoped for another view of his father's life and times in the heroic days he had heard so much about and for a glimpse of the beginnings of his parents' attraction to each other.

After he had finished the letters, Jim told Stannie that there was 'nothing' in them, an odd remark given the significance he would draw as a writer from many other far less promising details of family life. However, Leopold Bloom's son, Rudy, conceived out of wedlock and dead within a few days of his birth, may owe his existence to certain discoveries made in the garden that afternoon. What these discoveries might have been remains a question: it is just possible that it was only now that Jim realised that he was not the first-born; he may also have learned whether or not his mother had been pregnant when she married his father. As far as can be established, James Joyce never openly mentioned either the letters or John Augustine Joyce to anyone, not even, when the time came, to his authorised biographer. Bloom's early love letters to Molly are, however, an important motif in the texture of *Ulysses*.

Stannie could guess what was in Pappie's love letters: exaggerations, braggadocio, Byronic posturings, warm effrontery and unfulfilled promises. He later wrote that he had taken the bundle from Jim and burnt it unread. He may have done: indifference is one weapon of the vindictive. How his father might have reacted to this is unknown, but probably nobody felt it necessary or prudent to inform him of such a gross desecration of his private past. As far as Stannie was concerned, John's various acts of omission and commission over the years meant that he had forfeited the right to be consulted about anything.

If Stannie scorned to read the bundle, it was not for lack of interest in his father. Less than two months after his mother's death he began a new diary, the first having been deliberately destroyed at the same time as John Stanislaus's love letters. In this, he minutely examined his own responses to both his parents, their characters and habits. It has been published as *The Complete Dublin Diary of Stanislaus Joyce*, a book that, though it is full of useful insights on the family, is neither entirely accurate nor quite complete. The text is from a later copy of the diary, the copying process having allowed portions of the original to be adjusted or suppressed. Furthermore, even this later version has had pages removed in three places, whose context in each case suggests that they were once discussions of John Stanislaus. It remains a puzzle what Stannie wished to censor from the cold eye of posterity – especially given the scabrous nature of the material that he did not censor. However, what survives is enlightening. Stanislaus chronicled how his father coped during the first gloomy weeks after the bereavement. Sometimes, when under the influence, Pappie was 'domineering and quarrelsome', with 'that low, voluble abusiveness characteristic of the Cork people when drunk'. When there was no money he would stay at home in the evenings, sitting with a newspaper in the comfortable chair and chatting to whoever was in the room, or doing desultory work on financial matters or electoral lists. At these times his conversation could be 'reminiscent and humorous, ridiculing without malice, accepting peace as an item of comfort'. Stannie himself rarely spoke to him, but even when they said nothing it was obvious that his children formed an opposition, particularly Stannie and Poppie. At bedtime, as he collected together his paperwork, his mood would blacken and he would start 'complaining and promising changes over which he [had] no control'. He repeatedly told his children that he did not have long to live himself: his death would leave them all where Jesus left the Jews. For all his intemperacy while she lay dying, John knew that he had needed his wife to survive and many years later would still recall the day of her passing with extreme grief. At first, Baby was frantic with misery, rendering the house uninhabitable with her screams when she was not slinking into corners to sob. Though she was Pappie's favourite daughter, he was powerless to stem the tide of tears, but James sat with her on the stairs and told her that her mother was in heaven, 'far happier now than she has ever been on earth'. When she saw Baby crying she would be made unhappy again. After this sorry statement had finally succeeded in bringing some calm to the Joyce household, her father could sit her on his knee as he liked to do and gently caress her, bringing a degree of comfort to them both.

That a disembodied May Joyce might be observing the inmates of 7 St Peter's Terrace was believed by more of the family than Baby. One night, with Jim for company, Poppie kept a midnight watch for her dead mother at the top of the stairs, hoping for some sign. She was not disappointed. Some sixty years later, as a nun in a New Zealand convent, she recalled the occasion clearly. Suddenly, her mother had appeared, standing silently at the bedroom door in her brown shroud. Stephen Dedalus has a recurrent dream that owes its origin to this episode: 'In a dream, silently she had come to him, her wasted body within its loose graveclothes giving off an odour of wax and rosewood, her breath, bent over him with mute secret words, a faint odour of wetted ashes.'

The vigil with Poppie led Jim to look into *Human Personality and its Survival of Bodily Death* by Frederic W. H. Myers (Longmans, 1903), which appeared in the National Library in October. The book was an attempt to apply scientific criteria to a subject that is usually dogged by imprecision. Myers's book is a long one and Jim could scarcely have read in the library the whole of both volumes. Chapter Seven, however, entitled 'Phantasms of the Dead', contains reports of post-mortem phenomena, including an account of a ghost seen by one of the Lissadell Gore-Booths, W. B. Yeats's friends in Sligo. Jim may have noticed a case in which an Archdeacon Farler tells of seeing 'the dripping figure of a friend who, as it turned out, had been drowned during the previous day'. (The dripping figure of Mat Kane, who was to drown in Dublin Bay after a stroke less than nine months later, reappears in *Ulysses*.) Though nothing in Myers's book discussed shrouded mothers appearing to their children, there was a graph near the beginning of Volume Two showing that virtually all apparitions cease a year after death. About a year afterwards Jim mentioned in a letter that his dreams were still being visited by 'the skull'.

While her brother was consulting a book about the apparition, Poppie was consulting a priest. She was told that the figure she had seen in the doorway could indeed be her mother. The grounds upon which this clerical judgement was based were shaky: as she related later, everyone knew that Jesus Christ after his death had appeared to many and nobody had ever said that it could not happen again. This uneasy blend of Christology and the preternatural stifled her anxieties.

Stannie grudgingly admitted to his diary that he could not 'regard Mother & Pappie as ill-matched, for with Pappie Mother had more than mere Christian patience, seeing in him what only lately and with great difficulty I have seen in him'. Attraction and affection had flowed both ways – John had appreciated May's rich sense of the ridiculous, and her ability to mimic their friends had been a good complement to his more cynical and verbal wit. It was easy to forget all the fun when in the last months of her life she had been little more than an object of pity, but the whole family missed her earlier energy, gentleness and humour. Not the least bereft was her widower.

John's quiet days spent at home began to grow rarer, however. He usually found a way to get drunk when he really needed to and his offerings to Poppie of money for food became more and more erratic. Both Jim and Stannie helped out when they could, Stannie on the rare occasions his office paid him and Jim from what he earned from the book reviews he was still doing for the conservative Dublin *Daily Express*. Although these subventions were intended to ease Poppie's difficulties, in practice they made things worse, for when her father found out about them he kept more for himself to spend on whiskey, with predictable results. Or so Stannie would have it.

Jim too had now begun drinking heavily, usually on an empty stomach. He spent evenings in the Bodega on the corner of Trinity Street which served the evocative tipple, sack (the drink of Hal in search of his father in Shakespeare's *Henry IV*). Stannie describes him at this time arriving home 'glossy-eyed and slobbery-mouthed'. Charlie had found an agreeable job with a bibulous wine merchant in need of a drinking companion and when he too began staggering into the house with a skinful, there were ludicrous scenes in which drunken father berated drunken sons for drunkenness. The effects of these episodes on Eva, Florrie and Baby can only be imagined. The Joyces were falling apart.

A further factor in the sorry tale of the Joyce family finances was that by now John again evidently owed a good deal of money to several different creditors, money borrowed on the sympathy generated by his wife's illness and death. There had been several exceptional expenses recently, including the cost of the funeral itself, and John probably even paid the priests to say Masses for the repose of his wife's troubled soul, as he knew she would have wished. As her death receded into the past, these creditors began to put John under increased pressure to repay them. On 4 November 1903 he again approached the accommodating Sheridan and took out another mortgage, this time for £150, to be repaid with ten per cent interest by April 1904, less than six months later. This was his last chance to speculate on the security of the family house, but if he hoped for a bonanza it failed to materialise and he may even have lost – or simply spent – the lot.

The other members of the family were in difficulties too. Charlie might have enjoyed aspects of his duties with the wine merchant, but by Christmas he had left, no doubt (being Charlie) under a cloud. Following Jim's lead, he had already taken to whoring and now was even writing poetry as well – his brothers were convulsed by a verse that began: 'Her milky breast, so full of woe, / Doth rise beneath a fall of lace' and ended: 'I took down her drawers'. (The subject of the poem was either a prostitute – he spent three nights in a row in bed with one in Tyrone Street at about this time – or a girl to whom he was briefly engaged.) Then he landed a job as a touring actor and singer. Unfortunately, Stannie imagined that the rackety life of a 'fit-up' actor would lead to even worse behaviour and visited his prospective employer to warn him about his younger brother's unreliability, scotching his career opportunity for good. From now on, Charlie would live from hand to mouth, like his father spending any money he had. Much of it would go on drink. The following May, the 'spoiled priest' was sent to jail, presumably for some refinement of the usual 'drunk and disorderly' charge. Four days elapsed before anyone was found who was willing (or able) to get him out by paying the optional fine.

Stannie had also left his job by New Year 1904. The exploitative drudgery of his apprenticeship in the accountant's office, whatever his future prospects might be there, had become too much to bear. He went to work for a couple of unremunerative months at the Apothecaries' Hall in Mary Street, becoming entirely un-employed in February. It gave him all the more time to observe his father.

Jim was not making much progress either. In September 1903, he had turned down an offer to give lectures in French at his old College (though he would give a few French lessons elsewhere). Soon afterwards he was pronounced 'quite unsuitable' when he applied to Professor Dowden for a library job, probably at Trinity. (In return, Dowden – once described as the sort of *littérateur* who would write a life of Southey – would be ridiculed in *Ulysses*.) He attended a few law lectures, which must have given John a ray of hope, but soon gave them up and very briefly thought yet again about a medical career. The twenty-third of his *Express* book reviews appeared in November and, after an argument with the editor, proved to be the last. Then Jim again took after his father with a series of highly grandiose money-making schemes. He would issue shares in himself that could be realised when he had become a successful writer. He could find no investors. He would start a newspaper with his high-minded friend, Frank Skeffington. It would be called *The Goblin* and would sweep the country with its new 'continental' viewpoint. He could find no backers. He actually was appointed to the post of Assistant Editor of the *Irish Beekeeper*, but the job lasted only one glorious afternoon, apiculture's loss being literature's gain.

Apart from the remnants of John's pension, all sources of family funding had evaporated by December. The only good news was that Poppie, working on her own initiative, had managed to per-suade the Sisters of Charity of the St Vincent Female Orphanage Day School in North William Street (off Summerhill) to take in

Florrie and Baby, and perhaps Eva as well. Jim met one of W. B. Yeats's sisters at a performance of *Broken Soil* by Padraic Colum in the Molesworth Hall. She noted his 'tennis shoes' and marvelled how the young man had nonchalantly told her that 'he thought drink would soon end his father and then he would give his six little sisters to Archbishop Walsh to make nuns of'. When Christmas came, John Stanislaus had not died, but the grim contrast with the celebrations of the previous year, before anyone even suspected that there was anything wrong with his Maime, as he called her in moments of grief, made him wish that he had followed her to the grave already. And Jim and Stannie, who then had seemed to be heading towards careers, had both given up. A loving pair of sons, in John's ironic opinion. Not to mention Charlie. Something definite would have to be done.

CHAPTER 21

Shite and Onions

What John Stanislaus did was to submerge himself in drink. On 2 February 1904, it was Jim's twenty-second birthday. He had been alone and hungry in Paris for his twenty-first, so Poppie marked this occasion with not one but two decent meals in the 'bare parlour'. That evening the weather was wet and after tea they stayed indoors, sitting around the kitchen table over cards. While Charlie and Jim puffed on cigarettes and Stannie idly invented silly nicknames for the entirely recognisable characters in Jim's continuing novel, their father (whom Stannie had dubbed 'Sighing Simon') was out; when he returned later, sodden with rain and whiskey, he lurched off to bed without even pausing to greet or growl. Jim's suggestion that he should ask him down again to join them was vetoed by popular acclaim, and so John Stanislaus was left alone to serenade his eldest son's birthday in sighs and inebriated snores.

The mortgage had to be paid back in April and, if Stannie's descriptions are accurate, by March John's equilibrium had almost completely deserted him. Andrew Kettle, veteran of the Kilmainham 'Treaty', dropped in to see him, perhaps answering a call for help in extricating his old political ally from financial ruin, but John was out and nothing came of it. He left reminding them to say that 'Mr Kettle called. You know, what you boil the water in.' Poppie replied that they had to boil water in the teapot. They had no kettle. But there were not very many jokes being made these days in St Peter's Terrace. When Pappie was drunk, as he now usually was in the evenings, he would shout at the children. Charlie was a particular butt: 'Where are you going, Ch-a-a-arlie? Down to the Murrays I hope ... Going to sponge on them for porter, eh?

Sucking porter, that's all you're good for. You seem to be very fond of them. Ye'll get out of this, ye bloody waster of hell. Ye can go and stay with the Murrays, then. Ye can go and sponge on them as your brother did . . .' He called them bitches or bastards regardless of sex and picked on their weak points one by one: 'Curse your bloody blatant soul,' or 'Ye dirty pissabed, ye bloody-looking crooked-eyed son of a bitch. Ye dirty bloody corner-boy, you've a mouth like a bloody nigger,' he might bellow at the boys, and at the girls: 'Ye black-looking mulatto. You were black the day you were born, ye bitch. Ye bloody, gummy toothless bitch. I'll get ye a set of teeth, won't I'. (Except for their father, who had none at all, the whole family suffered from rotten teeth, which Stannie ('Jim's jackal', a 'bloody-looking Yahoo of hell') blamed on their insufficient and irregular diet. There were no visits to the dentist.) Only Jim escaped the worst of the abuse – though not his father's torrent of complaints.

Stannie loathed hearing the voice John used in these scabrous philippics: the 'balking little rat', as he called his father, haranguing his silent family, in 'that deep, open-vowelled, rasping, blatant voice, listening to which, I at least understand hate'. But it was not only his words. Sometimes John would fling objects across the room at his daughters – cups, plates, even pokers and frying pans. One day Stannie forcibly managed to stop him striking them with his fists. The younger girls in particular were terrified: Eva and Florrie would never get over the traumas inflicted on them now. But John could still be affectionate to Baby, whom her mother had called 'the peacemaker in troubled times'. Observing this, Stannie remarked to his diary: 'Pappie cannot have been a bad lover when he was newly married for I notice that his manner of fondling Baby, for instance, is very playful and endearing.' Beside this entry, either Stannie himself or Jim has written the word 'Fudge!' and immediately before it is one of the diary's 'missing' pages. The silence is eloquent, and enigmatic.

The girls now implored their brothers not to leave them alone in the evenings with their Pappie. Jim, Stannie and Charlie decided to police the house, Stannie taking on, he said, the lion's share of the surveillance work. The outcome of these efforts is unknown – at this point in the diary another page has been removed. John might now have been deprived of a physical outlet for his frustration by his vigilante sons, but he stepped up his verbal abuse instead, threatening: 'I'll break your hearts, but I'll break your stomachs first.' He was not bluffing: one night after the pubs had shut he returned foodless and penniless to a house full of children who had been hungry since breakfast, waiting for him.

Stannie admitted that his descriptions of family life were sometimes 'coloured too highly, like a penny cartoon', but despite this, his account remains a convincing picture of the pain Pappie was causing to those around him. Jim's portrayal of his father as Simon Dedalus is normally sympathetic by comparison. However, towards the end of 1903 he had written a short and damning poem about his father. It was called 'Cabra', after the area around 7 St Peter's Terrace. 'Cabra' has been described as summing up Joyce's feelings about the death of his mother, but it does nothing of the sort. It is about his father. Like most of Joyce's verse at this time, it appears to be quite simple. The first two verses describe a herdsman driving his cattle gently, almost affectionately, through Dublin, 'calling to them in a voice they know'. The third and final verse addresses the herdsman, telling him to sleep safe and well tonight at home, while his charges themselves are sleeping.

Around the corner from St Peter's Terrace ran the 'straight red road' of the poem, the red-brick North Circular Road, then the main route for bringing cattle through North Dublin. The animals in the poem are following the 'wintry sun' (towards the south-west) and so will soon reach the junction with Prussia Street and the Dublin Cattle Market on Prussia Street, with the abattoir opposite. These cattle 'know' the drover's voice, so he cannot have just bought them. He must therefore be driving them to slaughter, or to sale and slaughter. The herd may sleep the deepest sleep of all tonight. The key that opens up the poem, however, is not topographical. Urban cattle-droving was dangerous, dirty and brutal. The warning cry of 'Mad Cow!' was common in the Dublin streets – Bloom hears of an incident involving one in Prussia Street, and there is another, 'at Cabra', in *Stephen Hero*. The barbarity of the practice had aroused much comment in the public prints: the *Irish Society and Social Review*, for example, had spoken out the previous autumn:

These creatures are not mad at all: they are goaded to temporary frenzy by terror and ill-treatment. They are taken off the grass to which they are accustomed, and transported from quiet, noiseless, country fields to harsh roadways, slippery pavements, stony thoroughfares, and the lurid turmoil of a city – with the added terror of men and boys shouting angrily behind them, and beating them cruelly with sticks. Can you, or can I, buy a bit of meat in any victualler's shop, even the best class, that is not defaced with purple stains, and congested bloodmarks and bruises? . . .

This, not the poem's version, was the reality. It was also the reality of the herdsman of the Joyce children as he drove them 'along the straight red road', the road of life, of blood, of heredity. 'Cabra' is consistent with Joyce's early fiction, where realism coexists on equal terms with symbolism. Its contented animals and gentle herdsman are ironic, a pastoral fantasy. It is hardly surprising that the verses have so consistently been misinterpreted, since they are incomprehensible to anyone ignorant of the Irish beef trade at the turn of the century. Joyce himself later realised this and, when he had an international audience, he rewrote 'Cabra' under a new title, putting in classical allusions and giving it an entirely new significance. But the first version, an ironically inverted allegory, was his coded indictment of his father. The poem ends with the herdsman and his cattle-children at home, 'and the door made fast'. There was no escape for any of them, except in sleep – or death.

On April Fool's Day the notice appeared in the *Freeman* that Valentine Blake Dillon had died at his Leeson Park home at the age of fifty-seven. Another great raconteur gone. He was put to rest at Glasnevin at the beginning of April. John Stanislaus Joyce spruced himself up as best he could and turned out to honour the ex-Lord Mayor of great ability and great bulk, whose path had crossed and recrossed his own since the old days. He had been a considerable public figure, so the usual array of associates 'from all walks of life', as the papers said, turned up too. Between friends and time-servers, it was a large funeral of the old style. Val Dillon had been election agent for several of the triumphant Liberal candidates in the 1880s and solicitor and advisor to The Chief himself during the Parnell Commission's inquiry into the vindictive and unfounded allegations in *The Times*. If he had been forced to compromise a little to further his political career in post-Parnellite Dublin, most people had and, for John Stanislaus, Val had been another man who knew what Parnellism meant. And he was always impressive. The *Freeman* wrote: 'He was a man of splendid physique, great courage, and in case of a police raid or baton charge, he would move to the front of the crowd to remonstrate with the officer in charge, and put rioters and others aside as if they were children.' The big man's death brought back to John the lost triumphs and hopes of those exciting days, and the long evenings at his cousin Mat Dillon's, where Val was a considerable presence. Another link with May was broken. Let it end. Shite and onions.

Just what happened when in April the £165 that John owed became due has not yet been uncovered. On Wednesday, 27 April he attended the Four Courts as a defendant, but the case was postponed. Between 29 April and 13 May the *Freeman's Journal* reported that a Mr Joyce was scheduled to appear several times before Hon. Mr Justice Walter Boyd in a King's Bench Division bankruptcy suit, 'Joyce, motion M'Gonigall & Kelly' – the judge perhaps the uncharitable 'Touch me not' Boyd of *Ulysses*. Whether this case had to do with the Sheridan loan or not, John, however, somehow contrived to hold on to the house for the time being. But in the process he sold the family piano and a furious Jim (now planning a musical career) repudiated his father by abandoning Cabra entirely for an upstairs room in Shelbourne Road. (He rented it largely on borrowed money, supporting himself with an unsatisfactory and temporary teaching job in a Dalkey school. His friend Con Curran would eventually hire a piano for him.) Normal relations between father and son completely broke down. Before leaving St Peter's Terrace, Jim had given up even arguing with him: when Pappie vilified Aunt Josephine for the crime of being a Murray, Jim calmly flicked crumbs of food in the faces of the ancestors ranged disapprovingly around the walls, sacrosanct still. In conversation with friends, Jim now caustically referred to his father as 'that little whore up in Cabra'. Significantly, John does not seem to have turned up to watch him narrowly fail to win the gold medal for tenor solo singing in the Feis Competition on 16 May, certainly the sort of occasion he would not usually have missed. No doubt his friends congratulated him when they saw the *Freeman* the next morning: 'Mr Joyce showed himself possessed of the finest quality voice of any of those competing, but lost considerably in marks owing to not attempting the piece at sight.' What had those expensive piano lessons in Clongowes been for?

Though Stannie saw his elder brother occasionally, usually at the Murrays' house (4 Northbrook Villas, North Strand Road), John may not have spoken again to James until they met on 13 July for the funeral held after Mat Kane's body had been recovered from the sea at Kingstown. Charlie was there too (though not Stannie, who disliked most of his father's friends) and they met Alfred Hunter, the man who lit the first spark of *Ulysses* in James Joyce's mind. A large crowd was at St Michael's Church in Kingstown and John Stanislaus must have known nearly everyone. Of the old gang there were Captain Cunniam with his son Thomas Cunniam Jr, Alfie Bergan, Daniel Hishon, John Wyse Power, Tom Devin and Charlie Chance, Henry Campbell, 'Long' John Clancy, John Henry Menton, old Patrick Cotter, the solicitors Thomas Clegg and Roger Greene, Patrick Butler of the pub in Moore Street and many others. Collectively, these men were the material from which John's son would eventually fashion a world in the pages of the novel. After the service, the Joyces' cab joined the long cavalcade of vehicles which drove north across the city to Glasnevin, following much of the route taken in the novel for the burial of Paddy Dignam.

Although in the atmosphere of the funeral, relations had to remain civil, there was still no reconciliation between John and James. Towards the end of the month, though Charlie had been admitted to Whitworth Hospital with suspected pulmonary tuberculosis, his father had a three-day binge on the strength of the monthly pension cheque from Drimmie's. Stannie had to listen to him fulminating about kicking Jim's arse: 'O yes! Kick him, by God! Break his arse with a kick, break his bloody arse with three kicks! O yes! Just three kicks! . . .' The house was emptier than it had been for years. Wisely, Eileen had got out for the summer, staying with her great-aunt Ellen Callanan at 41 Aughrim Street, where the Flynns had gone after the break-up of their home on

Usher's Island. Mrs Callanan had not long to live and would die ('of stupidity,' said Jim) on 4 December. At the beginning of September Eileen went into Mountjoy Convent (technically St Joseph's Female Orphanage run by the Sisters of Charity, 60–1 Mountjoy Street), joining her sister May who had already been boarding there for some time. Then, a month later, after a short stay with Oliver Gogarty in the Martello Tower in Sandycove and a few days with the Murrays, Jim suddenly went back 'permanently' to St Peter's Terrace. He had important matters to discuss with his father.

John found Jim much more sympathetic than he had been lately: he seemed to have forgotten their differences. Over the next few days they spent a good deal of time talking man to man. It was something that young Jack Joyce had never quite achieved with his own father, who had died when they were both too young. It seemed that an agency in Lincolnshire had found Jim a job, teaching English in Switzerland. It might not be much, but it was a start. The only problem was that he needed money to get there. He had asked almost everyone he knew to help and had raised a little, but still there was not going to be enough. He did not know what to do. If Pappie could help him on to the first rung of the ladder, who could say how high he might not climb? It would be a contribution to an eldest son's rite of passage, a paternal duty performed and a token of the bond between them. John Stanislaus promised to do his best and a few days later handed Jim the considerable sum of £7. One small matter was not mentioned at all. Jim was bringing Nora Barnacle, his mistress, with him. The fare for two to Zürich was £7.10s.0d.

Seeing off the emigrant son was a ritual of Irish life: his years by the River Lee in Cork had taught John that. On the evening of 8 October 1904 he made his way down to the North Wall. Jim was leaving the country. The ferry was meeting the boat-train to London at Holyhead in the early hours of the morning. Stephen in the *Portrait* would remark that the shortest way to Tara, the ancient seat of the Irish high kings, was via Holyhead. But James Joyce was turning his back on Tara and all it symbolised, and setting his awkward face towards Europe and the world. His father wished him well.

The expedition was rather less romantic than young Jack's had been all those years before, off hunting Prussians. Whatever he might say, Jim was not going into exile: he was off to seek his fortune. John had a great deal of faith in his son. The lad obviously had brains to burn. It was only a matter of time before he 'struck oil', as John put it. And then he would not forget his old father. After all, there were all those years at expensive schools and at the university, when he might have been making a bit of money to help out the family like any normal son. Anyway, when he got his job, he would have no other claims on his wallet. He might even make a little spare cash from his endless scribbling.

With its double row of portholes high over the river, the ship could be made out through the doors of the sheds leading to the embarkation point. A stream of travellers heaved leather-strapped luggage past the iron barrier and struggled up the gangway. Among them were a good number of English soldiers, off home from their benighted Irish garrisons. Forces of the Crown, intent on England, home and beauty. On the other side of the platform, trains from Amiens Street pulled in with their passengers, and renewed rounds of lamentation and leave-taking began. Aunt Josephine, Stannie and the others had also come down to see Jim off, but it was his father to whom this moment belonged, and he dominated the conversation. Jim was his eldest and closest son, and it was only right that the proper ceremonies be observed.

Some time before the boat sailed, Jim cut short the advice and paternal pieties, said goodbye and hurried on board. He had, he said, enough money in his pocket to last him as far as Paris, where he would have to borrow more. Stannie, who like everyone there except John, knew Jim's secret, could relish the dramatic irony of his brother's departure: Nora had crept up the gangway some time before the ferry slipped its moorings. At nine o'clock, with a long blast on its whistle, the steamer edged out into the Liffey, to steer between the 'therrble prongs' of Dublin Bay, and John Stanislaus wept. He had again lost his son and heir.

Tom Devin happened to be on the ferry that evening. He joined the couple on board and, always a ladies' man, got on well with Nora, a handsome and intelligent country girl from Galway, with a convent education, a winning turn of phrase and a proud demeanour, who took no nonsense from her lover. She would have told him how she had left home in the west of Ireland and come to Dublin to better herself. She had been working in Finn's Hotel behind Trinity to make ends meet when she met Jim the June before. Jim no doubt asked Devin to say nothing about her to his father. The couple were right to trust him: Tom Devin would remain a good (if sea-divided) friend to both of them for many years. But the elopement was hot news in Dublin and it probably reached John's ears sooner rather than later. When it did, Jim's treachery came as a terrible shock. Jim with a common slavey from the back of beyond! He was dragging the family down. John knew that in a city so full of whispers he would not be able to go into a pub without hearing remarks. They would be making up limericks about it. It was not just that he had gone off to live in sin with some chambermaid out of a fleapit of a hotel; what really hurt was that all Jim's recent so-called interest in his father's opinions was no more than a ruse to extract cash out of him. He had been conned out of the money, which he could well have done with, and it was paying the shameless hussy's fare. It was all 'very nice'. John Stanislaus knew that he had been betrayed once again – but this time by his own son. It would be a long time before he would be able to forget what James had done to him.

Two or three days later, John was penniless and desperate. He called on Hugh Temple, who sold groceries and drink in 'The Hut' off Phibsborough Road, and borrowed two pounds. It was for a good cause. With the money in his pocket, he settled himself in a pub and proceeded to stand rounds for his friends. Among the thirsty company was old Patrick Casey, to whom Jim had brought greetings from his brother Joseph in Paris the year before. These days, Pat Casey, who lived in Cabra Park, had nothing to do except attend meetings of the Fenian Old Guard Benevolent Union and regale them with stirring tales of the past. John was always happy to exchange reminiscences with him and tell his stories, but now, after drink had been taken, the pain of the past few days was too much. Though he may not have mentioned the scandal, he subjected Pat Casey and the others to a pitiable performance.

An hour or two later, waiting outside the pub for his father, Stannie was trapped by Mr Casey, emerging full of whiskey and mawkish solicitude. Grasping his hand, in a thick Kilkenny accent the old man told him that his father loved him, loved all of them. As second son, it was now Stannie's responsibility to look after him. He was never to desert him. Stannie agreed that his father had been through many hardships and, to get Mr Casey to go away, promised to do as he said. He had no intention whatever of taking care of John: as he told his diary, 'I do not like being near Pappie and when I ask myself why, I cannot pretend to like him.' Why should he? After all, there was no sign that Pappie cared whether Stannie lived or died, whatever he might tell people in pubs.

Some little time elapsed before Jim contacted his father. The promised job in Zürich did not exist. He had then tried Trieste, where another imaginary teaching post beckoned. There, though he did not tell his father this, consoling himself in the drunken company of three English sailors, he contrived to get himself temporarily arrested. Finally the couple had taken a boat to Pola, a port on the Istrian peninsula (now in Croatia). The city was then an obscure Adriatic backwater of the Habsburg Empire (though Jim must have been pleased by its associations with Dante's *Inferno*). From here, at the end of October he sent home an Italian advertisement from the local newspaper in which the imperial and royal employees and officers at the Berlitz School were grandly informed that 'yesterday evening the second teacher of English [had] arrived, JAMES A. JOYCE B.A., Bachelor of Arts Mod. Lit.'. John had only a smattering of Italian, practised now only on any organ-grinders or their monkeys that he might meet. But there was no denying that his son's name was printed there in large and heavy type for all to see. Though Jim might have landed on his feet, Pappie did not write to congratulate him.

On 10 November, Jim wrote directly to his father for the first time since leaving Ireland. He first warned that he would expect John to repay sixty francs he had borrowed from a Dr Rivière on his way through Paris. If that didn't elicit an answer, perhaps the rest of his chatty letter might. Jim wrote it to impress: Pola was a good place to be, an important Austrian naval station, with a dozen men-o'-war in the harbour. The few English in the city were all 'lions' – which, by implication, Jim himself soon would be. Most of his pupils came from the officer class. (One of them would later become the Hungarian head of state, Admiral Horthy.) Another much larger advertisement had appeared in the paper, hailing the new teacher as '*dottore in filosofa*', though he did not enclose it. One of his poems had been printed in the *Speaker* (following the unacknowledged intervention of W. B. Yeats) and there would be more to come. And he could get Stannie a job in a Berlitz school if he wanted one. (Pat Casey would have had something to say about that idea.)

Nowhere in Jim's letter was there the least hint of Nora's existence. He wrote as if entirely alone, using the word 'I' nineteen times in twenty-two sentences. The tension between father and son was acknowledged by being ignored. If the news of Nora had leaked out, he wanted Pappie to believe that he was unaware of the fact, thus placing the responsibility for any rift between them firmly on his father's shoulders. John may have derived some grim amusement from Jim's complaint that he was being pestered all night by mosquitoes. Perhaps Jim's woman would be just a fly-by-night too. There was a PS: 'A letter will be read with pleasure.' There would be no letter.

'Stannie-in-honours', as the others used to call him for his seriousness, had undergone a change in status at home. He was now Jim's main contact and agent in Dublin. (Of Jim's friends, Curran was busy, Skeffington was regarded by Joyce as untrustworthy and Gogarty was an enemy.) He had a good – and usually justified – opinion of his own analytic abilities, but this was undermined by a distrust of his emotions. His calm, remote, blockish exterior was ideal for concealment: one thing it hid was his uncertainty about whether any of his feelings were genuine. In fact, when Jim left, Stannie's world had fallen apart. At the same time pressure from his father had increased. He was now the eldest male child in the house but there was to be no meeting of minds. Father and second son still spoke to each other as little as possible. From the others there was not much companionship for Pappie to be had either: Charlie, though he seemed to have recovered from his illness, was still erratic, sullen and shiftless, and often as drunk as his father wanted to be; Poppie remained unwillingly in charge at home, broke and frustrated; the other girls still in the house lived in fear as their mother's memory grew more distant. Life was not good for anyone in 7 St Peter's Terrace.

In Stanislaus's dogged chronicle of life with his father there is a 'Bile Bean' that is more eloquent about tensions at home than most of his usual gloomy *aperçus*: 'Listening in silence to another eating is most unpleasant.' Gone were the days when they all sat around the dinner-table listening to Pappie's rumbustiously performed stories, with everyone taking sides in the discussions. Now there was never much dinner. As Stannie complained in December 1904, they had been living on 'practically starvation rations' for a year. Often the only meal of the day was breakfast and that 'very small'. As John Stanislaus glared down in his shirt-sleeves upon the motherless remnants of his family around the untidy table, it was clear to all of them, himself included, that he had failed, that it was over and that the future lay with Jim. Stanislaus was, for once, in agreement with his father.

'The Holy Office', Joyce's venomous broadside against the 'mumming company' of Yeats and his pack of literary revivalists, had been printed in Dublin at the end of August 1904 for Stannie to disseminate immediately after Jim's departure. To pay most of the printing costs Jim had earmarked five shillings that were coming from the *Speaker* for a poem. Unfortunately, the cheque had already reached St Peter's Terrace, where it had promptly been cashed. At the end of January 1905, Jim wrote to Stannie asking him to 'examine Charlie' about the missing money. There was a much more likely suspect: Pappie. Jim had taken him for a fool – and taken his money to pay for a woman he had not even been told about. Cashing the *Speaker* cheque was no problem, even if it was not made out to 'Mr J. Joyce'. And if Charlie were blamed, so much the better.

Jim possibly never discovered what became of the missing five shillings in the end. If John had taken the cheque, he had also taken a more effective revenge against his son than he knew. The money never reached the Dublin Steam Printing Company and so the broadsides were never collected by Stannie. 'The Holy Office' would have to be set up and printed again more than nine months later. This delay seriously blunted the historic parting gesture of James Joyce; the satire, as a result, would have little effect when it finally appeared. By the time he got a copy, at least one target of the pasquinade assumed that the gift meant that James Joyce thought him to be a friend. By then the Dublin of literary soirées and theatrical gossip had half forgotten the precocious young poet. Anyway, he was 'difficult' and his background was suspect. 'The Holy Office' had missed its moment. It is unlikely that the poet's father realised the fact, however. For John Stanislaus nothing had changed: he would not easily forgive.

By Christmas 1904 father and eldest son were no longer directly in touch with each other at all. Pappie even ignored Jim's birthday in February, an unforgivable sin in the Joycean calendar of high days and holidays. Stannie was now enjoying the controlling position of censor, reading out at home judiciously edited (Noraless) passages from his brother's frequent letters to him and passing everyone's reactions back to Pola. He was also seeing the latest chapters of *Stephen Hero*, which he was allowed to show to Aunt Josephine, but to nobody else in the immediate family. He showed them, however, to Jim's medical student pal, Vincent Cosgrave, who commented sarcastically that when Jim's father read them, he would 'love' Jim. John Stanislaus was never to read *Stephen Hero*. He protested that something in one of Jim's letters was 'lunatic' – evidently a repeat of the suggestion that Stannie go on the European Berlitz trail. Though this would have meant one less hungry mouth in the house, John wanted his second son to stay put for the time being. The wastrel might be out of a job, but he was still potentially the best earner. Besides, without Stannie, he might hear nothing of Jim at all.

Financial problems were, if possible, even worse by the spring of 1905. John had fallen so far behind in paying his domestic rates that the Corporation at last took action. On 26 May the house had to be legally sold off by 'John S. Joyce and the Right Hon. Lord Mayor, Alderman and Burgesses of the City of Dublin'. It is unrecorded how much was paid for the house by the purchaser, Michael Moynihan (a few doors up at 17 St Peter's Terrace), but if anything was left after John's debt had been paid off the money would have been used largely to console him for the loss of the last property he would ever own: Stannie told Jim in a letter during this year that Pappie was now rarely sober. Within a few days, the family were out. John heard of a six-roomed two-storey house (with basement) to let for £5 a month in a short terrace less than a mile away. By the beginning of June they had transferred to 7 Whitworth Place, near the top end of Dorset Street beside Binn's Bridge over the canal. Just around the corner was one of John's favourite pubs, Leech's, whose proprietor, Peter Leech, was the landlord of the Joyces' new abode. One way or another, he was to take a good percentage of John's money over the next year.

The forced sale of the family seat marked the eclipse of John Stanislaus Joyce as a 'gentleman', in the eyes of others at least. An old man at fifty-six, he would either have to find work or to rely on the goodwill, or charity, of others. What charity were his children likely (or able) to offer? Then in the early summer, through Tim Harrington and Jack Hishon his 'Fides Achates' (as John called him), John was given work on the Registry of Electors in the wards of East and West Pembroke, part of the Stephen's Green constituency, whose MP had for the past two years been Laurence A. Waldron. By the time the job was complete in the autumn, he had earned altogether an extremely welcome £40. At first, John turned down the chance to get Stannie a job on the Registration as well, for fear of 'spurring the willing horse'. If this son were kept in poverty, he would be forced to find permanent employment in Dublin and subsidise the household. Finally, however, Stannie was allowed to help, but made only £2.

In June Jim encouraged Stannie to read a poem that he said was addressed by Wordsworth to the 'lost son' he had abandoned in France during the Revolution. Actually 'The Affliction of Margaret' is narrated by a woman. For Jim, however, the verses spoke of his own split with his father. In words that would be echoed by Pappie over the next twenty-five years, the poem begins 'Where art thou, my beloved Son, / Where art thou, worse to me than dead?' and ends:

> Beyond participation lie
> My troubles, and beyond relief:
> If any chance to heave a sigh,
> They pity me, and not my grief.

> Then come to me, my Son, or send
> Some tidings that my woes may end;
> I have no other earthly friend!

James Joyce was not only discovering his father in the literature of others; he was continuing to put him there himself. It was in the swelter of Trieste (where he had gone after Pola) that he wrote the 'frigidities' of another *Dubliners* story, 'Counterparts'; the portrait of a futile existence of scrivenery and sottishness around Fleet Street was drawn without sympathy and owed much to Jack Joyce's time there some fifteen years before.

In February, after getting a pair of pince-nez reading glasses, Jim had asked Stannie what strength Pappie's were in comparison. Nora was pregnant and his thoughts were beginning to dwell on the subjects of heredity and the rearing of children, of nature and nurture. The baby, he had decided, would not be baptised: 'Why should I superimpose on my child the very troublesome burden of belief which my father and mother superimposed on me?' John was to learn nothing of the impending birth until he was already a grandfather. It happened at the end of July. In the small hours of Friday the twenty-eighth a telegram addressed to Stanislaus Joyce arrived at 7 Whitworth Place. It read 'Son born Jim'. Stannie described the scene in a vivid reply to his brother:

I got up and answered the door and while I knelt down to read it by the light of my candle which I had stuck on the stairs, heads appeared at the nursery door, Charlie came out . . . shivering on the landing in his shirt, and Pappie who was sober whistled one never knows what one is going to hear next from you. I brought the telegram upstairs with a Christmas morning feeling. It gave me such unmixed pleasure that I didn't hesitate to show it to Pappie first and knew that you intended that I should. He said nothing while I was in the room but read the telegram two or three times. When I went out, however, he wept and on Saturday he went to some trouble to get me the money to send the telegram in reply to yours . . .

In the morning Stannie busied himself spreading the news. Aunt Josephine, in Whitworth Hospital with one of her periodic bouts of kidney trouble, was 'pleased beyond measure', but neither Pappie nor Poppie made much comment, appearing merely to take 'a very friendly interest perhaps pride in it and to be glad inconsistently'. Their muted reactions reflected two different reservations. Poppie found her nephew's questionable legitimacy difficult to accept, though she could not help being pleased for Jim; her father was swept with powerful but conflicting emotions and for once found difficulty expressing himself. The birth of his first grandson should have called for unstinted celebration, but he had been ignored. The telegram ought to have been addressed to him – it might have been a chance for Jim to make peace.

But Jim no longer wished to make peace with his father. Two days after the birth he wrote properly, but again the letter was sent to Stannie. Nevertheless, the surge of patrilinear pride in it was irrepressible. His son, he said, had inherited both his father's and his grandfather's voice and the baby had a great taste for music, responding to several operatic airs he had whistled to him. When Pappie was shown the letter, which went on to beg for a parcel from Dublin, it did not improve his mood. After he got his monthly pension cheque from Drimmie's he escaped from the house for a drinking spree with his cronies. He was tired of being judged by his children. Patriarchs were to be treated with respect.

While John was adjusting to his new status as a grandfather, Jim was defining his own role as a father, using Stannie as his 'whetstone'. He told his brother that he was determined not to make the mistakes with his new-born son that Pappie had made with him: 'Wouldn't it be awful if I had to hawk my son from one beggarly lodgings to another, from land to land? I mean, of course, for his sake. I hope to Christ he won't have to make allowances for me when he begins to think.'

Back in Dublin, Stannie was desperate to leave home. There was now a definite Berlitz job for him in Trieste. In October he went to his father and asked for the fare. Pappie exploded, telling him to 'go to Hell for it': Jim could send Stannie some of the £7 he had got out of him the year before. In a series of detailed letters to his brother Jim had been listing the expenses Stannie would have on the journey. In the last of these, dated 16 October, he told him to show the whole correspondence to his father and to ask him for the necessary funds. The instruction was not what it seemed. It was a ploy to tell Pappie his grandson's name, something Jim could not bring himself to do directly. The letter of 16 October was the first to mention Georgie by name. When, following these instructions, Stannie showed it to his father, the apparently casual mention of the name must have come as a greater shock to him than the fact of the child's birth.

The name was George. Surely the child ought to have been named after its grandfather? This was nothing but a vicious snub. For four generations the first-born had been baptised either 'John' or 'James'. It was true that George was a family name from Rose Cottage in Fermoy, but John knew that ancient family loyalties were not in Jim's mind: he was commemorating his brother Georgie, whose death had deprived the family of so much spirit and promise. Therefore it was impossible for John to object to the choice, but it can only have awakened painful emotions in him. He was all too aware that some of his children still blamed him for the death of their favourite brother. His first grandson would be a living reminder of this terrible accusation and more generally of the shame that John Stanislaus had brought to the once proud Joyce lineage.

CHAPTER 22

Parting Drinks

When Florrie was almost thirteen and Baby a year younger they together were confirmed as full members of the Church on 10 October 1905, in the presence of Charlie, Eileen, May and Eva, all doubtless superintended by Poppie. John is unlikely to have been there. Neither of them looked as well in their Confirmation dresses as Eva had in hers: both sisters were very small for their age (Stannie blamed malnourishment) and Florrie was already noticeably withdrawn. Less than three weeks later she would lose her chief protector. With money from Jim, Stannie was off at last to Trieste, wearing hastily gathered 'new-looking' clothes, apparel that he had been assured would do 'excellently'. Jim recommended that he bring a can of tinned meat to keep from starving on the four-day journey, but he could not afford one.

When the day came, Eva, Florrie and Baby waved goodbye to Stannie as they parted on the North Circular Road on their way to school. Baby was crying. The others went down with him to the boat to see him off and were joined by Aunt Josephine. Afterwards, as Charlie told him in a letter, there was more 'weeping and wet eyes' and Poppie went off with Aunt Josephine for a 'gala lamentation' at her house in Northbrook Villas. Aunt Josephine had been fond of Stannie, and her daughter Katsie, in particular, would miss the long walks she took with her serious cousin, who sometimes had thought he might be in love with her. Stannie may have been surprised to hear that his father 'wept and talked a great deal' over his first letter home a few days later. For all his apparent coldness, he would be missed by his father. But the departure of Stanislaus was another certain sign that the Joyce family was fast fragmenting.

If they could have done so, the five children still in Whitworth Place with their father (Poppie, Charlie, Eva, Florrie and Baby) would have followed their brother's example and found somewhere else to live too. But there was nowhere else to go. For Poppie, almost the only relief from domestic drudgery was in clandestine visits to the Murrays and the occasional trip to a show: she got out to the Christmas Pantomime at the Gaiety with Aunt Josephine and, after he had seen it five times himself, Charlie was kind enough to take her with him to see the *The Only Way* on the sixth time. But that was about it. Finally she plucked up courage to approach her father about her long-held wish to become a nun. He accused her of 'insolence' and flatly refused to let her go, reminding her of the solemn vow she had made to her dying mother. Poppie was never to forget the anguish of this time. In her late seventies she spoke of how he invariably had answered her annual requests to leave home with: 'If you wait another year everything will be all right.' Far off in her New Zealand convent, as she repeated Pappie's words to a friend, the old nun broke down in tears.

Poppie's dilemma was the basis for James Joyce's story, 'Eveline', a version of which had already been published in Æ's paper, the *Irish Homestead*. Eveline has promised her dying mother to stay at home for the sake of the younger children. She has to haggle with her angry and drunken father over every penny she spends on food for the family. When a rescuer appears in the shape of a young man, she finds herself incapable of going away with him. Though in the story the suitor was substituted for Poppie's vocation, Eveline's paralysed inability to break her promise and desert the others was taken directly from life. Four more years would pass before Poppie could escape to serve a more merciful master than John Stanislaus Joyce. In the meantime, much of what spare time she had would be spent stitching by the fire and singing to herself, like her poor mother. She was trying to save up to buy herself some teeth.

Stannie was worried about the mess he was leaving behind him, but Aunt Josephine was more worried about her nephew's state of mind. She wrote to reassure him in January that the family in Whitworth Place had had 'plenty of everything at Xmas'. Though Poppie had been laid up (ostensibly from 'excitement'), it was only for a day. Charlie reported that his father had been drinking less since Stannie's departure. He spoke too soon. In January, probably on the recommendation of Henry Campbell (still Town Clerk) or Jimmy Henry his deputy, John Stanislaus earned £9 in three weeks during the run-up to the 1906 General Election. He also got Charlie a job as Personation Agent at a polling station. Unfortunately, when John got his hands on both sets of wages and Charlie asked him for the £5 he had earned, after a heated argument John handed over only ten shillings. But with this work at last John had 'struck oil', though not on quite the scale that he had once envisaged. Since the election he had taken in (with his monthly pension cheque) quite a tidy sum – almost eight months' rent, in fact. Out of this he felt it wise to pay something to Leech ('*clarissima nomen*', as John once commented) and the landlord gratefully put an inside lavatory into the house. The milkman and another unidentified creditor they called 'The Man at the Top' could also modestly celebrate being paid. With a large chunk of the remainder John went on a 'royal drunk'. He was sometimes so bad that there were nights when the stairs to the basement kitchen became too perilous to be attempted. On these occasions the children at least were spared the usual assaults of their father's tongue. In the mornings he could sometimes be quite tolerable and the girls even persuaded him to give them enough for 'new second-hand' dresses, though the precariously clad Charlie got nothing. He commented coldly to Stannie, 'Pappie drank several pairs of boots, hats, trousers, collars, etc. Everyone to his taste.' When all the election money had run out, Pappie asked him if he had any of his ten shillings left to lend him. But it had all gone.

For all his supposed 'stupidity', Charlie, like his brothers, was a lively and perceptive letter writer. He kept Stannie up to date with Dublin news in a series of vivid screeds. One described an evening spent with Oliver Gogarty and Vincent Cosgrave, who bribed him with pints of stout and pumped him about Jim. Gogarty had announced that he 'had just had a "ride" and that he was about to perform a miracle by changing porter into seed'. More generally, however, Charlie's letters were a catalogue of woes. He was trapped at home, 'bootless, clothless and hatless', wearing odd shoes and Stannie's old trousers (now in 'a pretty state'). Repeatedly, obsessively, he blamed his father. The tales he told of Pappie could be epic:

The day Pappie was paid [for the election work] he came home sober at 3 in the day. 'Seigfreid' [sic] was on at the Royal. I was *invited!* As Pappie was sober and I wanted to see the opera particularly I went . . . We started at 6.25. When we got to the Canal Bridge a tram came up. I asked Pappie to get into it as there would be a great crowd at the theatre. No: 'Oh, it's early yet; plenty of time man.' Pappie (solus) went into Leech's and remained there for 15 mins. When he came out we got a tram and as there was no boosing shed in the tram Pappie had to wait till we got to the 'Scotch House'. He remained about 5 mins in there. When we went over to the Royal there was a man shouting: 'Only standing room inside.' I then told Pappie I wasn't going in, and I didn't. Pappie thought we should go to the Empire and have a smoke. He headed for the Empire via every public house from the Royal to Dame St. He was getting nicely drunk by this time so I refused to go into the Empire. By the way, I was waiting for Pappie *outside* the pubs. Pappie had not, up to this time, given me as much as a penny for cigarettes. Pappie wanted to see 'poor little Egan' in Kavanaghs. [James Kavanagh's Wine Rooms were upstairs at 16 Parliament Street. James F. Egan, who had served fifteen years' penal servitude for Fenian dynamiting, was now City Swordbearer.] He tried very hard to get me up with him but yours truly was too stupid. I sat down on Kavanagh's stairs (I was cold and tired) and after half an hour Pappie came down drunk. Dame St, College Green, Westmoreland St, O'Connell St, Abbey St, the 'Ship'. I did the patient, vigilant dog for 20 mins. Pappie and McDermot came out of the 'Ship' rolled round the door-post into Mooney's and did their best to pull me with them. As Pappie had someone to bring him home I thought i[t] was time to chuck me job so I told him [I] was going for a walk. At last he asked me did I want cigarettes and I told him I did. He gave me *6d.* I ask[ed] him for a shilling as I wanted to get an exercise [book], [illegible] and a 3d. cigar. He gave me the shilling and *took back the 6d. out of my hand.* Can you imagine my feelings. Had I taken all the drinks I was offered that night it would not have come to less than 2/- [two shillings]. Nice isn't it? The following day was Saturday and he asked me to go out till he got me a suit of clothes. No clothes. If you just read over what occoured on Friday you have read exactly what happened on Saturday.

In Britain the General Election had been a landslide for the Liberals under Campbell-Bannerman. There had been no mention, however, of the re-introduction of a Home Rule Bill in the Party Manifesto. In Ireland the old parliamentary (and municipal) political routes towards freedom seemed to be losing their direction. Anti-Englishness fed the desire for a Gaelic Ireland and both were increasingly in the air. John Stanislaus disliked the stench. These days he was spending a good deal of time with Jack Hishon, sometimes at work, more often in bars; Hishon was himself an expert drinker. Tim Harrington was still an MP and on the City Council but no longer as Lord Mayor (this was now J. P. Nannetti, also an MP), and through Hishon's friendly professional attachment to him John could pick up most of the Corporation and Westminster gossip. But otherwise he was isolated from – and suspicious of – the new generation of activists in his erstwhile stamping-grounds of business and the press. While James Joyce was wondering if Arthur Griffith's Sinn Féin might not dissipate some of the 'odour of corruption' that floated from his *Dubliners* stories of chicanery and self-deception, his father's cynicism about the city and its citizens was deepening.

As well it might have done. Harrington abruptly told him that his services would not be required in the summer for registration work as they had been last year; in the Pembroke Wards (around the Grand Canal) the sitting MP, Laurence Waldron, a successful government stockbroker, had a large enough majority not to need any more electorate. (Selective registration of different areas had for years allowed the City Fathers freely to manipulate the parliamentary and local government vote.) To add to John's troubles, his insurance agents, Drimmie's, discovered an overlooked bill for £2.16s.od and proceeded to remove it in instalments from his monthly pension cheque. In the four weeks of March he managed to earn £4.6s.1od on Dublin County Council work of some sort, but was then let go. If the present was bleak, the future looked bleaker. Even Nigger the dog had something wrong with him, yelping in heart-rending tones about the house, but as Charlie said: 'Whether the ailment is in his paws, ears or arse *je ne sais!*' Charlie told Stannie in May that Pappie had been reading out to his friends in pubs choice bits from his and Jim's letters home, in order to show 'the poltroons . . . what blackguards the Jesuits can "turn out".' Apparently John told them that his sons never sent a penny piece from their jobs abroad to help him provide their unfortunate sisters with something to eat. In fact, Stannie at least had been sending money home regularly. He despatched a furious letter of accusation to his father.

John may not have replied to Stannie's diatribe at once, or at all. He had more important things to think about. On 15 May Peter Leech served a formal demand for two months' rent (£5), with just two weeks' grace before they were all thrown out on to the street. Extreme action was called for. John swallowed his pride and the next day wrote his first letter to Jim since the split, describing the family circumstances in the most dignified terms he could muster. He would not reproach Jim – whose 'own secret thoughts' must do so already – for the terrible mistake he had made (leaving Dublin with Nora). He did not apologise either – one of his mottoes was 'never apologise' – but said that his feelings towards his eldest son had recently undergone a change, as the photographs of his first grandson had awakened old memories. Remembering the days of Jim's childhood, however, did nothing 'to assuage the torture I at present endure, associated as it is with all the happiest moments of my life'. He went on to say that, only half-way through the month, they were already without food, coal or light and faced certain eviction. He had asked J. J. Clancy MP to see if there was any chance of recovering the full pension that he believed he should have been granted in the first place. (Despite the advice of Clancy's pet barrister, nothing would come of this forlorn hope.) His health was rapidly deteriorating – he had seen his last Christmas – but he would have warmly welcomed his own death if it had not meant 'leaving my little motherless girls *friendless*, cast upon the wretched heartless world' – even those dreadful convents had to be paid to keep them on. Whatever else happened, Charlie and Poppie could live with him no longer. As for their poor father himself, it would be the 'Union' – the North Dublin Poor Law Workhouse, next door to the Richmond Lunatic Asylum in North Brunswick Street. Could Jim have Charlie in Trieste? Could Jim and Stannie between them pay the rent? If they could, they were not to send the money to him, but to Poppie. The existence of

Nora was, of course, unmentioned. The letter was signed simply, 'Your Father'.

As usual, it was Stannie who responded, sending 10s.0d., of which Poppie got her hands on 5s.6d. That day, Pappie lent most of the rest to Tom Devin (relying as John did on casual loans from friends, it was almost as important to lend as to repay) and they got drunk together. Aunt Josephine warned Stannie to send no more money, as his father was making 'very bad use' of his charity.

Charlie now began a journal for Stannie about life in Whitworth Place. It is a chilling document, showing John Stanislaus at his worst. It traces for a whole month the family's struggle against their father's alcoholism and their hand-to-mouth existence as they waited for him to give money for each day's food; these amounts are religiously chronicled:

26th May. (2nd day after you sent 10/-) 7.45 pm. Pappie home very drunk: Baby asked him if he had any money; he said he had not, went into his room and locked the door: out in the house rolling about abusing: wants to kill the priest: gone down to the kitchen: gave 2/6.

——

27th Sat. morng [actually Sunday]: Pappie gone out without any apt [appointment] with anyone in town: 6 pm. Pappie in drunk: threatening to go out and leave us without any money: gone to sleep in the kitchen: no tea: 9.30. Poppie home from the Chapel: Pappie awoaken: shouting and howling-match between Pappie and Poppie: Pappie jumping up to go out: Poppie running away with his hat: Baby sick for want of her tea: Pappie gone to bed: gave 4/-: no assault: calmness, pain in my head. Amen.

——

28th Monday. 7.30 pm. Pappie home very drunk: gave 3/-: gone to bed.

——

29th. Pappie gave 2/-: nothing thrilling.

——

Wednes. morg. 30th. No money: Florrie's dress pawned, 1/-: breakfast:. 8.30 pm. Pappie home sober: gave 2/6.

——

T[hur]sday 31st. Poppie gone out to meet Pappie in town: Poppie home, £1: 7. o'c. Pappie home very drunk.

―――

Friday 1st June. 7. pm. Pappie home blind.

―――

2nd June (Sat). Pappie gave 10/- 7.30. pm. Pappie home very drunk: gave Baby 2/- to get a dress, Eva the same: Eva took 5/- out of Pappie's pockets.

―――

3rd Monday evg. Pappie gave 1/-.

―――

4th Tuesd. morg. do. Pappie gave 1/-. 6.30 pm Pappie home sober: fighting in the kitchen.

―――

5th Wed morg. 2/6: night 3/-.

―――

6th Thurd. Pappie home: has had a few drinks: fighting with me or rather at me.

―――

Friday 7th. Pappie had some money and Pappie gave 3d.: breakfast: blouse pawned 8d.: 8ds worth grub: Pappie home sober: no money: gone out again: home again: no money: gone to bed: Poppie gone out: home again: got 6d. from Aunt Josephine.

―――

Saturd. 8th. Florrie's dress pawned, 1/-: Poppie gone to meet Pappie in town: home 10/-: Pappie home drunk: gone out again: home again more drunk: standing at the hall door abusing at the top of his voice: gone out again.

―――

Sunday 9th. 4 o'c pm. Shouting bawling Mary's Alleying between Pappie & Poppie: after dinner: Pappie gone out. Would not leave money for the tea.

―――

Monday 10th. Pappie home sober: 2/6.

———

Tuesday 11th morg. 2/6: night gave 2/-. Pappie home sober.

———

Wedy 12th. Pappie gone to election.

———

Thurdy 13th. No breakfast: Pappie gone with Baby to get paid for election: Baby home: Pappie won't get paid till 3 o'c: Poppie and children gone to meet the Murrays: Pappie home 4 o'c: left £1: gone into town again: P & children home: a feed: Pappie neither drunk nor sober: cursing at the top of his voice in the kitchen: gone out again: home drunk.

———

Friday 14th. Pappie home in a cab *rotten*, 4 o'c: gone to bed.

———

Saty. 15th. Pappie hopeless, 5.30 o'c: Abusing, says he has no money: Poppie has 4/- left: Pappie gave 2/-.

———

Sunday 16th. Pappie hasn't come home to dinner: 11.45 pm.: Pappie home half-drunk.

———

Monday 17th. Pappie gone out: gave 2/-. No more notes till 23rd June.

———

Saturday 23rd. Poppie gone to meet Pappie in town: P. home. 5/-: Pappie says he got 15/-: Pappie home half-drunk: would not give any more money: gone out again: home: gave 2/6.

———

Sunday 24th. Pappie home to dinner very drunk: shouting swearing etc: Pappie has thrown his dinner about the floor: Baby white as a sheet: Pappie gone out again: home again: sleeping off some of the drunk: gave 8d.: gone out again: home again at 12.20 pm.

———

Monday 25th. Pappie gave 1/-: no dinner: Eva's dress pawned 1/-: tea: 7. pm. Pappie home drunk: gave 2/-.

———

Tuesday 26th. Poppie gone to meet Pappie in town: P. home, 5/-: 5.30. Pappie home drunk: gone out again:

———

Wedy 27th. Pappie gave 1/-: afterwards 2/6 more: Pappie has not come home all night

———

Thursday 28th. Pappie not home yet. Eva's dress pawned, 1/-: breakfast: ... no dinner: 4 o'c Pappie home absolutely drunk: gave 2½d.: says he was at Dalkey with a friend last night: Florrie's dress pawned, 1/-:

———

Friday 29th. Pappie Poppie and Baby gone out to try and get some money: Poppie & Baby home: Pappie got 4/- & gave 2/10: 12 o'c breakfast: 7 o'c Pappie home drunk. Gone to bed.

———

30th Saty. (*today*) Baby and Pappie gone into town to get the cheque: Baby home £1: It is now 3 o'c and here my notes end. Pappie is not in yet but I suspect when he does come it will be in the usual condition. Clothes were continually going in and out of the *pawn*. Every time we were without money something was pawned and then got out when we got money. These notes are not very minuted but additions to them would be unnecessary and superficial, as Fogarty would say. [Fogarty was an incompetent grocer on Glengariff Parade (who is owed money by Tom Kernan, another John Joyce figure in *Ulysses*.)]

Tim Harrington (whose letter of recommendation James was still brandishing to potential employers) relented in May and offered John the 1906 Registration of the South Dock and West Pembroke Wards after all. John accepted the work on the condition, verbally agreed, that he would be paid the same rate as the previous year. As he was 'very shabby', a collection had to be taken among his friends to buy clothes, and he got new boots, socks, a straw hat and a £2.10s.0d suit of light-grey tweed. With the surplus the girls were bought new dresses or had their shoes mended, and a sweeping brush was purchased for Poppie, whose gratitude can be imagined. The work lasted until October. Charlie, who because of the state of his trousers had been indoors for weeks, complained that he was doing most of it himself, ruining his eyes by staying up half the night copying names and addresses from one book to another. (John assiduously paid back all the money to the subscribers after Henry Campbell appointed him Presiding Officer at an election on 12 June.)

It may have been the Registration income that stopped Leech evicting them: though the landlord served John with a summons to appear in court before the Recorder on 18 June, the Joyces were not finally shifted until 1 October. Jim eventually sent Charlie a suit and some collars, but he could make little use of them at first: his illness had returned and he was admitted as a casual tubercular patient to Beaumont, in Drumcondra, a convalescent home in a former residence of two generations of Arthur Guinnesses, which was affiliated to the Mater Hospital and catered mainly for 'those of the poorest class'. Here, cosseted by the Sisters of Mercy, he slept and was fed for a couple of months during the late summer. In September he fell off a borrowed bicycle on his way home and was rushed into the Mater after losing a lot of blood from an artery in his head. When he came out of hospital the family had moved to one of the 'small red houses' beside Drumcondra Bridge over the Tolka, 9 Millmount Terrace (close to their 1895 'villa' in Millbourne Avenue). The new rent was £32 a year and there were five rooms, a kitchen and even a bathroom with hot water.

At the beginning of December, John wrote to Jim (now in Rome), courteously requesting him to send £1 to Poppie to help the family Christmas. Jim, 'skinty' himself as usual, asked Stannie to borrow some money from his boss at the Trieste Berlitz School and to forward it to Rome, so that Jim would then take the credit by sending it on to Poppie. Stannie obeyed, sending more directly to Dublin himself. Thus on Christmas Day, as their grateful father wrote, 'what looked likely to be red herrings on the Saturday became Turkey and Ham, Goose and bacon, Plum Pudding, etc. and punch'. Envy of this yuletide catalogue may have been one inspiration for James Joyce's greatest short story, 'The Dead', written some months later, in which Gabriel Conroy (who is partly based on John Stanislaus) presides over the lovingly described festive board in his aunts' house at Usher's Island. Other details probably came from Charlie: he told Stannie about singing 'Watch with me Love Tonight' at the Murrays' to great acclaim from Uncle Willie, who said (like Freddie in 'The Dead') that 'it was a long time since he had heard anyone sing so well'. Charlie then (like Bartell D'Arcy) refused to sing any more songs as he had a cold.

At the end of the Registration, John had fallen out seriously with both Hishon and Harrington over £15 that he argued was still owing for his work on the South Dock Ward. They claimed that Waldron was the man in charge of the money: it had merely been dispensed by them. John stormed into Waldron's offices in Anglesea Street where he was told that the MP had nothing to do with the matter, having given Harrington a blanket cheque for all the work. John decided to sue Waldron. The case would leave, he wrote to Jim, the biggest 'Stink' that had been smelt in Dublin for a long time. It would show up Hishon and Harrington as the worst impostors then living in the country.

When the trial was held, in the first week of January 1907, the Recorder found against John, since nothing could be proven: the agreement with Harrington had not been written down. John comforted himself with the thought that he had revealed to Waldron the shabby finagling of his henchmen. It was a relief that costs were 'in the cause' and so could not be awarded against John Stanislaus. Aside from a few small paragraphs, the case made little stir in the papers. At the end of the same month Pappie sent Jim a birthday card for the first time for some years. He rapidly followed it with a letter to Stannie containing a sad tale of how he had spent all his money on rent, coal and milk, as he had been banking on the promise of work from a County Council official, Robert Blackburne. Then this 'Bastard' had suddenly postponed the job for another fortnight. Could Stannie, who with Jim was the only resource he had left, possibly manage £1?

On 9 February John also tried a similar request on his eldest son. Jim, depressed by repeated failures to get his stories (or 'epiclets') published in book form as *Dubliners*, complained to Stannie a few days later: 'My mouth is full of decayed teeth and my soul of decayed ambitions.' (He was, however, fascinated by reports from Dublin of riots at the first performances of his friend John Synge's *Playboy of the Western World*. The *Freeman's Journal* had called it a 'hideous caricature' that would be 'slanderous of a Kaffir kraal.' Joyce imagined that Synge would be condemned from the pulpit and pictured 'pore old Æ . . . nibbling cabbages up in Rathgar in quite an excited state of mind at the amount of heresy which is rife in Dublin'. The play, he noted, was about 'a self-accused parricide'.)

Though he had no wish to kill off his own father, Jim refused to send him a penny. However, he repeated his offer to take Charlie and a sister off John's hands, but there was nothing for their fares and anyway Charlie was nervous of his teaching abilities if he worked at the Berlitz School. Soon afterwards May left her convent with reasonable results in the Intermediate Examination and, ever capable, by March was at work in the Cash Desk in Todd Burns, the vast Mary Street drapers and general house furnishers. She was paid an initial three shillings a week, with three meals a day. Eileen, now adorned in spectacles, was coming home from school soon too, and would find a probationary post in the Telephone Office. As for Charlie, John had been promised a Corporation job for him, but it had not quite materialised yet. It never would.

With his 'hopes, – proud hopes – shattered', Pappie wrote yet another desperate appeal in April to Jim, now back in Trieste. It was possibly, he said, the last letter he would ever get from his lonely father. Jim had asked him precisely how much he was getting from what was left of his pension and John told him: £6 a month, of which £2.12s.4d was due in rent. When he was out of a job, he had only 2s.3d a day on which to feed and clothe everyone – 'five girls, one – well, Charlie, myself and Nigger'. It was not enough. He would have to break up the house (an easy task as everything was broken up 'quite sufficiently' already) and get Poppie and the 'aforesaid ex-ecclesiastic' (Charlie) off his hands. He told Jim that his friend James Kavanagh J P, proprietor of the Parliament Street Wine Rooms, was helping him to find a place for the three youngest girls in the Holy Faith Convent in Glasnevin for £24 a year: if between them Jim and Stannie promised to pay eight shillings every week, he would make up the balance. He did not explain that this balance amounted to only just over one shilling and sixpence a week – but as Jim had spent most of his recent waking hours as a bank clerk in Rome, there was no need to develop the calculations. John had an idea that Poppie had somewhere to go, and perhaps Charlie was still wanted in Trieste. As for May and Eily, if they really had to they could share his lodgings, though he felt more like returning to Cork – the idea was almost a maudlin euphemism for death. If he was there he could perhaps find some old friends who might should show him the 'respect & perhaps even affection' he so signally lacked in Dublin. Wherever he ended up for his very few declining years, it would be 'some relief from the miserable existence I have put over since *August 13th 1903*', the day he lost May. As the long letter drew to a conclusion, John gave the emotional screw another twist:

Perhaps in years to come, long after my release from this world, you may learn to feel some of the pangs I have endured, and then you will appreciate the feelings of a Father who loved his children and had high ambitions for them, and spared no money when he could afford it, to educate and make them what they should be, but who when adversity came and he could no longer gratify all those wants, was despised[,] disrespected, jeered at, scoffed at and set at defiance . . . Goodbye, Jim, and may God protect you, is the prayer of your still fond and loving, though broken-hearted,

Father.

Jim's reaction to his father's effusion was to try to get an Italian daily paper to send him to Dublin, ostensibly to report on the hugely successful Irish International Exhibition (complete with Kaffir kraal) that the Earl of Aberdeen as Lord-Lieutenant opened in Herbert Park at the beginning of May. After this scheme had failed, he posted Pappie a signed copy of *Chamber Music*, his first book of poems. Some months later he also sent copies of the Italian newspaper *Piccolo della Sera* containing articles he had written. John got one or two of them translated into English for publication in Dublin by an acquaintance, Hugh McNeill, but, despite promises, failed (if he ever really tried) to place them with Mr Meade, the then editor of the *Evening Telegraph*, or anywhere else. Eva, Florrie and Baby had to go back to their wretched old Loreto convent school in North Great George's Street after all.

In the summer of 1907 John got a permanent job at last, with a house purchase company, the Provincial Homes. Given his expertise in the art of moving house, it sounded ideal for him at first, but he was paid only about 25s. a week for his work. However, the money kept what Charlie called 'the old sheet of tissue paper' between the Joyces and the workhouse. John seemed to settle well into the routine, generally keeping himself sober despite having a little money, and he even opened a short-lived credit account with Leverett and Fry's, a 'toney' grocer's shop on Lower Drumcondra Road. Even so, it was not much of an existence, and he found himself hoping more and more that Jim would come home and set the ball rolling again. On John's fifty-eighth birthday, 4 July, the new MP, Tom Kettle (son of 'Mr Teapot', Andrew Kettle), who had been in College with Jim, spoke in the Commons on Irish university reform. If the university were to be expanded, there should be something there for Jim, but everything these days was uncertain. As if to prove the fact, the papers reported that the 'Irish Crown Jewels' had been stolen from the Office of Arms in Dublin Castle. Embarrassingly for the authorities, that same month the King and Queen visited Dublin for the Exhibition. Even the Castle was not what it had been.

On 2 August, probably dodging rent again, John moved the family to a smaller house, 4 O'Connell Avenue near Eccles Street (where across the road at No. 9 was the Boer War hero – and renowned toper – John MacBride). On the day of the move, Charlie, who was as lonely and miserable in Dublin as his father, wrote to Jim – currently in a Trieste hospital with severe rheumatic fever – congratulating him on the birth the previous week of his daughter (in the pauper ward of the same hospital). Charlie's money-making efforts now extended to begging unsuccessfully from priests. He informed his brother that Nigger was now suffering from mange. Pappie wondered aloud if Jim was 'quite mad' for choosing such a peculiar name as Lucia for his daughter.

John Stanislaus would have found more ammunition against the Murrays in the Irish Crown Jewels affair if it had ever become fully public. Though identified, the thieves were never arrested and the jewels never recovered. The inquiry into the robbery was suddenly abandoned after the perpetrators threatened to reveal secrets that 'would shake the government'. One of them, a homosexual, had been with the King's brother-in-law, the Marquis of Lorne, himself secretly gay, the week after the theft became public. Whether because his own brother-in-law resembled the Marquis, or because he had heard rumours about the aristocrat's morals, or both, John Stanislaus had for years been taunting John Murray by calling him 'the Marquis of Lorne'. In reality John Murray was now a most devout Mass-goer: his wild oats had been sown many years before. But still the feud continued unabated: that year Pappie accused Jim of writing to these 'highly respectable people' more often than he wrote to his own father. (The accusation was justified, as Jim was in frequent touch with Aunt Josephine, who had at last settled down at 19½ Foster Terrace, off Ballybough Road.) Other unwelcome, to John, information came from Poppie, who indignantly reported to her father that his friend Alfie Bergan had been entertaining Uncle Willie with tales about the disgusting state of the Joyces' new house. John promptly 'kicked up hell'. Uncharacteristically rushing to his father's defence, Charlie confronted Alfie in O'Connell Street about 'his low tongue', but the little clerk denied everything. He was, he claimed, quite in the dark about the matter. If he was in the dark, Charlie replied, 'he had only to repeat his little amusement & he'd see stars.'

While most of the family was living in squalor, May was soon up to five shillings a week in Todd Burns, occasionally splurging some of it at the theatre, where she was thrilled to see the legendary actor Martin Harvey. She used her employers' handsome notepaper to write to Stannie with news: Eva had been got out of the Loreto Convent and was moving to a far better school, Tyrone House, opposite the Pro-Cathedral in Marlborough Street. She was becoming very pretty. Eileen was out of work again, having failed her qualifying examination in the Telephone Office (where Charlie had also unsuccessfully tried for a job), and now she was applying for a temporary post in the Junior Army and Navy Stores. (She did not get it.) And as for Pappie, who gave less than half his wages to the household, 'a terrible little no-good is my Pappie.' Later in the autumn, possibly trying to appease her, John took May with him to Kingstown. There they ran into Pat Casey, now in complete penury. The old firebrand brushed off their concern: he was expecting any day to come into some property or money. May had heard this sort of talk before.

After the January municipal elections, at which Sinn Féin made a first substantial showing with fifteen seats, Pat Casey died penniless in the 'Union'. May, and doubtless her father, felt very sad about him. Though ignored for the last years of his life, he was buried in the Fenian Plot in Glasnevin, surrounded by most of Ireland's other glorious patriots. His Fenian brothers-in-arms were among John Stanislaus's first friends: now they too were dying off. John went on a ferocious bender, finally retiring to bed ill. At the same time he lost his job with the Provincial Homes and he was already months behind in his rent. With no piano at home, for entertainment his daughters were reduced to eavesdropping on the music of a talented young student next door, their ears pressed against the party wall. As May said, it was 'a case of the same old abject poverty again'. Were the Joyces, she asked Stannie, 'always to be the same paupers that we are now?' Well, if they were, in John's humble opinion, it was not his fault. He was doing his best. On 20 April he got another job, this time as District Inspector with the Equitable House Property Company of Manchester, and by his own account brought in two thousand pounds' worth of business to the firm in three months. Thereafter the company unaccountably refused to pay his salary and when John heard that after a court hearing in Manchester the Public Prosecutor was threatening to close it down for swindling and malpractice, that was the end of that. John never caught up with his recent arrears and in early July had to get out again, finding yet another small house nearby in Connaught Street, No. 24, an 'artisan's dwelling' that had not even been built when Charlie Chance had lived in the street in the early 1890s.

May had written to Stannie in February: 'Dublin decidedly is not the place for poverty-stricken geniuses & poets. Charlie finds this very much so'. For almost a year her last remaining brother in Ireland had been talking of emigrating to America, where more than one of his acquaintances were said to be doing well. But travelling cost money, of which Charlie had less than none. In the meantime he had been hanging around the city in Jim's old suit and, pauper or not, he had finally found a group of convivial companions (in Pappie's view, corner boys of the meanest sort, who belonged in the gutter). More enterprisingly, he had also met a pretty, fair-haired girl of eighteen with 'a fine pair of large blue eyes' who lived at 48 St Mary's Road in the North Docks, and it was a shock but no great surprise to Charlie when she announced soon afterwards that she was going to have a baby. Charlie at once said he would have nothing further to do with her, suspecting that he was being trapped into marriage. After Aunt Josephine stepped in, however, he agreed to see her and became convinced that, as he told Jim, 'the child is mine, and mine only'. Vincent Cosgrave advised him that 'if there was a choice between going to gaol and marrying, to marry'. And so, on 18 July 1908, in the dockland Church of St Laurence O'Toole's, Seville Place, Charles Patrick Joyce was married to Mary Josephine Meagher, the daughter of a grocer. On the register, he described himself as 'Gentleman'. Afterwards he wrote to Jim that his new wife did 'not care about my want of money. "With all my worldly goods I her endowed" on last Saturday. My worldly goods consisted of myself and the garments thereupon; but that was all she wished, poor thing.' Three weeks later, after a makeshift honeymoon in Lennox Street on the south side of Dublin near Portobello, the couple left for Boston, via Liverpool and Queenstown. Pappie, who had not been told 'the true details of the case', was cautiously approving and furnished Charlie with some 'first class' letters of introduction, including one for the American President of the United Irish League and editor of the *Boston Globe*, John O'Callaghan, which he got through James F. Egan, the City Swordbearer. He also arranged for Charlie to be enrolled in the Ancient Order of Hibernians, a Catholic triumphalist body with more than a whiff of Tammany about it, which might help him with the powerful Boston Irish. (That same month, sponsored for similar reasons by Jimmy Henry, 'Boss' Croker of Tammany Hall was given the Freedom of the City of Dublin.)

After Charlie had gone, his father summed him up for Jim, announcing that from a young age he had never attempted to be a gentleman. Latterly he had sunk into the 'Slough of Cadism, *"facile descensus Averno"* '. But his bride was a decent girl from Tipperary, plain but proper, who had a 'Bit o' money'. When Cosgrave, Aunt Josephine and 'the usual *rabble*' had gone to see them off at the boat, there was 'the usual weeping, real and *feigned*' and the usual drinks given and taken, Cosgrave being especially thirsty. Some of the new Mrs Joyce's dowry had already been spent: Charlie had cut a fine figure on the quayside, in silk hat, clean shirt and stockings, and with other 'rareities' like gold glasses, watch and chain. Mary Joyce had also paid the fare. Stannie was less optimistic than the groom about the couple's chances: he foresaw Charlie in Boston sticking up posters while his wife looked on, holding his brat and his tea can. He was being more accurate than he knew. John Stanislaus's hopes for Charlie were equally forlorn. To be honest he would not miss him very much.

CHAPTER 23

The Language of Music

At least as far as his landlord was concerned, John Stanislaus's tenancy of 24 Connaught Street was not a success and by December 1908 the troublesome tenant had already been moved on. The remaining Dublin Joyces spent Christmas at 44 Fontenoy Street close to the Blessington Street Reservoir, otherwise known as the City Basin (which watered much of the north city). The new dwelling was even more pinched than the last, just four rooms and a kitchen, with lavatory facilities in a back garden that was less than ten yards long. At some stage during the autumn John had managed to pick up a salesman's job with an insurance company, offering, alas, only the 'splendid salary' of ten shillings a week; as he failed to find anyone to insure, it soon came to an end. So he wrote his usual pre-Christmas letter to Jim, wishing his two sons and Giorgio (though not Nora or Lucia) a very happy Christmas. At home, he said, things had at last come to a climax. A pound or two would help, but only a little.

What this climax amounted to in the end was one thing: Poppie, now turning twenty-five, was finally leaving him. At first she thought that she would go to a convent in Texas, but then it was decided that she would spend some time at the Mercy Convent Missionary School in the little town of Callan, south of Kilkenny City. She set off eagerly in the early spring of 1909. Her five sisters were all now old enough to be safe from Pappie at home: she had kept her promise to her mother and made her long penance. Her father would miss her housekeeping and cooking, but he would not miss her sharp tongue. He looked forward, in fact, to when they would all be off his hands. May could take a bed in the large staff dormitory under the roof of Todd Burns in Mary Street. The next in line, Eileen, however, could not be turned into the family slavey, as he told Jim. She was too intelligent, too difficult – too much *Eily* – for that ever to work. She wanted to be a singer and had the makings of a good one. No doubt she would soon be gone too.

If a convent could then be persuaded to take on his remaining daughters full time, John realised that he would be able to go into lodgings on his own. With the money he saved on rent and food, he could have a good try at making a success of his few remaining years. There was some life in the old dog yet but, of course, it all depended on his health. He was not yet sixty, but for years he had been claiming in his letters to Trieste that he was at death's door, while his children (and Aunt Josephine) invariably reported him to be perfectly well, which to all appearances he was. When John moaned to his sons about failing health he was certainly seeking their sympathy (and a correspondingly generous remittance by return of post). He may also still have been worried about having syphilis. As much as five years before he had been taking up to five minutes to urinate and sometimes was heard complaining to fellow-drinkers in pubs that there was something wrong with his waterworks. Then there was Uncle Willie. All recent reports of him were that he was disintegrating even as Aunt Josephine and their children looked on. Gout was blamed. Whether or not John knew that William Murray had syphilis, the disease cannot have been far from his thoughts. But the fact remained that none of his own children seemed to have the infection, which was frequently hereditary, and his wife had not died of it: perhaps the carbolic treatment he had tried in Cork had cleared it up – or could there be any truth in the belief that intercourse with a virgin was a cure? In reality John Stanislaus was no syphilitic. It is far more likely that his problem was enlargement of the prostate, a common complaint among men that worsens with age, sometimes leading to extreme discomfort and even incontinence. The prostate gland was not much talked about in Edwardian Dublin. It was certainly not a topic of John's conversations with his daughters, who would have learned nothing of their father's worries in this area.

Although John had alarmed Jim before Christmas by saying that he would soon be going into hospital ('which I sincerely trust I may leave soon – feet foremost'), in fact he had no immediate plans to die. It is clear that he harboured an ambition to end his days with Baby, still very much his favourite daughter. Neither Eva nor Florrie would be willing to mind him in his old age; nor would they be much welcomed if they tried. But Baby would always be good to him: she was sensible and she knew how to cheer him up. In the meantime, till she joined him after her schooling he could get back to making money unencumbered.

In February 1909, a Nationalist gathering (later known as the 'Baton Convention') was held in the Mansion House. Representatives came from all over Ireland and beyond, including the eminent William O'Brien MP and Cork contemporaries of John Stanislaus. 'Mollies' from Westmeath were there with cudgels and cattle-drovers with hazel sticks. According to the sometime Parnellite O'Brien, orders had been given: let no one with a Cork accent get near the platform. But John Stanislaus was no longer interested in the minutiae of Irish parliamentary progress.

In March, Mary Ellen Callanan died of heart disease in Dr Steevens's Hospital. She was only just into her forties and she was the last remnant of the 'dark gaunt house' on Usher's Island, a house of women and music and almost forgotten Christmas dances. Her mother and Aunt Julia were long gone. Lately, she had been organist in St Catherine's Church, Meath Street (Fr James Flynn's old parish in 'The Sisters') and it was from there that she was buried. John shared the mourning carriage politely with John Murray. He was surprised to find that there was nobody else at all at the funeral, except a man by the name of Mr Mullett, one of the Invincibles, in whose public house on Dorset Street the assassins had shared out the surgical knives that they were to use. (After his release from prison he moved to Bridge Street (not far from the Flynn sisters) where he set up another pub opposite the Brazen Head, one of John Stanislaus's favourite old haunts.) Why a member of the conspiracy that killed Lord Cavendish and his colleague in the Phoenix Park, and in the event almost brought down Parnell as well, should have attended the obsequies of a genteel young piano teacher who had been only about eleven when the atrocities took place remains an imponderable. There may or may not be significance in the fact that, before killing him, the conspirators intended to bring their intended victim, 'Buckshot' Forster, to a house directly next door to the Flynns, then in John Street. Mr Mullett may simply have become a family friend. Whatever the truth, it was buried with Mary Ellen.

Charlie wrote from Boston with news. He too now had a son, and his wife Mary (or May, as he usually called her) was expecting a second child. His four-month-old baby had been named after Jim and was extraordinarily 'precocious and quick' (quickly born, anyway): 'The woman in the house here was kind enough to tell May she thought he was too bright to live,' Charlie commented ominously. He hinted that if he were to come to Dublin for a visit it might be very hard to go back to Boston again: he was not exactly having a roaring success there. Currently, he was planning to get his voice trained for the professional stage: it was, he said, bright, clear and so powerful that people marvelled at his imitation of Caruso's rendition of 'M'appari', which he had heard on a gramophone. He might even have begun a course of singing instruction if they had not just been evicted from their lodgings (through no fault of his own, obviously). Charles Joyce's New World had clearly not changed him, as his father had almost hoped it might.

Charlie asked for a photo of Jim's family. He knew that he had been sending pictures home for his father to look at. Pappie received those of 'Georgie', as, to Jim's irritation, he called his grandson, with an outpouring of sentimental affection and pride. According to May Joyce, the most recent photograph made him 'rather crazy' and he would not be able to contain himself when he saw the real thing. For some time, Jim had been feeling that his son ought to meet his grandfather and, if Pappie really was not well it had better be sooner rather than later. He announced that Stannie would take Giorgio to Dublin for six weeks in the summer. This led to lengthy and emotional negotiations with John and the sisters, in which Jim suggested that the boy would not be made very welcome in Dublin – a slight or an inference that John Stanislaus found unacceptable. The old wounds between father and son had still not healed. May, in a friendly intervention, insisted on how much all of them were looking forward to the visit of her little nephew to the 'mansion' in Fontenoy Street. She pointed out that Pappie had written several enthusiastic letters to Jim on the subject.

If John and his daughters all eagerly awaited a sight of Georgie (and of Stannie, of course), their father was also a little nervous at the prospect of meeting the heir apparent of the Joyces, the first-born male of the next generation. What if the three-year-old Austrian polyglot disliked him or, indeed, found 'that his Ould Grandfather was a bloody ould Cod'? After all, 'a bloody ould Cod' was the consensus in Fontenoy Street. When Jim expressed concern that Giorgio might be made to feel like a lost sheep in Fontenoy Street, his father wondered about his own feelings, like a 'found Ass'. Though he expressed himself as comically as he could, it was one of the very few occasions when John Stanislaus let his truest feelings slip in a letter.

Jim had been battling with his pride in Trieste. He might be sending Giorgio to his father as a token of peace, but he was not going to be there himself. His last opportunity to close the rift had been too early, when Giorgio was born. When would the next one be? The fourth of July 1909 would be John's sixtieth birthday. At the last possible moment, in late July, Jim commandeered Stannie's ticket and set off with Giorgio, father and son, to Dublin. John and the girls, determined to give Jim's son the welcome they had promised, were all at Westland Row Station to meet them off the train from the Kingstown boat and even Poppie was on her way up from Kilkenny for a few days. When the 'foreign-looking' pair appeared, the girls chorused 'Where's Stannie?' But their father was delighted by the change of plan.

A little while later, leaving Giorgio at home, Pappie and Jim went out for a walk in the country together. They caught a tram to Rathfarnham, south of the city, then headed off on foot towards the Dublin mountains. They had got only as far as the edge of the village when they found themselves outside the Yellow House, a large roadside pub. Inside, they discovered an empty room with two pianos. When drinks had been bought, John, without saying anything, sat down to play a baritone cavatina from the second act of *La Traviata*. Jim, generally as traditional in music as he was to be avant-garde in literature, loved Verdi's 1853 opera and recognised the piece. He knew that the words of the aria (sung by Alfredo's father) were:

From the land and sea of dear Provence,
What has caused your dear heart to roam?
From the love that is ever with you there,
From your father and your home.

In the song, the father is imploring the son, who has left home for the sake of a woman, to come back to him. The same old father goes on to acknowledge how much he has suffered: eventually there will be a reconciliation between them. Some years later, James Joyce told Padraic Colum that he had replied to his father on the other piano with another appropriate tune – though Colum could not remember what it was. Thus, in this characteristically unconventional fashion, John Stanislaus and James Augustine Joyce at last forgave one another for all that each of them had done and not done, said and not said, over the previous five years. It was something that could not have been achieved so quickly through the awkwardness of crude verbal apologies.

James Joyce learned another, literary, lesson from his father that afternoon, for experience would be similarly focused through the use of musical quotations in the 'Sirens' chapter of *Ulysses* and throughout *Finnegans Wake*. In the 1930s, a close friend of his in Paris, Louis Gillet, came to the conclusion that the 'peculiar rapport' between *père* and *fils* was 'the central factor in Joyce's life, the basis, the axis of his work'. For Joyce, said Gillet, love 'appeared to be an exclusively male function, a virile abstract affection which . . . was placed entirely outside the domain of the senses: a current going from man to man, without passing through the intermediary of maternal entrails, a type of genealogy similar to the imposing introduction of Saint Matthew.' Though John's wish for his son to come home was to continue through the next two decades, the recollection of the wordless communication between them that day in the Yellow House would remain significant to both Joyces, father and son, marking as it did the end of their estrangement and the acknowledgement of their love.

For the rest of his stay in Dublin, Jim bustled around town trying to organise the publication of *Dubliners* and drinking lemon-sodas with friends and ex-friends. He took Giorgio to see the 'Marquis of Lorne' and his wife, Lillie, who were courteously hospitable. After so long an absence from the city that was his subject-matter, James Joyce the writer was hungry for impressions of Dublin, its street lore as well as its physicality. The sense data of 1909 still included stenches and operas and incense and cattle-drives through the streets. But Dublin was not as paralysed as once it had seemed. There were marches for the rights of the working man and woman, and there were motor cars – in August Gogarty's chauffeur killed a child in Donnybrook. No doubt Pappie's rich commentary on the changes that five years had brought about was worth hearing.

On 19 August the great Caruso was performing before the Lord-Lieutenant at the Theatre Royal. The concert included two arias by Verdi in a long programme and the *Irish Times* readily acknowledged that 'it could not be claimed that he short-changed Dubliners'. Unfortunately, none of the Joyces could be there as they could not afford tickets – nor could Jim manage to wangle any press passes out of the three newspapers he tried. The music-loving city won five encores from the singer and brought back memories (for some) of the great bel canto occasions of thirty years previously and more – of Campanini and Giuglini, Parkinson and Aramburo and Ravelli, of hand-drawn carriages and songs in the small hours, sung from hotel windows to a hushed crowd . . .

On 9 September Jim left Dublin to return to Trieste with Georgie Porgie (as Pappie now liked to call his grandson) and a suitcase full of bedlinen. He also unburdened his father of another member of the family. Oddly, this was not Eileen but the younger and more timid Eva. The day before they set off she had her tonsils removed at the Richmond Hospital by the soon to be knighted Mr Robert H. Woods MB FRCSI of 39 Merrion Square (no less). This was done in order to cure her adenoidal snorting when she spoke and to improve her singing voice, which she had been promised would be given proper training in Trieste; the operation was paid for by Jim (or rather by Stannie, who had been sending him money). The recovering patient behaved 'idiosyncratically' on the journey, which took five days (they ran out of money in Milan and had to leave their luggage as deposit on a loan) but for Jim and Nora it was all worth it: Eva knew the rudiments of dressmaking, which would be useful and, as Jim said, she would be hardly any extra expense: 'I should have had to get a servant in any case.' For his part, John was not sorry to see his house a little emptier. When he heard a couple of weeks later that Eva was already suffering from homesickness (a disturbing thought given her home circumstances), he assured Jim that since she had got over the measles all right, this would probably be no different.

So things went back to what passed for normal. Quite often now, John spent the day at the offices of George Lidwell, a solicitor and old friend at 30 Upper Ormond Quay (next door to Reuben Dodd's office). Since April or May, Lidwell had been giving him casual employment as a messenger or scrivener and, at the end of each day, put a shilling or one-and-six into his hand. It might not be very much but, as May said, the job kept him out of mischief. Of course, it tended to be spent the same evening, as Lidwell was a regular drinking partner of John's, including at lunch-times in the nearby Ormond Hotel. Accordingly, the Joyce finances were always near 'chaos', as John put it. On 8 October (the fifth anniversary of Jim's flight with Nora) he wrote to Jim, diplomatically asking him to send some money. This was to go direct to Eileen, who willy-nilly was now running the household. She had begun voice lessons at the Leinster School of Music in October (for which Jim and Stannie were paying the fee of five shillings a month).

In Trieste, Eva happened to mention that Dublin had no proper cinematograph. Jim decided to shake the place up by giving it one. Continental films could not fail to succeed in a city where the best that was being offered for entertainment were plays like *The Mist that does be on the Bog* (at the Abbey that year). Most people did not go to plays in any case. He soon found investors for the scheme and left again for Ireland, this time on his own. He arrived on 21 October, only six weeks after his previous leave-taking, moved in with his father at 44 Fontenoy Street and set to work, his hat at the jaunty 'Kildare' angle befitting the man of business. Premises were soon found in Mary Street, near Todd Burns, where May was still living and working. Charles J. Murray of Verbena House, Saint Alphonsus Road, a useful relative of the late May Joyce, was engaged as company solicitor. Upstairs in the building a room was turned into an office and here Eileen, and no doubt her father, would come, one to help and the other to give advice. For once with some cash – belonging to his backers – in his pocket, Jim gratefully took the pair of them to a bad play on the twenty-seventh, probably *Sweet Lavender* at the Gaiety, where they would have seen Edward Terry.

Poppie had now finished her time in Callan and had taken the religious name of Mary Gertrude. Though at first she thought that she was going to be sent to a Sisters of Mercy convent in Germany, the plan had changed and now it had been decided that she would go to New Zealand. In mid-November she was seen with due ceremony on to the boat by her sorrowing family. Particularly pleased that Jim could be there, Poppie was not disabused of the idea that he had come back to Dublin primarily to say goodbye to her. She would never see any of the Joyces again. Years later she looked back on her decision to leave Dublin: 'I thought to myself, "Well now, I haven't much to sacrifice" and the only thing I had to sacrifice was my love for my own people, and that was my sacrifice.' She would miss them all very much.

Her father had more than one reason to thank the Sisters of Mercy. They looked after the patients in Jervis Street Hospital, where a few days after Poppie had left he found himself 'on the broad of his back'. He had been having problems with his eyes for years and had at last visited an oculist – perhaps persuaded to do so by Jim. Immediate treatment was needed for conjunctivitis and slight iritis (ailments that were already beginning to plague his son). John Stanislaus was a charity case and as such was treated by Patrick W. Maxwell MD, a typically distinguished Dublin ophthalmic surgeon. The hospital was literally around the corner from the Volta, as the new picture palace was to be called, and Pappie in his bandages became almost a rival attraction to his son's venture. Family and friends visited both. Jim saw a bit of Tom Devin and, still grateful for his friendliness and silence on the occasion of his elopement, could not avoid lending him money – twice. When Rebez and Machnich, two of the Volta's Triestine financiers, arrived in the city to see how things were progressing, Devin even tried (unsuccessfully) to get Jim to guarantee a loan from them as well. As soon as he was up again and able to see, Pappie nicknamed one of them, presumably Machnich, 'that hairy mechanic in a lion-tamer's overcoat'.

With John in hospital, Jim found himself to be a Dublin paterfamilias in Fontenoy Street. The landlord had given notice that the family was scheduled for eviction on 1 December, but money must have been found somewhere and they were able to stay a little longer. John would even manage to give Jim some cash to wire to Nora on Christmas Eve, one indication of how much things had changed between father and son. Though Jim was working himself to exhaustion with the endless arrangements for the new business and had no time for any serious writing, he was continuing to build up an alphabetical series of sketches of the people he knew, including members of the family. It was to be used in the new fiction that was beginning to turn in his mind. Among the longest entries is one entitled '*Pappie*'. Collected over a period, the notes cumulatively render the charm and irascibility of John Stanislaus, his son's impossible father.

He is an Irish suicide

He read medicine

He cannot keep his pipe alight as the buccinator muscle is weak.

He gave me money to wire Nora on Christmas Eve, saying: 'Non ignarus malorum miseris succerere disco.'

One morning he played the fiddle, sitting up in bed.

His college friends were: Tom O'Grady, Harry Peard, Mick Lacey, Maurice Moriarty, Jack Mountain, Joey Corbet, Bob Dyas and Keevers of the Tantiles.

He calls a prince of the church a tub of guts.

The verses he quotes most are:

> *Conservio lies captured! He lies in the lowest dungeons*
> *With manacles and chains around his limbs*
> *Weighing upwards of three tons.*

When he is satirical he calls me sonny and bids me think of my maker and give up the ghost.

He offers the pope's nose at table

He was proud of his hop step and jump

He calls Canon Keon Frosty Face and Cardinal Logue a tub of guts. Had they been laymen he would condone their rancied [*sic*] fat.

When something is mislaid he asks softly: *Have you tried the ashpit?*
He inquires: *Who said?*
He read Modern Society and the *Licensed Victuallers' Gazette.*
He threatened to make me smell hell.
He called Eileen a confirmed bloody idiot
He quarrelled with my friends
When drunk he composes verses containing the word *perchance.*

Many of these jottings were put verbatim, or almost, into Joyce's writings: the pope's nose was to be in the *Portrait.* Fr Keon (a Fairview parish priest and friend of the Murrays) had already come velvetly into 'Ivy Day' and its Committee Room. The lines on Conservio are in *Ulysses*, 'Circe', while the Latin quotation (or rather, misquotation) would be reused in 'Eumaeus': it comes from Virgil's *Aeneid* (1, 1.630), which John very likely knew from his school-days. One old translation (by Conington) of the line goes: 'Myself not ignorant of woe, / Compassion I have learnt to show.' There could be no doubt now that in John's mind Nora was at last a member of his family and that she would be welcome in 44 Fontenoy Street or wherever Pappie's next precarious perch might be.

After various frustrating delays, on 20 December the first show in the Volta was given to an invited audience including John and his daughters; Eileen guested on the piano at some stage. Next day the cinema opened to the general public, who came in such numbers that the police had to be called to control the crowd. *The Bioscope*, the London film-trade magazine, had reported that the new cinematograph would put '... representations on the screen from the best-known operas, accompanied by a gramophone recital by artists representative of the numbers actually being sung in the scene depicted.' However, in the event Jim went one better, engaging a four-piece band to accompany the films and to provide interval music. After a week, when his City of Dublin Cinematograph Manager's Licence (for 'music only [i.e., no dancing] and not at all on Sunday') had finally come through with the help of C. J. Murray, it looked as if Jim's scheme was an assured success: his father, who had for years been urging him to put his talents into a more lucrative trade than teaching, can only have been pleased. At least one of the family was able to make money.

CHAPTER 24

A Shout in the Street

Whether the Volta caught on commercially or not, in early 1910 Jim wanted to get back to Trieste and leave the cinema in the hands of Novak, another of the backers. His efforts on behalf of *Dubliners* had also borne fruit, or so he thought: a contract had been signed with George Roberts of Maunsel and Co., a 'red-headed Scotchman', and the long-anticipated book was to come out soon. But, as Jim told Nora, Ireland was no longer his home: 'A strange land this is to me though I was born in it and bear one of its old names,' while in a letter to Stannie, he wrote: 'This is such a dreadful house that it is a God's act to rescue Eileen from it.' The cramped and uncomfortable surroundings of his father's home, on top of its physical chill and a certain psychic unease, were hastening his steps back to Trieste. This time Jim had decided that his sister Eileen would be better off in Trieste too, and her company on the journey would be welcome as he was also now suffering badly from iritis. He later claimed to have done the entire journey with black bandages over both of his eyes. It is easy to suppose that the parting on 2 January 1910 was another somewhat wet-eyed affair. Now, left behind in 44 Fontenoy Street with Pappie, there were only two: Florrie and Baby.

John Stanislaus's Dublin continued to shrink. At the Mater Hospital, the impish newspaperman Chris Callinan had died before Christmas, as had Roger Greene, a leading figure in the Dublin legal world whom John Stanislaus had known – the stairs to his office would receive the glory of a mention in *Ulysses*. Then, on 10 March, Tim Harrington died, aged fifty-eight. As Parnell's own lawyer and a Dublin MP since 1885, the 'Organiser of Victory' (as he had once been popularly dubbed) was buried with predictable and proper pomp. Respectful obituaries recalled details such as his work in rescuing the posthumous reputation of Myles Joyce of Maamtrasna (though did not mention the political capital he made from the case) and heroic tales were told, such as how in 1883 he had been elected Mullingar's MP while languishing in the town gaol. A sorrowing D. J. Hishon, his old partner-in-crime, accompanied the remains from the Harcourt Street residence of the deceased to the University Church on St Stephen's Green, before the cortège moved on to Glasnevin. John was at the funeral with George Lidwell, from whom he seemed to be currently inseparable, and the great crowd included *le tout monde* of political, municipal, commercial and artistic Dublin, from Captain Cunniam and Tom Devin to William Reddin and Roderick O'Connor. Shortly afterwards, there ended the life and reign of Edward VII himself. If the city was changing, so was the Empire.

Much closer to home, John Murray was the next to go, suddenly on 30 May and still in harness with the accounts department of the *Freeman's Journal*. This was a shock to everyone, for though he had been an asthmatic, it was his brother William who had been most seriously ill. Among the chief mourners were Valentine Murray (son), Albert Browne (cousin) and two brothers-in-law of the lamented, David G. Barber and John S. Joyce. At the cemetery gates the superintendent, still John O'Connell, was there to receive the funeral party, among which were a generous number of the old crowd including Jack Hall and ex-Mayor J. P. Nannetti. They were all getting rather ancient. From Trieste, Jim sent a letter of sympathy to Lillie Murray. He touched diplomatically on the tension between the two branches of the family, but emphasised how glad he was to remember the friendly visit he had made with Giorgio to the Murrays' house the previous summer. John Stanislaus's reaction to the gondolier's death has not survived.

Under Novak's inept direction, the Volta had rapidly declined. Knowing little English, the businessman failed to organise the necessary publicity properly: there was sometimes not even a mention of the new cinema in the entertainment columns of the Dublin papers. The initial surge of curiosity had died down and audiences dwindled badly, so in April the Triestine partners decided to cut their losses. Jim told them that his father would be just the man to sell the cinema as a going concern and asked Pappie to arrange for the Provincial Theatre Company, an English firm then expanding into Ireland, to buy it. There would be a £20 commission in it for him. However, whatever action John took in this matter, if he took any, by June the business still had not been disposed of and Novak took over the task, quickly disposing of it himself to the Provincial for £1000. Once it had been put on a more businesslike footing, the cinema would operate quite profitably for nearly another forty years.

Some time in the early summer of 1910, most probably at the beginning of June, Pappie and his pair of daughters gave up (or were ejected from) the house in Fontenoy Street. He decided not to rent another one and moved with them into the Eblana Private Hotel at 11 Great Denmark Street, a few doors up from Belvedere College. Hishon's Hotel, or the Eblana as it was officially called (after one of Dublin's ancient names), was run by Mrs Nora Hishon and her family; it was not an unpleasant place to stay for a while. There was also the advantage that, unlike a rented house, rooms could be paid for by the week, or even, at a pinch, by the day, though there were discounts for longer stays. With Jack Hishon himself (now thankfully back on speaking terms with John) and one of the Lidwells on the premises, he was in no great hurry to leave. Domestically, things were much more pleasant now. Meals were eaten in the hotel, there were no threats from bailiffs and the Hishons, his friends, could scarcely put them out on the street. However, as in many Irish hotels and boarding-houses of the time, standards of hygiene were low and with a floating population of unattached gentlemen it was not really the most suitable place for Florrie and Baby. As May later wrote, Baby 'got on very well with men and used to have great fun talking and laughing with them, much to Pappie's annoyance'. John's immediate ambition was still to get both girls into 'some school' for twelve months. After that, as he wrote to Jim in July, he would be '*all alone*'.

Despite such remarks, ever since the reconciliation with Jim the previous year John's letters had lost their self-pitying whine. There were no more death threats and he gave every sign of being genuinely interested in the welfare and whereabouts of his scattered children – even of the silent Charlie, now in a shocking state of poverty in suburban Boston. Not that John was averse to the occasional shaft of sarcasm – after Eileen and Eva sent him greetings from the Adriatic for his sixty-first birthday, he conveyed to them (through a letter to Jim) his heartfelt appreciation of their 'awakened memory'. But now he felt valued again: Nora Joyce had sent him a birthday present and he looked forward to meeting her before too long, promising to put them both up in the hotel, and he could now refer to his grandson, little 'Georgie Porgie', as his 'pal'. He was also drinking much less. Almost seven years had elapsed since his wife's death: at long last John Stanislaus Joyce was reaching equilibrium.

The welcome change was noticed in Trieste and Jim invited his father to come and stay for a while. John, replying gratefully, hoped to do so as soon as his two youngest daughters were settled and his duties to them as a father were over. How Stanislaus viewed the prospect of seeing his father again was another matter. Pappie was one thing at a distance and quite another in the flesh. But, though Stannie had never confided in him before, he now chose him as someone to turn to. During the summer, after a serious fight with Jim, he wrote Pappie a long letter. In it, he described in minute detail the pain and misery that he had been suffering at Jim's hands since following him to the Continent and he even reminded his father that he had wisely urged him in 1905 not to leave Dublin in the first place. In Stannie's opinion, Jim's drunkenness, selfishness and reckless extravagance were quite as bad as Pappie's had ever been: he himself had got no thanks for making his own life a poverty-stricken 'hell' while he subsidised, or rather supported, his brother's profligate one. Eileen and Eva were heavily under Jim's influence and could be devious and unpleasant to him, complaining, for example, that they had not come all the way to Trieste to cook for their brother – not this one anyway; and Stannie was the only one who had to pay money to eat with the family. On the recent visit to Dublin, John and everybody else had asked Jim to pass on their messages to Stannie, but when he got back to Trieste Jim could not remember what any of those messages had been. Stannie's whole letter was a howl of frustration and bitterness. But he decided not to post it, and perhaps simply writing it helped him to feel a little better. (He would keep it squirrelled away for decades afterwards.) The old man would be able to do nothing to help him anyway. Furthermore, how might Pappie react to such an approach? He would probably look on the letter as a betrayal of Jim, or as unwarranted and long-suspected weakness by him, or put it all down to fraternal jealousy. Stannie knew enough to be certain that Jim would always win any battle for his father's affections.

Unaware of the tensions in Trieste, John wrote an entertaining letter to Jim on 23 July, inquiring what exactly had happened in the end over the sale of the cinema business. '*Swindled, I presume?*' he asked rhetorically. He had met the Volta solicitor, 'that drunken Cad' Charles Murray, and after quizzing him for information had come to the conclusion that he was playing Jim false. Jim was to have no further dealings with him, if he took his father's advice – the man was no friend. (Nor was he one to John himself, either, being a Murray.)

In early August John must have come into a little money from somewhere, for he decided that a holiday was many years overdue, left the girls in Hishon's and set off alone for a fortnight. He was leaving the Dublin area for perhaps the first time in a decade. He caught the train down to Fermoy and booked into the Bridge Hotel, facing north across the river towards the Ballyhoura Hills. It was the height of the season and the hotel was full of fishermen, pleasant enough company in the bar after their days spent knee deep in the Blackwater. When he wandered up through the town to St Colman's College he could see that it was almost unchanged since his time there, though the building had been tastefully expanded a little and the boys were on holiday. Rose Cottage was less than half an hour's walk on the other side of the bridge that his relations had helped to build and no doubt he made the pilgrimage. He may also have explored the graveyard where generations of his forefathers lay. There were other family connections still in the area as well, such as the Joyces of 'Acres' a few miles outside the town, and perhaps John visited one or two of them, an odd sight with his cane among the farmyard poultry and manure heaps. Jim had asked him to do some research for him while he was there, probably on ancestral matters, and he may have pored over the records at the Courthouse or the Church, for he promised his son a long letter detailing his findings. He also offered to dazzle Jim with 'all' views of Fermoy of which he could find picture postcards. Only two such postcards survive and the long genealogical letter may never have been written: if Jim was hoping for early material about his family to weave into his writings, there is little or no evidence to be found there that he ever got it. His father's main reason for choosing to go to Fermoy seems to have been in order to pay homage to the memory of the family dead: he may also have been considering whether to move there himself for good. A residential country hotel would have been cheaper than a city one.

When John returned to Dublin and summer faded into autumn, it was business, or the lack of it, as usual. On Jim's behalf he had asked Hishon to sort out a confusion relating to the Volta electricity bill and the Dublin Electric Committee had agreed to issue a cheque for overpayment. As for his son's forthcoming *Dubliners* book, George Roberts of Maunsel's had delayed publication again, typical Dublin lead-swinging in John's opinion. And he had no more success than before in his ambition to find a school to take Florrie and Baby as boarders. For the time being, at least, there would be no moving to Fermoy, or Cork City, or anywhere else. He was still their father, after all.

In November 1910, the House of Lords rejected the 'People's Budget'. For the Liberals, it was a signal that the power of the Upper House would have to be curtailed. It was no longer acceptable that their (unelected) lordships should be able to kill off Commons Bills entirely. Two months later a General Election divided seats in the Commons almost equally between the Liberals and the Conservatives, so once again the Irish Parliamentary Party, now reunited under Redmond, found itself in a position of strength. The Irish MPs helped the Liberals under Asquith to hold on to government and the prime minister put through his successful Parliament Bill to emasculate the Lords. The word was that another Home Rule Bill (already drafted) was on the way in reciprocation. In an article (translated as 'The Home Rule Comet') that he wrote at the end of 1910 for an Italian newspaper, James

Joyce, observing from Trieste, was sceptical. In Dublin, his father probably was too.

John and his daughters were now for all practical purposes 'of no fixed abode': though over the next couple of years John would often end up staying at Hishon's Hotel, it was by no means a permanent address. In April, the 1911 Government Census found John Stanislaus, Florence Elizabeth and Mabel Josephine Anne Joyce (Baby) temporarily residing at 20 Gardiner's Place, in a boarding-house that may have been a little cheaper than the £5 per month that they were paying for their rooms to Mrs Hishon. May, who had turned twenty-one in January, was still working for Todd Burns but had left the staff dormitory there: she was now lodging with a family called Sherlock at 4 Lower St Columba's Road, Drumcondra. Both her younger sisters had at last left their convent and, though they did not yet earn a wage, had embarked on training as typists. Baby was pleased to have got into an apprenticeship with the printers, Gerrard's of Stephen's Green, the firm that in 1901 had printed the pamphlet containing Jim's essay 'The Day of the Rabblement'. Their father's idea of being free of them all at last was going according to plan. If the worst happened and his health began to give out, Baby could come back to look after him: she would always be there for him. Then, on Thursday, 19 June, Baby fell ill.

After the weekend John brought a doctor, George Francis Mac-Namara MD, to Hishon's (where the Joyces were again staying) and asked him to have a look at his daughter. MacNamara was physician to the South Dublin Union Workhouse and, since Great Denmark Street was outside his normal catchment area, John very likely had got to know him socially and asked him to come as a favour. Baby was already in considerable discomfort, with headaches and an agonisingly painful throat. The doctor quickly recognised that she had contracted typhoid and telephoned the Fever Hospital ('and House of Recovery') in Cork Street to have her admitted at once. This time there were no objections by her father: poor Georgie was still in everyone's minds. Since conventional modes of transport barred typhoid patients from using their vehicles, the 'fever cab' had to be sent round to convey her across the river. When it arrived, Baby wept and protested that she wanted to stay where she was, but it was her only chance. Once she was in the ward, the family's visits were confined to an hour a week on Sundays, as the patient had to be kept quiet, with as little stimulation as possible.

After the news that Baby was in Cork Street reached Eva in Trieste, she set off on her own to Dublin. Unlike the more confident Eileen, she had failed to settle down properly amid the penury and squabbling that always surrounded Jim and though she would miss little Lucia, to whom she had grown very close, this seemed to be the right time to come home. When she arrived, on 3 July, she was met at the station by May, Florrie and her father, who looked, as the traveller wrote to Trieste, 'particularly dirty and shaby'. John immediately borrowed a shilling from her. She was assured that Baby was doing well, but after her journey was upset to be told not to visit her, as knowing that she was back in Dublin might over-excite the patient.

Pappie was not very welcoming. At first he announced that Eva would have to find herself somewhere to live, since there was nowhere for her in Hishon's (he had not seen the point of paying for Baby's bed when she was in hospital), but after some persuasion he relented and went to considerable trouble to find her a room (on credit) in an Abbey Street boarding-house for a week – no easy task, as Dublin was overflowing with visitors to welcome the new King George V and Queen Mary, who were about to arrive at Kingstown on a Royal Visit. However, when May met them all in town after work she vetoed her father's arrangement – nobody knew anything about the Abbey Street place and it would be full of 'black strangers' who might take advantage of a young lady on her own. It was by now half-past nine in the evening and May's intervention was the last straw for Pappie. As Eva told Stannie later, he reacted like a madman and 'jumped about the middle of O'Connell Street' in frustration. When he had stopped shouting, he enlightened them (and passers-by) that he had done all he could and that it was now May's job to find somewhere for Eva to spend the night and to pay for it too. Eventually, May found nine shillings to get her sister a week's board with the Sherlocks in Drumcondra, whom she had just left in order to keep the distraught Florrie company in Hishon's. Since Eileen had gone, May had been feeling the strain of being John's eldest daughter in Ireland, with the mantle of Poppie and her mother on her shoulders, and a weekly wage of only ten shillings.

Despite what Eva had been told, Baby was not doing well in the Fever Hospital. When John, May and Florrie had visited her at the end of June they found her very weak. Her hearing was badly affected and it was upsetting to have to shout at her to be understood. While they were there she had asked May in an almost inaudible whisper whether she thought she was going to recover and when May replied that of course she was, just lapsed into silence again. On 6 July, they saw Baby for the last time. In a letter to Stannie, May described what happened:

... when we went into the ward she was asleep and I wanted to come away altogether and let her sleep but Pappie stood looking down at her and she suddenly woke with a start and stared at us for a minute. Then after a minute o[r] so she commenced to talk but all we could understand was 'May, I am dying. I am dying, its a positive fact.' ... Stannie, have you ever seen an animal in pain, do you know the look they have in their eyes? well it was with just a look that our little sister followed us out of the ward after we had said Goodbye to her ...

Six days later, on Saturday, 12 July, Baby died. She was seventeen. From Trieste Jim sent a wreath and some money and at the funeral, as his father told him in a letter of thanks a few days afterwards from Hishon's Hotel, 'everything was carried out as it should be and as you would wish.' The tone of the rest of this letter must have been dismaying to Jim. It was less than two years since the pair had been reconciled in the Yellow House, the moment when Jim could feel that the father he had lost had returned to him, the old father he had hardly seen since May Joyce died in 1903, and now Pappie was obviously back to square one again. John's letter continued:

... I can't go into the details of her lingering illness. She became unconscious the day before she died and remained so to the end. I was with her for over an hour the day she died and I think she knew *me*. She got her sickness in this accursed hole. But this [is all] perhaps for the best, as she was too sensitive and highly-strung to endure the troubles of this

319

wretched world. She is with her Mother who idolized her, and has left me to linger on, a broken hearted old man, but only for a short time now until I will follow my darling Maime and my 'doatie darlie' to where partings are not known. I am now most anxious to die, having lost the only one (*except you*) who loved me . . . So much for the past – now the present has been made so unbearable to me by the callous, unnatural treatment I am receiving from my three daughters, that I am resolved to leave Dublin and them on the 1st prox. Since my poor baby died they have left me alone, and refuse even to take a walk with me. Everyone here, as in the last house we stayed in, crys shame on them for their cruel conduct towards their Father. I will allow Florrie £2 a month out of my cheque, and Eva will have £1 or 25/- from you and May has nearly 10/- per week all found, so that the three can live well until they get some employment – but live with them any longer, after the eight years of misery I have endured, is out of the question. Now all that I loved, or loved me, has been taken from me, I am anxious you should have the family portraits &c. how can I manage that? I know *you* will set proper value on them when I am dead and gone. Do, Jim, for the sake of the *old love* we had for each other. My health is breaking down and my eyes are bad again, as you see by this writing, but when I come out of Hospital, if I do – I will go to Cork and perhaps never see one of you again – I should wish greatly to see you and Stannie and Georgie once more before I die. But I fear it is not possible. *Now* Jim, as time is short let me have a few lines *by return*. You and Stannie have *acted nobly* towards paying a last fond tribute of your love for your darling sisters memory. I feel proud of you both – Give my love to all and for the short balance of my life think of me as your fond, though heartbroken

FATHER

May too wrote about Baby in a moving letter to Stannie on the twenty-fifth, telling him: 'There is one thing I know, and that is, none of us will ever be as happy again as we were when we had her with us.' She continued:

. . . [W]hen we used to go out in the evenings for a walk we spent our time talking of you all, Baby praising everyone, (she always did) and saying that she would go to Trieste, that was the dream of her life. The poor child used to dance along the road at the very thought of going over there. It was a peculiar thing that this whole year passed we never went with anyone but ourselves and never wanted anyone. We used to go for long walks, round Santry or Ballymun or Killester, but always by ourselves. You say you would have been fond of Baby had things been different. She was winning as a child but no one could help loving her since she grew up. She was so affectionate and thoughtful and had such a sweet disposition that everyone, even strangers in the house, took a fancy to her. And then after it all to see her lying there dead, the image of Georgie, it would break your heart to see her. However, whether it is for the best or not that she is gone at least she is at rest. It is a consolation that the first of the month [when John's pension cheque was being spent] or Pappie's humours cannot affect her now. She is gone with her brightness and there is nothing for us to do but try and face whatever else there is in store for us. . . . [M]y throat gets sore when I think of Baby and all she intended to do for everyone. . . . [W]hen I see you I will tell you all some nice stories. They used to make us laugh but they would not make me laugh now.

In her letter to Stannie, Eva had said that Baby's illness had been caused by 'the surage in Hishon's'. Her father agreed, and had a fight with Jack Hishon about it (and probably also about money matters – Hishon actually owed him something, for a change). He found somewhere else to live, though he refused to vacate the hotel until he had used up what he considered was due to him. While John, and initially Eva, might blame the suspect drains for Baby's death, May and Florrie had other ideas. Their attitude to their father, and his to them, had not been exaggerated in his recent letter to Jim. May told Stannie that she had very little sympathy for Pappie:

. . . Had Baby always had plenty of nourishment and food, and less worry, she most probably would have pulled through as it was she was strong enough but her constitution must have been undermined from constant starvation and misery. And still he is just as selfish as ever. Since Eva came home he did not give a penny for her . . . Now it is this sort of thing that first wore Mother out, then Poppie, then Eileen (whose appearance you remember when she went to Trieste) then Baby and now, at long last it has come to my turn . . . Pappie is a thorough no-good and the quicker we are all able to do without him the better. He does nothing but drink and fight and moan and groan from the time he gets up till he goes to bed again.

For many of his surviving children, and particularly for May, Pappie had had his last chance. It was no mitigation that he was grieving as deeply as any of them.

After Baby's death, Jim had sent a 'rather strange and bitter' letter to his father, which John seems not to have kept. (In fact, John never managed to keep anything for very long. James Joyce's letters to his father, and there were many, would now be an Irish national treasure if they ever were to surface.) Richard Ellmann considered that Joyce blamed Ireland itself for the tragedy of his sister's terrible passing, rather than Pappie's character (or Jack Hishon's sewerage system), and certainly John bore Jim no resentment for whatever he said in his letter. The fact was that, as Jim knew, family bereavement was still very common in Ireland. A. J. Kettle, for instance, had recently lost his daughter at the supposedly stable age of twenty-five and even Dublin's Chief Medical Officer of Health, Sir Charles Cameron, who the year before had been made an honorary Freeman for his work on improving the public health of the city, saw five of his six sons predecease him. But that was of no comfort to John. Baby had been the one to give him hope for a comfortable and contented old age. Now he had lost her and he felt very alone.

CHAPTER 25

The Old Story

As the summer drew to a close, John and his daughters kept an eye out in case *Dubliners* suddenly appeared in the bookshops, but though an advertisement for the book would appear in an Abbey Theatre programme, the year would end without seeing its publication. Jim had been sending frequent hortatory letters about the delay to George Roberts of Maunsel's, but had been getting infrequent replies. He was rapidly losing what was left of his patience. Already he had threatened in July to sue Roberts for breach of contract, using his 'solicitor in Dublin'. Taking his father's advice, he had dropped Charles Murray and taken on George Lidwell instead as his Irish legal representative. Since John was still often in Lidwell's office, during the subsequent negotiations about *Dubliners* he would be closely involved (though not always with the encouragement of Jim). Had John taken up the cudgels on his son's behalf, the dispute with Roberts might have become a reprise of his feuds with Dodd, Waldron and many others. In fact it never quite did so: John Stanislaus Joyce was tired of battle and his spirit was almost broken.

But not completely. There was laughter in the city when the story got around that on 26 August, Reuben J. Dodd's son, Reuben Junior, had jumped into the Liffey in an attempt to drown himself after falling for a girl from a quayside shop of whom his family disapproved (though he later claimed to have been retrieving his hat). He was pulled out by a Jewish docker, Moses Goldin, who had to be treated in hospital with pulmonary trouble as a result. For all that, Dodd Senior gave Mrs Goldin two shillings, after she went to see him in the hope of recouping earnings lost while her husband was recovering. Dodd reputedly told her that he should have minded his own business. On hearing the value that Dodd had put on his son's life, John Stanislaus snorted, 'One and eightpence too much.' The remark was much appreciated by Jim, and it would be repeated by Simon Dedalus when the story of Dodd's Liffey swim was anachronistically told in *Ulysses*. The implication was that no son of Reuben J. could be worth fivepence.

At the end of August, John moved out of Hishon's to 12 Gardiner's Place, bringing Florrie and Eva with him and paying a month in advance for them all. They lodged there under an accommodating Mrs Baird, who Eva was pleased to find owned a piano that she was allowed to practise on. Florrie still had no job, but Eva took an apprenticeship with Gerrard Brothers, the same Stephen's Green printers where Baby had been the previous year. Fired by her stay in Trieste, she also intended to enrol for evening classes in typewriting, shorthand and arithmetic at the Municipal Technical School just off Rutland Square, and in her spare time hoped to take music lessons as well. She wrote to Stannie explaining how much these various courses would cost, and she was not disappointed: he and May between them covered all Eva's fees for the coming year. For his part, John warned Eva that he was not prepared to pay any more of her accommodation expenses. He could no longer endure living with his daughters and their reproaches, spoken and unspoken. His relations with them all had now become actively hostile in both directions. Even innocent remarks could lead to trouble: as Eva wrote to Stannie, 'When I ask Pappie about Jim's book that I thought would be published in September he either tells me to go to – – – – or to write to Jim.'

May had been sending Jim newspapers containing reports of industrial unrest in the streets: there had, she said, been up to a hundred policemen killed or injured as a result of recent strikes, and 'it was as much as your life was worth to go near the city at night.' However, some things never changed in Dublin and the memory of Charles Stewart Parnell was still alive. On 1 October 1911, just before the twentieth anniversary of Ivy Day, the Parnell Monument was finally unveiled by John Redmond. With 'Boss' Croker alongside, Redmond spoke confidently about the impending prospect of Home Rule. The statue (by Augustus Saint-Gaudens) overlooked the intersection of O'Connell Street and

Great Britain Street, close to the scene of many of The Chief's triumphs in and around the Rotunda. At the same time Great Britain Street was renamed Parnell Street. For D. J. Hishon it was the culmination of many years' work on the Parnell Monument Fund Committee, which had met weekly (primarily under the chairmanship of the late Tim Harrington) since the laying of the foundation stone twelve years before – though as with Daniel O'Connell most of the money to pay for it had been raised in America. For John it must have been gratifying to know that he was still not quite the only one to remember. His solid idols now dominated both ends of Dublin's main thoroughfare.

Aunt Josephine's house was still a haven for John's children, though they never mentioned their visits there to their father. Of her six living children, Stannie's friend Katsie had already left home and her eldest son John (somehow always known as Jim) had just got married, much to everyone's surprise – five years earlier his mother had been visiting him behind bars in a prison or asylum, where he had been sent with severe emotional problems. Josephine Murray's greatest worry now was her husband. Uncle Willie was in the horrific final phase of syphilis, but, perhaps frightened that his secret might get out, he refused either to visit a doctor or allow one into the house. In November his younger brother, Joseph Murray (Uncle Joe), died in London, but there was no question of Willie travelling over to the funeral: he was now eating very little and would soon be having difficulty articulating his words. Nothing, however, not even this, interfered with Aunt Josephine's devotion to the Joyce children: she wrote regularly to Jim, Nora and Stannie, and always had a spare shoulder to cry upon for those left behind in Dublin. After Baby's death she had been a tower of strength and as May said, had been 'very good & kind to us, indeed only for her I think we would be in a madhouse'. But to Pappie Aunt Josephine was still an interfering old busybody.

As 1911 drew to an end the girls in Dublin felt ever more envious of their siblings in Trieste, who, though they may have been short of money, at least had a semblance of family life together. They looked forward to Eileen's proposed visit to Dublin in the New Year. Eva sent her a 'stickyback' photograph on 21 December and asked her to remember them at Christmas, but 'not to think on past times, as it will do none of us any good'. For them, she remarked, Christmas Day in Dublin meant 'all the places shut up, and what harm if it was a case of "be it ever so humble there is no place like home"'. Having nowhere they could call a home, the sisters' thoughts were also with Poppie, far off in her convent on the other side of the world, and with poor Charlie in Boston, who was rumoured to have been in gaol. Still entertaining a forlorn hope that Jim or Stannie might find him a position in Trieste if he could be got back from America, May had written to Stannie that she hated 'to hear of any of the family coming to the wall as he did'. Charlie finally broke silence with a postcard to Jim on 22 December, written in what looks like a drunken scrawl. In its entirety, it read: '32. E. Brookline St Boston Mass Dear Jim, Do not ask me for an apology for not writing. I have none. But if you can spare a word, your derelict brother would appreciate it. Charlie.' Jim, of course, knew that it was not words, of which he had plenty, but money, of which he had none, that Charlie would appreciate most. But to his credit, Charlie had not asked him for any.

By January 1912, Jim was optimistically using his father as intermediary in his dealings with George Roberts, sending him papers and receiving short postcards signed 'Pater' confirming that his instructions had been carried out, or would be soon. John was still spending most of his days with George Lidwell and had made friends with another lodger in 12 Gardiner's Place, a Mr Walshe, in whose company he spent most of his evenings. Eva was now doing her piano practice at Aunt Josephine's, but one day her aunt told her that the instrument was going to have to go back to the shop since Uncle Willie was no longer earning anything. Eva persuaded her to write to Stannie with the suggestion that if he sent the rental, Aunt Josephine's piano could be left where it was and Eva could treat it as her own. Stannie sent the money and on 8 February Eva showed off her new typing skills in a letter that she sent to thank him. She purported to miss the 'Adonises' by the Adriatic, but despite everything she was beginning to enjoy life and had been to a few good films in Dublin, though they were no substitute for the magnificent Triestine opera. She mentioned that there were now seven or eight cinemas in Dublin, including one in the Rotunda, and that, if the queues outside were any indication, they all seemed to be doing well. This was news that Jim can hardly have been overjoyed to hear.

News came from Eileen, who had not been very well. From her wages (as a governess in and around Trieste) she was still saving up for her visit to the family in Ireland, who had not seen her for nearly two years. The trip was planned for June. May strongly advised her against coming back permanently – there was nothing for her in Dublin. But the good news was that Florrie had found a job at long last. Thanks to May, she was on the Cash Desk of Todd Burns, where she seemed to be getting on quite well. One of her tasks was to operate the store's mechanical system of overhead wires and springs that propelled hollow wooden balls at high speed to all corners of the shop, carrying payments, change and receipts to and from assistants on the floor. Her diminutive size meant that she needed a stool to stand on when pulling the levers. Florrie was delighted with the three or four shillings per week (plus all meals) that she was getting there.

Now that all his daughters showed signs that they might soon be self-sufficient, Pappie revived his complaints about feeling neglected. He pestered Eva for a week with his old threat of going back to Cork to die. Eva warned Stannie to take no notice if his father mentioned Cork to him: it would never happen. Of much more concern to her was the plight of Charlie. Although he never wrote to any of them in Dublin, she had been given a letter that he had sent from Boston to a friend of his named Redmond. It was 'too bad to describe': his wife had been ill and he himself was 'in a deplorable way'. Eva passed the letter on to Pappie, who forwarded it to Jim. The consensus was that Charlie should never have left Dublin in the first place and that some way ought to be found to bring him back again to Ireland.

At the beginning of May, the three Joyces left Gardiner's Place. Eva and Florrie took a room in a large hotel at 65 Eccles Street, run by Mrs Mary Jane Whelan, mother of Leo Whelan the painter (who was still living there as well). It was probably at this point that Pappie grasped the nettle and took a room somewhere else to live in alone, for what seems to be the first time in his life. But they all were gathered together again a few days later when, on

11 May, Charlie appeared back in Dublin with his family, to the extreme delight of his sisters. He had somehow laid his hands on enough money to pay the fare from Boston. It may be that Stannie (or Jim) had finally decided to help him out. He looked thinner and, thanks perhaps to his Joycean ear for music, his accent had picked up a transatlantic twang. Otherwise they were glad to see that he was little changed. Ill health and the ravages of life on the breadline in Boston had noticeably altered his wife Mary, however: she did not look either healthy or happy and was thinner than her husband. They had been forced to leave behind their eldest child, Jim, to catch up with them later, probably because he was ill as well, but the Dublin Joyces, always appreciative of children, were pleased to meet Georgie, who was nearly two, and his four-month-old sister Eileen. In his choice of names for his offspring, as in several other less commendable ways, Charlie appeared to be emulating his father. Auntie May noticed that they might have been better dressed.

For the reasonable rent of six shillings a week, Charlie and family quickly found a couple of furnished rooms at 37 Great Charles Street, off Mountjoy Square East. Eva, imparting the glad tidings to Stannie, was optimistic that if 'some sort of a suit' was found for her brother to wear, he would soon get work in Dublin: with this Home Rule business on the way people were saying that shortly there would be any number of vacancies. Pappie looked more respectable now than he had when Charlie had left and he might even be able to use what little influence he still had to obtain a position for him. She was not wrong: within a matter of weeks Charlie would be working for the Telephone Company. As this was part of the Post Office, he would officially be a civil servant.

Home Rule did indeed seem imminent. Two days before Charlie's return, the third Home Rule Bill had been passed in the House of Commons. Everything was now on schedule for a parliament in Dublin within two years. But it appeared plain to many that this would be a largely puppet government, swearing allegiance to the British monarch and leaving important purse-strings in the hands of the British Chancellor. It would be neither the government that Messrs Parnell and Joyce had (in their different ways) fought for, nor the one that Arthur Griffith's Sinn Féin was demanding. The prospect also failed to satisfy Jim. Soon after the Commons vote he published in the *Piccolo* an article entitled '*L'Ombra di Parnell*' ('The Shade of Parnell') and sent copies to his father, Charlie and May. Had John been able to read it, it would have interested him, but unless Eva managed to puzzle out some of it for him (and her Italian was rudimentary), he probably never did. The article imagined the ritual opening of the new Irish parliament, a parliament with only the 'appearance of autonomy'. The ghost of Parnell, unnoticed amid the celebrations, looks on sceptically. It was not 'English wolves', James wrote, that had brought down this 'extraordinary personality': he had been ripped to pieces by the Irish themselves. John would have emphatically agreed, though adding that the politicians who had inherited Parnell's great example were, almost to a man, time servers, impostors and traitors. Tim Healy was not mentioned by name in the piece, but the writer blamed Parnell's habitual melancholy on the leader's 'profound conviction that . . . one of the disciples who dipped his hand in the same bowl with him would betray him'. John Stanislaus would have had no doubt about whom his son saw as Judas to Parnell's Jesus Christ. When, after a fortnight, Jim had received no acknowledgement of his article, either from his father or from anyone else, he wrote to Eileen at her job outside Trieste that he hoped shortly to send 'an old pair of trousers to Dublin which is more in their line'.

Charlie's feelings towards Pappie had changed very little while he had been in America. After his sisters had regaled him with their piquant tales of the foolishness and selfishness of the old man, he came up with a plan. They should all pool their resources, rent a roomy house and live together again – all, that is, except for Pappie. It was as if he was trying to recreate the home he had grown up in, but with himself in his father's shoes. The idea had several advantages for Charlie: with four adult women in the house and only one man, himself, he should be well cared for and since some of his sisters would be earning money, it was unlikely that he and his family would ever starve again. Most attractive of all was the thought that the arrangement might dilute the constant emotional and financial pressure that Mary had been putting him under. In truth, Mr and Mrs Charles Joyce were not having a very happy life together. She may already have been ill.

Charlie's suggestion gave rise to what Jim called 'a good three-cornered fight' in Dublin. Jim's view was that his brother 'should take a labourer's cottage and live in it with his wife and children, alone'. Pappie likewise did not welcome the thought of his children united against him and May had her own reason for doubting the advisability of the scheme: as the only one with a decent steady job, the chances were that she would end up supporting the entire ménage. Eva and Florrie were happy enough to do whatever they were told, but they were being told different things by different people. In the end, nothing came of Charlie's plan.

On the evening of Monday, 8 July 1912, Nora Joyce arrived in Dublin with Lucia. They were on the way to Galway to visit their relations there, particularly Nora's mother and her uncle, Michael Healy (a customs official and nothing to the political Cork brothers), whom she had not seen for over eight years. When they reached Westland Row Station they were both pleased to recognise Eva among the gaggle of Joyces meeting the Kingstown train: the others waiting on the platform, Pappie, Charlie and Florrie, they knew only by reputation and some old photographs. John Stanislaus, looking healthy ('but poor', Nora said), was most welcoming and played the part of genial host. He liked the look of Nora, who was wearing a wedding ring to stop snide comments being made in Ireland about her (and Lucia's) status, and the sight of his granddaughter reduced him to sentimental tears, tears that, as Nora told Eileen later, were really 'all about Jim'. It never took much to make John cry about Jim. He escorted the party up Westland Row and round the corner to Finn's Hotel, where Nora had been a chambermaid when she first met Jim, and there they had a welcome dinner. Over the meal John must have produced his oft-repeated witticism of years before – that with a name like Barnacle, Nora was bound to stick to Jim. No record survives of who paid the bill. It was probably Nora. Elegant in the somewhat ostentatious Continental fashions that Jim had paid for, she relished the thought of being a guest where she had previously been a slavey, and booked in for two nights: John's earlier offer of a bed for her and Jim whenever they were in Dublin was no longer an option anyway.

The next day was a busy one for everyone. Pappie and Charlie picked up Nora and Lucia in the morning and they marched off to Maunsel's offices in Middle Abbey Street to confront George Roberts about what he intended to do with *Dubliners*. Catching him in for once, they 'just pinned that charming gentleman' to the spot and Nora gave him a piece of her mind. While she was in full flow, John could not resist breaking in to add one or two further points. Thereafter, Roberts treated Nora as if she were not even present, addressing himself exclusively to her father-in-law and making his escape as soon as he could. He would have more time to discuss the matter, he said, the next day. The episode did not endear John to Nora.

For the moment, there was nothing more to be done, so as the weather was good John suggested that they all take a tram or train out to the Hill of Howth for a picnic. May was at work all day, but Eva and Florrie joined them, and were doubtless put in charge of bringing the sandwiches and flasks of tea. The party spent a pleasant afternoon among the heather and rhododendrons, chatting and gazing out over the sea and the city. Before they left, Lucia was persuaded to sing them a song and everybody signed a picture postcard which they posted off to Jim in Trieste. They got back to town about six and managed to shake Pappie off, before going to see Eva's and Florrie's new room at 2 Sackville Gardens off Ballybough Road. As Nora later appropriately wrote, the girls seemed 'quiet happy' to be living on their own there, finally free of the uncertainties and, for Florrie at least, the terrors that life with Pappie brought with it. Once May had joined them after work, they walked round the corner to Aunt Josephine's for more songs, notably from Charlie. By this time Nora had had quite enough and could hardly wait to take Lucia back to Finn's: she did not take to any of the Murrays, not even Aunt Josephine herself. John, if he ever heard her opinion of his 'very respectable' in-laws, would have approved of Nora even more than he already did.

On Wednesday Charlie and Nora decided to leave Pappie behind when they called on Roberts as arranged. There was, of course, no sign of the recalcitrant publisher. After one further futile attempt to catch him, Nora gave up, checked out of Finn's and caught the train to Galway with Lucia. Charlie promised to lie in wait for Roberts every day until he succeeded in questioning him properly on his intentions. In Trieste, meanwhile, Jim was seething with curiosity about how Nora had got on at Maunsel's: when the Howth postcard arrived a day or so later, with Nora's, his father's and a lot of other signatures on it and no news, he at once angrily set off for Ireland, bringing Giorgio and a walletful of borrowed money. If he wanted something done, he obviously had to do it himself.

Father and son appeared in Dublin on the evening of Monday, 15 July and must have squeezed in for the night with Charlie, Mary and their children at 17 Richmond Place (just round the corner from their old home in North Richmond Street). The brothers had not met since 1904. Charlie had already been sacked from the Telephone Company and was out of work again, struggling to support his family on the meagre 'outdoor relief' or dole. Though Jim believed that this had happened 'through his own fault' (a family euphemism for drunkenness), he thought his brother a 'decent poor fellow' and offered, if he got an opportunity, to look for something else for him to do. Pappie's famous 'influence' was not what it once had been.

But Jim's chief business in town was with his publisher. The next morning Roberts granted him an audience, finding the writer, as he remarked later, even less malleable than the Giant's Causeway. He was most willing, he told Jim, to publish *Dubliners*, but only with cuts; alternatively he was prepared to sell him unbound sheets of the book (which had been set up in type by the O'Connell Street printers, John Falconer's, more than two years before). The first John Stanislaus knew of his son's arrival in Dublin may have been a little later in George Lidwell's offices. Walking round the block to 30 Upper Ormond Quay, Jim was unlikely to have been in the best of moods to meet his father. If he did consult him now on the subject of Roberts, John had a good many graphic stories about the publisher's untrustworthiness to tell him. That afternoon Jim was on the train to Galway and Nora. He needed to think.

While Jim was off exploring Connemara, ancient home of his distant ancestors (where he found a gravestone in Oughterard inscribed with the name 'J. Joyce'), in Dublin John was seeing practically nothing of his immediate descendants. There was no longer much reason why any of his children should have wished to seek him out, as he had by now entirely stopped giving them money. It is even uncertain where he was living at this time: the only hint is in a letter that Charlie sent to Stannie on 6 September 1912, which mentions that 'Pappie has left the Iveagh House'. On the south side of the city, not far from Dublin Castle, this was a supervised hostel that provided over five hundred beds a night for homeless labourers and other male indigents. In fact, his father had almost certainly been in the Ivy Hotel, a north-side lodging-house beside the Children's Hospital in North Temple Street which had once been the Parnells' Dublin residence. This was an establishment he would use again six or seven years later, and it was no worse than Hishon's or Whelan's in Eccles Street or a hundred other similar places in the city. For Charlie to dub Pappie's residence 'the Iveagh House' was only to be expected, given his father's habitual impoverishment. For John one attraction of the ivy-covered hotel was that it was named for Parnell; another was 'Buckety Bill' Beardwood, resident, a large, bandy-legged man, in unusual trousers with a bass voice – 'bockedy' Ben Dollard of *Ulysses*. There were still some left.

In mid-August, leaving Nora, Giorgio and Lucia in Galway, Jim came back from his adventures in the west to continue the negotiations over *Dubliners*. During the next fortnight he made various concessions to a short-tempered Roberts on condition that the book be published in time for Ivy Day, 6 October, less than two months later. John Stanislaus's shrewd judgement was that capitulation to Roberts would lead to other demands – and so it proved. Jim used Pappie's table in George Lidwell's offices as a centre of operations, but the more he consulted Lidwell himself, the less practical use he found him. Most of Lidwell's work was in the police courts, not in business, and the solicitor spent most of his time either in court or in the Ormond Hotel, where it was difficult to get him to pay attention. It was equally difficult to get him to pay for drinks: if he wanted a consultation Jim was expected to buy rounds for the solicitor and everyone else who happened to be with him. These invariably included John, who by now was calling Roberts 'a swindler' and urging his son to 'buck up', forget about Maunsel's and try another publisher. John's private opinion (which Charlie obligingly passed on to Jim) was rather different; he had now seen the manuscript, and called *Dubliners* 'a blackguard production'. Lidwell's contribution to the debate was to tell Jim that 'An Encounter' (in which two boys meet a sadistic elderly paedophile josser in Ringsend) was a 'disgusting' tale. He said that even Jim's father, 'a man with experience of life, ha[d] no idea what kind of individual you are writing about'. If a story about Ringsend really had to be in the book, that district had 'many historical associations' which could be drawn upon instead. For a second opinion on the josser, Jim took the short stories to his friend Tom Kettle MP, who, though he did not like them, confirmed, 'I know, we have all met him.' As indeed he had: the Captain was a familiar figure as a reader in the National Library. After seeking the advice and taking the recommendation of Arthur Griffith (who as editor of *Sinn Féin* had published in the previous summer a long letter by him about the ill-treatment he had received over *Dubliners*), Jim transferred the case to another solicitor, who he hoped would be more sympathetic.

The meetings in the Ormond Hotel, though frustrating, had not been entirely unprofitable to James Joyce the writer, however. The 'Sirens' chapter of *Ulysses* would be set there, drawing on many details observed in the hotel at this time. Waiting to talk to George Lidwell, Jim found himself listening to extended sessions of story-telling. One unlikely tale of John's that never found a place in his son's work (though he passed the anecdote on to Stannie) showed something of Pappie's old anticlerical sparkle:

A bishop visited a P.P. [parish priest] and stayed too late to go home. The P.P. asked him to stay and said there were only two beds in the house, his own and that of his housekeeper. The bishop said he would sleep in the P.P.'s bed for one night. They went to bed. In the morning the P.P. half awoke and hit the bishop a smack on the backside saying:
– Get up, Mary Ann, I'll be late for mass –
And, by God, the very next day His Grace was made an archbishop.

Since his father no longer had a house, in Dublin this time Jim probably stayed with Josephine Murray for the first day or two,

Parnell's funeral passing the old Parliament Building in College
Green. His death in 1891 marked a turning point in John
Stanislaus's life
(Illustrated London News)

James Joyce at college in 1902
(Photo: Constantine Curran, courtesy
Special Collections, UCD)

H. C. E. CHILDERS.

" H(ERE) C(OMES) E(VERYBODY)
CH-LD-RS."

H.C.E. Childers ('Here Comes Everybody'), one
of the models (with John Stanislaus) for the
central figure in *Finnegans Wake*
(Courtesy Peter Costello)

After the Easter Rising - the ruins of the offices of the *Evening
Telegraph*, *Freeman's Journal* and *Sport:* only The Oval (Phil Gilligan's
old bar, second building from the right) survives
(Courtesy Peter Costello)

Eugene Sandow, the body builder admired by
John Stanislaus and Leopold Bloom. This was
how John imagined himself, even down to the
moustaches
(Strand Magazine)

John Stanislaus's inscribed copy of the recording of James reading
from *Ulysses*, sent to Claude Road in November 1927
(Courtesy Dr Garret FitzGerald. Photo: Peter Costello)

The Schaurek children – one of the photos John
Stanislaus kept on his mantelpiece in Claude Road
(Courtesy Yvonne Conroy)

Eva and Florence Joyce with some of their Murray and
McNestry relatives
(Courtesy Yvonne Conroy)

Eva Joyce in the 1920s
(Courtesy Yvonne Conroy)

'Tatto' Schaurek in *Trial by Jury* in
Belvedere in 1942
(Courtesy Central Catholic Library Dublin)

May Joyce in the 1920s
(Courtesy Yvonne Conroy. Photo: Keogh Brothers)

The Joyce family in Paris: another photograph which John Stanislaus kept on his mantelpiece
(Wide World Photos. Poetry Library, State University of New York at Buffalo)

Giorgio Joyce and his wife Helen, photographed by Man Ray after their marriage – also displayed on the mantelpiece
(By permission of the Man Ray Trust, Paris. Poetry Library, State University of New York at Buffalo)

Alf Bergan, from a drawing by William Conor
(Courtesy Arethusa Greacan)

25 Claude Road, where John Stanislaus lived in the last years of his life
(Photo: Peter Costello)

Four generations of Joyces,
Paris 1938
(Photo: Gisèle Freund. Courtesy
John Hillelson Agency, London)

Gravestone in Glasnevin cemetery; the
granite boulder in the background
marks the grave of Parnell
(Photo: Robert Allen)

The memorial bench to John Stanislaus Joyce and James
Joyce on St Stephen's Green

IN MEMORY OF JAMES JOYCE, DUBLINER
AND HIS FATHER JOHN STANISLAUS JOYCE
CORKONIAN, 6TH INTERNATIONAL
JAMES JOYCE SYMPOSIUM, 1977

The inscription
(Photos: Peter Costello)

despite the further deterioration in Uncle Willie who was currently in and out of hospital. On at least one occasion Jim kept his long-suffering aunt up 'all night' listening to him talking about Nora. Then, after another short stay with Charlie, now in severe danger of being imprisoned for debt, he found accommodation for rent a few doors up at 21 Richmond Place, and wrote to Nora in Galway asking her to join him there with the children as soon as possible, which she did. (He planned to take her to the Horse Show and to point out various places that were mentioned in his book – the first Joycean tour of the city.) A room for Pappie was also found in the same house, and he left the Ivy Hotel and took up residence with his beloved son.

In a matter of days Jim had surrounded himself, as he always seemed to do, with a teeming and argumentative family. With Pappie in the mood he was, it cannot have been agreeable for any of them. John was now grumbling that 'all the girls in Dublin were prostitutes' and, as he had shrugged off any responsibility towards his daughters, Jim somewhat unwillingly took on the burden himself. Eva was nearing the end of her apprenticeship and both she and Florrie were so badly off that he felt he had to give them money to save them from complete starvation.

Nor did Jim forget his promise to find work for Charlie. He extracted from the manager of David Allen's advertising firm a lukewarm offer of a job for his brother during Horse Show week, on the strength of having paid Allen £50 in 1909 to publicise the Volta. He also set up an interview for him with a solicitor, Robert Keohler, and for good measure sent him to demonstrate his singing voice to an acquaintance of his father's known as 'Rochford of the quay'. (This was the man who in 1905 had been nearly asphyxiated down a manhole outside the Scotch House on Burgh Quay, an entirely unheroic accident that would be heroically commemorated in *Ulysses*.) Rochford was looking for a tenor for the choir of his local parish church, the Star of the Sea, Sandymount, and although the £10 a year on offer was not very much, Jim hoped the post might help his brother to get other more lucrative engagements at secular concerts. But, like his father long years before, there is no evidence that Charlie availed himself of the opportunity of advancing himself through a career in singing and he does not appear to have impressed any of his other potential employers either. Instead, Jim got him to write long letters on his behalf to Stannie with news and instructions, and to copy documents relating to the increasingly complex *Dubliners* business. This may have been because Jim was having another bout of eye trouble: the writer James Stephens had a drink with him around now and thought that his strong spectacles 'made his blue eyes look nearly as big as the eyes of a cow'. These tasks also prevented Charlie from feeling too guilty about accepting money from his brother.

On 5 September, a decision was made at last about *Dubliners* which bore all the hallmarks of the sort of financial gamble that John had been falling foul of for years: Jim agreed with Roberts to buy 1000 sets of the sheets from Maunsel's for £30 (though where the money was to come from remains a minor enigma). He could then publish them himself under the imprint of The Liffey Press and once they had been bound, Maunsel's were prepared to distribute the books. The Liffey Press would operate from Jervis Street close to the old hospital, where he intended to rent two rooms, one as an office and one which Charlie could occupy with his family, if in exchange he would deal with the firm's paperwork. Charlie, glad to have somewhere to live and now hoping that 'this business of Jim's books' might lead to permanent employment in the book or publishing trade, was enthusiastic about the scheme. He informed his landlord that he was leaving. Jim was now completely broke, and had even pawned his watch and watch chain, but such a feeling of relief and good spirits flowed through all the Joyces that they did a little celebrating, in which John no doubt joined with gusto. May was so pleased that she lent her eldest brother £1 for a good warm overcoat now that the long wait was over.

Disaster struck on 10 September. The managing clerk of Falconer's, who had now got around to reading the disgraceful book his firm had printed, also thought that it was a 'blackguard production' and flatly refused to hand over the sheets to Maunsel's or to anyone else, saying that the lot would immediately be burnt. Nothing could be done to make him change his mind. Legal action would be prohibitively expensive. It was futile to protest and Jim knew it. Finally taking his father's advice, he decided that the book would have to be published by someone else after all. He bamboozled Roberts into letting him take away a set of his proofs, went back to Nora, his father and the children at Richmond Place and delivered his blow to them: he was leaving Ireland the next day with Nora and the children. It is improbable that Pappie had ever seen him before in such a state of cold fury. It would not be the fond farewell he had been hoping for.

James Joyce later melodramatically claimed that as the boat bore him away from Dublin he could see the bonfire smoke from the pages of his book rising above the city they described. In fact the unbound sheets were not burnt, but beheaded: with the running heads chopped off in the printer's guillotine, the 125,000 odd pages would soon be widely distributed, general over Ireland, in the form of wrapping around other books printed by Falconer's. It would be very many years before any of James Joyce's works would achieve as big a circulation again.

John Stanislaus had not changed his mind about giving his eldest son the portraits to take to Trieste, but they had probably not come with him to Richmond Place. He may in fact have been keeping them stacked against a wall in Lidwell's Upper Ormond Quay offices. Along the river at 26 Lower Ormond Quay, Daniel Egan, 'carver, gilder and printseller', was given instructions that the battered Joyce ancestors were to be restored, the bill to be paid after the job had been completed. When they were ready, they would follow their new owner abroad. Since John seemed so unsure of where he would next be living, to remove the pictures for safe-keeping was obviously a practical move, but it was more than that: when he finally made his son custodian of the Joyce family portraits – the last link with the Cork roots of the family – it was a symbolic act, a turning-point in his life, and it was a turning-point in the life of James Joyce as well. In the inexorable progress of the race, the baton was passing from father to son.

Neither of them knew it, but as Pappie wept his customary quayside valedictions to his son and the little group of Joyces with him, it was the last time the men were ever to see or speak to each other again. After that other little group of Joyces, the portraits, had also left Ireland a short time later, John Stanislaus would never look upon their faces – his father and his grandfather – again either. But John and James Joyce would remain actively in each other's minds as powerful presences, James's distance increasing John's love, and John's nuance of speech and gesture preserved alive in the writer's extraordinary memory. The new head of the family was one day to make the Joyce name famous, but until then, in the North Dublin streets filled with summer sunshine or winter snow, Mr Joyce the elder would still be about his business and pleasure, carrying brown paper parcels of documents from Ormond Quay down to the Four Courts, running sometimes into May or Eva though never caring to see any of the others, dodging from pub to street corner in his old coat and scuffed shoes and, like the 'Nameless One' of Mangan's poem 'amid the last homes of youth and eld', slowly fading into an ancestor himself. And often, after he had rolled a friend around the pillar into Mooney's, his familiar voice would begin the story again, an old man telling of his Mamie and his Baby and his Sunny Jim.

With the passing of time, the living man in Dublin and the man his son remembered as Pappie would merge in James Joyce's imagination and move into the realm of dreams, and John Stanislaus Joyce, an old man in a changing city, would become every father and hence, in the Joycean way of it, every son.

PART THREE

Old Josser

John Joyce as Simon Dedalus in *Ulysses*, 'Circe': 'His Eminence Simon
Stephen cardinal Dedalus, primate of all Ireland, appears in the doorway, dressed in red soutane, sandals and socks. Seven dwarf simian aco-
lytes, also in red, cardinal sins, uphold his train. . .'
Illustration to *Ulysses*, by Hector McDonnell. Private collection.

CHAPTER 26

The Patriarch Game

It was never the plan that John Stanislaus and his favourite son should say goodbye for the last time as they parted on 11 September 1912. The relationship continued on the page and in the head, and, in ways, would be sustained better as an idea than as a reality. Having spoken to his father many times since their reconciliation in the parlour of the Yellow House, James Joyce sensed that in his development as an artist he had to be about his father's business and John Stanislaus was sometimes – close up – not a very pleasant person to know. The occasional friction between them was in part due to the similarity of their temperaments. Mystical kinship, rather than the routine of daily life, suited father and son better. James remembered from Shakespeare that it was a wise father that knew his own child.

> The anchor's weigh'd, the anchor's weigh'd
> Farewell! Farewell! Remember me.

Each remembered the other and the song went into *Ulysses*.

At Flushing, while waiting for the train on the long journey back to his other home in Trieste, James began to write 'Gas from a Burner', a bitter denunciation in verse not only of Dublin printers and publishers, but of the city's culture in general. In the spirit of 'Parnell' (*'Et Tu Healy'*) and 'The Holy Office', he paid a Triestine printer to run off copies. These were sent back to Dublin for Charlie to distribute. If this was vanity publishing, it arose from an exquisite form of self-regard. John Stanislaus's misgivings about the wisdom of James's chosen course crept out again and Charlie wrote to Stannie reporting that when Pappie saw 'Gas from a Burner' he had pronounced his son to be 'an out and out ruffian without the spark of a gentleman'. Harsh words, but no harsher than those in the squib itself. Such comments were to become a pattern: in the years to come John would often sneer behind his back at James's efforts in print, while yet retaining his pride in his son's growing fame.

May Joyce in October reported that Pappie wanted her (and Eva and Florrie) 'to go back' to live with him. But she had gained their liberty and had no wish to run a household for the old man's convenience. Family cynicism was grounded in hard experience and May knew that her father would change his mind before the first day of the next month. The allowance from Drimmie's was still the central feature of his financial cycle, which, as ever, revolved from being flush with cash to being penniless. This turbulence was echoed in James's own irregular dealings. Having given money to Charlie and Eva during the summer, he demanded repayment from Stannie. May was to be found complaining angrily to Stannie about the £1 she had lent James to buy a coat, money he had promised to reimburse her without delay: 'I dont know what he means by treating people in such a way unless indeed he is of the opinion that being so extraordinarily clever manners are superfluous.' These were Pappie's faults too. The money was never repaid. With all James's talents, other considerations were unnecessary. The world did indeed owe him a living: John Stanislaus was his son's imago.

Charlie, after failing as a disinfectant salesman, had taken a cottage at 14 Langrishe Place, off Summerhill, in a poor quarter of the city. By November John had moved to 41a Upper Blessington Street, beside the City Basin near Eccles Street, persuading Eva and probably Florrie to join him there for a time. His ill-regarded brother-in-law, William Murray, was sinking fast; in December 1912 he finally died, a driveller and a show. On his death certificate were the shameful initials 'GPI' – General Paralysis of the Insane, the third dreadful stage of syphilis. Though James sympathised with Aunt Josephine for the sore trial of her husband's long illness, his father did not share the sentiment. His long-standing derision of the good-natured Willie Murray may have been intensified by his old apprehension that he himself might harbour the same contagion. The disease was almost unmentionable in polite society outside official statistics, especially in Catholic Ireland. Murray's fictional self, the Ritchie Goulding of *Ulysses*, appears there bedridden, complaining of his back pain and singing 'Down among the Dead Men'.

John Stanislaus, however, did not include himself among the dead men just yet, despite his own complaints. He was still active, still to be found in drinking places as diverse as the Bachelor Inn, the Brazen Head and Barney Kiernan's. On the whole he now preferred hotels, however, even if the whiskey was dearer, and he and Lidwell continued to be regulars in the Ormond Hotel, a step away from the office. But they were also friends with James Brady, another police court solicitor, whom Stanislaus as far back as 1904 had characterised as 'a rare type of the common, cute, Irish fool'. Actually Brady, who was Alfie Bergan's brother-in-law, was very far from being a fool: his services were greatly in demand by trade unions as he was an expert in workman's compensation. Brady was one of a group who met daily near Dublin Castle in the Dolphin Hotel just off Parliament Street, where they discussed the affairs of the city and the world over coffee, brandy and cigars at the centre table in the smoking room. Among this group were the MP William Cotton, Alderman John Clancy, the solicitor and MP Patrick A. Chance, the veteran journalist Charles Hands (Boer War correspondent and librettist of the musical play *Madame Sherry*), Henry Doig and others, including (when flush) John Stanislaus. John apart, Brady was the life and soul of this group, who were agreeable enough fellows, even if some of them had once been Anti-Parnellites. Since the Irish Parliamentary Party had been reunited under John Redmond some of the past divisions had been healed. Newspapermen from the nearby offices of the *Evening Mail* would also congregate here, as would many from the city's sporting fraternity. Michael Nugent, owner of the Dolphin, was a character long celebrated in Dublin. He was the brother-in-law of the unfortunate Phil Gilligan of the Oval and both had been friends of John Stanislaus over a period reaching from the heady days of his political ambitions to these declining years of his life. Much of this congenial socialising John Stanislaus still kept from his family.

On 28 February 1913 Charlie's wife, Mary Joyce, gave birth at the Rotunda Hospital to a little girl who was christened Lilian

Gertrude on 30 April. It was unusual then for a child not to be born at home, but the tiny cottage would have been crowded and perhaps not very pleasant. Since the turn of the century, after a long period of decline since the Famine, the population of the city had been rising sharply and many of these people, like Charlie and his family, were desperately poor, though few of them had fallen from a comfortable middle-class life, bringing with them a sense of loss and failure that made life all the more difficult. When Jim thought of Dublin he saw it as a centre of paralysis, but in fact it seethed with potentially turbulent discontent.

In 1913 the city of Dublin was revalued for the rates; this may have provided John Stanislaus with some work. But 1913 was also a year when the international profile of Dublin and its poverty grew. May Joyce's unease about going near the city at night was more than vindicated by what was happening in the streets. The opera seasons of John Stanislaus's youth had been eclipsed by music-hall and plays from London. Cinemas, including the thriving Volta, were popular with young people that winter, the 'flicks' proving at least as agreeable for courting couples as the patriotic pretexts of the notorious Fenian gatherings of John's Cork days. But the city was about to be engulfed by a turmoil such as few European cities had ever seen. The Great Dublin Lock-Out of 1913 gave lurid confirmation of the city's ugliness and want, much of which could be laid at the door of the corrupt Nationalists who ran the city council.

On 2 September seven people were killed and six injured by the collapse of a tenement house in Church Street. A commission of inquiry into urban poverty was established, whose eventual report made appalling reading. Over the course of the year the city had been troubled by a labour dispute centred on the efforts of James Larkin to unionise the transport workers, the draymen and other delivery men, upon whom the complex economy of the city depended. Larkin championed the cause from the balcony of the Imperial Hotel, owned by the Anti-Parnellite son of Bantry, William Martin Murphy (alongside the old McSwiney store he still owned as well). This led to an organised lock-out by the united employers under Murphy, determined to resist trade unionism. Twenty-five thousand people were put out by the employers. It culminated in

September with riots in O'Connell Street in which 500 people and fifty policemen were injured and two killed. Revaluation was turning into revolution.

The social cohesion of the city, largely an illusion of pious Nationalists, was unravelling. As a trade unionist, Larkin was seen as a dangerous syndicalist and he was much disapproved of by men such as John Stanislaus – and his old *bête noir* Archbishop Walsh ('Lord Leitrim's coachman') who condemned the workers' actions. The riots led to the Labour movement establishing its own Citizen Army, a sort of workers' militia, a forerunner of both the Ulster Volunteers and the National Volunteers. The enemy was not always the British Empire or the Church, but the attitudes of the new Catholic middle class. A grim struggle over the nature and condition of what it meant to be Irish was rapidly escalating.

The lock-out ended on 19 January 1914. By now James had managed to find a publisher and in February *A Portrait of the Artist as a Young Man* began a serial run in the pages of *The Egoist* in London. In several passages of this book the character of Simon Dedalus was delineated with care; James's picture of his father, at once fiercely outspoken and lachrymosely sentimental, was shown forth for all the world to see. John Stanislaus's daughters were to hate the book for its emphasis on the poverty and squalor of their family life. That March, James Joyce began writing the first sketches of *Ulysses* and his collection of stories, *Dubliners*, was finally published in London in June.

News of these achievements filtered through to John Stanislaus. Like a demented Lear, he complained in an old and continuing refrain of the ingratitude and irreverence of his daughters. He took no interest in the children of the only son to stay in Dublin. Charlie and his little platoon might just as well not have existed. John's repertoire maintained a certain wit: 'Jesus wept, and no wonder by Christ.' But he himself had no tears or wit to spare for the city or its benighted children. He was not the benign patriarch he had once hoped to be.

However, the ill health he had for so long complained of was now real enough and his weight had begun to fall. In the spring of 1914 he spent two months in the Mater Hospital suffering from some gastric problem. In May he was in the Beaumont convalescent home out in Drumcondra, where Charlie had been a patient years before. Time was beginning to take its long overdue toll on John Stanislaus Joyce.

Whether fearing for his sire's mortality or attempting to boost his morale, James proposed (following the allusive title of the *Portrait*) to have a painting done of his father to enlarge the ancestral collection and show how things were meant to be done. In Trieste his friends could see from the portraits now hanging on the walls of his flat that he had been born a gentleman. Pappie was eager to comply: 'as soon as I get up some flesh &c. I *certainly will* get it done for you, and as you *again* ask me to go over, perhaps, as things have turned out here, and the cruel treatment I have received from my daughters here, I may go over to you on a visit for a month. Of course only on the understanding that I would not be any incumbrance to you or Nora and that I should pay my way, as I have to do here.' But the war in the Balkans, which had broken out the year before, and the Curragh Mutiny over Home Rule, meant that this suggestion went no further.

These local crises were about to merge into the overarching turmoil of the Great War. At Westminster, the Home Rule Bill had not only been passed, despite strident and armed Orange resistance ('Ulster will fight and Ulster will be right'), but had actually received the Royal Assent to become law. Here, albeit in muted form, was Parnell's dream, but the act was suspended for the duration of the war (initially expected to last months rather than years). It was an extraordinary Irish development – like Moses on Mount Pisgah written by Lewis Carroll. A trip to Trieste would have been a nice diversion for John. His claim that he would not be a burden to Jim and Nora echoed the Englishman's proudest boast, as repeated in *Ulysses*: 'I paid my way.' The visit was never to happen.

In the spring of 1914, Eileen became engaged to her beau Frantisek Schaurek, a Czech bank assistant who worked in Trieste, where he had been one of James's language pupils. He seems to have been agreeable but financially unsound. In May, John Stanislaus wrote to his son, mentioning his own experience of ephemeral betrothals and stating his concern about the proposed marriage. He described Eileen as 'the *only one* of my daughters (*now alive*) who never gave me insolence, or showed contempt for me'. He was being more perceptive than he knew about her fiancé. Alluding to Stannie's distant and disapproving silence, he used a tag that was recycled by James as he revised *Stephen Hero* to make the *Portrait*: 'I dare say "Tempora mutantur" &c.', and signed off gloomily, 'What is left of Your Father.' But Stannie would never change in his feelings towards his father and years later would still be suggesting that Pappie had been one of the 'deserving poor' – meaning that he was poor and he deserved to be.

In another letter a little later, John Stanislaus, recovering from a return of his gastritis, wrote in empathy to an also convalescent Jim and thought idly of a week or two at the seaside ('how about *Galway*'). He relented too of his harsh reaction to his prospective son-in-law after he had studied his character in a photograph. The method ('he has a good face, good eyes and mouth . . .') seemed to owe something to the conventions of appraising bloodstock. In character was destiny, and Joycean luck tended to be consistent. While Pappie, stuck in Dublin, forswore self-help, James stepped nimbly from one crisis to another: when conflict came to Trieste, James was able to arrange transit for himself and his family to neutral Switzerland. Stolid Stannie, however, was rounded up as an enemy alien and so became a cook internee.

John Stanislaus was sent a signed copy of *Dubliners* on publication. He knew that the title was almost a neologism, as the citizenry still tended to refer to themselves as Dublinmen. But the scandal feared by George Roberts and Maunsel & Co. did not materialise, though some of those readers who were themselves Dubliners began to notice that the book carried a number of recognisable people – Fogarty, Cotter, Corley, Maria the laundress, Fr Flynn, Browne, Fanning, Fr Keon, Henchy, Malins . . . This was hardly the orthodox fashion for fiction, but it was James's manner of making: John Stanislaus's verdict that *Dubliners* was 'a blackguard production' can only have been confirmed by the knowledge that thinly disguised descriptions of himself were now on sale in the city. The stories were less than warmly received in *The Irish Book Lover* in November and their grim tone was disliked by more than the author's immediate family.

As John's generation was being revived in fiction, it was dying out in fact. His distinguished kinsman, the literary scholar and historian Patrick Weston Joyce, died in early 1914; so too did T. D. Sullivan, Bantry 'Gangster' and author of 'God Save Ireland'. The song's title was an ever-ripe theme. Contingencies were developed by both Unionists and Nationalists as a prelude for an Irish civil war that seemed increasingly unavoidable.

Politics in Ireland was becoming frenetic. During the July gun-running into Howth by Erskine Childers, soldiers opened fire and killed three civilians beside O'Connell Bridge at Bachelor's Walk. This was the scene of many of John's past jollifications with friends like John Phelan in the old Carlisle (later the Bachelor Inn), just by Dillons' auction-rooms where Mr Dedalus goads one of his daughters on Bloomsday in 'Wandering Rocks'. Diverse pretexts of reform and radicalism had multiplied, spawning Horace Plunkett's co-operative movement for practical improvement to the dairy industry, James Connolly's trade unionism, and the romanticism of Nationalists who saw the cause of brave little Belgium as analogous to Ireland's. Even so, homelessness and ignominy still abounded in Dublin. In January 1915 the Dublin Shelter for Men had an attendance of 3554 indigents, about 110 a night. The Dublin Committee for the Prevention and Relief of Distress sent cheeses to prevent and relieve distress. Sean O'Casey would describe even those fortunate enough to have other accommodation as 'wriggling together like worms in a putrid mass in horror-filled one room tenements'. One such family was Charlie's.

The war had not ended at Christmas, as people had hoped. While the soldiers began to dig in along the Western Front, in Dublin, on 24 January 1915 yet another son was born at the Rotunda to Charles and Mary Joyce, who by now had moved to 20 Lower Gardiner Street. A month later this child was christened in the Pro-Cathedral. He was given the name John Stanislaus Joyce. The accolade should have cheered the baby's grandfather, at last with someone in the family to carry his name. But the home where the child would live was miserable with the squalor inevitably caused by poverty and multi-occupancy. Pappie, at least, was better housed than this: by March, he was living at 1 St Vincent Street (just opposite the monument to the Four Masters in front of the Mater Hospital), a property owned by a Mrs Bridget Moriarty.

(By chance, 'Biddy Moriarty' is also a character in the old song 'Finnegan's Wake' and the name can be found again on page 453 of Joyce's book.) Though this address may sound like a Catholic stitch in the largely Protestant official tapestry of Dublin, Irish history is rarely so straightforward: the name actually commemorates the British naval victory at the Battle of Cape Saint Vincent in 1797 and the admiral who became Earl St Vincent had the family name of Jervis – the street and its hospital echoing another of John Stanislaus's sojourns.

From this new vantage point, John Stanislaus watched as contemporaries continued to pass away. Arthur Guinness died at his mansion in Clontarf. John had outlived his old opponent, a practitioner of the old corruption, unseated from Parliament in the days of hope, only to join the Upper House as Lord Ardilaun – the title came from his extensive landholding at Cong in the Joyce Country. The following week Alderman 'Long' John Clancy died, just after being elected Lord Mayor; he had been very close to James Stephens the Fenian and had employed Alfie Bergan as his assistant around the turn of the century. Messrs Lidwell and Joyce and Hishon turned out for the funeral from the Pro-Cathedral, along with John Henry Menton, John O'Connell (still Superintendent of the cemetery), J. J. Clancy KC MP, Jimmy Henry (briefly John's boss in 1903 and vetter of potential Freemen of Dublin), John Redmond MP, Alderman Sir Joseph Downes the baker (whose seedcake John liked), Henry Campbell, John P. Cuffe JP (of the Cattle Market), Mrs McGuinness (probably the pawnbroker of *Ulysses*), Thomas Cunniam, Reuben J. Dodd and the evocative Messrs Kapp and Peterson, celebrated Dublin pipe-makers. Here was a roll-call of the remnants of John Stanislaus's past. In a graphic intimation of his own mortality, the Joyce plot was head to head with the Clancy plot and doubtless John reflected (as Simon Dedalus does in 'Hades') that he would soon be joining his wife there. J. J. Nannetti, *Freeman* man and MP of Whitworth Road in Drumcondra, shortly afterwards passed away too. His forebears had been Italian craftsmen, practitioners in plasterwork and he, though a Dubliner born and bred, must often have heard the remark, 'With a name like that, are you Irish at all?' Despite the traditional rhythms of these Glasnevin funerals, Dublin was fast changing and had already changed from the paralysed city of *Dubliners*, or the old order emanating from the Castle.

On 13 March the birth of his grandson and namesake, and the deaths of so many of his peers, led or drove John to make his first will:

I, John Stanislaus Joyce, now residing at No. 1. St Vincent Street, North, Berkeley Road, Dublin, Retired Rate Collector, declare this to be my last Will and Testament, hereby revoking all former Wills and Testamentary Dispositions heretofore made by me. I give devise and bequeath all my real and personal property to my son [James (inserted)] Augustine Joyce absolutely and I appoint him and John George Lidwell, Solicitor, Executors of this my will.

John's self-description here as 'Retired Rate Collector' was less florid and pretentious than some of his previous identities. The witnesses were J. G. Lidwell and Terence Cooney, his law clerk. It is not clear how the sole beneficiary's first name came to be omitted and had to be interpolated. The name of James Augustine Joyce was already becoming notorious in Dublin. Oddly rapidly after making this will, John Stanislaus made a replacement one (on 22 May 1915). Eileen's wedding a few weeks earlier may have prompted him to restate his intentions clearly: there are signs of the family tension between him and several of his unhappy children at this time, which births and marriages did little to assuage – May, for example, was not even on speaking terms with him now. However, the main difference between the documents was in the lack of punctuation in the new will and the replacement of the now overweight and ailing George Lidwell as executor with Alfie Bergan, who also witnessed it. This time the second witness was Bergan's formidable Protestant landlady at 2 Claude Road, Mrs Kathleen Refaussé, the widow of an official in the General Post Office. In agreeing to be a witness, Alfie was forfeiting any hope of a legacy, but none of John Stanislaus's real friends could really have expected one. After all, unlike most of his fellow Dubliners, John was not even leaving anything to pay for Masses for the repose of his soul (or that of his late wife, May).

Though the times were changing, John Stanislaus Joyce was ceasing to change with them. His world, his social set, was shrivelling and he found comfort in sober or musical or fantastical reminders of the old days. More significantly than any legal bequest, John had already passed on to his favourite son nearly all that he had to give, not money or property, but his traits of every description – among them humour, litigiousness, eye-trouble, a fondness for alcohol and lions, a sense of anniversary, a low regard for official-dom and a gift for story-telling. By now safe in Zürich, James Joyce was revolving in his mind the same past, the same stories, the same city streets, turning memory into literature as he continued with *Ulysses.*

CHAPTER 27

'A Gentleman No Longer in Politics'

In 1916 John Stanislaus was still using Lidwell's office, 33 Upper Ormond Quay, as his postal address. Letters sent there were at least private. At this time it is likely that he had not yet left his lodgings in the little house on St Vincent Street, but this was just somewhere to sleep. His real life was lived out and about with his cronies, where he could still feel part of the main current of events in the city.

Lidwell's office beside the Four Courts buzzed with talk of the new Nationalist movement. The establishment of the Irish National Volunteers in the south of Ireland in November 1913, as a response to the organisation of the Ulster Volunteers by the Unionists in the north, looked as though it might bring the country to civil war in the summer of 1914. But with the coming of the Great War in August, John Redmond offered the services of the Volunteers (who had passed into the control of the Irish Parliamentary Party in the summer) to the Imperial Government. They then amounted to about 100,000 men. As he saw it, they would be Ireland's army defending Ireland's rights against a common enemy. Many Volunteers followed this lead and joined up. But a smaller group, some 10,000 men, repudiated him and this rump passed under the influence of the Irish Republican Brotherhood. In fact the Brotherhood and not the council of either branch of the Volunteers would make the real decisions from now on.

Hand in hand with his job as a Police Court solicitor, George Lidwell was Treasurer of the 5th (Dublin) Battalion of the Volunteers, based in Sandymount. He was one of the majority who stayed with Redmond. Positions would shift with the rapid developments of the next few years, but neither George Lidwell nor John Stanislaus was in favour of armed rebellion at this stage in the country's history. Lidwell was a placid gentleman, whose company and advanced Nationalist sympathies John found congenial. But once again, John had found himself involved on the edge of the current National movement. With the attention of the populace focused on the battlefields of the Great War, the 1916 Easter Rising, when it came, was a profound shock for most of the country; John Stanislaus probably knew that it was going to happen.

By the time it was launched, the Rising was more an act of bloody street theatre than a military enterprise with any prospect of success. Its origins lay in the split in the National Volunteers. At the heart of the group that had repudiated Redmond the inner core of Irish Republican Brotherhood men could trace their allegiance back to the Fenians of John Stanislaus's youth. Indeed, one of them, old Tom Clarke, was a veteran of that era. It was their plan to use the Volunteers' routine Easter manoeuvres to launch an insurrection, unbeknownst to the theoretical leadership of Professor Eoin MacNeill. When he discovered what was planned, and that guns were about to be landed by Sir Roger Casement in Kerry, he cancelled the manoeuvres. Hastily the Republicans managed to get some units into the field, but only about 700 men rose in Dublin.

On Easter Monday, 24 April, they seized the General Post Office in the heart of the city and a ring of other buildings around Dublin. The following day there were German raids on the English coastal towns of Yarmouth and Lowestoft, a reminder to the War Office that London's difficulty was Berlin's opportunity. Reacting angrily to the Republicans' claim of aid from 'our gallant allies overseas', the authorities imposed martial law in Ireland within days and advocated a strong military response on the ground. But from the very first hours the Rising was doomed: the rebels failed to seize the telephone exchange, where Charlie was again working, on the corner of Crown Alley off Dame Street. It was taken by British soldiers, who managed to divide the rebels and then to pin them down. Charlie was soon back at work, providing the communications essential to the suppression of the rebels.

For John Stanislaus, as for most Dubliners of the day, the Rising was a terrible event. Very near his lodgings a road-block was put up by the rebels, just where the Phibsborough Road crossed the North Circular Road, but by the Tuesday of Easter Week a British Army '18-pounder', added to raking machine-gun fire from the Broadstone Railway Terminus nearby, had made the position untenable, and they retreated (or advanced, according to perspective) along the Cabra Road to the Phoenix Park and soon enough dispersed in the driving rain. For days, citizens remained shut up in their houses or restricted in their movements. When it was over and he could walk the streets again, he could see for himself the three million pounds' worth of damage that had been done. This had been a consequence unforeseen by the rebels: Patrick Pearse believed if they held out as a government for three days they would receive *de jure* recognition, while James Connolly believed that the British government would never wantonly fire upon the property of capitalists. They were both wrong. The military authorities tried and executed them and most of the other leaders with brutal swiftness.

Though the military casualties were light enough by wartime standards, eighteen civilians had been killed. James Joyce's co-essayist from University College, Frank Sheehy-Skeffington (a pro-feminist change of name), was among the victims of the week. As a principled pacifist (he was the model for McCann in the *Portrait*) he was trying to prevent looting by civilians when he was detained by an army patrol and taken to Portobello Barracks in Rathmines. Soon, garbled rumours reached his family. He had been murdered by an insane army officer named Bowen-Colthurst: the name was familiar to John Stanislaus through this family's connections with Fermoy and Chapelizod. He remembered them as a good family, one of whom owned Blarney Castle.

The ruination of his city was a sad sight for John Stanislaus. Acres south of the Imperial Hotel and Clery's store were burnt out. In Abbey Street, Phil Gilligan's old pub, the Oval (albeit reconstructed after his death), stood almost alone. Beside it the offices of the *Evening Telegraph, Sport* and the *Freeman's Journal,* where both John Stanislaus and his son James had passed many agreeable hours, were completely destroyed, razed to the ground. Lawrence's studios and some of its irreplaceable photographs were no more. Like most Dubliners, John was neither an advocate of nor a sympathiser with the armed insurrection. 'Let me Like a Soldier Fall', one of his favourite songs, was grand opera, not real life. He had no qualms that his daughter Florrie was currently working in the Army Pay Office, ensuring that the thousands of Dublin women whose men were in the Dublin Fusiliers and other army units got their money week by week. John Stanislaus now walked the city among the shattered glass and toppling masonry that his son was writing about in the phantasmagoria of *Ulysses*.

After the Rising, which ended on 30 April, it took time to re-establish contact among the family. It was not until the beginning of September that May Joyce wrote to James from Todd Burns with news of the last two years. She did not have a great deal to say about the activities of her benighted father. Pappie had not been very well for a time, 'but is looking alright again'. Maunsel's had been driven out of Abbey Street to offices in Baggot Street and Eva had applied there for a job. George Roberts felt that if she had the brains of her brother she would do well, but he did not hire her. He had been curious, however, about the fate of the book he had rejected and was interested to learn that it was now due to come out at last. 'We are all quite well here. Charlie is still in the Telephone Company. He has now five children, the little girl Eileen is very delicate, but the others are healthy. Georgie promises to be very clever, the eldest Jimmy, is Charlie on a small scale.' She did not tell Jim that the latest one of them had been named John Stanislaus: it was not May's business to mend fences between her father and the rest of the family. That her own life was soon to change radically she was as yet unaware.

While all this was happening in Dublin, James Joyce was in touch with Edward Marsh in No. 10 Downing Street, London, hoping for a grant from the Royal Literary Fund. Behind the scenes, W. B. Yeats had written to Edmund Gosse to facilitate this benevolence. Gosse, the author of *Father and Son*, may have found congenial the published portions of *A Portrait of the Artist as a Young Man*, for presently young Mr Joyce was awarded £100, further to the £75 he had received the year before. Such recognition from the very top (the Royal Literary Fund) tickled John Stanislaus's old swagger and he wrote to James at once, congratulating him on the great honour that the King had bestowed on him. He showed the letter to a contemporary, once a member of the United Liberal Club, Professor John Gordon Swift MacNeill MP, who was Professor of Constitutional Law and of the Law of Public and Private Wrongs in University College, Dublin. Swift MacNeill (not to be confused with UCD's other Professor MacNeill, of the Irish Volunteers) was as grandiloquent as his title, and was noted in Dublin for his exuberant chat and excited light-blue eyes. John thought him 'a very clever man'. His first professorship had been at King's Inns and he had joined Isaac Butt's Home Government Association in 1870, later becoming a Parnellite MP for South Donegal (for thirty years). (Among his Joycean associations were that his mother had been born a Tweedy – Molly Bloom's maiden name – and that he had campaigned for the abolition of flogging in the Royal Navy. The practice is discussed at length in 'Cyclops', two years before the reform was finally effected.) Swift MacNeill was even connected to the Richmond Jail, from where James Stephens had escaped, but what brought John Stanislaus to him was primarily the fact that he was also Clerk of the Convocation of the National University of Ireland. John knew that if the letter from the Royal Literary Fund impressed such a well-connected man sufficiently, James might be offered a chair at UCD like some of his contemporaries and inferiors, and would come back to Dublin again, making decent money at last. The Professor, who, as well as being a celebrated parliamentarian, was descended from Jonathan Swift's uncle and guardian, was properly impressed to see a college man getting on, but that was the end of the matter. 'If you should wish to get a paragraph in Dublin papers,' wrote the proud father nonchalantly in his letter to James, 'let me know.' He may also have entertained hopes that some of his son's windfall might come his way, but little or none of it did.

In the reorganisation of civil government that followed the Easter Rising, Nora Joyce's uncle, Michael Healy, as a competent servant of the Crown, was transferred from Galway to Dublin and moved to Clontarf with his mother. The authorities had need of reliable functionaries: public opinion had shifted against them, not so much because of the Rising, but because of the disproportionate response to it – specifically the execution of so many of the leaders. John Stanislaus, who, after all the upsets of the last year was now understandably claiming to suffer from neurasthenia ('My nerves are quite shattered'), would be glad of the presence of a reliable family friend – more reliable than those daughters of his – close by in Dublin, a man who was a reader of *T.P.'s Weekly* and whose administrative skills were now at his service. The jovial Michael Healy who in 1912 had visited James and Nora in Trieste was already one of James's most loyal supporters. He would also prove to be a good friend to old John, always willing to lend him something from his salary.

Though there was to be no conscription in Ireland, thousands of Irishmen had volunteered to fight in the Great War for the rights of Belgium. Bertie Murray, one of Aunt Josephine's brood, was among those who were soon on the Western Front in a Pals' Battalion 'got up for commercial men', as May reported. The war, with its grim telegrams, often came closer to home than Flanders, or even than Florrie's job in the Army Pay Office. In September 1916 John Joyce's erstwhile Parnellite colleague Andrew Kettle ('Mr Teapot') died, less than a fortnight after his gifted (if by this time disillusioned) son Tom was killed in action in France. Tom Kettle was more than just an MP or an academic: at the outbreak of the war he had been in the Low Countries buying guns for the Irish Volunteers, then became a war correspondent, then a Dublin Fusilier. For these diverse accomplishments a memorial to him was later erected in Stephen's Green, but 'Killed in France' was not allowed in the inscription. (Nonsense like this normally provoked from John Stanislaus one of his vivid dismissals: 'Agonising Christ, wouldn't it give you a heartburn on your arse!')

In the late summer of 1916 John Stanislaus recovered relatively from another period of ill health, very likely to do with his stomach (or his 'nerves'). But the ageing John had an unfortunate problem that would not go away, the one consubstantially anticipated at the beginning of the *Portrait*: when you wet the bed first it is warm, then it gets cold. The complaint was revisited in *Ulysses*. Like all Dublin men he needed washerwomen for his laundry and if he could not afford them he may have changed landladies as often as he changed sheets. His invariable use of Lidwell's as a postal address suggests a transience or instability in his accommodation arrangements at this time. It was during this confused era of his life, perhaps in the course of one of his still periodic bouts of heavy drinking, that John lost the famous case with the teeth in it – and the putative 'certificates' from Queen's College, Cork. Other Joyce family heirlooms very likely disappeared now, too, such as photographs of John's father which Stannie remembered seeing. Certainly he was now becoming even more withdrawn from his Dublin children and there are no authoritative reports of anyone else spending much time with him either during these miserable months. John Stanislaus Joyce was at his lowest ebb.

As he was no longer supporting his children and the ones who had lived were grown up, they were not as cowed or compliant as in the years gone by. 'Pappie also I am sure has told you pretty tales,' May retaliated, perhaps before the event, in a letter to James. Her practical forthrightness did not warm Pappie to her: 'He sometimes looks up Eva & Florrie but seems to think me much nicer at a distance.' These children, whom he now routinely called 'unnatural', had separate existences, and he complained bitterly of not seeing them and of not hearing from the far-away ones. But he could always acknowledge his dependence on James. Apart from the fixed days of the father–son calendar, the birthday greetings exchanged and the seasonal good wishes, there were moveable feasts too. James kept close to Pappie by sending him a group photograph of the growing family taken in Switzerland. Pappie inquired about the only two grandchildren important to him; he also wondered about the safe-keeping of the Joyce portraits: 'Let me know.'

May was close only in the literal sense: when Pappie had come round one Sunday in September – perhaps James had paraphrased to him her complaint – it was the first time they had seen one another in almost two years. His problems with 'nerves' she crisply attributed to the fact that he was getting old. But any family feeling was channelled in the usual way: Pappie produced his photographs of James and family. The personal aspirations of his other children, regarding marriage for example, were as nothing against the magnet and focus that was their eldest brother. This dominance by James was a stance that John Stanislaus shared with several of his own children: the first-born sons of both Stanislaus and Charles were to boast the name James Joyce.

In hospital again in late 1916, John Stanislaus (still on Lidwell stationery with its jaunty telegraphic address, ACQUITTALS DUBLIN) practised some traditional refrains: 'this will be my *last* Xmas . . . If you could spare me £1 you would greatly oblige . . .' In military and political apprehension, all letters were liable to scrutiny by the government censor and had to be fully signed. Accordingly, Pappie gamely abandoned his now usual style of 'Pater' and made a flourish in signing off: 'Your Fond Father, John Stanislaus Joyce!!'

Submarine attacks permitting, James's first published novel was about to appear. He wrote out the names of intended recipients of complimentary copies of *A Portrait of the Artist as a Young Man*: Pappie was first in a long list and among the few who knew that the book, being a 'Portrait', reflected in an oblique way Joyce family tradition. Early in 1917 the novel was finally published in Europe (with American sheets). Because of the war, the copy John Stanislaus received was unsigned this time, being sent directly from London. If John read it, even the first page would have brought memories surging back, of Brighton Square and West Rathgar, when he was young and prosperous and lived in south Dublin with May. The opening was of Baby Tuckoo. Now James was telling the world stories about him telling James stories. The same opening passage had a version of his song, 'Lilly Dale', that he had taught James:

> Oh Lilly, sweet Lilly, sweet Lilly Dale,
> Now the wild rose blossoms o'er the little green grave,
> Neath the trees in the flowery vale.

As so often, the musical repertoire was tinged with death. The songs tended towards the elegiac as the novel recorded the decline and fall of the Dedalus family and the squalor of contemporary Dublin. Pappie also may have noticed with a snort that the Royal Irish Academy in Dawson Street had erroneously been transferred to parallel Kildare Street – something never put right in later editions despite Joyce's request. But while he would have had his criticisms, not least in the portrayal of himself in the book, he was pleased that it had at last come out: he could remember James and Stannie talking about it before their mother had gone. It must be good to have taken so long.

The *Portrait* gave the name of Joyce a Dublin reputation far beyond *Dubliners*. A story went around about how John Stanislaus brought a copy of the *Portrait* in to Paddy Hooper, editor of the *Freeman*, now removed to Townsend Street offices. Because his Cork father, the Alderman, had been on such good terms with old Mr Joyce, Hooper agreed to the request for a notice and passed the matter over to a minion for prompt attention. This journalist adjourned, in accordance with tradition, to a nearby pub with his colleagues and returned to the office behind schedule and somewhat befuddled. Opening the book in the middle, he found the many pages of the long sermon on Hell and, duly impressed with the rigorously orthodox tone, he began his review: 'This is a book which should be in every Catholic home . . .' Seemingly not literally true, the story remains vigorous in Dublin oral tradition and is a medium-early instance of Joyce folklore spreading through the city. By 1919 D. P. Moran's acolyte Arthur Clery was taking issue with Joyce in his *Dublin Essays* published by Maunsel's, while Aunt Josephine was gently but firmly reminding Jim of the impact of his writings on the Joyce girls. Eva and Florrie, devout and respectable spinsters, felt embarrassment and shame at the ventilation of family difficulties in the *Portrait* and were beginning to avoid mentioning their brother to people they met. In time, they would blame any social difficulties they encountered on his scandalous reputation.

On 2 March Charlie's wife added to the family a little girl, Eva Mary Joyce, who was baptised on 23 March 1917. The child's sponsor was her Aunt Eva. Another child can only have added to the hardships, but Charlie bore them stoically. Though it was at this time that Jim's life was dramatically improved by the first gifts of money from his patroness, Miss Harriet Weaver, very little of this largess made its way to John Stanislaus. It is simple to imagine that, deep in his father's past world as he continued with *Ulysses*, James found that the reality of his father's situation interfered with his writing and that he preferred to remember Pappie as he had been in his prime. Aunt Josephine's warning, that John would spend unwisely anything he sent, may also have been a factor in James's apparent stinginess.

That summer had seen not only the attempt by the Irish Convention to rescue Home Rule (a failure), but also Sinn Féin demonstrations in Dublin during which a police inspector was killed with a hurley stick. On 21 September the death occurred of Major Malachy Powell ('Major Tweedy') at the age of ninety-six, who had unknowingly provided material for Molly Bloom's father in Jim's new book. He received a public military funeral. After the emergence of a reorganised ultra-Nationalist movement that autumn, piety about older soldiers of the British Imperial Army would be less lavishly observed.

Like religion, music was still more important in the city than Joyceness, though this had not saved the Antient Concert Rooms in Great Brunswick Street from closure in 1916. However, John Stanislaus's concert-going days were long gone. He would not have seen, either, at the Abbey Theatre in late 1917, Oliver Gogarty's *Blight*, 'a tragedy of Dublin', which addressed the related scandals of the pullulating Dublin slums and of venereal disease. As an Abbey controversy it ranked between Shaw's *Blanco Posnet* and the imminent dramas of Sean O'Casey. (James Stephens's story *Hunger* and Francis Cruise O'Brien's *Starvation in Dublin* were other indicators at this time that the urban problems were physical before spiritual. The leaders of the Rising had hardly addressed this all-important issue.)

Though *Blight* was a serious piece, James's old rival had used it to ridicule the Joyces. It featured characters such as a labourer named Stanislaus and a crippled son called Jimmy, and contains a knowing or mocking reprise of elements taken from the home life of the Joyces as it was known to Gogarty. Oliver Gogarty had once at least had to go to John Stanislaus's house, when Eva had refused to walk through Dublin carrying the man's suit that Gogarty was lending to James. *Blight* also featured as light relief 'Medical Dick' and 'Medical Davy', comic turns from the college banter between Jim and Gogarty that Joyce would also use in *Ulysses*. It is highly likely that the Joyces recognised themselves here, for a little time after the play opened in early 1918 Charlie Joyce wrote the author a letter: 'Dear Mr Gogarty, Can you lend me £1 . . .' They had been awkward drinking pals back in 1904. Perhaps Charlie was showing his true Joyce colours by claiming royalties; the money, if it came, would naturally have been welcome, however: his son, George Alfred, now eight, was about to make his first Communion. A further indication of the confused nature of Charlie's family life was that they had lost George's baptismal certificate from Boston and he had to be rebaptised on 13 March. Neither Jim nor his stately ex-friend, now engaged with Arthur Griffith and Michael Collins in the creation of a new Ireland, would have been much amused by Charlie's appeal.

In October there was a note in *The Irish Book Lover* about a forthcoming work by James Joyce, the play called *Exiles.* It was an indication that even in the most conservative of Irish literary circles attention was being paid to his sudden rise to prominence. (In the play, as mentioned, Jim had recycled material from his father's past as well as his own: the theme of the young man's love for his Protestant cousin stems from John Stanislaus's earliest relationship, as it appears, with the Justice girl whose mother, then in Youghal, had been O'Connell or Hearn.) A first edition was sent to Pappie when the play was published in May 1918. Because his residence was so unsure, it was posted care of Lidwell's offices. Again because of the war, the book came unsigned from London, though once again Pappie had been top of James's list for complimentary copies. Of all the books that James sent his father, this would be the only one still in his possession when he died, its cover damaged by candlegrease. The results of his son's industry were becoming abundant. In America that spring, episode one of *Ulysses* appeared in *The Little Review,* it was the first published glimpse of the book.

Such things were to be expected from Jim, with his education. John Stanislaus had come a long way from his own palmy days as a university man sneering at counter-jumpers and their sons (an epithet he applied to Oliver Gogarty). In 1918 May Joyce (now aged twenty-eight) married into the Monaghans, a business family from Oughterard in County Galway. The couple had met at Todd Burns, and the Monaghans disapproved of the match and were prepared to give this forceful woman from Dublin a hard time on her removal to the west of Ireland. The wedding might have been a respite from the round of funerals, but John Stanislaus was not invited.

In London, R. Barry O'Brien died, whom John had known in

the dear dead days almost beyond recall. He had published James Joyce in the *Speaker.* O'Brien, who had worked with H. C. E. Childers, was by now best known as the author of his biography of Parnell, in which John Stanislaus appears by all accounts as the unnamed figure in the second volume ('a gentleman no longer in politics') who had told O'Brien the story of the retaking of the *United Ireland* offices by loyal Parnellites during the heady days of the split back in 1891. How long ago it all seemed, when Parnell would sweep through Dublin so regularly, from Westminster, from Kingsbridge Station, from the North Wall or Kingstown, to Morrison's Hotel or the National Club, or Westland Row, or indeed that unlikely nest of Nationalists facing the GPO, the Imperial Hotel (prop. William Martin Murphy). And still, despite everything, there was no Home Rule.

By May 1918 James had finished 'Hades', the first episode of *Ulysses* in which Simon Dedalus appears in full fig. He also appears in 'Aeolus', in the newspaper office and in the musical episode, 'Sirens', set in the Ormond Hotel: all of these were completed by mid-1919. Yet, since much of Bloom's life in its misadventurous detail was also drawn from John Stanislaus, and since many of the people who inhabit the book are John Stanislaus's friends, his spirit pervades all chapters of the book from the opening of the fourth episode, 'Calypso', which had been written by March 1918.

Being so far from Ireland, James could take advantage of his isolation from the country, and from his father. He relied on memory, letting the facts fall as they would. While Simon Stephen Dedalus came to life on the page, his alter ego, John Stanislaus Joyce, was slowly retreating from it on the streets of Dublin.

The Great War came to an end in November with universal rejoicing. But on 14 December 1918 the General Election provided a new shock. When the final results were counted, the old Parliamentary Party of Parnell and Redmond had been swept aside along with its leaders, as the south of Ireland voted solidly for Sinn Féin; in the north they voted as solidly for the Unionists. By their ballots the people had reinforced a division of the country which had been apparent from 1886 onwards, when the widened franchise had brought Parnell and his party into effective power. This election marked the end of many political careers, among them that of old William Field, the Blackrock meat merchant.

The Sinn Féin MPs would not go to Westminster. Instead they chose to sit in Dublin, meeting in the Mansion House (that place filled with happy memories for John Stanislaus of glorious parties in the 1870s). There they constituted themselves as the assembly of the Irish people, reaffirmed the Proclamation of 1916 and passed a social programme. This was all very fine and political. But on the same day the IRA attacked a guarded explosives cart, killing two policemen. One of those who took part explained that they did not want the politicians to make all the running. What would come eventually to be called the War of Independence had begun, though then it was known merely as The Troubles.

What John Joyce thought of Sinn Féin is uncertain. He was most likely fairly sceptical of these rough fellows, who seemed to think that if they sat on the parliamentary sides of their arses for long enough, then, with the help of God and a few policemen, they might learn how to run a country. At least he was still staggering through Ireland's history, but only just; he complained how difficult walking now was for him. In July, a letter was sent by him from Lidwell's offices to his favourite son on a favourite theme: it would again be his last birthday. George Lidwell was dying – and John Stanlislaus was not in great shape either, and was very 'shappy', he said. But what concerned him most was how he had been traduced by his own children, all of whom – apart from James – had abandoned him '*for years past*'. He blamed the treatment he had received from them on a single fact: that they were 'Mongrels'. If they would not acknowledge him as their father, he would deny them too. With his mind on death, he announced in the most brutal terms that if his 'unnatural' spawn did not want to be Joyces, they could not be buried with their parents in the family grave. Instead, he said, they could be flung into the 'Murray Sink', where they could revert to the hated family from which they came in the company of Uncle William and the rest: they were no Joyces. The vile image came from the depths.

Two weeks after John wrote this intemperate letter, George Lidwell was dead. John turned out for the big funeral from Corrig Road, Kingstown, to Glasnevin. Legal men abounded – mostly barristers, solicitors and magistrates of the younger generation, rather than politicians. John Stanislaus Joyce had never made magistrate and the occasion was in some ways a last hurrah. He would not be in this milieu again, where he had spent so much of his life, among functionaries and lawyers and the civic middle class of Dublin. He was old.

The death of George Lidwell (only forty-nine, he had been ill for some time) meant a complete change in John's life. Perhaps he and Tom Devin, Lidwell's best man at his wedding back in 1890, had been his oldest acquaintances. Dublin's rowing fraternity – Lidwell had been a member of the Neptune which rowed against Devin's club the Dolphin – as well as Sandycove Swimming Club had been all well represented at the funeral. This combination of sport and the law harked back to John Stanislaus's earliest days in Dublin. Lidwell before his death had taken a newly qualified solicitor, Stephen H. O'Reilly, into the practice and O'Reilly now took over, initially as Lidwell and O'Reilly, then in his own name. Both Lidwell and O'Reilly were well connected with the parties in the newly emerging establishment of the Irish Free State. John may have stayed on with O'Reilly into 1920 to ease the transition in the firm (or he may simply have held on to some of the firm's headed writing paper).

Medically, personally, domestically, societally, John Stanislaus was unsettled. He continued to draw about £150 annually from his pensions, still a respectable income despite the serious price inflation caused by the war, especially so for one with no dependants. His frequent poverty can be attributed to his habitual vice of improvidence. As he had shown for much of his life, it took resources to be prodigal, and prodigality was another cast of mind (along with a penchant for self-pity, verbal dexterity and a habit of comic exaggeration) that he passed on to his favourite son. He retained a strong sense of where he fitted in among the nobility, gentry, clergy, professional gentlemen, merchants, manufacturers and other classes of his city: it was not among the artisans, soldiers, labourers or those at the lowest levels of subsistence – in theory at least. The later hints of James Joyce's Dublin friends about his father's 'ignominy' and 'breakdown' seem to be concerned with a combination of his own poor plumbing and Dublin's bad housing.

Con Curran referred to a 'complete collapse'. The loss of Lidwell must have been a factor. John Stanislaus, man about town, was now down-at-heel and, at intervals, odorous, and may briefly have sampled complete destitution. (The *Wake* later cited a 'dweller in the downandoutermost where voice only of the dead may come, because ye left from me, because ye laughed on me, because, O me lonly son, ye are forgetting me!') Yet there is no evidence whatever of any criminal procedure such as a prosecution for vagrancy or being drunk and disorderly. Like the dark offence of *Finnegans Wake*, in its vagueness the fault grows with the imagination.

The unresolved question of Irish independence meant an atmosphere of tension and implicit violence. James Joyce, sensing this from afar more acutely than some resident Dubliners, inquired after the well-being of his father. Getting no reply, it seems that he rapidly recruited his brother as a sleuth (what Pappie might have termed a Fides Achates). Charlie Joyce, who had no wish to meet him himself, sent his wife to the Fairfield Road area in Ballybough to search for John Stanislaus. Mary, too, failed, but she ran into Josephine Murray and her daughters coming out of one of the picture-houses nearby. They did not know where he was either. When Jim learnt of Pappie's apparent disappearance (his brief season of ignominy), his efforts to locate him would have increased – through Con Curran and Alfie Bergan for example. Menace was in the air.

In fact, at this date John Stanislaus, now an old age pensioner, was back living at the Ivy Hotel in Temple Street. This quiet little private hotel, run by Mrs Hollywood, was only a few doors down from the nearby children's hospital and in the evening John liked to converse in the pubs on the corner of Dorset Street with the medical students doing their stint on the wards of the hospital. One of these was Dr Francis R. P. Walsh. Dr Walsh (then in his final years as a student) remembered old John Stanislaus's colourful comments on the frosty morning weather, for his language was as exuberant as ever it had been. Well aware of who the old man was, the students would draw him out. He talked about his own days as a medical student in Cork in the late 1860s. This was when he claimed that he had cured himself of syphilis at that time by using carbolic. But as we have already seen, John Stanislaus never had syphilis. He suffered from a simple venereal chancre. Given his son Jim's fascination with syphilis, which has attracted the attention of many critics, this revelation by Dr Walsh when made in 1975 caused delighted ripples among literary critics eager to hunt out the effects of the disease in all its stages among members of the Joyce family. But as there never was any syphilis in John, there were no effects either.

In the first clash of the new war a patrol of British light infantry was audaciously ambushed going to church in Fermoy. The raid was led by Liam Lynch and there were military reprisals. Fermoy was 'proclaimed' under the 1887 Criminal Law and Procedure Act, an active relic of Harrington's Plan of Campaign, and within three days all of Ireland followed suit, as Great Britain formally found the Dáil to be illegal. (Further away, in Paris and Philadelphia, the wheels of diplomacy and *realpolitik* were turning slowly with regard to recognition for an Irish state. President Woodrow Wilson was awarded the Freedom of Dublin without coming near the city.) Unsurprisingly, John Stanislaus took to his sickbed for a variety of reasons. James was soon to coin the word 'Drumcondriac'. John announced to his son in 1920 that he was 'in a *dreadful state* for clothes and boots' and said that his time was very nearly up. But it was not. He was still not dead yet.

If the sitting of the Dáil was seen by some as an important political development, the appearance of *Ulysses* in the March–April issue of *The Egoist* marked an equally important literary one. The interest which the publicity about the novel aroused led to the circulation of rumours in Dublin about Joyce himself, which he commented on with some asperity to Aunt Josephine on 6 August 1919. Doubtless, as with so many people who come to prominence in Ireland, these took the form of *Who does he think he is? I knew his father when* . . . In October 1919 Jim and his family returned to Stannie in Trieste, reaching his old home in November. Here he would stay until July 1920 – working further on the ever more complex text of *Ulysses*.

James Joyce's first biographer, Herbert Gorman, would arrive in Dublin too late to talk to John Stanislaus, but in time to meet those who still recalled him. In the book he summed up John Stanislaus

Joyce as 'in his later years, at least, an Irish exemplification of Mr Micawber':

Those who remember him in Dublin, and he appears to have left his mark on a city that brimmed with impressive and eccentric personalities, assert – albeit with a tender reminiscential glow – that he was an inebriate and a fop, wore a monocle in one eye, was blessed with a quick natural biting wit, was continuously popular and always notorious for his penuriousness and improvidence.

This was John Stanislaus as he had appeared before he vanished from the public knowledge of the city after 1920. At the beginning of 1920 the international difficulties that beset the publication of Jim's book can have meant little to John Stanislaus or to his daughters in Dublin. On 23 February 1920 a curfew from midnight to 5 a.m. came into effect in Dublin, in an attempt to curb the numerous shootings and killings in the city and suburbs. Not all of these were directly political, for the troubled times encouraged lawless elements to rob a bank or two under the guise of patriotic motives. Around the country, labour troubles, strikes and 'soviets' flared up. Whatever about his health, this state of affairs would have affected John Stanislaus's comings and goings.

In May 1920 Pappie was in hospital again, 'suffering from impecuniosity' according to Charlie and Mary, who visited him there. In addition to his self-neglect, it may be that these institutionalisations were part of John Stanislaus's survival strategy, a sort of urban transhumance, a move to occasional fresh pastures where the nuns and young nurses would provide him with the care he felt was his by right. Charlie, with his own problems, had little time to spare for his brother's doings: his world at least did not revolve around the progress of his brother Jim. These Joyces had for some time lived at 30 North Great George's Street, but nobody informed Pappie, who found out Charlie's whereabouts only some years later, when James told him. Charlie complained about how little news he himself got from the rest of the family too: now, six years after work on *Ulysses* had begun, he remarked, 'You are writing another book I hear.' His wife Mary was ill, struggling with a bout of pneumonia. She had contracted her husband's tuberculosis and would never be really well again. Though still in the Telephone Exchange, he was, he said, 'on the road to James's Street', the south Dublin workhouse, and asked Jim for help. Jim did send him a little, but it did nothing to change the situation. In 1918 Richard Charles had been born, and matters if possible, became even more difficult.

It was clear that John Stanislaus's health precluded a return to his former independent life. Hotels, convenient as they were, did not welcome guests who were old and often ill. Through the good offices of his young friend, the ever-present Alfie Bergan, he moved from Temple Street to new lodgings with a Protestant family named Medcalf at 25 Claude Road, a cul-de-sac between Whitworth Road and the railway line in Drumcondra.

Bergan's own lodgings were still with Mrs Refaussé at 2 Claude Road, on the other side of the street from John Stanislaus's new dwelling-place. Mrs Refaussé, a Church of Ireland lady, must have known the Medcalfs, who were very High Church in tone; indeed one of their abiding interests was their parish church. The house was owned by Mrs Mary Medcalf. She had been born about 1864 in the Falkland Islands. She had trained as a nurse in Florence Nightingale's nursing school and then worked in Steeven's hospital in Dublin. She married William Medcalf, who worked in the Dublin printing trade, in 1884. He was a good twenty years older than Mary. They lived first in Grattan Terrace, just off the Drumcondra Road, and then when their family came, at 3 Whitworth Road. When their daughters married they moved to Claude Road. Mrs Medcalf had always had elderly lodgers, offering her nursing skills as part of the services. Her husband was eventually fired from his job in Armstrong's because he would not stop singing in the workshop, where he was paper cutter. However she did not mind having him at home. Music and song were as large a part of their lives as they were of old Johnny Joyce, as they came to call their lodger. They kept a piano in the front parlour and William sang in choirs and at parish events. The musical ambience must have been agreeable to John Stanislaus. Though her husband was unemployed and her youngest son, Albert Edward ('Bertie'), earning very little as a clerk, it is unlikely that she was entirely dependent on his fees. Every month a messenger called with a brown paper envelope, which the family thought contained money paid her from the Tetley's tea family. What the real source of the money was remains a mystery, as the Medcalfs were a secretive family and kept themselves to themselves. She was by all accounts a genteel, respectable, kind-hearted lady. If John Joyce had been in better health she might have ensured that he kept up with his religious practices as a Catholic. What with family troubles and two old men in the house Mrs Medcalf cannot have had too easy a time. It is likely, too, that an aura of prim respectability hung over the little house.

According to Padraic Colum, who talked with Albert Medcalf, the youngest son of the house, John 'had come to live with them after some kind of a breakdown – either an accident such as befalls old men or a shock that had left him somewhat astray'. This seems to have been a minor stroke of some kind, something that was always likely, given the high colour of his complexion. Certainly there was no question, now that he had the old age pension, of going out to work at the Municipal Elections that were held in Dublin's new district divisions in January 1921.

Old John Stanislaus Joyce was given the second bedroom on the first half-landing, and it overlooked the back garden. It was just beside the lavatory-cum-bathroom, which would be convenient for any of the little problems that now beset him. The only distinctive feature in the room was a small cast-iron fireplace, along the mantelpiece of which he was able to arrange his pictures of James and his children. He seems to have moved about very little from this date on.

The security of this room in Drumcondra, after years of improvisation and shame, was doubly welcome. Dublin had become a city of confusion and disinformation, treachery and violence, the whole island was currently polarised and confused and tense. The Troubles, later to be dignified as the War of Independence, were an ugly business, with brutalities, squalid little shootings and ambushes, which on both sides were justified by an appeal to a higher cause. A cycle of violence and reprisal went on: blank cheques drawn on history. The centre of Cork City itself had been set alight by British Auxiliaries, destroying the City Hall and the Library. New personalities dominated events, such as Erskine Childers and Desmond FitzGerald. These events and these people were to be seen as through a gloss darkly in *Finnegans Wake*.

Meanwhile Jack's old employer, Henry Campbell, Town Clerk of Dublin for so many years and once Parnell's secretary, finally retired. In his later years he had been having undignified squabbles with Sinn Féiners, as he fought a rearguard battle against the Gaelicisation of names in public use. To no one's surprise he accepted a knighthood a few years before his death in 1924, when it was proffered by Lord French, the Viceroy whom the IRA had recently attempted to murder. The compromises into which he had been forced made a strange contrast with James's and John's view of The Chief, who increasingly seemed as remote as an Irish Moses, who had seen, but never visited, the Promised Land.

Through 'Big' Jem Dagge of the GPO (who lived two doors away from Alfie Bergan in Claude Road), John Stanislaus must have learned of another Mr Joyce in the vicinity, a former Dublin Castle man. He too had been 'eased out' in the early 1890s, and now he was seeing representatives of the new government at a special meeting in Whitworth Road, Drumcondra and telling them some Home Rule truths, tales of skulduggery among G-men in the old days. Soon this Mr Joyce was to meet the President of Ireland, Arthur Griffith, who was 'interested' in this revelation of the secret history of his country, but did not see a way of using the material. This Mr Joyce was a small, sharp-featured, rather stooped and badly dressed old man with a moustache, who smelt of drink and had a shake in his hand, and lived in a house that smelt strongly of boiled cabbage. The Messrs Joyce were not related, except spiritually and in their shared experiences and ambiguous relationships with the forces of authority. A meeting of both Mr Joyces can be imagined about now, each with his own tales of chicanery in high places to tell. Though increasingly isolated from the gossip of the city, John Stanislaus Joyce was still a man who enjoyed his talk.

The death of Archbishop Walsh on 21 April 1921 was another break with the past, the man whom John Stanislaus's savage wit had skewered as 'Billy with the Lip' thirty years before at the time of the split. Though the Archbishop was an enemy of the *Freeman's Journal* (as were the IRA now), and richly despised by John Stanislaus for his timidity, his qualified support for Parnell was judged by many to have cost him a cardinal's hat. British influence was always strong at the Vatican. Before his death he had been promoting a campaign (sometimes known as the 'Angelic Warfare for Maintaining the National Virtue of our Country') against evil literature (especially in the form of British Sunday papers) which would go on gathering force up to the introduction of the Censorship Act in 1929. This reaction against all things British spread not only to personal names and papers and books, but to buildings and statues, and to the names of the city's streets and public places: geographical Dublin, a largely English construct, was to be remade as an Irish palimpsest. Some felt that 'British' buildings should be demolished (or at least not restored), but Dublin's topography was the main forum of change towards Irish names of places: in 1925 Sackville Street would at last be officially renamed O'Connell Street. Despite its new identity it continued to boast at least three adulterers on its public monuments – and a few more on its pavements.

After the final months of 1920 with the dreadful events of Bloody Sunday, during early 1921 the Troubles in Ireland were moving to their climax. On 28 February six Republican prisoners were executed in Cork, after which six soldiers were murdered in the city. On 7 March James's old college pal, George Clancy, now Mayor of Limerick City, was murdered by gunmen outside his home. The murderers were never identified but were widely thought to have been the (British) Black and Tans.

The Local Government Board which now paid John's pension was based in the Customs House, which was attacked by Republicans on 25 May and burnt. Prisoners were taken and lives lost. The idea behind this was to render British administration of the country impossible, but all it did in reality was to affect the payment of pensions for a little while. But in effect the British era in Ireland was coming to an end. Shortly after Pappie's seventy-second birthday, a truce was reached on 11 July 1921 between the Irish government and the British authorities.

In June 1920 Ezra Pound had persuaded James to move to Paris, which the family did that month. There he received a letter (1 July) from a friend of John Stanislaus in Dublin – perhaps Alfie Bergan, Tom Devin, or even young Dr Walsh. The letter told James that his father was 'still of opinion that you alone care for him and believe in him, and his whole thoughts are centred on your coming over so that he may see you before he dies.' But though he was now nearer home, James's fears of visiting a war-torn Ireland were realistic enough. He later told Gorman that he had been urged to leave Trieste by his father (but did not mention that the old man meant him to come home). In Paris they were at least in immediate contact with London and New York, where a few months later an official complaint was laid against *The Little Review* for running the increasingly shocking parts of *Ulysses*. Dublin too was in easier reach of Paris, though there was no prospect of a visit there by James, given the state of the nation and his urgent need to complete the book.

Certainly one event there had passed the family in France by. On 30 November 1920, an eighth child, Frederick Joseph, was born to Charles and Mary Joyce, once again at the Rotunda. The family were still living in rooms at 30 North Great George's Street – the Georgian house was only doors away from what is now the James Joyce Cultural Centre. At least Charlie had held on to his job as a minor civil servant on the telephones.

Florence and Eva were now in rooms at 81 Summerhill. John would from time to time look in on them. One of the last sightings of him in public was as an old man toiling up Summerhill to visit them, his tatty coat flapping behind him and his tie out untidily: there was nothing left of the fop John Stanislaus Joyce had once been. For Michael Lennon, too, John had been a familiar figure about the city while he was working for Lidwell. Lennon's politics differed from Lidwell's, whom he called a cheap police court solicitor. As a judge in the secret underground Republican Courts, Lennon had spent the previous years on the run, hiding for six months with John Stanislaus's O'Connell relations in Cork from whom he picked up garbled impressions of the family history.

The July truce meant that finally the politicians would have to try to patch together a settlement which would prove satisfactory. The curfews which had been imposed, as well as the shootings and killings, stopped for the time being. But this civil peace would have had little effect on John Stanislaus, who by now rarely went further than the Brian Boru pub, or the pubs on the lower Drumcondra

Road, where he could enjoy the gossip and rumours about the future that flourished in the city during this time.

The future of Ireland, however, was of little interest to the Paris Joyces. James, who in April 1921 had agreed that Sylvia Beach should publish his novel there, wanted only gossip about the past. On 13 September, Lucia, whom her grandfather admired, acting as her father's amanuensis, sent John a typewritten list of questions concerning Major Powell and the social connections of Stamer Street from the 1880s, the answers for insertion into *Ulysses*. John did not answer this letter: it would be found among his few papers after his death. James's father was now beyond such efforts. On 14 October James wrote more urgently to Aunt Josephine, also asking about the Powells. He inquired, too, if she knew anything about Alfred H. Hunter, the acquaintance on whom Bloom was partly based, and about Alfie Bergan, whom he had introduced into the book as a practical joker. James had not known that his father had for some time been in 25 Claude Road, and was a near neighbour of Bergan, who would remain a confidant of the old man to the end. However, now that he had renewed contact with his father, James and John would write to each other several times a year, usually around Christmas and their respective birthdays.

To many who had not been acquainted with Mr Joyce in his prime, he was known and increasingly referred to as 'John Stanislaus'. Venerable, a citizen of renown and credit, he verged on being a public curiosity. He remained interested in the younger generation, as his friendships with Bergan and Dr Walsh show. Even so, only one of his children had given him 'proper' grandchildren. At a time when his family as a whole amounted to over twenty-five individuals, John Stanislaus thought only of the Paris four – or three: Nora was good for James, but she was not one of John's obsessions. Of the children, John was most fond of Lucia, and through her and Giorgio, he could even look forward to 'proper' great-grandchildren one day. Though his diatribes still constituted a Joycean broadside (the rhetoric of *Ulysses* caught some of it), when he was being kind the old wit and charm would resurface. His reply to Lucia at this time, an amusing screed in his careful copperplate handwriting, suggested that if he were ever to leave the house, he would need a bodyguard or protector. The city was not safe (and James's verdict was that the country had become a slaughterhouse). Meanwhile, he continued to denounce his other children, and their children, as Mongrels destined for the 'Murray Sink'. All this was heartless, selfish and cruel. His rejection of and by those children, his own flesh and blood, and the distance which even his grandchildren maintain from him to this day, speaks volumes.

On 6 December 1921, the Treaty between the representatives of Great Britain and Ireland was signed in London. The next day, in Paris, Valéry Larbaud gave a public lecture on *Ulysses*. Already Dublin literary circles, picking up on items in the British and French press, were beginning to talk about Joyce's new novel. While one event signalled the birth of a new state, the other indicated the arrival of a new literature. James Joyce's final words in *Ulysses* were not Molly Bloom's *yes I will Yes*, but his own extra-textual *Trieste–Zurich–Paris, 1914–1921*. The years during which James had written his masterpiece out of the shards of his father's fractured universe had been for John Stanislaus years of bitter and undignified decline. His Dublin, with its people and memories, its quirky practices, its diversions, was truly a city of the past, a place in history. The Treaty brought to an end eight centuries of British rule, and Irish self-government – Ireland Free, O'Connell's Repeal, Parnell's Promised Land – had finally come to pass. That was the theory, anyway. For John Stanislaus it could not begin to realise his ancient hopes. But at least he had survived to see it happen and he could enjoy contemplating it with the scepticism of experience. In Yeats's words to the cheering man, 'Ireland will get her freedom, and you still break stones.'

While Jim struggled over the completion of *Ulysses* for publication in the new year, in Dublin the old year ended in tragedy. On Christmas Day 1921, Richard Joyce, the three-year-old son of Charles and Mary Joyce, born in the last days of the Great War, died. From the shabby but respectable lower-middle-class atmosphere of *Ulysses* they had fallen into the grim poverty of the tenements of Sean O'Casey's plays. But worse was to come. . .

CHAPTER 28

Learning to Die

As Dublin Castle was being vacated in 1922 and the British Army marched towards its boats, *Ulysses* was published in Paris on James Joyce's fortieth birthday. The most avant-garde manifestation of the new Ireland was a re-creation of the old Dublin under the Union Jack. The author sent his father one of the very few presentation copies. (The book, with its inscription, is now lost.) Father replied, remarking politely on his son's Paris success. (Aunt Josephine was another recipient.) Some Dubliners asked others nervously, 'Are you in it?' Many were. Often these people were almost unknown except to the Joyces and their circle, but others were city eccentrics, like Cashel Boyle O'Connor Fitzmaurice Tisdall Farrell, who walked the streets bristling with swords, umbrellas and fishing-rods, and there were some who were more eminent, such as Andrew J. Horne FCPI, Master of Holles Street Hospital in 1904 and once an Assistant Secretary in John Stanislaus's own Local Government Board. One report of *Ulysses* was that it was a book that could be read on the lavatory walls of Dublin, but in public at least, the author's Pappie was not going to side with the begrudgers. Ever his father's son, James compiled an impressive list of potential subscribers for *Ulysses*. It began with Baron Ralli and Count Sardino, before mentioning Italo Svevo (who, with John Stanislaus, Alfred Hunter and James himself, was another of the real people whom Joyce dovetailed into the character of Leopold Bloom). Professor Stanislaus Joyce in Trieste, whose career had flourished since he and James parted and the war ended, was at number six, with Baroness St Leger at number eight followed by Lady Cunard and the singer John McCormack, soon to be a Count of the Holy Roman Empire. The Joyces continued to mix with the best, but James would not have been too surprised to learn that his father's mild but uncomprehending reaction to this strange new book was the traditional one: 'He's a nice sort of blackguard.' Mrs Arthur Griffith, moving with her husband in the city's musical circles, heard that the dreadful James Joyce, whom Arthur had known since 1904, had written a book that 'even his old father could not read'. John's dismissive remark, however, in fact followed his intensive scrutiny of the large blue volume through his monocle.

Undoubtedly, John Joyce never did read *Ulysses* from cover to cover. His own presence in the book was unmistakable, however, and he would scarcely have been human if he had not leafed through it looking for scenes containing Simon Dedalus. But he was surely unaware of the important part he had played in the fashioning of Leopold Bloom, that idiosyncratic middle-aged Irish Everyman with a would-be fatherly relationship with Stephen Dedalus the young writer. Bloom's first appearance in the novel, for example ('Mr Leopold Bloom ate with relish the inner organs of beasts and fowls'), reflects a preference not of the author but of his father. Many other traits of Bloom's character and events in his past also come from John Stanislaus, such as the reading of *Tit-Bits* and, more significantly, the loss of his first-born son after less than two weeks of life. However, in the sightings of Mr Dedalus himself there was already a good deal for John to be getting on with in the book.

Apart from his singing, it is in the colourful nature of his conversation that Simon Dedalus shines in *Ulysses*. John Stanislaus would have recognised his own voice in phrases such as 'Fit as a fiddle, only he has a lot of adipose tissue concealed about his person', 'Melancholy God!' and 'I'll tickle his catastrophe, believe you me'. John's attacks on his in-laws are also repeated by Simon, who calls one of their children 'Papa's little lump of dung' and her father a 'drunken little cost-drawer'. The weather is 'as uncertain as a child's bottom' and Bloom's wife 'has left off clothes of all descriptions'. One of John's attacks on his daughters also appears: 'You're like the rest of them, are you? An insolent pack of little bitches since your mother died. But wait awhile. You'll all get short shrift and a long day from me. Low blackguardism! I'm going to get rid of you. Wouldn't care if I was stretched out stiff. He's dead. The man upstairs is dead.' The sailor W. B. Murphy's report of Simon Dedalus in a circus in Stockholm shooting eggs off bottles fifty yards away can obviously be taken as pure fiction, however, and it may be noted that the judgement from 'Cyclops' referring to Mr Dedalus's son Stephen was excised by James before publication: 'He'll never be as good a man as his father anyhow'.

To Louis Gillet in Paris, James Joyce later remarked of his father, 'The humour of *Ulysses* is his; its people are his friends. The book is his spittin' image.' Of course, it was more than phrases that the writer took from John. Since he had begun writing as a young man, the unique dynamics of the father–son relationship had enthralled James Joyce. Stephen's discussion of *Hamlet* in the National Library comes close to it, in which 'he proves by algebra that Hamlet's grandson is Shakespeare's grandfather and that he himself is the ghost of his own father', as Buck Mulligan sneers. *Ulysses* is in many ways a book about failed fatherhood, but it took the author's own failed father to engender it. And in the process, it became increasingly evident to James Joyce that his Pappie's life, spanning as it did two centuries and two political systems, was a resource he was going to have to tap again.

Following the late Archbishop's lead, the country was awash with a politico-religious campaign for 'Clean Literature', fostered by the Catholic Literature Service Guild, the Irish Vigilance Association (which was a neighbour of Charlie's at 39 North Great George's Street) and other organisations. Newsagents and booksellers were urged to carry no literature which insulted modesty or mocked religion. It was an unpropitious moment for the appearance of *Ulysses* in its home city, but a number of booksellers fearlessly stocked it, including P. S. O'Hegarty's nationally minded shop in Grafton Street. In Listowel in the wilds of County Kerry, Dan Flavin's surprisingly ordered twenty-four copies of the expensive first edition. The bookshop was only a few miles from the ruins of Old Court, where Séan Mór Seoighe, the first-known of the line of John and James Joyce, had once held sway. It was a form of return, what was to become known in the next novel as a vicus of recirculation.

Despite the talk of yet another war, between the Irish themselves over whether to accept the Treaty, John expected visitors from Paris, carefree now that James had at last produced his damn great square book. In April 1922 Nora and the children visited Dublin. It was a great success, dampened only by the absence of James. Ten chaotic years had passed since John Stanislaus had seen any of James's family. The first person they went to see was Nora's uncle, Michael Healy. The next on the list was to be John Stanislaus, but neither Nora nor her uncle could find his address. Then Lucia, a bright girl, now nearly fifteen, remembered from her letters where her grandfather lived and they called round to a great welcome. The Galway man made amends by taking John Stanislaus, Tom Devin and his second wife, and the Parisians out for dinner. James Joyce wrote afterwards to his Aunt Josephine who, when she heard that Nora and the children had been in Dublin but had not bothered to visit her, had been extremely hurt: 'The only enlivening feature of their journey appears to have been their interview with my father who amused them vastly by the virulence, variety and incandescence of curses which he bestowed on his native country and all in it – a litany to which his eldest son says Amen.' Over the meal John was in good form, and among the stories he told may have been the oft-told tale of the Norwegian captain and the tailor – a good one, worth telling again. It had originally come from Philip McCann, about the Dublin tailor who tries to make a suit for a hunchbacked sea-captain. Fitting after fitting is unsuccessful and the two men argue: when the captain says the tailor can't sew, the tailor retaliates by saying that the captain is impossible to fit. As Richard Ellmann commented, it is one of those anecdotes that are potentially much funnier than they sound: it would be retold in *Finnegans Wake*, where, if John had seen it, he would have said of James, 'He can't tell that story as I used to and that's one sure five!' The situation in the tale was related to the one in Balfe's *Maritana*, where the devil-may-care nobleman Don Caesar jokes irresistibly about his tailor's bills. So story and song would roll on, one stimulating the next, or the next variation.

Giorgio was now seventeen and tall, and something of a singer. Joyceness proceeded – continuity with discontinuities. In August of 1922 James Joyce was in London, but apprehensive about being shot if he went to Ireland where more than one old friend from college had been murdered already. (Even in London, there had been successful Irish assassins that summer.) When Nora and Giorgio had been driven out of Galway by a skirmish, only to have the train they left in shot at, Joyce insisted on seeing it as at least a deliberate anti-Joycean threat. James Joyce had an unshakeable faith in his people – that they would betray him.

That summer of 1922 marked one peak of the Irish Civil War. It was fought between two sets of patriots. After some months of feinting preliminaries, Free State forces opened fire on anti-Treaty Republicans who were holding the Four Courts (and a National Army general hostage). The bombardment was partly from the Phoenix Park (and the detonation of explosives at the Four Courts and the adjoining Public Record Office shook Tim Healy's house in Chapelizod). In August, the death of Arthur Griffith in Dublin, and the killing of Michael Collins in Cork, were serious losses for the new state that was struggling to be born. Notwithstanding, on 6 December 1922, in accordance with the Treaty, the Irish Free State officially came into being. It was thirty-two years to the day since the last meeting of the unbroken Irish Party under Parnell. The following day, another Corkman and parliamentarian, Deputy Seán Hales, was shot while leaving the Ormond Hotel, where John Stanislaus had once whiled away many a musical afternoon. In retaliation for this murder, on the day after that the government shot, with others, Rory O'Connor, Clongownian and UCD contemporary of James, in Mountjoy Gaol. In November 1922 Erskine Childers (denounced by Tim Healy as 'quite unIrish', though he was not) was tried by a Military Army Court (which included another of James's friends, Eugene Sheehy) and executed in Dublin by the new Irish Government as an enemy of the people. History, as ever, was moving in cycles, with repetitions and variations and cumulations: Childers's son Erskine Childers would become Irish head of state in the 1970s. Just as O'Connors, Sheehys and Stephenses could recur, Joyces could recur, and Monsieur Joyce the Parisian could sense that whatever made him what he was, he had derived it from the strange and wonderful man who had once set out on his Cork legs to fight for France, but got no further than London. Now he himself was in London from France, but had no intention of getting any nearer to the war in Ireland. The old gentleman in Drumcondra very much wanted to see him.

The living past was in the son's mind and he decided to make it the subject of his next book. This time it would be something yet more ambitious than his exhaustive account of an Edwardian Dublin day in *Ulysses*: it would be an endless Dublin night, the centuries of it, an encyclopaedia of world history to rival the *Book of Kells* in its intricate and ornate detail. Its primary disguised presence was to be the spirit of John Stanislaus Joyce, with all his fun and impossibility and outrageousness. The central character, HCE, even started in the notes as 'Pop'. The new book would develop and shift over the years, but its driving constant was the history of the Joyce family, their triumphs and their many reversals, as an example of the human condition in all times and all places. The genealogical tradition of the seanachie was to be rendered in rococo. In the *Wake*, Dublin's hinterland included the world. The Phoenix Park was many things, including a stage of the imagination. Somewhere in the vast space of the 'Fifteen Acres' there, it was said, Daniel O'Connell had once killed a man in a duel. There, too, much later, John Stanislaus had his heroic encounter with the pipe-smoking cad, the burglarious old josser. This nineteenth-century mugging became his explanation of his low 'takings' that day of the municipal rates. Though there had been only one incident, the story already came in an abundance of guises. Several of these came from the lips of John Stanislaus himself: to the Collector-General, it suited John to be the victim, but to his audience of children, he was naturally the hero. To the other Apostles, in a public house, he might soup it up with some choice expletives. When no longer in the employment of the Rates Office, his language would remain choice in other ways about what had 'really' happened. And there was the truth, whatever that might have been. One version of the story now begins on page 35 of *Finnegans Wake*, but there are 1001 other stories of the same event in the book. Furtiveness in the Park is a version of the Book of Genesis and of modern life. Parnell himself had been accused of a crime in the Park – complicity with the Invincibles. So James Joyce's Work in Progress grew into a literally endless story and was filled with his

Pappie's songs and stories and addresses and personality (in all its contradictoriness). Here Comes Everybody.

And from where? From Cong and Lixnaw, and Cork and Fermoy and the Ballyhoura Hills. Youghal and Windsor and Brighton Square, Mullingar and Galway, Pola and Chapelizod. Paris and back. Soon, Pappie's grandson Giorgio would marry into a distinguished family in New York, where some distant cousins had helped build Saint Patrick's Cathedral. And there was Dublin itself. Dublin was a stage and not just a staging post. In the Phoenix Park was the same anew – as the very name suggested. For the Joyces, the Phoenix also suggested the red bird of their coat of arms. Family history (with its national and literary interstices) was never far away. Indeed, it was Weston St John Joyce who revived the Gaelic etymology that the Park was named after the sparkling spring there – *Fionn uisce*. Chapelizod, nearby, took its name from the Chapel of Isolde, and the second drafted passage of what was to become *Finnegans Wake* was the Tristan and Isolde fragment. The theme of Chapelizod in turn picked up on John Stanislaus's enthusiasm for Sheridan Le Fanu's *The House by the Churchyard*. The novel had a comic duel in the Park, and much else, and was set at the house overlooking his once successful distillery. Appropriately, John Stanislaus's Chapelizod distillery was later known as the Phoenix (and the word also had a resonance for what Captain O'Shea had once called 'hillside men', the Fenians). Possibly the title for Work in Progress (kept secret as the book grew) was derived by Joyce from Weston Joyce's and Wakeman's *Evening Telegraph* articles (and popular reprints) of the late 1880s, as much as from the exhortation, 'Phoenix Awake!', young Jim's comic song, 'Hooligan's Cake' or 'Finnegan's Wake' itself.

The first sketch for the future *Wake* was of King Roderick O'Connor, two pages done on 10 March 1923. The story was of the last Irish high king ('suburbanites he didn't care a spit out of his mouth for'), who had died in Cong in 1198. The name also invoked his namesake fighting in the Four Courts in 1922 for absolute Irish freedom, Rory (or Roderick) O'Connor. King Roderick O'Connor was described in James Joyce's draft as being between fifty-four and fifty-five years of age – the age of Pappie when James had last lived with him in 1904.

The day after he began sketching the O'Connor piece for this, his most ambitious book, James wrote Pappie a friendly and constructive, even cultivating, letter. With many teeth just removed, and abscesses and more eye trouble developing, as he approached his mid-forties the writer could remember his father clearly at the same age, as he was in the years of Parnell's rise and fall, and experienced a feeling of even greater affinity with this remarkable man. James remarked that he had read in the newspapers that Hugh M'Intyre, one of the Twelve Apostles, had died and surmised that his father would not be sorry to see the departure of such a mean fellow. In the same historical-allegorical letter, Joyce also reported (from another newspaper detail sent by Michael Healy) that Pappie's old office at 43 Fleet Street had been blown up in the bitter fighting of the Irish Civil War. The Offices of the Collector-General had been taken over by the Government Stationery Office and the aim of the bomb was to destroy the forms and licences without which no modern administration can function. Still Dublin was a no-go area for James Joyce: glass was still shattering and masonry toppling. Even the DMP, helmeted and brightly buttoned, were not long for this world, and would soon be abolished under the 1925 Police Forces Amalgamation Act.

Thus was Irish history in the making or remaking. His Pappie's experiences and expressions were to help James formulate a race memory for the new Ireland. John Stanislaus had gone from being a dilapidated old man to being the progenitor of the old uncreated conscience of the race. The father figure in this first-most draft was showing a regal thirst for 'chateaubottled Guiness's [*sic*] or Phoenix brewery stout it was or John Jameson and Sons . . .' As the writer knew, the Guinness *château* was by the Joyce Country at Cong. Irish history shows that many roads lead there, just as many lead to Fermoy.

The city in which John Stanislaus had once walked and now, more often than not, lay, remained full of conversation and he still found ways of talking about what was going on, usually in terms of vibrant disapproval. A Republican raid on the Molesworth Street headquarters of the Freemasons led to intense embarrassment for certain of the Dublin burgesses when the substantial number of Catholic Freemasons was revealed. The episode illuminated the intensity of the rumours about the masonic status of many Dubliners. (In 1896 *The Irish Catholic* had accused French Freemasons of Devil worship.) Henry Campbell was said to be a Freemason – by Tim Healy. Isaac Butt, Father of Home Rule, certainly was and so too was John Stanislaus's long-dead friend, Dick Thornton. (It is even broadly hinted that Leopold Bloom is a Mason.) The Freemasons were a more successfully oathbound secret society than the Irish Revolutionary Brotherhood had ever been. The funeral of Liam Lynch, the last major diehard of the Civil War, was held in Fermoy in April 1923. Appropriately, Fermoy had been the final permanent holding of the anti-Treaty forces the previous August. It was also the site of Castlehyde, one of the grand ancestral homes of Douglas Hyde who, for constitutional reasons, shares with Arthur Griffith the title (or style) of first President of Ireland. (There are other candidates too.)

   While John Stanislaus was getting used to this new, more peaceful life, Charlie was facing a severe crisis, one that has left no trace in the family correspondence with James. On 5 May 1923, Mary died of tuberculosis in the North Dublin Union – the workhouse. Since he was working nights on the telephone exchange, Charlie had to place the older children in care with the Christian Brothers at Artane, as the family recalls. In fact the 'Brothers' ran two separate establishments in the vicinity, the most famous being the Industrial School in Artane Castle. It is more probable that the boys went to the other one, however, the O'Brien Institute, an orphanage close to the Casino at Marino, as does the little Dignam boy in *Ulysses*. The girls found refuge with the nuns. The youngest, Stanislaus Mary, who had never been well from birth, was placed with the Sisters of Charity of St Vincent de Paul, at their 'infant asylum and children's infirmary' (actually a home for unmarried mothers) at Pelletstown on the northern side of the Phoenix Park, just outside the city boundary beyond Cabra. There, aged nine months, he died on 15 August 1923. He was buried with his mother and brother in a now unmarked grave in Glasnevin, another forgotten Joyce. These terrible nineteen months of suffering and bereavement were all part of the tragedy of Dublin, and were symptomatic of the blighted lives of its poorest class, lives that scarcely concerned the politicians of the day.

When assessing the attitudes of his children to John Stanislaus Joyce, it should always be borne in mind that those who lived through and witnessed this horror felt that it had been brought upon them by their father. James, now in receipt of money from a rich British Communist, could afford to admire his father from a distance, almost indifferent to the miseries of the others. For his brother and sisters, scraping their livings in a hostile and poverty-stricken Dublin, the wish to judge was entirely understandable.

For all the need and impoverishment under its guardianship, Municipal Dublin still found resources for ceremony. The Freedom of the City was given that autumn to John McCormack, by then one of the most famous tenors in the world. The Lord Mayor was Alfred Byrne (who duly reappeared in his chain of office as Lord Mayor of Beaugency, France, in James Joyce's story for his only grandson Stephen, now known as 'The Cat and the Devil'). John Stanislaus knew about Dublin's greatest civic honour, having worked for Jimmy Henry, and was aware that merit was not always the main criterion. He also knew about tenors. Always he had advocated clear enunciation in singing, advice that was passed on to Giorgio. John's repertoire had included 'Ah si ben mio', 'A te cara' (a favourite of Stanislaus's), 'M'appari' naturally, and 'Salve dimora'. The old man had once been the next Campanini and had made Barton McGuckin jealous. He had been told that his voice was like Jean de Reszke's with its 'velvety tones, fresh, clear and mellow as a bell': he was not inclined to be complimentary about such a vulgarly successful entertainer as McCormack. Though his son had once had a certain regard for the tenor, James too later felt that McCormack's operatic talent was exaggerated by the Italian–Irish–American set who made the important decisions.

Though civic awards could be tainted, family honours could be deeply deserved. In keeping with James Joyce's new-found (and hard-won) status as an international literary lion, that same spring he revived his 1914 plan to add to the family collection of paintings of gentlemen by having a richly earned portrait done of his father. At the suggestion of the Irish would-be painter, Arthur Power, the commission went to Patrick J. Tuohy, a native of North Frederick Street (between Rutland Square and Eccles Street), whose father, the noted Dublin doctor known to John Stanislaus since the death of Freddie in 1895, had been a medical hero of the Easter Rising. (In turn, Dr Tuohy's father was 'Jimmy' Tuohy, the *Freeman*'s parliamentary correspondent in London.) With so much shared background, the artist as a young man and his aged subject got on with complementary liveliness. Tuohy had enjoyed an adventurous life for one so young. He had been educated at Saint Enda's, Patrick Pearse's establishment in Rathfarnham, near the Yellow House. An early scholarship for £40, predicting 'a brilliant future' for Tuohy, had been reported in the *Freeman* under the title 'A Young Dublin Artist' some years before. He studied painting at the Metropolitan School of Art under Sir William Orpen, who had recently painted Gogarty's son Oliver Odysseus (and was soon to paint Count John McCormack). In 1916, aged twenty-two, Tuohy had helped Pearse in the Rising. After a discreet spell in Madrid he had returned to Dublin and gone back to the Metropolitan School of Art as a teacher. One arm was withered, but the other one was all he needed to be increasingly recognised as a highly able painter and drawer. According to Æ, Tuohy was 'an obstinate artist', and though he did his portrait of the old man in the front parlour, would follow John with palette and filled easel into his bedroom when he retreated there in exhaustion. He was not a quick worker: some of Tuohy's other portraits had taken up to eighty hours of sittings, daily progress being scraped off in the evenings. As a conversationalist, the painter tended towards the tedious, but it seems that John Stanislaus welcomed his visits for the fact that he had an audience for his own remarks.

After the painting was finished (a reproduction is on the cover of this book), the portrait and artist went to Paris. John Stanislaus was the latest and grandest of the collection of family icons. Tuohy's efforts were much appreciated and Joyce reported proudly in early May that the portrait had caused something of a sensation in Dublin. The finished painting was entered with three of the artist's other portraits for an art competition of the First Tailteann Games (a Celtic Olympics), sponsored by the culturally aware new state: it was exhibited at the Royal Dublin Society in Ballsbridge, the city's most illustrious institution, founded in 1731. In August 1924 Sir John Lavery RA awarded Tuohy a bronze medal for his entry. With greater filial pride than accuracy, Joyce wrote that the painting won second prize and the newspaper itself said that the outcome was 'keenly criticised' (not least because Jack Yeats had not entered). Though the painting is often known as *Portrait of an Irish Gentleman*, Padraic Colum called it *Portrait of a Dublin Gentleman*, and the *Irish Times* reproduced it with the caption 'Mr P. J. Tuohy's portrait of Mr John S. Joyce'. According to Thomas McGreevy (a friend of Æ and future Director of the National Gallery of Ireland), by accident or design the picture was known as 'Simon Joyce, Esq.', a happy blend of his actual and fictional identities. When McGreevy met Joyce in Paris, Joyce rather coldly said, 'I believe it was you told Tuohy my father's Christian name was Simon.' McGreevy blamed Tuohy for the confusion. (The mixed identity eventually reappeared in Myles na gCopaleen's 'Cruiskeen Lawn' column on Joyce's birthday in 1942.) Others in Dublin knew John Stanislaus by sight: Harry Clarke, the flamboyant stained-glass-window artist whose work was in Belvedere (and later in Cong), was among those who referred to him as 'Old Simon'. Underneath his customary *froideur*, the writer seems to have been rather pleased that his art was shifting the collective imagination of his native city. How John Stanislaus might have reacted to the change of name is another matter.

The portrait, now at Buffalo and recently cleaned, captures John Stanislaus magnificently. It is one of the great Irish paintings of the twentieth century. His eyes are quizzical, the eyebrows somewhere between humorous and irascible. The hairline has receded since the only other known pictorial image of John to survive, the photograph taken before James's start at Clongowes. One reminder of John Stanislaus's more gracious days, however, is the spectacularly wax-pointed soup-strainer moustache. James Joyce made it his practice to carry a photograph of this painting in his pocket. Even Stannie liked the painting and called it 'a wonderful study of that little old Milesian ... The likeness is striking.' (The allusion to Pappie as a follower of the Irish-Greek hero Milesius, kingly father of three sons, is apt: the Milesian standard of the flag of Munster is invoked in 'Cyclops'.) Tuohy followed up his portrait of John Stanislaus with a painting of the son, but the unanimous opinion was that this was a failure.

His portrait as an old man added to John Stanislaus's 'peculiar' fame (James Joyce used the adjective in acknowledging – to Miss Weaver – his moral debt to Tuohy). The painting was reproduced in the *Dublin Magazine* as well as the *Irish Times* at the time of the Horse Show, when Dublin was busiest with visitors. Despite his indigence, John Stanislaus was still remembered as a character around Dublin – with a growing repute as the father of the notorious writer. Piaras Beaslai, who was a political activist as well as a journalist, described him: 'He was a familiar figure, a real man about town with his monocle, spats and air of faded gentility. He seemed to be treated with respect by everyone who knew him.' Eugene Sheehy remembered 'a dapper little man, with military moustache, who sported an eyeglass and cane, and wore spats, and I can quite believe that on the stage he could do "George Lashwood" [a name from the music-hall artiste or song] to the life'. Constantine Curran also described James Joyce's father well, and his relics of old decency:

His father has since become something of a legendary character but the legend hardly outruns the facts. I knew him only in his last days, though like many north-side Dubliners I was familiar with his bristly, stocky figure in the Prince Albert [frockcoat] and low topper worn by men of his generation (though in his case the top hat and frock coat, spruce enough on the first of the month, grew a bit seedy towards its close . . .). He was a man of unparalleled vituperative power, a virtuoso in speech with a unique control of the vernacular, his language often coarse and blasphemous to a degree of which, in the long run, he could hardly himself have been conscious. A notable singer, with a wide knowledge of Italian opera, he would hold the attention of any room all night if there was a piano . . .

Another witness commented more succinctly on his impression of John Stanislaus: 'he was quite a character you know.' James Joyce agreed. Eager to draw on his father's memories and extravagant idioms in his new book, he arranged – possibly through Tuohy – for him to be interviewed by a shorthand writer, probably a journalist. That first interview is now lost (and there may have been several others).

In the early summer of 1924, Charlie Joyce married again, just over a year after Mary's death, this time to Annie Hearne, in Haddington Road church (which had been mentioned in 'The Dead'). The name of the bride evoked for John Stanislaus the zealot of his spacious days in Bray, 'Dante' Conway, née Hearn. With glum appropriateness, John's new daughter-in-law was an advanced Catholic, the automatic stepmother of Charlie's seven children, including John Stanislaus. Soon afterwards, Charlie left his job and removed the family to England. That autumn he visited James in Paris at about the same time as Stannie visited James from Trieste. It was the youngest brother's first meeting with his eldest brother since the Maunsel crisis over *Dubliners* more than twelve years earlier. The occasion was a serial triple reunion, an opportunity to exchange old stories by and of Pappie. Charlie's wedding seemed to set an example to another son of John Stanislaus, as not long after, Stannie got engaged to Nelly Lichtensteiger, a Triestine of Swiss origin. (James himself would go through the ceremony 'for testamentary reasons' a few years later.)

John Stanislaus was now seventy-five. His old acquaintance, the composer Geoffrey Molyneux Palmer, had moved on from settings of *Chamber Music* to write *The Sea of Moyle*, an opera on at the Gaiety the previous year, and this was revived for the 'Tailteann Games' in Dublin in August 1924. An invitation to James Joyce to revisit Dublin for this Celtic jamboree, championed by W. B. Yeats, was politely declined. Among the other attractions put on by the Games was *Shaun the Post* by Harold White, a Belvedere man. The musical entertainment was inspired by a play by Dion Boucicault, the late Dublin dramatist, which would soon be transmuted in turn by James Joyce himself.

Another local influence was more important. Aunt Josephine died that autumn. In Paris, James was truly distressed – she was an important link with his childhood. Her strong involvement in propping up John Stanislaus's sorry family was otherwise never much acknowledged, though some letters of the time suggested otherwise. The two had something in common besides unfulfilled ability: they had both married Murrays and she had helped John selflessly with what passed for family life when he became a widower. Her integrity and forthrightness were rightly respected by all but John himself. In 1919 she had written to James that she knew he had never lied to her, adding blankly, 'I thought it was rather late in the day to start.' After *Ulysses* was published she even called at the two main Dublin libraries, and in the face of institutional hostility inquired about its availability. However, she did not approve of the book herself, keeping it hidden in a cupboard. Shortly before Aunt Josephine went to hospital for the last time, she destroyed some letters from James, and on her deathbed was heard repeating the words: 'The book . . . the book . . .' If her brother-in-law in Claude Road felt any emotions when she died, he kept them to himself: it may be that among them there was a tinge of guilt.

Padraic Colum thought that John saw very little of the Paris funds of his son and that the old man lived on his 'realized insurance, with, perhaps, an old-age pension'. But if James sent money even occasionally he could not bring himself to visit. Of his other children only Eileen visited him regularly and then just a very few times a year. The rupture with his younger daughters was now almost total.

One practical consequence of living in the new state was shown in May 1925 when 'Monto', the brothel district, was finally forcibly closed down by activists of the Legion of Mary. The raid was reported codedly by the press, if at all. Centuries of ill fame were at an end. Sex was not the only issue, however, as Nighttown had also become a congeries of ex-military men of all kinds, some of whom indulged in armed robbery to support themselves. The finality of the end of the Civil War was uncertain, though the consensus of hindsight was that the diehard cause had been buried militarily with Liam Lynch in Fermoy two years earlier. Additionally, some in the new state were keen to impress visiting Roman dignitaries. One of those liaising between the Vatican and Dublin was Con Curran's brother, Monsignor Michael Curran, who for years had been Secretary to Archbishop Walsh, then became Privy Chamberlain to His Holiness the Pope. Presently he would become head of the Irish College in Rome. When a full-scale Eucharistic Congress was held in Dublin just after John Stanislaus's death and the city was awash with cardinals and ecclesiastical finery, it confirmed posthumously John's view of religion behind the satirical anticlericalism – that it was a splendid way of getting on in the world.

The archetypical Dublin Gentleman was doing just that on canvas. In the summer of 1925 Tuohy's portrait of John Stanislaus was exhibited at the Royal Academy in London. By October the painting was touring the United States with its painter (who would soon relocate there). The old man's fame was spreading, and helped the reputation of *Ulysses* and of its author. Meanwhile, for his next book, Joyce needed even more urgently (after the loss of Aunt Josephine) the memories and idioms and speech rhythms of his father. The letters and the reports were not enough: he would have to get an accurate transcript to yoke to his creative method. Accordingly he arranged again for the stenographer to visit John Stanislaus and record his divertimenti. Welcoming the company, John complied as naturally as he always did when in an expansive mood. This unknown interlocutor worked his way through the set of diverse questions which James had provided and received a rich haul of answers. Though old John was speaking from his bed, his verbal vim was unimpaired, right from the opening 'Begor', which is stage-Irish now but was not then. The pungent reactions and droll asides of his flow of speech captured the querulous gusto of his presence, and the monologue was a fountain of gossip about Irish history and personal narrative. When asked about Jonathan Swift's lover Vanessa (Esther Van Homrig) he had this to say:

Van Homrig, who the Hell was he? my God I could not tell you. Why does he want to know these things. Jim must be getting mad. There are some of Dean Swift's family still living in Dublin. Swift McNeill is a relative of his and he is a very clever man. Of course I didn't know the Dean because he was in Hell long before my time. The Dean had one of the Van Esses as a sweetheart and he had a second one but I don't know her name.

Indications of phonetic transcription do not suggest the work of the Dublin students who in later years Brian O'Nolan let it be thought were involved in the venture: the misspelling 'Guiness' in the Interview would be retained consistently through various revisions in the Roderick O'Connor fragment of the *Wake*. The mention by John Stanislaus of Hugh Kennedy as Lord Chief Justice immediately dates the Interview to not earlier than 11 June 1924. A letter by Joyce to Miss Weaver (of January 1925) also seems to echo Pappie on Lord Ardilaun and may delimit the date to the second half of 1924 therefore. The sneer at the Free State government ('they'd make a mess of it') very likely owes something to the cut made in the old age pension in 1924. The latest possible date (a *terminus ad quem* as John Stanislaus might have said) is October 1925, when James paraphrased his father's words in writing to Miss Weaver about his father's expected opinion of 'Anna Livia Plurabelle': 'He has gone off his head I am afraid. He has overworked himself. Why did he not go to the bar? He speaks better than he writes.' So did John Stanislaus Joyce.

The extensive lore about the gentry and others in the spiel provided many unexpected connections and reminders for James Joyce. In its cumulative effect the Interview resembles a forthright, imploded nucleus of the *Wake* – from Joyce trivia to discussions of politics and memories of Ireland's past. Some family pride also crept in irresistibly: 'You know James had a great flow of language?'

Snug in Claude Road with the meticulous Mrs Medcalf, John Stanislaus was still pleased to receive visitors and had quite a number of them. Some of these visits were orchestrated by his son. The American writer, Robert McAlmon, came in late 1925, brought by Patrick Tuohy. Between them the visitors would have regaled him with stories of his son's Paris high jinks and international celebrity. To McAlmon, from his patrician New England background, this was an unfamiliar and barbarous world. He later described his visit to see this 'amazing old man':

He sat up in his bed and looked Tuohy and me over with fiery eyes, and complained of his weakness. The fact was he didn't like to exert himself too much, but he rang the bell and his landlady brought barley water, and the three of us sat ourselves down to a bottle of Dublin whiskey which we had brought. He assured me that he was fond of his son James but the boy was mad entirely; but he couldn't help admiring the lad for the way he'd written of Dublin as it was, and many a chuckle it gave him. I have never seen a more intense face than that of old man Joyce.

The landlady was a none too cleanly good-natured and rather shiftless Irishwoman, who complained about the trouble and work the old man caused her. But she appeared to like his presence in the house, and boasted of her own self-sacrificing nature. Before I left, Mr Joyce had become for me the street-corner politician and aged man about town as revealed in *Ulysses* . . .

As for Tuohy, despite his occasional spasm of awkwardness, he was loyal enough to James Joyce to send telegrams contributing details to Work in Progress. The patterns by which James Joyce's Irish or Irish-bound visitors were asked to call on his father is unclear, but errands were successfully sought from many such visitors: Hanna Sheehy-Skeffington, Frank O'Connor, District Justice Kenneth Reddin, John Dulanty, Desmond FitzGerald and Eugene Sheehy were among them. Of other visitors to John, most have left no trace, but Alfie Bergan probably arranged that people like Tom Devin occasionally dropped in. Certainly, J. F. Byrne and Con Curran did, as well as Michael Healy and Bergan's old friend, Jim Tully, whose father had been Healy's predecessor as Collector of Customs in Galway. Tully later said that the old man he saw in bed had 'delusions of greatness and grandeur'. He also told a friend that *Ulysses* was 'crammed with stale chestnuts we fell out of our cradles laughing at before he ever saw the light'. No doubt John Stanislaus gave him some more.

From Dublin, a theatrical enthusiast named Thomas Pugh visited Paris often and may have brought James Joyce news of his father. Michael Lennon also met James at this time and had several long conversations with him about his background – and especially his father whom Lennon probably knew or had known. Lennon was a Justice in the new Ireland whose interest in the Joyce family was to have its counterpart in his professional life: both ended in outrage. Later, he successfully asked for an inscribed copy of *Ulysses* and received it, according to James Joyce, with 'expressions of gratitude'. But Lennon was not trustworthy (and Richard Ellmann was to find him wholly unreliable as a witness): even in the 1950s, after his enforced resignation from the Bench (for other reasons), Lennon was burbling his fantasies about James Joyce's illegitimate offspring by an usherette at the Volta.

The Medcalf family too had tensions and disruptions. In January 1926 Mrs Medcalf suffered a heart attack and soon died. She left to her bereaved husband William the cost of a new suit from her insurance money. Her son Albert Edward and his young wife Grace took over the running of the house, and their paying guest, to whose ways they had become accustomed, was not asked to leave. John Stanislaus now stayed firmly in his bedroom and often in his bed, surrounded by mementos of his son and his past. Gummy and supine, ruminant on his diverse experiences, he was much in his son's thoughts, and his son in his. Back in Paris, the writer, when drinking with Robert McAlmon, would dwell on the fertility of his forefathers and their families of twelve to eighteen children. 'Joyce would sigh, and then pull himself together and swear that by the grace of God he was still a young man and would have more children before the end.' It was comforting for him to think of emulating his fecund father.

James remembered Pappie's birthday again that year. The following day, John Joyce replied: '. . . I have at least one son, and he *the one* I so love, who does remember me on what, perhaps, is my last birthday . . . I am anxiously looking forward to *seeing* you once before I die.'

Though Pappie often implored James to visit so that they could meet again, his son feared to return to Dublin and the 'slaughterhouse'. He had no wish to be shot or to emulate Parnell in having quicklime flung in his precious eyes by any literary-political-religious enemy. Although Ireland had at last attained independence, its topmost figure was intensely familiar from the early days: the Governor-General was Tim Healy, who occupied the old Viceregal Lodge, now known to some Dublin wags as Uncle Tim's Cabin. Healy's eminent (if honorary) position cannot have endeared John Stanislaus to the new Ireland. One of those for whom he was literally Uncle Tim was Kevin O'Higgins, a government minister whose best man at his wedding had been the diehard hero Rory O'Connor. O'Higgins was to be assassinated in July 1927 in placid, respectable Booterstown in south Dublin (and was commemorated in Yeats's poem 'Death').

At the same time Tuohy twice sent a solicitor's clerk to take notes, probably again at the instigation of the writer, but John Stanislaus did not co-operate until Tuohy himself appeared to renew their lively acquaintanceship. The artist (now with a proper R.H.A. after his name) was also highly knowledgeable about music.

He had been a soloist with the Palestrina Choir at the Pro-Cathedral, and could swap notes and opinions with the old man indefinitely. Probably John told him about the great singers he had heard, and of the great occasions like the retirement concert of his hero Sims Reeves in May 1891, when the platform included Mr McGuckin and his fellow Irishman Signor Foli, and the legendary Adelina Patti.

For John Stanislaus these days, memories tended to stop before the new century began. Dublin hostility to John's son now proliferated. Typical of its tone was the following, 'The Author's Lament', by M. J. McManus:

> I might write clotted nonsense
> By strenuous endeavour,
> And make the puzzled critics
> Ejaculate, 'How clever!'

> I *could*, like Mr Joyce,
> Confound the prim reviewer
> If my timid nose would let me
> Dive headlong into a sewer.

> But my work is undistinguished,
> And my royalties are lean,
> Because I never am obscure,
> And not at all obscene.

Ridicule such as this, and worse, meant that Eva and Florrie were at this time actively denying that they were related to *that* James Joyce. Fortunately the name was quite common: on the Censorship Board would soon be John's distant cousin, W. B. Joyce, the Dublin historian, while one of the members of the National Council of the Eucharistic League was the Very Rev. Monsignor Joyce PP VG. Florrie was now even more noticeably timid and withdrawn. Whereas others in the family had the Joyce fizz (May's forthright, sometimes angular letters are a good instance, as are the idiosyncratically Joycean ironies of Charlie), Florrie was too young to have had the benefits of the more stable life before her mother's death. In County Galway meanwhile, the widowed May Joyce's in-laws referred to the writer as 'that Antichrist', and cut her dead in the street and out of all family wills, though they remained friendly to her late husband's children.

That summer of 1926, John Stanislaus's old butty, Patrick Hoey, formerly of the library in Charleville Mall, ran into James on holiday in Ostend. Through such contacts the son continued to savour zestfully, though indirectly, the flavour of his Pappie's Dublin. When J. B. Hall brought out a small volume of memoirs centring on the Dublin of the 1870s and '80s, he promptly bought a copy. With Irish visitors (and many others) James Joyce loved to share his father's stories and tell tales about him and sing his songs. He even dressed in the style of the 1880s, as the journalist Nino Frank observed when he professionally noted the detail of Joyce's jacket-over-waistcoat style. Like his father too, he carried a cane.

James's acknowledgement of his Victorian Irishness in his writings and social evenings found a response. Regard worked both ways. In the Irish Free State even in the early 1920s, James Joyce had iconic status for young Irish writers. Even as the Free State was coming into being his European reputation tended to reflect well on their view of modern Ireland, the new 'old country'. However, the consensus was usually different. (See opposite.)

Eileen came to Dublin in late 1926 on a visit to her family and friends. While she was there the shocking news came through to James of the suicide of her husband Frank Schaurek, in Trieste. He had been embezzling from the bank where he worked and to shoot himself had been the only way out. John Stanislaus's intuitive sense about Schaurek had been sound (as it had been with Gogarty and Roberts). Eileen was now a widow. James, though effectively the head of the family, evaded all responsibility for dealing with the crisis. When Eileen was in Paris on her way back to Trieste, he spent much time with her but pretended he had not heard the terrible news, and she was not to learn it until Stannie told her later. As usual James's mind had been on higher things. He had made a recording of a patriotic speech from 'Aeolus' about Ireland's hopes of getting to the Promised Land. The speech, a genuine historical document, was celebrated but dated, and was by reasonable inference probably one already known to Pappie. (In a 1905 pamphlet, *The Language of the Outlaw*, Sir Roger Casement had mentioned it as a favourite of his.) John Stanislaus and the

Warder: 'We took you off the oakum picking half an hour ago and gave you Joyce's *Ulysses* to read. What do you want now?'
Convict: 'More oakum!'
Cartoon from *Dublin Opinion* in January 1924 satirising the local view of Joyce's masterpiece

author of the speech, J. F. Taylor, had been neighbours in Rathmines during the brave days of Parnell's Plan of Campaign, and Taylor, an associate of both W. B. Yeats and John O'Leary, had been an unsuccessful lawyer and journalist. Only thirty copies were made of James Joyce's one-sided record, and a signed one was sent to Pappie. Some listeners to this rare artefact of Joyceana have discerned a Cork accent in James Joyce's reading of the speech, an idea that repeats a boyhood detail of the *Portrait* and may stand as an unconscious tribute to his father.

After two years of betrothal, Stanislaus got married (abroad of course) to Nelly Lichtensteiger, choosing the anniversary of his mother's death to do so. It is doubtful, as with others of his children's weddings, that Pappie was even invited. The date seems like a rebuke, or even a conscious tribute – though he said it was an accident. By 1927 John Stanislaus was entirely bedridden anyway, and had been since the previous year. His lingual strength, however, was celebrated on the book jacket (and page 92) of Robert Graves's new book on swearing and blasphemy, *Lars Porsena* (so called because of the arch invocation of the second line of Macaulay's *Lays of Ancient Rome*: 'By the Nine Gods he swore'). Graves was favoured in the Parisian and Joycean magazine *transition* at this time, and was returning the admiration. The book ended with a brief discussion of the character of Simon Dedalus in *Ulysses*: 'the only man who is able to harmonise religion, politics and obscenity into something like artistic reality. Old Dedalus swears admirably.'

James's achievement grew. Twenty years after *Chamber Music* he produced his second and final slim volume of verse. (The critical consensus has endured that James Joyce, like his father, was more skilful at invective.) In July 1927 the presentation copy of *Pomes Penyeach* was not acknowledged by John Stanislaus. This seems unusual and possibly a letter went astray in either direction. But if James could occasionally forget his birthday, Pappie could some-times forget to write too. The bond was more than ritualistic, though it was that also. The book was to be the last full one thus received from James, and its 'Tilly' was the first poem, Joyce's adaptation of the 1904 'Cabra' which celebrated (after a fashion) the family's grim life under their mercurial herdsman. The city and its inhabitants never left Joyce's imagination – nor Joyce's imagination it. Visiting Holland at this time he even recorded his place of residence as Dublin, where he had not been for fifteen years.

A Civic Week was held in September 1927. Among the events was a concert by John McCormack (whom James Joyce was presently to contact regarding help for Giorgio as a singer in New York). An essay by Con Curran appeared in the *Official Handbook*, which boldly mentioned James Joyce at the beginning and end, in the august company of other Dublin men of letters such as Swift, Sheri-dan, Le Fanu and Goldsmith. Many of the *Handbook*'s details, including the advertisers, were incorporated in Work in Progress. Also among the visitors to James Joyce's salon-in-exile was his Col-lege friend, J. F. Byrne. John Stanislaus's first copy of James's gramophone record may never have reached him, for in November 1927 John wrote to Byrne to answer his proposal to visit him with a copy of the disc. Reflecting his training and status, John Stanislaus wrote formally: 'Dear Mr Byrne, I shall be glad to receive the gramophone record of Jim's oratory . . . confined to my bed for the past twelve months . . .' When Desmond FitzGerald several years later was given this record by Eileen, he found that the record did not work, and concluded that it had been played to exhaustion by Joyce's father. (FitzGerald was another Irish public figure who knew James Joyce in Paris. He had wished the Irish Free State to nominate him for the Nobel Prize.) The picture of James Joyce's old father and muse in Claude Road listening over and over again on the Medcalfs' gramophone to the voice of the son he loved, the son whom he now surely expected never to see again, is a beguiling one, but the suspicion remains that, since the disc was recorded on one side only, FitzGerald may have been trying to play the wrong side. Be that as it may, for John Stanislaus, the recording of James would have been no substitute for the real thing.

CHAPTER 29

Old Man Gone

The old and long-lost world of political high hopes continued to fade out for John Stanislaus. From the newspapers he learned that that disputatious Corkman William O'Brien was dead, then J. J. Clancy. Then the great T. P. O'Connor, who had become Father (Senior Member) of the House of Commons, went, shortly after writing the introduction to J. B. Hall's *Random Records of a Reporter*. Life could be random, John may have felt, surprised that he himself had lived so long and recalling the time he and James had called on 'Tay Pay' in London to try to get some writing work for the boy. John had never realised (except, of course, physically) his ambition to get to Westminster, or to a restored Parliament House on College Green. Jack Hall himself went next, once a figure as familiar as John Stanislaus in the Dublin streets which he walked 'in all weathers, with his overcoat slung over one shoulder'. John's dancing days were done. In Paris, meanwhile, as his father lay in his Dublin bed with his memories, the son developed his concept of a nightbook: the tale of a giant man stretched out across the north of the city from Howth to the Phoenix Park, with nothing but his past and his dreams.

The role of the Medcalfs was a benign and supportive one. There was no religious friction, and they seem to have liked the old man for his irreverent wit, which was more robust than he was. John Stanislaus, though nominally a Catholic, was no pietist as his wife had been. Despite the indicators of the unusual nature of their lodger, however – the portrait painter, the letters and cards stamped from around Europe (depending on James's latest jaunt), the arrival of the first edition of *Ulysses*, exotic visitors such as Bob McAlmon or the Habsburg–Italian–Swiss–French Joyce grandchildren – the Medcalfs seem to have had little sense of who the old man was. Padraic Colum said later they saw him simply as 'a battered shabby old person' (and James was distressed at hearing this). They had been unable to imagine his sporty youth. But many old men can seem wholly unconnected with their dashing prime (sometimes even to the aged themselves), as their isolation increases and they retreat into their memories.

John Stanislaus was also in touch with the solicitors, David Charles of 4 Clare Street, where Alfie Bergan had worked as a clerk since the early 1920s. They helped him a little with correspondence about his insurance and his pension. The office, close to Finn's Hotel and the former practice of Bloom the dentist's, was next door to the building surveyors' company Beckett & Medcalfe, run by the father of Samuel Beckett. James Joyce had recently got to know Beckett and the two expatriate Dublin writers developed a silent communion, often indoors in the fading light of a Paris evening. Beckett, never (knowingly) a father, was somehow always a son, while Joyce, like his father (and Odysseus) could be both – and was also more obsessive about these themes. During their closest times, what Joyce drew on from his father, Beckett seemed to draw on from Joyce.

The theme of the father operated at many levels in James Joyce's mind and hence in his work. He was steeped in the controversies of the early Christian Church which had debated whether God the Father and His Son were separate Persons, Rome in the Filioque clause in the creed upholding the equality, and the consubstantiality, of the Father and the Son, and Greece, Russia and the East Orthodox churches believing, as Joyce put it in a letter a few years later, 'that the procession is from the father alone, ex patre without Filioque'. This argument fed directly into his books. Stephen, in *Ulysses*, asks: 'Who is the father of any son that any son should love him or he any son?' Paternity is regarded as a legal fiction because of the uncertainty – the impossibility – of knowing it. If the identities are accepted nevertheless, there is a necessary competition between father and son, to be resolved only in the son becoming a father himself. That then brings about the recommencement of the cycle.

This is why Stephen finds (as Joyce did) the heresy of Sabellius ('subtlest heresiarch') so appealing: the idea that the Father Himself was His Own Son. Consubstantiality. Tim Finnegan as John Stanislaus as James Joyce as Hamlet's father's ghost as Hamlet as Shakespeare as John Shakespeare. In the *Wake*'s fable of the Mookse and the Gripes, the struggle between HCE's two sons (and the struggle between Greece and Rome for Christian supremacy) is concerned with this issue of filioque, and of how fathers and sons relate to one another. But, oddly, though James Joyce loved his own son Giorgio, his fixation remained with his father at home in Ireland.

For James Joyce, fatherhood, being so evasive of confirmation, shaded into being a metaphor for creativity. Of Shakespeare he wrote that when he wrote *Hamlet* he was not merely the father of his own son but, being no more a son, he was and felt himself the father of all his race, the father of his own grandfather, the father of his unborn grandson. As Aeneas bore his aged and infirm sire Anchises from the ruins of Troy at the end of the war, so James Joyce took the memory of his Virgil-quoting father out of the decay and oblivion that was turn-of-the-century Dublin and gave him a home in his work. *Ulysses* teems with direct and indirect commemorations of his Pappie as Simon Dedalus: he is found in the *Evening Telegraph* office, though with no apparent function – probably because Bloom is doing the job that John Stanislaus did eight years before; he goes past Bengal Terrace where Aunt Josephine's Papa Giltrap had lived and the Childs murder case took place – a continuing interest; his son gets drunk on Bloomsday in the Ship in Lower Abbey Street: one owner of the licensed premises formally known as the Ship Hotel and Tavern had been the well-known publican Mr Connery, whom John Stanislaus (the well-known sinner) had befriended 'in the matter of taxes'.

When James Joyce first planned *Ulysses*, he may have envisioned an even larger role for Mr Dedalus: one unused note for the novel reads 'Simon Dedalus blackthorn cudgel'. Simon Dedalus is both a true father and a false father. In Stuart Gilbert's book on *Ulysses*, shaped by James Joyce himself, it is suggested that 'Mr Dedalus, Stephen's father, is, perhaps, the noblest Achaean of them all', a conflation of family history extending to the work of P. W. Joyce, who in his *History* had the Achaeans come to Ireland. But the important father figure in the finished book was not Simon Dedalus but Leopold Bloom – though they meet in 'Sirens' as Siopold! Bloom is born precisely half-way between the two Joyces, which may suggest that he is consubstantially both father and son. In the 1904 of *Ulysses* he is old enough to have been young and vigorous in the 1870s and 1880s and remembers the Parnellite excitement. Many of John Stanislaus's richer and quirkier traits – such as the Sandow's bodybuilding course, the succession of improvisatory jobs and the outlandish money-making schemes – were borrowed by James to enrich the character of Bloom. While Simon Dedalus's external appearance, and some of his characteristics, nostalgia, a susceptibility to self-pity, his variegated cursing and the like, are John Stanislaus's indeed, the narrative never enters his thought processes and, as a result, in contrast to Leopold Bloom, he can seem almost flat.

However, the flow of linked thoughts in Bloom's head that forms much of the 'interior monologue' of the novel owes perhaps as much to the tipsy muttering that John Stanislaus engaged in after a day out on the town as it does to anything else and, indeed, something of a similar flow may be seen in the late Interview. Simon Dedalus, as a character, lacks the very element that made his father of such consuming interest and value to his son: his mind. That, or part of it, was bestowed on Leopold Bloom.

Like John Stanislaus's, Bloom's favourite operas are Flotow's *Martha* (with its admixture of Tom Moore) and Mozart's *Don Giovanni*. 'M'appari' from *Martha* is their most beloved song:

> All on earth I then could wish for
> Was near her to live and die:
> But alas! 'twas idle dreaming,
> And the dream too soon hath flown;
> Not one ray of hope is gleaming;
> I am lost, yet I am lost for she is gone.
> When first I saw that form endearing . . .
>
> Farewell base world, thy sins oppress me
> With footsteps fleet I haste away
> Where foes or friends no more distress me;
> My spirits' higher call obey.

Even Stannie acknowledged how well Pappie had sung the song. That was his song. But John was not hasting away quite yet.

Now, in Dublin, songs, stories and memories were virtually all John Stanislaus had left; but like Bloom and Simon Dedalus on Bloomsday, fathers without proper sons, he would not acknowledge defeat. Such fortitude appealed to James Joyce. He mentioned his great enthusiasm for Dostoevsky's *The Brothers Karamazov* to his friend, Arthur Power, who reported his words:

Do you remember when Aloysha goes to see his father after Dmitri has attacked him? His father's head is still wrapped up in a red silk scarf and he gets up every now and then to examine his wounds in the mirror while he declares he will go on living as he has always lived, passionately, evilly – his pride, his boasting, his desire for the young Grouschenka, the strumpet and the virgin in one.

Such vigour was to be celebrated, not judged or condemned. James's father was just as much alive, and his exuberance was clearly not extinct. It was, however, metamorphosing and moving onto an active mental plane, now that the old body had failed him. As he said in the Interview, these days he regularly revisited in his head the jollifications of the past, hunting again the fields of north Cork, walking again the streets of two cities, and relishing all over again the fun he had enjoyed. But even in the Dublin of the late 1920s, the old days were rarely far away. The memoirs of Tim Healy, for example, came out and were reviewed even-handedly by Con Curran in the *Irish Statesman* in early 1929. Though Curran went on to acknowledge some of Healy's strengths, he was not very sympathetic. In imitation of Barry O'Brien, he made a reference to an unnamed gentleman, no longer in politics, who remembered The Chief. John Stanislaus Joyce was surely behind Curran's comments on Tim Healy's demeanour during the Split: 'his mildness could give way to blasts of unique vituperation (one of his former colleagues, now, perhaps, censorious, said that in this respect he leaves [James] Joyce standing). He has the terseness of the peasant's speech and its coarseness . . .' (It was left to later scholarship to show how much the Healy memoirs had been doctored.) John Stanislaus's early assessment of Healy had turned out to be right. The public commemoration of Ivy Day might have died out, but not (for some) the memories of the damage done by this Hibernian Judas. In the city that James Joyce was to call 'Healyopolis', Curran's portrait of Tim Healy in the review was a choice accolade, given Irish standards of betrayal.

In Work in Progress, John Stanislaus (the old artificer) was becoming the old artificee. The stories Pappie had told were being worked upon and could be retold in any number of ways, for stories are about themselves. Currently, one ancient story was being retold in the various journals of the neo-Celtic state, as Cong Abbey in County Galway reached its eighth century. In 1128, during the heroic reign of Turloch O'Connor, King of Connaught, the Abbey had been refounded by a filicide (who also commissioned the Cross of Cong). The King's son Roderick O'Connor was inaugurated in Dublin in the city's first Irish regal pageant as High King of Ireland. He would be the last. A fighter in the Anglo-Norman troubles who killed his own brother, he suffered what P. W. Joyce called 'domestic discord' and retired from the world to live at Cong Abbey. The Abbey, on the fringes of what would later be called the Joyce Country, was the main repository of religious fine art in Connaught. In ambition and execution, as in complexity, *Finnegans Wake* was an emulation of Ireland's sacred illuminated manuscripts and the O'Connor story gave James Joyce another template of life that served to echo and broaden the primary one in the book, that of the Joyces, their past, and in the person of John Stanislaus, their present.

For John Stanislaus, by this time, his children in Ireland were not in fact as distant or indifferent as he often alleged. May, as a widow, had much adversity and three children to cope with in Connemara, County Galway. Eileen, after the tragedy of her husband's suicide, had moved back to Dublin with her own more exotic young trio. With so much family business to discuss, Pappie was now corresponding almost warmly even with Stannie (though he could no longer impose complete silence on the household before putting pen to paper as he had when Stannie lived with him). Poppie wrote to her father from New Zealand occasionally. Eileen, with her daughter Bozena Beatrice Berta – she had been flamboyantly named after *Exiles* – sometimes visited John Stanislaus in his bedroom and saw a small man who liked drinking whiskey.

Every time they went they brought a bottle of John Jameson and Son's, his favourite. He was often reading when they arrived, and invariably held forth about James. By 1928 Eva was living very near her father in Whitworth Road, but there are few, if any, reports of visits from either her or Florrie. Though John did not see Eileen more than two or three times a year, he usually enjoyed it when she came, both for her manner, which retained some of the dramatics of her long stay on the Continent, and for the fact that she was practical and non-judgemental.

On 16 June 1929, the centenary celebration of Catholic Emancipation achieved by the Liberator began with much rejoicing and went on for a week. Four hundred thousand people attended Mass in the Phoenix Park. Little 'Bertha' Schaurek was taken to see the huge bronze statue of her famous relative at O'Connell Bridge: she expected it to be of her Uncle Jim rather than Daniel O'Connell. In Paris, meanwhile, James Joyce's followers turned Bloomsday into a high day of the literary calendar and had their own celebration of its twenty-fifth anniversary (and the new French edition of the book, *Ulysse*) with an excursion. James Joyce waited until the special day of 4 July, his father's birthday, breezily to inscribe a copy to his publisher and benefactress, Miss Beach.

On the day of his eightieth birthday, John wrote to James. Despite the occasion, he continued to complain of ungrateful daughters (though he did not define what they had to be grateful for). Estranged or cut off from four out of five of them, and from all his sons, he longed only to see James. It was virtually all he had left to hope for in life, being no longer mobile himself. But James kept his distance, though he continued to half-suggest he might come, and Pappie kept believing in the possibility. As if mustering courage to take the plunge, James went as close to Ireland as he could, and spent holidays in Celtic Cornwall and Wales, even once getting to Holyhead (from where the mailboat crossed to Dublin). Work was in Progress however: Books I and II of the final publication were substantially formed – two-thirds of the *Wake*. It is inconceivable that he did not write to his father as he reached fourscore, but the letter has not survived. A few weeks later, however, he sent to Claude Road from Paris the *de luxe* version of the booklet of *Tales Told of Shem and Shaun.* John Stanislaus looked at his present, adorned with Brancusi's geometrical and semi-abstract spiral sketch of his son, and remarked gravely, 'Jim has changed more than I thought.' He was not wrong.

Festivity and levity instead of war was catching. Another Civic Week was held in Dublin in September 1929 to show the world and the city itself that it had recovered from the devastations of the previous decade and a half. Con Curran had been promoted to the Council, alongside Senator Guinness, Gerald Sherlock (the Town Clerk), Lord Glenavy, Bulmer Hobson and other dignitaries. (Hobson, among much else, had been involved in founding the Irish Volunteers in 1913 and in the Howth gun-running with Casement and Childers in 1914.) The city, like the Phoenix, was renewing itself. But John Stanislaus was not much in sympathy with what he had seen of modern Dublin on his last outings, with its gougers and gurriers (more cheeky than ever), and its petrolly ways, though he might have appreciated some of its street cries: one of these burlesqued Verdi's 'La donna è mobile':

> My name is Paddy-O
> I sell ice creami-O
> Outside the G.P.O. . . .

If John was able to play his record of Jim's oratory, he must also have had the chance to listen to whatever musical fare the Medcalfs favoured. It is possible, but unlikely, that this was his beloved opera. Whether or no, records of McCormack, Caruso and the rest would have given him enormous pleasure, but nobody, not even James, seems to have thought of it. But then the only thing Pappie had ever asked for was a little money.

On the wall of the Joyces' Paris apartment, as well as the family's holy pictures, was a scene of John's other city. 'What's that?' the writer Frank O'Connor asked, visiting over Easter 1929. 'Cork,' was the answer. O'Connor had recognised his own home city well enough, but was asking about the odd wood used for the frame. 'Cork,' said Joyce again: the *rebus* was a double filial tribute – as well as a Wakean quip. O'Connor was one of the new wave of Irish writers. Just a few years earlier he had been on the run with Erskine Childers in the hills beyond Fermoy during the Civil War. While relating those adventures to Joyce he was probably grilled about the County Cork families he knew, as James Stern was about the Fermoy Cremins and Bechers. O'Connor and Dan Breen (whom Joyce also met in Paris) had a Cork and/or political background that James Joyce, writer and son, was eager to explore. Dublin detail was savoured too, and in return Joyce discreetly and indirectly emphasised his intense sense of family tradition and dignity. The portraits hanging on Paris walls were a confirmation of what was known by John Stanislaus and his son (and understood by many others), that James Joyce too was after all 'a gentleman'.

There were other gentlemen. William Dwyer, a solicitor of Roscrea in County Tipperary (where Dan Lowrey of the famous Dublin music-hall came from), was in touch with John Stanislaus. Probably as a friend, possibly as a smuthound or an investor, it appears that he may have somehow obtained from John Parisian letters and artefacts concerning his son. Jacob Schwartz was doing something similar in London, privately republishing Joyce's early essays on Mangan and Ibsen from his Ulysses Bookshop in Bloomsbury, a shop that had connections with the Jolas magazine *transition*. Schwartz too visited Dublin to see John Stanislaus, and if he got anything, it was more than likely sent out to his family in Manhattan who sold literary collectibles. It was the advent of such snoopers and potential betrayers that encouraged James Joyce to consider an authorised biography.

For any visitor to John Stanislaus, in search of Joyceana or not, the old man needed no encouragement to discourse on his controversial son. Old John was bedridden and toothless, but his decidedly odorous room was filled with pictures and newspaper cuttings of James. His sense of the patriarchal tradition was shown by the photographs on his cast-iron mantelpiece, of James and of James's son Giorgio: these had now unprecedentedly been joined by one of Eileen and her little troupe. Beckett's uncle, Harry Sinclair, was in touch, as well as other associates of James – though Michael Healy, whose sustaining friendship with John was later commended by Curran, had left Dollymount and moved back to Galway. Most of these visitors were soon to help Herbert Gorman on the biography. As son and heir, James Joyce could know what the nascent Joyceans did not – that Gorman had eased his appointment as biographer by happening to have the same surname as the priest who had married his father and his mother. An atmospheric photograph of this period records James Joyce and the gnomelike Irish writer James Stephens as *flâneurs* in Paris, standing talking on the pavement with John Sullivan, the French–Irish tenor. James's 'Sullivanising', his brief but intense, even obsessional, campaign to achieve recognition for John Sullivan at the major opera houses, was conducted in part to explore an alternative version of success – of himself and Pappie as international tenors. 'Bravo Cork!' Joyce would cry in the opera house, waving his hat and cane as he announced that Sullivan had by his singing of blindness cured him. The singer, though he had grown up in France, had been instilled by his mother with the notion that he could be nothing better than a Fenian. Joyce's character sketch of Sullivan at fifty seems oddly familiar:

In temperament he is intractable, quarrelsome, disconnected, contemptuous, inclined to bullying, undiplomatic, but on the other hand good humoured, sociable, unaffected, amusing and well-informed. He supports a family connection of eleven people . . .

Ever the master manipulator, of people as well as words, Joyce marshalled a claque of associates to cheer Sullivan, who included Selskar Gunn, the son of Michael Gunn of the Gaiety in Dublin, and Michael Lennon. He would play the tenor's records 'over and over'. Drawing on the gentlemanly duels of Daniel O'Connell over a century before, he challenged other tenors to match Sullivan's accomplishments. He extracted from John Sullivan one priceless favour as thanks for the tireless promotion of his voice ('beside which Chaliapine is braggadocio and McCormick [*sic*] is insignificant'): he asked Sullivan to visit his father in Dublin. As a Corkman, Sullivan had somehow become a substitute father for James and, suitably, his most famous role was as Arnold in Rossini's *Guillaume Tell*, an opera whose theme is a reprise of the stories of Abraham and Isaac, and of God, and indeed of Ulysses – the father's seeking of the son, the son's seeking of the father, in tension and reduplication. The emotional lament, 'Asil héréditaire', was commonly regarded as the opera's high point, in which Arnold remembers his childhood's happy home – his father's name, his father's blessing. The theme of regret at the end sung by Arnold was an empathising one too: 'Ah father, why are you not here in this moment of joy . . . ?'

John Sullivan had his first ever engagement in Dublin on 27 April 1930, the visit during which Sullivan called on John Stanislaus. Like the performances of Campanini and de Reszke and the old greats, what passed between them is not recorded, but both men were much given to laughter and John Stanislaus no doubt enjoyed the attention of the star, with whom he had a good deal in common: Cork would have been discussed, and singing, music, and perhaps Killiney and Dalkey, where Sullivan also had family and which John had known since the 1870s. And there was always James Joyce to talk about: by then, revitalised, he was back at work on Work in Progress, weaving in the names of the Lord Mayors of Dublin, extracted from the list in *Thom's Directory*. He remained on good terms with Sullivan but his campaign had, consciously or unconsciously, largely served its purpose in communicating with Pappie. That June he published the extract, *Haveth Childers Everywhere*, the book of the Father in the *Wake*.

Other Dubliners were communicating. Mrs Sheehy-Skeffington visited James from Dublin: she had known him since the At Homes in Belvedere Place long before. (He claimed that her maiden name was a variant of his own: Sheehy/Seoighe.) It was she who, asking him why he did not return to Dublin, received the famous answer: 'Have I ever left it?' He may well have asked this old friend to call on his father too.

In Ireland, as usual, the past continued to reverberate. John Stanislaus Joyce's name was in the papers again when they reported the shocking death of Patrick Tuohy in New York in August 1930. Officially it was an accident caused by a gas tap, but the truth was otherwise. Among that minority of Dubliners who had distinguished themselves at rebellion at Easter 1916, Tuohy merited a Glasnevin funeral and his remains were shipped to Galway and then taken on to Dublin for honourable burial. John Stanislaus was no longer fit for such outings, but the lawyer Kenneth Reddin was among the leading mourners and told Jim subsequently of the occasion. And it was an occasion. Vincent O'Brien, the distinguished son of the distinguished music teacher, and James Montgomery, the Film Censor, were there and so, too, were Seán T. O'Kelly TD, the future President, Patrick Pearse's mother and sister, and Brinsley MacNamara, whose novel-writing had cost his father his job. John Stanislaus was among that handful of Dubliners who had sat for Tuohy and he could add the experience to the historical richness of his memories and his narratives.

In January 1931 old John wrote a letter to his son for his birthday, remembering 'Babie Tuckoo' and the tale of the 'moo-cow' from Brighton Square days. Though his handwriting was no longer what it had been, he was cogent still for an eighty-one-year-old. The letter confirms that Pappie knew that his story preceded the version in the *Portrait*. He also commented on the excellent news that Giorgio was on honeymoon and added that he proposed to write to his grandson. The Joyces had much to look forward to again. The patrilineal succession had been renewed by Giorgio's wedding in December 1930. The proud father wrote from Paris how Giorgio would become 'by French law monarch of all he surveys'. In Dublin John Stanislaus added a Man Ray photograph of Giorgio and his wife, Helen, to his mantelshelf gallery.

The celebrity of James A. Joyce Esq. BA (as Pappie habitually wrote) led some undergraduates of his old College to go to see him. They were Niall Sheridan and Brian O'Nolan, and they set off with 'a half-dozen stout' to see Old Man Joyce one evening in the academic year 1930–1. Their gentleman host had other ideas, however, and the stout was disdained as 'a jarvey's drink': the implication was that John Stanislaus was not like one of those low fellows (such as Skin-the-Goat) who drove a horse-cab around Dublin to survive. Nor was he, but his bladder coped better now with spirits. The lively visit was not one that had any prior approval by James Joyce and the students did not think to set down notes on what was said. Sheridan remembered it much later as stuff about Dublin's old days, and about Parnell and elections. (It was this visit that led Brian O'Nolan, *alias* Flann O'Brien, *alias* Myles na gCopaleen, to claim that the famous Interview was a hoax when it was published in 1949.)

Disinformation was already a Dublin tradition. At this same time James Joyce's ostensible friend, Michael Lennon, published in the American *Catholic World* a curious account of the Joyce family. John

Stanislaus came in for special ridicule: he was presented as some sort of a sham squire and an embezzler. Among the details of ungrounded abuse was that Joyce Senior had worked for the Conservative Club and that James A. Joyce BA had not graduated. With its hostile lies and half-truths, the piece would have offended John Stanislaus, except that it is likely that he never saw it or heard of it. His son, however, for years viewed it as a Healyite example of Irish treachery, a propaganda tool of the Irish-American lobby against *Ulysses*, intended also to defame his father and to damage Giorgio's hesitant career as a singer. Joyce's distrust of his compatriots had other vindications too. The Irish diplomat, Thomas J. Kiernan, eventually Ambassador to the United States, told Richard Ellmann a strange (but just feasible) story about James Joyce screaming aloud in a gents' lavatory. Later he informed John Garvin that James Joyce had confided in him that his bedridden father was near to death with GPI – general paralysis of the insane: tertiary syphilis. Perhaps Kiernan was briefed by Lennon, but it may be that Joyce simply mentioned that his father was paralysed and diplomatic imagination did the rest. As this was confided to no one else, the story must be dismissed.

Consubstantiality, John Stanislaus's eternal bond with James, continued. He wrote to his son concerning Nora's uncle, 'I often hear from Mr Healy, who's [*sic*] generous gifts I should be grateful if *you* would also acknowledge.' Complicity bonded father and son. Old and useless as he was, life still afforded some satisfactions for John Stanislaus. He was not dead yet, by Christ. On 26 March in Chapelizod, however, the death occurred of the former Governor-General, Tim Healy. Having finally seen off the foul-mouthed old bastard, John must have reflected, '*Et tu Healy*'. It was one Glasnevin funeral he did not regret missing. If he felt that he had seen his last Christmas, however, a style that had served him for many decades, he was again wrong.

James Joyce's by now internationally famous decision to fly past the nets of family and nationality and religion – forces which define and sometimes enable – was reversed when that summer he got married on 4 July, Pappie's eighty-second birthday. The date was a significant gesture to his children (illegitimate in the eyes of English law) and to any children of theirs (and there was also pressure from the new Mrs Joyce, Giorgio's wife Helen). Most importantly, the gesture was to his father. The wedding of James Joyce, after nearly thirty years of life with Nora, was a birthday present. Pappie was an old man, and the son was acknowledging the importance to his father and to him of legitimacy and primogeniture. (When his biographer took to going round Paris later that year with a lady not his wife, James Joyce was mildly scandalised.) Not long before, John Murray's widow, who had married perforce in 1891 a man nearly twenty years her senior, died. John Stanislaus had forthrightly referred to that Murray offspring as a bastard, not only a personal insult but a family insult. Whatever the ambiguities or evasions of the past – James claimed certificates of legitimacy for his children under Austrian law – there could be no doubt now about the bona fides of the Joyce line. Charlie, though ill with a recurrence of his tuberculosis, was there and Eileen visited the oldish newlyweds in London and returned to Dublin, where she reassured Pappie with the good news. Not only was the line legitimate but there was soon more news: Giorgio and Helen were expecting an heir. With a fourth generation pending of his proud line, John Stanislaus could feel that he had not failed entirely. James Joyce was world famous. Giorgio Joyce would soon be exercising his bass voice on NBC in New York and other stations. His father and grandfather had not succeeded as singers, but here was the new Joyce to supersede them and he had been singing Italian arias since he was four. Who could say what the next generation might not do?

On Tuesday, 22 December John Stanislaus was taken seriously ill at 25 Claude Road. Albert Medcalf brought in a local doctor (Dr J. F. Delaney of 7 Gardiner's Row) to see him and also a priest from St Columba's, the local parish church in Iona Road, who anointed John and gave him the last rites of the Roman Catholic Church. As Mrs Medcalf had only just come out of a nursing home after a serious operation, the Medcalfs felt that, with the best will in the world, it would not be possible to care for the old man as he should be cared for since he required constant watching. They called an ambulance and had him taken the short distance to the Drumcondra Hospital, around the corner on the Whitworth Road.

His removal was witnessed by a neighbour, the theatre man and writer, Gabriel Fallon (whose home was at 58 Whitworth Road). When the stretcher came out of the front door of the house, Fallon recognised with a start the man on it, as he had once used the Tuohy portrait as the basis for his old man's make-up in a play (Strindberg's *Ghost Sonata*). Given John Stanislaus's own former theatrical ambitions, it is odd to think of his face, if not his spirit, on a Dublin stage, already a ghost in a city which had forgotten him. The stretcher was accompanied by the young priest.

Albert Medcalf went to see the patient that evening. John Stanislaus made him promise to write to his eldest son in Paris and this he did the next day. He suggested that James should communicate at once with his father, as he did not think he would last very much longer. 'As you know his heart is centred on you, and his last words before I left him last night were, Don't forget to write to Jim and wish him a Happy Xmas for me.' There was also the matter of the doctor's medical fee and the charge for the ambulance, and he hoped that Mr James Joyce would settle these and the outstanding rent: 'I would be grateful for an answer one way or the other.'

Until the end of John Stanislaus's life James Joyce hoped that he would receive a sign of his father's approval for the extraordinary screed that was Work in Progress, or for his writing in general. His father (as well as his city) was the source of his artistic ability. He longed for a gesture of some understanding from him, his own flesh and blood, for the strange struggles and achievements of his life as a writer. That never came. Though this detracts in no way from their mutual devotion, the awkward silence impinges nevertheless on the nature of the celebrated understanding. Father and son admired the principle of consubstantial love, one for the other. The practice was sometimes different – not just through human frailties such as missed birthdays (which are just as attributable to the vagaries of the postal service or a war) but in the evasions of any better commitment. For years, Pappie had not been visited by his special son, and he secretly regarded James's books as smutty and dreary compared with the racy reads of Frank E. Smedley or with the books of Bulwer-Lytton, whom he had liked for his praises of Daniel O'Connell and whose insistence in *Pelham* on 'the gentleman' fed into Carlyle's peculiar tract, *Sartor Resartus*, a markedly anti-Irish book in places. Human frailty aside, the failure on both sides to reach a fuller understanding becomes noticeable. But none of that got in the way of their mutual regard. In the devotion of John Stanislaus and his son to their principle, which was consistent, the practice was less so. The strange sense of consubstantiality was the most important element to each party in the strange relationship.

They shared a fascination with the Dublin streets and their past. Across the road from the hospital, on the other side of the Royal Canal, lay the lowering bulk of Mountjoy Gaol, bitterly known as 'the Joy' and the subject of many an Irish song. Whitworth Road had a rich history of bishops and doctors, executed felons and patriotic escapers (including Piaras Beaslai). It was even the site of a synagogue, a Dublin rarity. A century before, a supporter of Daniel O'Connell's, no blackguard but a barrister, had fought a duel in Whitworth Road, in a dispute with a Cork Conservative that had begun in the General Post Office.

As John Stanislaus declined into history, Con Curran, too, was in touch with his son by telephone about his condition. The news was increasingly less hopeful.

The usual little Christmas presents had already been despatched from Paris to Claude Road. In the *Evening Herald*, the 'Mutt and Jeff' comic strip was still prominent. At the Gaiety, where John Stanislaus had spent many evenings with the Gunns, the Grand Annual Pantomime that season was *Humpty Dumpty*. But though he was struggling to beat time, the ebullient munificent father portrayed in the *Portrait* was intermittently still discernible.

On the Wednesday Albert Medcalf looked up Eileen Schaurek (then living at 16 Mountjoy Square, a few doors along from Eva and Florrie, both now at No. 12). Eileen had not been to see her father for several months. She was out when he called, but he left word that she should contact him as soon as she returned home. She appeared at the Medcalfs' some time after midnight and Albert gave her all the details. The next day, as Albert was writing to Paris, Eileen went over to the hospital. Albert had also asked her to collect from Claude Road certain of her father's belongings that he had said he wanted, but she must not have been able to do so, for in the end it was Albert's father, old Mr Medcalf, who brought

John his pipe, tobacco and matches, and the book he was reading.

In the evening, when Albert himself called in to the hospital to see how his old friend was doing, John told him with a smile that he had had a visit from Boxer, the Medcalfs' dog. It seemed that when old Medcalf had brought in his book and bits, Boxer had come into the ward as well and, suddenly sniffing John Stanislaus, he had made a great affectionate fuss over the discovery. John was charmed by this canine loyalty, and told Albert it reminded him of when he was young in the university in Cork when his own little dog, Jack, used to follow him to and from the college.

On the evening of Thursday (Christmas Eve), the day that James in Paris must have received Albert Medcalf's letter with the news, John announced that he was coming back home to Claude Road on the Sunday. Alfie Bergan had, it seems, visited earlier, and perhaps also May who came up from Oughterard to say goodbye: facing the real possibility of death, he told her now or a little later 'that he had got more out of life than any white man'. Though Eva would visit before the end, Florrie is unlikely to have braved seeing her father again. Albert Medcalf dropped in later though and found him in great form, sitting up and having his tea. However, in the morning, when Eileen went to see Pappie after Mass, she found that he had deteriorated so badly that she could not make out what he was saying or talking about. She sent one of her daughters round to the Medcalfs to ask Albert to come and help. There was little that Medcalf could do but talk gently to the babbling old man.

Eileen went with him back to her father's room to collect his valise, in which there were some letters and other papers, and took also for safe-keeping the three family photographs from the mantelpiece, her own of the three little Schaureks, James's (taken in Paris in 1923), and the Man Ray of Giorgio and Helen. She told Medcalf he could give away her father's suit of clothes, but when he said that John Stanislaus might need them she said she would send her 'maid' for them. Yet well into the New Year the suit would still be hanging up in John's room.

At about 8.30 on Christmas Night a nurse came from the hospital to say that John Stanislaus was in a very bad way and to ask for Mrs Schaurek's number, which she had neglected to leave with them. Medcalf himself went round at once to Eileen's flat, but as it was the Christmas party season there was no one there. He left word with a lodger that her father was dangerously ill and that she should go at once to the hospital, no matter what time she got back. On his own way home Medcalf called in to see John Stanislaus, where he stayed a while. He told John that a letter had arrived from Paris with Christmas greetings, and held the envelope over him to look at, since the old man was too low to read it for himself or take it in.

On St Stephen's Day (Saturday) John had rallied a little. At lunch-time Eileen appeared at Claude Road and Medcalf explained about the letter. She opened it and found there was a postal order for a pound in it. She said she would keep that and send her brother a telegram saying 'Pappie failing'. But Medcalf, in his realistic way, told her to say 'Pappie dying' and to ask James what arrangements to make if he should die. Unknown to him the words were a direct counterpart of another telegram, also to Paris, in 1903. But this time Jim would not come home.

In the evening Medcalf called on the patient and told him that James had sent not only Christmas greetings in his letter, but a postal order as well. John was touched that his son had not forgotten him and told Medcalf that he always remembered him. 'I knew Jim wouldn't forget me.'

On Saturday he seemed low again and asked Medcalf to bring his wife, Grace, and his 'little pet': he may have temporarily forgotten Boxer's name. When Medcalf arrived he found John Stanislaus already had a visitor, for Tom Devin was there, who asked Medcalf if he was a Joyce relation. Medcalf explained that he was not. John Stanislaus had entirely failed to recognise his old friend and Devin was upset that he did not know him. Devin had met Eileen at a party the night before and she had told him that her father was sick.

In the days after Christmas, James sent messages by wire and letter and telephone to the Drumcondra Hospital. He was also in touch with Dr Kerry Reddin of Fitzwilliam Square, whose brother Kenneth he had got to know in Paris, when he came with Paddy Tuohy to tell him how his Pappie was getting on and to show the portrait. (Tuohy of course was dead, though memories of the old days never quite died for John Stanislaus. The dead, in one sense, did not die.) On 27 December a perturbed James Joyce telegraphed Dr Reddin:

MY FATHER DANGEROUSLY ILL DRUMCONDRA HOSPITAL DIAGNOSIS UNCERTAIN WILL YOU PLEASE ARRANGE HE GETS BEST MEDICAL SPECIALISTS ALL EXPENSES MY CHARGE MY THANKS ADVANCE = JAMES JOYCE

Perhaps his attentions, or those of another specialist whom James had also called, had some effect, because when Medcalf next arrived, bringing his sister to see John, he seemed a little better. He said he had heard from Jim in Paris, and requested that Medcalf write and let him know he had received it. This Medcalf was pleased to do.

The following evening (Monday, 29 December) Medcalf called in after tea and was told that Eileen had been there in the early afternoon. John Stanislaus was now very low. The nurse said that the house surgeon had just left and that he did not think that John Stanislaus would live through the night. Medcalf stayed on as his old lodger looked so bad and at about ten to eight it became evident to them all that it would only be a matter of minutes. One of the nurses lit a candle and placed it in John Stanislaus's right hand and the ward sister put a crucifix in his left. Then the nurses, the other patients in the ward and the Church of Ireland Albert Medcalf said the prayers for the dying together. Afterwards he sent a telegram to Paris with the sad news.

By a typical Joycean coincidence, the date of John Stanislaus's death was the birthday of little Rudy, Leopold Bloom's only son – a fictional self, his son's *alter ego*'s spiritual father's dead son. On his deathbed, John had thought only of his own distant son. Perhaps his last known remark of all had been to Eva, giving the answer to yet another query from James: 'Tell Jim he was born at six in the morning.' In the father's death was the son's birth. Birth and death, father and son, remained conjoined. The last end of John Stanislaus Joyce, at the age of eighty-two, had been as peaceful as anyone could have wished for him. After a lively life he had passed as quietly as the river at the close of *Finnegans Wake*.

CHAPTER 30

Recirculation

In the *Portrait*, Stephen Dedalus is asked by a friend to define his father. With exasperated yet loving attention he replies:

– A medical student, an oarsman, a tenor, an amateur actor, a shouting politician, a small landlord, a small investor, a drinker, a good fellow, a storyteller, somebody's secretary, something in a distillery, a taxgatherer, a bankrupt and at present a praiser of his own past.

He was never technically a bankrupt, but the list remains an exemplary synopsis of the life of John Stanislaus Joyce, though many of its elements could be further refined by placing the word '(failed)' after them. Two other words are conspicuously missing: 'father' and 'son'. Those were already a presence, inspiration and goal behind almost everything that his son had ever written. It would continue so. Now that he had gone at last, John Stanislaus Joyce could praise his own past no longer: it had become James Joyce's responsibility.

In Paris on the day that John Stanislaus died, James Joyce heard the news by wire. His father dead, he was no more a son. Thomas McGreevy had a prior arrangement to meet him at his temporary residence, the Hotel Bassano in Passy, to help in talks with an Italian company. Joyce was calm and Nora was subdued. With different appointments McGreevy and Joyce left together in a taxi and the dropping-off point was agreed: 'We hardly talked as we drove. When we reached the entrance to the Metro at the Trocadéro, however, Joyce said, "Don't go just yet." I waited. He began to talk but suddenly he broke down. He cried and cried and cried for several minutes . . .' Rapidly, however, Joyce's composure, his international insouciance, was regained and he continued on his journey.

The funeral, on New Year's Day 1932, added quixotically and automatically to the sense of the passing of history. The old man had been born in the 1840s, the decade of the Famine, when his great kinsman Daniel O'Connell had agitated for the Repeal of the Union with Great Britain. Now Ireland had taken her place among the nations of the world and was a prominent member of the League of Nations. The newspaper notices referred to 'John Stanislaus Joyce (late LGB), deeply regretted'. (One cynic remarked that the notice should have referred not to the Local Government Board but to GPI. Dublin lore had already gone deep.) The funeral turnout was meagre for a man once known throughout the city, whose son was famous in Ireland and internationally. Not that the beloved son dared to attend, and special circumstances, the forces of history even, caused him to make the ceremony to be made a private one. In Ireland, Catholic and free, James Joyce was by now virtually unmentionable (though there was always a residuum of admirers both in and out of a coterie). According to James Joyce, the editor of the *Irish Independent* objected to any reference to him in 'the obituary notice' of his father – yet he is mentioned there in a brief report on the funeral, in terms no more hostile than 'the well-known writer'.

The obsequies were conventional enough regarding the rite at Glasnevin cemetery: *de mortuis nil nisi bonum.* The children were there, except for the dead and the fled. In a change from earlier practice, women were now accepted as mourners too. Eight of his children survived John Stanislaus Joyce: James Augustine, Margaret Alice, John Stanislaus, Charles Patrick, Eileen Isabel May Xavier Brigid, Mary Cathleen, Eva Mary and Florence Elizabeth. His grandson, with the central-European name Patrizio ('Tatto') Schaurek, was there with his mother, who would wear black for a long time afterwards, and there were friends such as C. P. Curran (and his wife) and Michael Healy, who had travelled back specially from Galway. Even some Murrays turned out and a McNestry relation of theirs. The great or notorious writer sent a wreath of Parnellite ivy, inscribed austerely 'With Sorrow and Love from Jim'. (Three other family wreaths came from abroad.) He had not seen his father since the summer of the year 1912. On Joyce's behalf, Padraic Colum wrote to his patron, Miss Weaver, asking for the release of £100 to help cover the miscellaneous costs associated with a family death. She readily complied.

For the funeral, a coffin of polished elm had been chosen. ('Tell me, tell me, tell me, elm!' Anna Livia Plurabelle said in a 1930 published fragment, as night and death came on.) The cortège left from Saint Columba's in Iona Road (in the *Wake* as St-Iona-in-the-Fields). The hearse was pulled by four horses. A mourning coach and a carriage and pair followed it along the familiar road to the Prospect Cemetery, Glasnevin. It was John Stanislaus's last time. Often he had made this journey, to the place founded by Daniel O'Connell exactly a hundred years before, for the funerals of John Augustine Joyce, of Parnell, of Joe Gallaher, of John Kelly, of his wife May, of Freddy, Georgie and Baby Joyce, of Philip McCann, of Mat Kane in the summer of 1904, of Mary Ellen Callanan, Tim Harrington, John Clancy and George Lidwell, and all the half-forgotten others. With effortless Joycean symbolism he himself was now buried between O'Connell and Parnell, and far closer to the grave of Parnell.

Albert Medcalf reported in Beckettian terms to Joyce what had been left in his father's room: 'an old suit of clothes, a coat, hat, boots and stick'. Apart from the candlewaxed *Exiles*, all the presentation copies that James had sent to his father had somehow gone missing (and his letters). The biographers and the book dealers and the cameramen of the yellow press were believed to be snooping around for dirt on a banned writer and his rackety past. None of these books – the ultimate in 'association' copies – has yet surfaced. Certainly, the Medcalfs, proper to a fault, would have had nothing to do with their disappearance. Even before the matter of the will, James Joyce's immediate concern was what had happened to his father's personal effects, including not only private letters and personal papers, but the valuable signed copies of his books. Paul Léon (who by now had become for Joyce his essential *homme des affaires*) wrote to Alfie Bergan, and later to Con Curran, about this. Alfie Bergan also undertook, as John Stanislaus's named executor, to probate the will, using the services of his own firm, David H. Charles of Clare Street.

In the meantime, some pressmen were less chary than the Irish papers about recording Joyce news. The Paris edition of the *Chicago*

Tribune carried a report on the funeral and the significance of John Stanislaus:

He was a master of English vernacular and a fine story-teller. His versatility enabled him to adapt his style to all surroundings, whether that of a drawing-room or a saloon. He was full of reminiscences of Irish life of the last half century and his stories were unusually embellished with rare artistry.

The story was credited to the Tribune Press Service: the Left Bank newspaper was noted for its arts coverage (far better than its Right Bank rival, the *New York Herald*). The detail and warmth of the piece strongly suggest the involvement of James Joyce, and his friends Eugene Jolas and Elliot Paul were both *Tribune* men and Joyceans. As the latter, they were minded to do his bidding and the piece was undoubtedly contributed to in some form by Joyce himself. The headline read:

Final services
Held for Father
Of James Joyce

To friends, in letter after letter, James Joyce acknowledged his grief over his unquiet father, John Stanislaus Joyce. To Ezra Pound he wrote that his father had loved him deeply more and more as he grew older. The letter was silently prefaced by a stanza added by 'Father Prout' to Milliken's 'The Groves of Blarney', which appears to be directly biographical of John Stanislaus:

> And there's a stone there that whoever kisses
> HE never misses
> To grow eloquent.
> 'Tis he may clamber to a lady's chamber
> Or become a member of Parliament.
> A clever spouter
> He'll soon turn out or
> An out-and-outer to be left alone.
> Don't seek to hinder him
> Or to bewilder him
> Sure he's a pilgrim from the Blarney stone.

To T. S. Eliot, James Joyce wrote that his father had an intense love for him and that it added to his grief and remorse that for so long he did not go to Dublin to see him. 'I feel that a poor heart which was true and faithful to me is no more,' he went on. More darkly, James Joyce wrote to Herbert Hughes in Belfast that he could not go to see John Stanislaus 'because he lived among savages'. Miss Weaver was written to about Pappie's silliness and shrewdness, and his extraordinary affection and incessant interest in his son, even up to his last breath. 'I was very fond of him always, being a sinner myself, and even liked his faults. Hundreds of pages and scores of characters in my books came from him,' Joyce wrote, adding that his father's dry (or rather wet) wit and his expression convulsed him often with laughter. In the same letter, the writer insisted that he derived from his father 'an extravagant licentious disposition (out of which, however, the greater part of any talent I may have springs)'. James Joyce wrote to Alfie Bergan to say that no man could be worthy of such intense love as his father had for his son. Filially, in the spirit of the more vindictive John Stanislaus, he wrote also a bitter sneer at 'some of his unnatural selfrighteous kindred'. Even Stanislaus, who saw John as a millstone for James, did not deny the unconditionality of his elder brother's love for Pappie.

When Joyce's own grandson was born shortly after the burial of John Stanislaus, this conjunction (just after his own fiftieth birthday) seemed more like a family version of the apostolic succession. There was root, there was branch. James sent a telegram to Stannie which read GRANDSON BORU TODAY ... This odd misprint may well have been intentional and if it was not, Joyce certainly would have appreciated the invocation of the most famous High King of Ireland, Brian Boru, as the latest of his proud line. The king was already prominent in the *Wake*. He wrote the poem 'Ecce Puer' at the time of the baby's birth, welcoming Stephen James Joyce to the world. The new grandfather's regard for the baby's great-grandfather was, however, an equal concern of the poem. (Copies, on publication, were sent to Dublin.) The forces of paternity fascinated James Joyce just as they had fascinated John Stanislaus. 'The most important thing there is,' said Joyce, meaning when another Joyce was born into the world. The poem, almost the last he ever wrote, celebrated four generations of Joyces, adding a crucifixion to a nativity, and deftly linking grief and joy, past and future, goodbye and hello, forsaken and forsaker.

In March 1932 a cartoon of James Joyce was published in the Paris magazine, *transition*. The artist, César Abin, acting under Joyce's instructions, portrayed the writer as his father's ghost, a patched and cobwebbed would-be boulevardier, with the sheet music of 'Let Me Like a Soldier Fall' protruding from his side pocket. In a later comment, again straight out of *Hamlet*, Joyce told Eugene Jolas that he could hear his father talking to him. 'I wonder where he is,' he said. Later he would write to Miss Weaver that the voice of his father ('Poor foolish man!') had somehow got into his body or throat, especially when he sighed.

For all his devices and many qualities, John Stanislaus's death was nearly beyond his means. Dublin probate addressed his second will of 1915 and not an elusive will he made in 1920. But the difference was without distinction. 'All for Jim' was the essence of all his bequests. He had left £665.0s.9d. The bare 9d was a splendid John Stanislaus flourish (and traces of Falstaff or Mr Micawber can be imagined). Most of this money was from his insurance policy with Eagle Star and about £15 was his famous pension. There were sundry expenses, naturally: five guineas was owed to Dr Delaney of Gardiner's Row, for instance, and three guineas to Drumcondra Hospital. Albert Medcalf, with a sick wife of his own, submitted a bill for £43.19s. for board and lodging and the medical expenses he had conscientiously covered. On top of that there was loan interest of £7.1s.8d for the quarter. Crucially, £550 was outstanding as a charge on the Eagle Star policy, a residual detail of his property-owning in Cabra, thirty years previously. But the old accountant had died solvent: the sole legatee was James Joyce and the residual estate he received was £36.12s.1d.

There were no offerings for Masses, as was usual in so many Catholic wills of the day: the repose of his soul had not concerned John Stanislaus at any time. Nothing was left to anyone else, nor were his other children, nor his numerous grandchildren, mentioned in his will. Aside from Giorgio and Lucia, they had been effectively no longer part of his universe; now, he was no longer part of theirs.

In accordance with instructions from his father's ghost (so the son suggested), the gravestone for Glasnevin was soon commissioned (via Alfie Bergan) from Harrison's, who had done the arms of Dublin for the North City Markets in 1892. Bergan had heard directly from John Stanislaus that the inscription was to mention only John himself and his wife, May. There would be nothing about the other Joyces in the same plot, not even poor Georgie or Baby. Ignoring them, John Stanislaus's own role as a father was ignored. To put up the gravestone as requested left James Joyce (or his patron) in the end about £12 out of pocket. Alfie Bergan sent him photographs of it.

With organisational efficiency that reflected the spirit of Old Jack Joyce, a public bench in Whitworth Road, Drumcondra, that his son intended would commemorate him, was never actually placed. (One obstacle was the prospect of a wide bench on a narrow pavement.) James Joyce corresponded fitfully with Con Curran in Dublin for some years about this project, but they tended instead to reminisce about old Dublin and his father's de Reszke voice. John Stanislaus's true memorial is of course *Ulysses*. In Dublin Bay in the 1930s a pleasure-boat (technically a steamship), the SS *John Joyce*, took visitors and holiday-makers on excursions – an association that pleased James Joyce mightily. Coincidence it may have been, but *Ulysses* had spoken of a similar, Parnellite, vessel, *Erin's King*, and so the progression was apt – from Bloom and Parnell to HCE to John Stanislaus Joyce. Dublin Bay had been properly charted first by Captain Bligh (later of HMS *Bounty*), whose greatest shortcoming was not violence but a reckless fluency in abrasive language. It was a characteristic shared with John Stanislaus, who was often misunderstood and often understood too well. Some of his relations imagined him drinking with all his dead friends in the bar of the *John Joyce*, as it plied around the bay and the little islands and harbours he had known so long ago.

Herbert Gorman, deep in his biography of James Joyce, came to Dublin to learn more. Friends and associates tried to explain: Tom Devin, 'Blind' Pugh, Cyril Corrigan, Gerald Griffin, David Charles, the Sinclairs – Dublin contemporaries of father and son – told him of the Joyces they had known. Even so, Gorman was 'directed' (and then edited) regarding the roles of father and son by James Joyce, who inserted phrases like John Stanislaus's 'exquisite calligraphy of which he was very vain'. The biographee abandoned his usual polite (if devious) languor towards the other writer and insisted that certain passages 'be better deleted'. For James Joyce, in public, his father's competence and even financial integrity were beyond reproach. A slight suggestion that John Stanislaus had not been a good father was vehemently countered, as was the drafted mention that John would have regarded a position in Guinness's as acceptable for young James (the son of a gentleman). By contrast, when Gorman described Mrs May Joyce as 'a patient ghost drifting into inanition', Joyce did not bother to improve the harshly unrevealing opinion in the biography.

As time went by, James Joyce did not relax his obsession with the family past. In the mid 1930s the portraits were reframed and the Tuohy portrait of a Dublin gentleman was given pride of place. The writer had the photographs taken of himself seated beneath the image of his father, with his son and his grandson. The photograph of John Stanislaus in 1888 was included in the biography at Joyce's behest. But when Gorman wanted to use the Joyce arms on the cover of his book – as Jim had done for a special copy of *Chamber Music* for Nora – the request was curtly refused. This may have been from a sacral sense of what was personal between him and Nora. Alternatively, it is possible that James Joyce, a heraldic enthusiast like his father, had realised that such a cover might advertise the non-canonical nature of the arms and expose John Stanislaus's pretensions to be a gentleman. The misdemeanour was an HCE-like one, which yet suggested the man's vitality.

Pappie was never far away. James Joyce attempted to have the finished version of Work in Progress published on his father's birthday in 1938, but without success. Later in the year the Parnell Grave Memorial Subscription Fund acknowledged from Rathmines a contribution from the writer in France. The gesture to The Chief was indirectly also a memorial to John Stanislaus. There were other gestures too: James Joyce's practice was to ask friends, including Samuel Beckett, Paul Léon and even Maria Jolas, to go out on the Fourth of July into the streets of Paris and give a hundred francs to the first down-and-out they encountered, in honour and in memory of his father's birthday.

When the new book was finally ready, its title was revealed. As in *Ulysses*, John Stanislaus and his exuberant milieu were everywhere in *Finnegans Wake*. Charlie Chance, Father Prout, Tom Devin, Messrs Brooks and Lyons, Brennan on the Moor near Fermoy, the Gunns and their sons, Alfie Bergan, Reuben J. Dodd and the old crew were all presented in one way or another. Humpty Dumpty in 'The Ballad of Persse O'Reilly' (on pages 45–7) was Pappie lightly disguised and he was Finn MacCool and Tristram too. The Guinnesses and the Jamesons were there, and Hengler's Circus Entertainment, and the house by the Chapelizod eyrie, and Grace O'Malley from the west, piratical visitor to Howth Castle and environs. Amid the strange Joycean affinity for war and history, in that summer of 1939 James Joyce revealed his father, as HCE, the *Wake*'s most vital and polymorphous character reborn in *Finnegans Wake*. The red bird of his coat of arms had risen rejuvenated from the ashes. On the last page of the book the great river of the *Wake* runs into the sea from which it had once come: 'And it's old and old it's sad and old it's sad and weary I go back to you, my cold father, my cold mad father, my cold mad feary father, till the near sight of the mere size of him, the moyles and moyles of it, moananoaning, makes me seasilt saltsick and I rush, my only, into your arms.' The mutuality of father and son had changed literature. Frailties, misunderstandings, laughter and all, the one was the other.

But perhaps in the end, nowhere was John Stanislaus Joyce, singer, rebel, joker, Irish chieftain, wordsmith, old Milesian and, above all, father, more spectacularly to be celebrated than in his son's hundred-letter thunder-word on page 332 of *Finnegans Wake*:

Pappappapparrassannuaragheallachnatullaghmonganmacmacmacwhack-
falltherdebblenonthedubblandaddydoodled
and unruly person
creeked a
jest

●

EPILOGUE

The Joyce Family Seat

A Dublin Benchmark

Death is not the end of the story.

Just as John Stanislaus Joyce saw himself as an extension of the lives of his ancestors, so his children and grandchildren bore the old man with them into the years after his death. Though dead and buried, John Stanislaus continued to lead a fading afterlife in their memories and in the memories of his remaining friends. Later, the increasing fame of his son would bring him his own kind of fame, as the begetter of genius, the father of James Joyce.

The friends were few. In early 1937 Tom Devin died. For fifty years, since the age of fourteen, he had worked for Dublin Corporation, latterly (after a disagreement with the authorities) in the Corporation Cleansing Department on Wood Quay – the office alluded to in *Ulysses*. Though that novel represents him (under the guise of 'Jack Power') as something of a ladies' man and he did marry twice – and certainly charmed Nora Joyce – from the 1920s he had been a member of the most pious and proper Knights of St Columbanus, like the Ancient Order of Hibernians a Catholic response to the Freemasons. A decent, kindly man, clearly upset when his old friend Jack Joyce failed to recognise him on his deathbed, he retained the loyalty of both James and Nora.

When Tom Devin's death was reported by Alfie Bergan to the Joyces in Paris James said that Bergan was now the last survivor of his father's old circle of friends. The connection between the Bergan and Joyce families seems to have gone back to the 1870s. Still sprightly and dapper, the once mischievous little Alfie Bergan had retired as a clerk in David H. Charles's law office and had then done work for the Radiological Society of Ireland in the City of Dublin Skin Hospital. This had been founded by David Charles's father and members of the family remain associated with the institution to this day. Bergan had been born in 1870, of the generation between John Stanislaus and James, hence his friendship with both. He would still be lodging with Mrs Refaussé at Claude Road when he died among friends in the same hospital in December 1947.

By the end of 1939, when James Joyce had been hoping that everyone would be keenly discussing *Finnegans Wake*, the Second World War had broken out instead. The Joyces left Paris and found refuge for a time with the Jolas family in a village two hundred miles to the south-east. Then, in 1940, James, Nora and Giorgio escaped to Switzerland, leaving Lucia, whose travel permit had expired, under psychiatric care elsewhere in France. It was in Zürich that James Joyce was taken ill and died, on 13 January 1941, less than a decade after his father.

When his brother Charlie, in England, heard the news, he himself had less than three weeks left to live. After leaving Ireland with his new wife Annie and his children, as an ex-telephone operator he had technically been able to describe himself as a retired civil servant and it had been relatively easy to find work, again on night shifts, with the Post Office in London. There, by day, he had become involved with the Catholic Evidence Guild, a propaganda group established to spread the faith through public speaking. On Sundays during the 1930s, Charlie Joyce could often be found mounted on a soap-box at Speakers' Corner in Hyde Park, extolling the verities of the Roman Church to the puzzled and amused crowds that gather there. After he had a lung haemorrhage in 1931 Lucia, in London for her parents' English wedding, had been taken to visit Charlie's sanatorium, but he was kept away from their Kensington flat for fear his disease might infect her. He and Annie made plans to set up some kind of boarding-house, which they hoped Jim would help with, but Charlie's health remained too poor.

In 1937 they went to live beside the sea at Hastings, in the hall and basement levels of 13 Marine Parade. When the war came, Hastings was in the front line and suffered extensive damage from German bombers. Anyone who was not a native or connected with war work was evacuated. The Joyces removed to St Albans in Hertfordshire. They were living in lodgings at 6 Lower Dagnall

Street when Charlie was taken ill again and entered the St Albans and Mid-Herts Hospital. He died there on 4 February 1941, of 'chronic fibroid tuberculosis' according to the doctor who treated him. Charlie had contracted his fatal illness far back during the family hardships at the turn of the century. He, his handful of deceased children and his first wife were as much victims of John Stanislaus Joyce's improvident ways as his younger brothers, his sisters and his mother had been.

Annie Joyce returned to Ireland, where her youngest surviving stepson, Frederick, married in 1944. He qualified as an optician two years later and practised in north-central Dublin, in premises on the corner of Blessington Street and Dorset Street – what is now thought of as the heart of James Joyce's Dublin, only steps away from Eccles Street. He retired in the early 1990s. Under the influence of Annie Joyce he never mentioned the past and his children were even surprised to learn at the time of the James Joyce Centenary in 1982 that they were related to the famous – though in their father's eyes infamous – James Joyce. His son, Bob, and his family, however, are now among those most involved in running the James Joyce Cultural Centre in North Great George's Street, a few doors away from his grandfather Charlie's old habitation, and Paul Joyce, Bob's son, is an accomplished painter.

The rest of Charlie's children broke the connection with Ireland and, it seems, with the faith: at any rate none of their baptismal records carry the normal endorsement of a marriage in a Catholic church. The child named for his grandfather, John Stanislaus Joyce, now lives in the south of England, little involved in the Joyce legend.

In April 1951 the tenth anniversary of James Joyce's death was marked (a little belatedly) by *Envoy*, the leading Dublin literary magazine edited by John Ryan, with a special number devoted to a tribute to the writer. Among the articles was a notable essay by W. B. Stanford, relating the Homeric theme in Joyce's work to his schoolboy studies at Belvedere College. Sadly, just as this appeared, on 10 April Nora Joyce, who had never returned to Ireland after James's death for fear of, at the very least, unpleasantness, died from uraemic poisoning in Zürich. She had stayed in the city, close to her husband's grave, and had been living with her son George, whose marriage to Helen Fleischman had broken down. In 1946 she had made an agreement with Faber and Faber and the Viking Press that there should be an edition of James Joyce's letters. Though ostensibly this would be edited by Stuart Gilbert, much of the work of collection and annotation was done by Harriet Weaver and the young Irish writer Patricia Hutchins.

George married again on 24 May 1954, to Dr Aste Jahnke-Osterwalder, with whom he went to live in Munich and for a time he found employment there in a bank. His son, Stephen, who had been educated in America and was a graduate of Yale, was now working in Paris for UNESCO. He seemed to Patricia Hutchins, who met him at this time, to wish to escape from the shadow of his grandfather, yet to feel the strength of the connection. On 15 April 1955, aged twenty-three, Stephen James Joyce married Solange Raytchine in Paris. They have no children.

Professor Stanislaus Joyce, still in Trieste, had been publishing pieces about the background to his brother's stories and the early years in Dublin. His impressions of the Joyce family around the turn of the century would inform the new image of James Joyce that was coming into focus. In the summer of 1954 he visited London with some of his students, but did not go on to Dublin as expected: it would have been his first visit to Ireland since 1905, but heart trouble forced an early return home. The next year, on Bloomsday, 16 June, Stanislaus Joyce died in Trieste aged seventy. He left a widow, Nelly, and a son, James (known as Jimmy), born on 14 February 1943: both went to live in London, where they too eventually died, Jimmy not long after his marriage.

On 16 June 1954, the BBC Third Programme presented readings from *Ulysses* to mark the fiftieth anniversary of the date on which the novel was set. The radio broadcast had a strange sequel. In the High Court in Dublin, the following October, Reuben Dodd Junior claimed before Mr Justice Murnaghan (a college friend of James Joyce's) that one of the extracts from the novel had libelled him and he sought leave to serve a writ of libel outside the jurisdiction of the Irish state. He swore an affidavit detailing the circumstances surrounding John Stanislaus Joyce's relations with his father, Reuben Dodd Senior, and alleged that he had been held up to ridicule by the passage describing his rescue from the Liffey in despair over a girl. Though Dodd swore that he had merely been trying to retrieve his hat, his family now admits that the Joyce version was quite true. (One of the lawyers who helped Dodd to sustain the charge was Ulick O'Connor, later the biographer of James Joyce's great foe, Oliver Gogarty.) The BBC was given four weeks to enter a plea, but settled the case out of court, leaving Dodd some £500 to the good. It was in a manner the final revenge of the Dodds: sixty years after Dodd Senior had screwed the last of John Stanislaus's family money out of him, Dodd Junior still managed to get money from the Joyces, even if it was only by proxy.

Appreciation of James Joyce on a wider scale dates from 1956 when, with the July publication of *Dubliners* as a Penguin paperback in England, the mass-market interest in his writing began. This first book was eventually followed by all of Joyce's main works. To this period may also be traced the real rise of American academic interest in Joyce.

However, these matters impinged little on John Stanislaus's surviving children: they had their own lives to lead and deaths to die. On 25 November 1957 Eva Joyce, who had spent her working life as a clerk with the firm on Stephen's Green and had still been living with Florrie in the flat in Mountjoy Square, passed away at the age of sixty-six. Despite her feelings about her father, she was buried in the family grave in Glasnevin.

In Dublin, though Joycean scholarship might have been all but abandoned to the Americans, Joycean commemoration had not. The James Joyce Tower in Sandycove was opened during the Joyce Festival in 1962. Eileen Schaurek had only contempt for many who attended. She felt with some asperity that it was very much a case of 'late have I loved thee'. Fixed in her mind there was a very different James Joyce from the man being remembered. Shortly before, she had spoken of the religious young man of her childhood and her recent experience of hearing Jim's devotion to Our Lady praised from the pulpit by a young priest at the Convent of Perpetual Adoration in Merrion Square. For Eileen, her brother was returning to the church he had never really left.

The presentation of the famous Joyce waistcoat to the Tower

took place in 1963, on 25 January: it had been given by George Joyce to Samuel Beckett, who passed it via Con Leventhal to Padraic Colum, President of the Committee. This talismanic garment, perhaps the earliest family relic of all, might have been repaired and rebacked but, with its golden heads of hounds and stags, it remained a symbol of the rural Irish roots of the family that had given the world a writer of international stature, as well as being irrevocably associated with the links between John Stanislaus and James. Two days after the presentation Eileen Joyce Schaurek died from a heart attack after slipping on the ice on the way home from Mass and was buried in St Peter's Cemetery, Little Bray, once the great Fr James Healy's parish. After many years in Dublin flats, she had been living not far away in a bungalow on Newcourt Road, Bray and, in the months before her death, had given to the Irish writer Alice Curtayne a series of interviews, published after her death. In these she recounted her impressions of her father – they were not kind.

Eileen's own children had now grown up. Bertha was married to a Polish jeweller she had met in England during the war and they had a jewellery shop at the top of Bray's main street. Eleanora was now Mrs O'Driscoll and had moved to Canada. Tatto (Patrizio), who had lived with Eva and Florrie while he went to school in Belvedere, and of whom they became very fond, had left for England after the war. He had first joined a band called 'Three Dots and a Dash' which had some degree of success, then he became an actor in London where he now lives, appearing on television and elsewhere under the name of Paddy Joyce. He thus has succeeded to fulfil the stillborn theatrical ambitions of his grandfather John Stanislaus and of his uncles James and Charlie.

Poppie (Margaret) Joyce died in her New Zealand convent in March 1964. She had written to James (and prayed for him) until his death in 1941. The convent, whose nuns had been extremely fond of her, generously issued Fr Ainscough's late interview with her to the very few interested callers. On 8 May 1966 May Joyce Monaghan, who had left her Oughterard in-laws for the Dublin suburb of Terenure, died at Mount Carmel Hospital after a short illness. She was buried in Mount Jerome Cemetery, on the opposite side of the city to Glasnevin. Remaining proud of her eldest brother's achievements, once free from rural pressures and prejudices, May had made friends with several biographers and other such Joyceans, and from time to time had joined enthusiastically in various Joyce-related events.

May's son, Kenneth, who had come to live in Dublin with his aunts in the late thirties, went to work (like Florrie) in the Bank of Ireland, soon rising from a junior position. Both his sisters now live abroad, but Ken, when he retired, took on the promotion of the James Joyce Cultural Centre, as well as organising walking tours of Joycean Dublin, mainly in those districts which were the setting of the Joyces' lives after 1894. Married, with children, he has become the Irish representative of the family whenever a press comment is required.

In 1967 the inaugural James Joyce International Symposium was held in Dublin. Perhaps for the first time the full dimensions of the interest of the wider world in Joyce and his works were brought home to Dubliners. What had until then been something of a joke now became far more important: something to make money out of. That June, George Joyce visited Dublin to attend the Symposium. It was not a visit he enjoyed. Part of the time he was hardly sober, lying in a hammock in Arthur Power's garden in Sandymount. There is a sad photograph of George Joyce at this time, looking down at the deathmask of his father that he has been given to hold. He was driven around the city, but found this very confusing, and when the party headed towards 'Bloom's house' in Eccles Street, by then a rather seedy quarter of Dublin, he asked, 'Why are you taking me here?' At Sandycove, surrounded by Joyce fans, his bewilderment was evident. He had little in common with the surviving family members he met, and the haunts of his father and grandfather were almost devoid of meaning for him. After the failure of his singing career his own life had been an unhappy one. He died on 12 June 1976 at Konstanz in Germany and is now buried (along with his wife) beside his parents in Fluntern Cemetery in Zürich.

A few years earlier, on 3 September, the last of John Stanislaus Joyce's children, Florrie, had died at the age of eighty in a nursing home in Rathgar, where she had lived for some ten years after leaving 12 Mountjoy Square. She had retired in 1950 from her job in the Law Department of the Bank. Her dislike of her father was carried into death, for she was buried not in the Glasnevin grave, but at Mount Jerome, in the same Monaghan grave as her sister May.

In accordance with James Joyce's old wish for a Dublin memorial seat to his father, on 14 June 1977, during another Joyce Symposium, a public bench was dedicated to John Stanislaus Joyce and his son James. The ceremony was conducted by the playwright Denis Johnston in the distinguished company of Mme Maria Jolas and David Norris. It was not on Claude Road, however, but on St Stephen's Green – once for John Stanislaus a symbol of the displacement of the old power of the Guinnesses – and it was opposite Newman House, where he had come to see Jim's debating triumphs at the College L & H.

In February 1982 the centenary of James Joyce's birth was marked in Dublin with state and civic pomp. It was a signal of his absorption into the national pantheon. By contrast, the death at Northampton on 8 December 1982 of John Stanislaus's senior granddaughter, Lucia Joyce, passed almost unnoticed. Another unhappy life, lived in the long shadow of John Stanislaus Joyce, was ended.

During her visit in 1977 Maria Jolas had sought local information about the exact quality of John Stanislaus's voice, but there seems to have been no public response to this. There was no one left who remembered it. The generation of John Stanislaus Joyce had all passed on; the voice was silent at last.

But his bloodline remains. Several families of John Stanislaus's descendants will soon bring his vibrant lineage into the twenty-first century. The undoubted injury and anguish that he caused to his family have now all but healed. Soon, these new representatives of the Joyces, inheritors of the line, may look back with some pride at this most extraordinary of human beings, the man who enabled their existences. Perhaps, as James Joyce himself did, they will even refrain from passing judgement. John Stanislaus Joyce was who he was. Can anyone be otherwise?

While his heirs go forward, his ancestors, in their golden frames, have come to rest. They had hung in turn over the family in

Anglesea Terrace, Cork, in the many Dublin homes of John Stanislaus, in the lodgings and flats of James Joyce in Trieste and Paris, and in George Joyce's house. The portraits passed out of the family after a sale in the early 1950s to raise money for Nora Joyce who, in poor health, needed it to survive. They all now grace the walls of the Poetry Library in the State University of New York at Buffalo, safe but doubly exiled, from Europe and from Ireland. So too has James Joyce himself, through his own efforts, passed out of his family into the possession of the wider world.

The Irish family property – in which John Stanislaus had once taken such pride as being, like the portraits, the mark of the gentleman – has shrunk to the family plot in Prospect Cemetery, Glasnevin: the family seat to the one on St Stephen's Green. The real and living memorial to Pappie is in the pages of his son's books – books to which he imparted the stuff of his life, the vivacity of his own personality, the full-blooded invective of his phrase-making, the social density of his daily round. Through Simon Dedalus, readers of Joyce can share some large part of his uniqueness, but even James Joyce's words give little impression of how much John's close friends delighted in his company. That, like his voice, has been lost for ever.

Though moralists, beginning with his own family, have not been kind to John Stanislaus, now it does not matter what they said or say about him. To at least one of his children he had seemed an overflowing fountain of personal human history, worthy to be turned in *Finnegans Wake* into the teeming history of the world. The genius of John Stanislaus Joyce has become a universal possession.

Bibliography

These are among the published sources used in preparing this biography. More are within some of the publications cited here and others can be found in the References section. The *James Joyce Quarterly* was founded in 1963, and the year of any article cited may be calculated from the volume number.

1 ADAMS, Michael, *Censorship: The Irish Experience* (Scepter, 1968)
2 ADAMS, Robert Martin, *Surface and Symbol* (OUP, 1962)
3 ALGER, J. G., 'An Irish Absentee and His Tenants', *English Historical Review*, vol. x (1895), pp. 663–74
4 ALPHA AND OMEGA, *Blight: The Tragedy of Dublin* (Talbot Press, 1917)
5 ANDERSON, Chester, G., *James Joyce and his World* (Thames & Hudson, 1967)
6 ANDREWS, J. H., 'Henry Pratt, Survey of Kerry Estates', *Journal of Kerry Archæological and Historical Society*, No. 13 (1980), pp. 5–38
7 [ANON.], *Memories of Father Healy of Little Bray* (Bentley, 1898)
8 [ANON.], 'Interview with Mr. John Stanislas Joyce, 1849–1931', in Maria Jolas (ed.), *A James Joyce Yearbook* (Transition Press, 1949)
9 ATHERTON, James S., *The Books at the WAKE* (Southern Illinois UP, 1959
10 AUGUSTINE, Rev., *Footprints of Father Theobald Mathew, O. F. M.: Apostle of Temperance* (M. H. Gill, 1947)
11 BANTA, Melissa, and Silverman, Oscar A., *James Joyce's Letters to Sylvia Beach, 1921–1940* (Plantin, 1990)
12 BARRINGTON, Jonah, *Personal Sketches of His Own Time* (Routledge, 2 vols, 1869)
13 BARTON, Dunbar Plunket, *Timothy Healy: Memories and Anecdotes* (Talbot Press/Faber, 1933)
14 BARRY, Valerie, *Houses of Kerry* (Ballinakilla Press, 1994)

15 BAUERLE, Ruth (ed.), *The James Joyce Songbook* (Garland, 1982)
16 ——*Picking Up Airs: Hearing the Music in Joyce's Text* (University of Illinois Press, 1993)
17 BEECHER, Seán, *The Story of Cork* (Mercier, 1971)
18 ——*Day by Day: A Miscellany of Cork History* (Collins Press, 1996)
19 BECKETT, J. C., *The Making of Modern Ireland, 1603–1923* (Faber, 1963)
20 BEJA, Morris, *James Joyce: A Literary Life* (Macmillan, 1992)
21 BENSTOCK, Bernard (ed.), *James Joyce: The Augmented Ninth* (Syracuse UP, 1988)
22 BENSTOCK, Shari, and Benstock, Bernard, *Who's He When He's At Home: A James Joyce Directory* (University of Illinois Press, 1980)
23 BERRONE, Louis, *James Joyce in Padua* (Random House, 1977)
24 *The Bioscope* (London)
25 BLUNT, Wilfred Scawen, *The Land War in Ireland* (Stephen Swift, 1902)
26 BOWEN, Elizabeth, *Bowen's Court* (Longmans, 1942)
27 BOWEN, Zack, *Musical Allusions in the Works of James Joyce* (Gill and Macmillan, 1975)
28 BOWMAN, John, and O'Donoghue, Ronan (eds), *Portraits: Belvedere College 1832–1982* (Gill and Macmillan, 1982)
29 BRADLEY, Bruce, *James Joyce's Schooldays* (Gill and Macmillan, 1982)
30 BRADY, L. W., *T P O'Connor and the Liverpool Irish* (Royal Historical Society, 1983)
31 BRIVIC, Sheldon, 'The Father in Joyce', in Bernard Benstock (ed.), *The Seventh of Joyce* (Indiana UP/Harvester, 1982)
32 BROWN, Carole, and Knuth, Leo, *The Tenor and the Vehicle* (A Wake Newslitter monograph no. 5, 1982)
33 BROWN, Malcolm, *The Politics of Irish Literature* (George Allen & Unwin, 1972)
34 BROWN, Richard, *James Joyce and Sexuality* (CUP, 1985)
35 BRUNICARDI, Niall, *John Anderson: Entrepreneur* (Eigse Books, 1987)
36 BUDGEN, Frank, *James Joyce and the Making of ULYSSES, and other writings* (OUP, 1972)
37 BUNYAN, J. J., *A Sense of Fermoy* (2 vols, n.d.)
38 BURGESS,, Anthony, *Here Comes Everybody* (Faber, 1964)
39 BURKE, Bernard, 'Joyce of Corgary' in *Burke's Landed Gentry of Ireland* (Harrison, 1904)
40 BUSSY, F. M., *Irish Conspiracies* (Everett, 1910)
41 BYRNE, Edward, *Parnell: A Memoir* (Lilliput Press, 1991)
42 BYRNE, J. F., *Silent Years: An Autobiography with Memoirs of James Joyce and Our Ireland* (Farrar Straus and Young, 1953)

43 BYRNE, Patrick F., 'A Note from Dublin on 'Bloom's Job' ', *JJQ* (2), p. 108

44 CALLANAN, Frank, *The Parnell Split, 1890–91* (Cork UP, 1992)

45 ——*T M Healy* (Cork UP, 1996)

46 CAMERON, Charles, *Autobiography* (Hodges Figgis, 1921)

47 CAMPBELL, Julian, *The Irish Impressionists: Irish Artists in France and Belgium, 1850–1914* (National Gallery of Ireland, 1984)

48 CARLYLE, Thomas, *Sartor Resartus* (Grant Richards, 1902)

49 CATO, Bob, and Vitiello, Greg, *Joyce Images* (W W Norton, 1994)

50 CAULFIELD, Max, *The Easter Rebellion* (Frederick Muller, 1964)

51 CHART, D. A., *The Story of Dublin* (Dent, 1932)

52 CHENG, Vincent, J., *Joyce, race and empire* (CUP, 1995)

53 CHILDERS, Edmund Spencer Eardley, *The Life and Correspondence of the Right Hon. Hugh C. E. Childers, 1827–1896* (John Murray, 2 vols. 1901)

54 CHRISTOPHER, Father, *Father Charles of Mount Argus* (Catholic Truth Society of Ireland, 1938)

55 CIXOUS, Hélène, *The Exile of James Joyce* (John Calder, 1976)

56 CLAYTON, Jay, 'Londublin: Dickens's London in Joyce's Dublin,' *Novel*, Vol. 28 No. 3 (Spring 1995), pp. 327—42

57 COLLINS, R. G., 'The Second Dædalus: Simon the Testifier', *JJQ* (8), pp. 233—35

58 COLUM, Mary, *Life and the Dream* (Macmillan, 1947)

59 COLUM, Mary and Padraic, *Our Friend James Joyce* (Victor Gollancz, 1959)

60 *Complete Peerage*, 'Kerry' and 'Lansdowne' (St Catherine Press, 1929)

61 CORFE, T., *The Phoenix Park Murders: Conflict, Compromise and Tragedy in Ireland, 1879–82* (Hodder & Stoughton, 1968)

62 CORLESS, Damian, 'Take Me Up to Monto', *In Dublin*, March [c.14th] 1996, pp. 8–9

63 COSGRAVE, Dillon, *North Dublin City and Environs* (Irish Academic Press, 1977

64 COSTELLO, Peter, *James Joyce: The Years of Growth, 1882–1915* (Kyle Cathie, 1992)

65 COSTELLO, Peter, and van de Kamp, Peter, *Flann O'Brien: An Illustrated Biography* (Bloomsbury, 1987)

66 CRONIN, Anthony, *Dead as Doornails: a chronicle of life* (Dolmen Press, 1976)

67 CULLEN, L. M., *Princes and Pirates: The Dublin Chamber of Commerce, 1783–1983* (Dublin Chamber of Commerce, 1983)

68 CURRAN, C. P., *James Joyce Remembered* (OUP, 1968)

69 —— *Under the Receding Wave* (Gill and Macmillan, 1970)

70 CURTIS, L. P., *Coercion and Conciliation in Ireland 1880–1892* (Princeton UP, 1963)

71 DALY, Leo, *James Joyce and the Mullingar Connection* (Dolmen Press, 1975)

72 ——*James Joyce at the Cross-Keys, Mullingar* (1992)

73 DALY, Mary, *Dublin: The Deposed Capital* (Cork UP, 1985)

74 DAWSON, Hugh J., 'Thomas MacGreevy and Joyce', *JJQ* (25), pp. 305–21

75 DAVIES, Stan Gébler, *James Joyce: A Portrait of the Artist* (Stein and Day, 1975)

76 DELIMATA, Bozena Berta, 'Reminiscences of a Joyce Niece', *JJQ* (19), pp. 45–62

77 *Dublin Civic Week, September 17–25 1927: Official Handbook* (1927)

78 *Dublin Civic Week, September 7–14 1929: Official Handbook* (1929)

79 *Dublin Penny Journal*

80 DUNLOP, Andrew, *Fifty Years of Irish Journalism* (Hanna & Neale/Simpkin Marshall and Co, 1911)

81 EGLINTON, John, *Irish Literary Portraits* (Macmillan, 1935)

82 ELLMANN, Richard, *James Joyce* (OUP, 1982)

83 EPSTEIN, Edmund L., *The Ordeal of Stephen Dedalus* (Southern Illinois UP, 1971)

84 ERVINE, St. John, *Parnell* (Penguin, 1944)

85 *Evening Herald* (Dublin)

86 *Evening Mail* (Dublin)

87 *Evening Telegraph* (Dublin)

88 FAHY, Catherine (comp.), *The James Joyce-Paul Léon Papers in the National Library of Ireland: A Catalogue* (NLI, 1992)

89 FAIRHALL, James, *James Joyce and the question of history* (CUP, 1995)

90 FERRIS, Kathleen, *James Joyce & the Burden of Disease* (UP of Kentucky, 1995)

91 FINEGAN, John, *The Story of Monto* (Mercier, 1978)

92 FITZMAURICE, E G P, *Life of William, Earl of Shelburne, afterwards first Marquess of Lansdowne* (Macmillan, 2 vols, 1912)

93 FLEISCHMANN, Aloys, *Music in Ireland* (Cork UP/Blackwell, 1952)

94 FLOOD, W. H. Grattan, *Introductory Sketch of Irish Musical History* (William Reeves, 1922)

95 FLYNN, Arthur, *History of Bray* (Mercier Press, 1986)

96 FORD, Jane, 'Why is Milly in Mullingar?', *JJQ* (14), pp. 436–49

97 FORDE, Robert, 'A Brief History of the College up until A.D. 1900', *The Centenary College Annual* (Fermoy, 1960)

98 *Freeman's Journal* (Dublin)

99 FREUND, Gisèle, *Trois Jours Avec James Joyce* (Denoël, 1982)

100 GARVIN, John, *James Joyce's Disunited Kingdom and the Irish Dimension* (Gill and Macmillan/Barnes & Noble, 1976)

101 ——'James Joyce's Municipal Background', *Administration*, Vol. 33 No. 4 (1985), pp. 551–72

102 GATT-RUTTER, John, *Italo Svevo: A Double Life* (OUP, 1988)

103 GIBSON, Andrew (ed.), *Joyce's 'Ithaca'* (Rodopi, 1996)

104 GILBERT, Stuart, *James Joyce's ULYSSES: A Study* (Penguin (with Faber), 1969)

105 GILLET, Louis, *Claybook for James Joyce* (Abelard-Schuman, 1958)

106 GLASHEEN, Adaline, *A Third Census of FINNEGANS WAKE* (University of California Press, 1977)

107 GOGARTY, Oliver St. John, *As I Was Going Down Sackville Street: A Phantasy in Fact* (Rich and Cowan, 1937)

108 ——*It Isn't This Time of Year At All! An Unpremeditated Autobiography* (Macgibbon & Kee, 1954)
——(See also Alpha and Omega)

109 GOLDMAN, Arnold, 'Send him canorious', *Listener,* Vol. 88 No. 2262 (August 3rd 1972), pp. 142–4

110 GORMAN, Herbert, *James Joyce: a definitive biography* (John Lane The Bodley Head, 1949)

111 ——*James Joyce: His First Forty Years* (Geoffrey Bles, 1926)

112 GRAVES, Robert, *Lars Porsena; or, the future of swearing and improper language* (Kegan Paul & Co. 1927)

113 GRAY, Tony, *Ireland This Century* (Little, Brown, 1994)

114 HALL, J. B., *Random Records of a Reporter* (Simpkin Marshall/Fodhla, 1928)

115 HARRINGTON, T. C., *The Maamtrasna Massacre* (Nation Office, 1884)

116 HARRISON, Henry, *Parnell Vindicated: The Lifting of the Veil* (Constable, 1931)

117 HART, Clive, and Knuth, Leo, *A topographical guide to James Joyce's ULYSSES* (A Wake Newslitter Press, 1981)

118 HARVEY, John, *Dublin* (B. T. Batsford, 1949)

119 HASLIP, Joan, *Parnell* (Frederick A. Stokes, 1937)

120 HAYMAN, David, *The WAKE in Transit* (Cornell UP, 1990)

121 HEALY, Timothy, *Letters and Leaders of My Day* (Thornton Butterworth, 2 vols, 1928)

122 HECKARD, Margaret, 'The Literary Reverberations of a Fake Interview with John Stanislaus Joyce' *JJQ* (13), pp. 468–71

123 HEDERMAN, Mark Patrick, 'The "Mind" of James Joyce: From Paternalism to Paternity', in Richard Kearney (ed.), *The Irish Mind* (Wolfhound Press, 1985)

124 HENCHY, Deirdre, 'Dublin Eighty Years Ago', *Dublin Historical Record* XXXVI:1 (1972)

125 HERR, Cheryl, *Joyce's Anatomy of Culture* (University of Illinois Press, 1986)

126 HERRING, Phillip F. (ed.), *Joyce's* ULYSSES *Notesheets in the British Museum* (UP of Virginia, 1972)

127 ——*Joyce's Notes and Early Drafts for* ULYSSES (UP of Virginia, 1977)

128 HEUSER, Hermann J., *Canon Sheehan of Doneraile* (Longmans, Green & Co, 1918)

129 HODGART, Matthew J. C. and Bauerle, Ruth, *Joyce's Grand Operoar: Opera in* FINNEGANS WAKE (University of Illinois Press, 1996)

130 HODGART, Matthew J. C., and Worthington, Mabel P., *Song in the Work of James Joyce* (Temple University Publications/Columbia UP, 1959)

131 HOFHEINZ, Thomas C., *Joyce and the Invention of Irish History* (CUP, 1995)

132 HOLLOWAY, Joseph, *Joseph Holloway's Abbey Theatre: A Selection from His Unpublished Journal* (Southern Illinois UP/Feffer & Simons, 1967)

133 HOPPEN, K Theodore, *Elections, Politics and Society in Ireland, 1832–1885* (Clarendon Press, 1984)

134 ——*Ireland Since 1800: Conflict & Conformity* (Longman 1989)

135 HOWARTH, Herbert, *The Irish Writers: 1800–1940: Literature Under Parnell's Star* (Rockliff, 1958)

136 HUTCHINS, Patricia, *James Joyce's Dublin* (Grey Walls, 1950)

137 ——*James Joyce's World* (Methuen, 1957)

138 ——'James Joyce's Correspondence', *Encounter* Vol. VII No. 2 (August 1956), pp. 49–54

139 HYMAN, Louis, *The Jews in Ireland* (Irish UP, 1972)

140 IGOE, Vivien, *James Joyce's Dublin Houses* (Mandarin, 1990)

141 *Irish Ecclesiastical Record* (Dublin)

142 *Journal of the Cork Historical and Archæological Society* (Cork)

143 JOYCE, James, *Stephen Hero*, ed. Theodore Spencer, (Jonathan Cape, 1956)

144 ——*James Joyce's* DUBLINERS: *An Annotated and Illustrated Edition*, ed. John Wyse Jackson and Bernard McGinley, (Sinclair-Stevenson, 1993)

145 ——*A Portrait of the Artist as a Young Man*, ed. Seamus Deane, (Penguin, 1992)

146 ——*The Critical Writings of James Joyce*, ed. Ellsworth Mason and Richard Ellmann, (Viking, 1964)

147 ——*Poems and* EXILES, ed. J. C. C. Mays, (Penguin, 1992)

148 ——*Poems and Shorter Writings*, ed. R. Ellmann, A. W. Litz and J. Whittier-Ferguson, (Faber, 1991)

149 ——*Ulysses*, ed. Hans Walter Gabler, (Garland, 1984)

150 ——*Finnegans Wake* (Faber, 1966)

151 ——*Letters of James Joyce*, [Vol. I] ed. Stuart Gilbert, (Faber, 1957)

152 ——'Five More Pages of *Stephen Hero*', eds. John J Slocum and Herbert Cahoon, in M. Magalaner (ed.), *A James Joyce Miscellany:* Second Series (Southern Illinois UP, 1959)

153 ——*Scribbledehobble*, ed. Thomas E. Connolly, (Northwestern UP, 1961)

154 ——*Letters of James Joyce*, Vol. II, ed. Richard Ellmann, (Faber, 1966)

155 ——*Letters of James Joyce*, Vol. III, ed. Richard Ellmann, (Faber, 1966)

156 ——*Selected Letters of James Joyce*, ed. Richard Ellmann, (Faber, 1975)

157 JOYCE, Mannix, 'The Joyce Brothers of Glenosheen', *Capuchin Annual* (1969), pp. 257–87

158 ——'Na deartháireacha Seoighe ó Cho. Luimnigh – a saothar ar son na hÉireann', in *North Munster Studies*, (Thomond Archæological Society, 1967)

159 ——'Fragments from the Lost Census Returns: entries relating to Kilfinnane District', *North Munster Antiquarian Journal*, Vol. 17 (1975), p. 6

160 JOYCE, Patrick Weston, *The Origin and History of Irish Names of Places* (Educational Co of Ireland/Longmans, 3 vols, 1913)

161 ——*Old Irish Folk Music and Songs* (c.1890)

162 JOYCE, Stanislaus, *My Brother's Keeper* (Faber, 1958)

163 ——*The Complete Dublin Diary of Stanislaus Joyce*, ed. George Healy, (Anna Livia Press, 1994)

164 ——'The Background to *Dubliners*', *Listener*, Vol. LI No. 1308 (March 25th 1954), pp. 526–7

165 ——*Recollections of James Joyce by His Brother* (James Joyce Society of New York, 1950)

166 ——'Early Memories of James Joyce' *Listener*, Vol. XLI No. 1061 (May 26th 1949), pp. 896–7

167 JOYCE, Weston St. J., *The Neighbourhood of Dublin* (Skellig Press, 1988)

168 *Journal of the Cork Historical and Archæological Society*

169 KAIN, Richard, *Dublin in the Age of William Butler Yeats and James Joyce* (David & Charles, 1972)

170 ——*Fabulous Voyager: James Joyce's ULYSSES* (Chicago UP, 1947)

171 KAYE, Julian B., 'Simony, the Three Simons and Joycean Myth' in M. Magalaner (ed.), *A James Joyce Miscellany* (James Joyce Society, 1957)

172 KEARNEY, Colbert, 'The Joycead', in Morris Beja and Shari Benstock (eds), *Coping With Joyce* (Ohio State UP, 1989)

173 KEE, Robert, *The Laurel and the Ivy: The Story of Charles Stewart Parnell and Irish Nationalism* (Hamish Hamilton, 1993)

174 ——*The Green Flag* (Quartet, 3 vols, 1976)

175 KENNEDY, Brian P. and Gillespie, Raymond (eds), *Ireland: Art into History* (Town House, 1994)

176 KENNER, Hugh, *Dublin's Joyce* (Columbia UP, 1956)

177 ——'The importance of being definitive', *TLS*, No. 4, 159 (December 17th 1982), pp. 1383–4

178 ——*Joyce's Voices* (Faber, 1978)

179 KETTLE, A. J., *The Material for Victory* (C. J. Fallon, 1958)

180 KETTLE, T. H., *Irish Orators and Oratory* (T. Fisher Unwin, 1916)

181 KLEIN, Herman, *Thirty Years of Musical Life in London, 1870–1900* (William Heinemann, 1903)

182 LARKIN, Emmet, 'The Roman Catholic Hierarchy and the Fall of Parnell', *Victorian Studies* iv (June 1961), pp. 315–36

183 LEE, J. J., *The Modernisation of Irish Society, 1848–1918* (Gill and Macmillan, 1989)

184 ——*Ireland, 1912–1985: Politics and Society* (CUP, 1989)

185 LENNON, Michael, 'James Joyce', *The Catholic World*, Vol. CXXXII. No. 792 (March 1932), pp. 641–52

186 ——'Paris of the Irish', *Irish Ecclesiastical Record*, Vol. LXXIII (January–June 1955)

187 LEVINE, Jennifer, 'Rounding up the usual suspects', *Novel*, Vol. 29 No. 1 (Fall 1995), pp. 100–13

188 LEWIS, Samuel, *A Topographical Dictionary of Ireland* (2 vols, 1837)

189 LIDDERDALE, Jane, & Nicholson, Mary, *Dear Miss Weaver: Harriet Shaw Weaver 1876–1961* (Viking, 1970)

190 LOBNER, Corinna del Greco, *James Joyce's Italian Connection: The Politics of the Word* (University of Iowa Press, 1989)

191 LUENING, Otto, *The Odyssey of an American Composer* (Charles Scribner's Sons, 1957)

192 LUND, Steven (comp.), *James Joyce: Letters manuscripts and photographs at Southern Illinois University* (Whitston, 1983)

193 LYONS, F. S. L., *Ireland Since the Famine* (Weidenfeld and Nicolson, 1971)

194 ——'James Joyce's Dublin', *20th Century Studies* (November 1970) pp. 6–25

195 ——*Charles Stewart Parnell* (Fontana, 1977)

196 ——*Culture and Anarchy in Ireland 1890–1939* (Clarendon Press, 1979)

197 LYONS, J. B., *James Joyce and Medicine* (Dolmen Press, 1973)

198 ——'*What Did I Die Of?*' (Lilliput Press, 1991)

448

199 ——*The Enigma of Tom Kettle* (Glendale Press, 1983)
200 ——*Thrust Syphilis Down to Hell and other Rejoyceana* (Glendale Press, 1988)
201 LYONS, Mary Cecilia, *Illustrated Incumbered Estates in Ireland, 1850–1905* (Ballinakella Press, 1993)
202 MCALMON, Robert, *McAlmon and the Lost Generation: A Self-portrait* (Nebraska UP, 1976)
203 MCALMON, Robert, with Boyle, Kay, *Being Geniuses Together: 1920–1930* (Doubleday, 1968)
204 MACANDREW, Donal, 'Mr and Mrs Windham' in *The Saturday Book* (Hutchinson, 1951)
205 MCCAFFREY, John, 'James Joyce's Father', *Irish Times*, February 1st 1960
206 MCCANN, Sean, *The World of Sean O'Casey* (Four Square, 1966)
207 MCCARTHY, Michael J. F., *Five Years in Ireland, 1895–1900* (Simpkin, Marshall, 1901)
208 ——*Priests and People in Ireland* (Hodges Figgis, 1902)
209 MCCARTHY, Patrick, *et al.*, 'James Joyce and the Phoenix Park Murders: A Forum', in Zack Bowen (ed.), *Irish Renaissance Annual IV* (University of Delaware Press, 1983)
210 MCCARTNEY, Donal (ed.), *Parnell: The Politics of Power* (Wolfhound, 1991)
211 M'CREADY, C. T., *Dublin Street Names, Dated and Explained* (Hodges & Co, 1892)
212 MACDOWELL, R. B., *The Irish Administration, 1801–1914* (Routledge & Kegan Paul, 1964)
213 ——'The City of Dublin', in James Meenan and David A. Webb (eds) *A View of Ireland* (British Association for the Advancement of Science, 1957)
214 MICHAEL MCEWAN, Michael, *Ten Great Irish Hunts* (Punchestown Books, 1996)
215 MCGINLEY, Bernard, *Joyce's Lives* (University of North London Press, 1996)
216 MAC GIOLLE CHOILLE, Brendan, 'To James Augustine Absolutely', *Martello* [Dublin, c.1985]
217 MCHUGH, Roger, 'Hangmen and Divine Assistance' *JJQ* (2), pp. 314–16
218 MCHUGH, Roland, *The FINNEGANS WAKE Experience* (Irish Academic Press, 1981)
219 MCINTYRE, Dennis, *The Meadow of the Bull: A History of Clontarf* (1987)
220 MACMANUS, M. J., *Dublin Diversions* (Talbot Press, 1928)

221 MCNEILL, J. G. Swift, *Titled Corruption: The Sordid Origins of Some Irish Peerages* (T. Fisher Unwin, 1894)

222 MADDOX, Brenda, *Nora: A Biography of Nora Joyce* (Hamish Hamilton, 1988)

223 MAGALANER, Marvin, *Time of Apprenticeship: The Fiction of Young James Joyce* (Abelard-Schuman, 1959)

224 ——'The Anti-Semitic Limerick Incidents and Joyce's 'Bloomsday', *PMLA* 68 (December 1953), pp. 1219–23

225 MAGALANER, Marvin, and Kain, Richard *Joyce: The Man, the Work, the Reputation* (John Calder, 1956)

226 MANGANIELLO, Dominic, *Joyce's Politics* (Routledge & Kegan Paul, 1980)

227 MARSHALL, C. F., *Syphilology and Venereal Disease* (Baillière, Tindall and Cox, 1914)

228 MAUME, Patrick, *D. P. Moran* (Historical Association of Ireland/ Dundalgan Press, 1995)

229 MIKHAIL, E. H. (ed.), *James Joyce: Interviews and Recollections* (Macmillan, 1990)

230 MILLER, David W., *Church, State and Nation in Ireland, 1898–1921* (Gill and Macmillan, 1973)

231 MORAN, D. P., *The Philosophy of Irish Ireland* (James Duffy, 1905)

232 MORLEY, John, *The Life of William Ewart Gladstone* (Macmillan, 2 vols, 1906)

233 *The Municipal Year Book* (London)

234 MURPHY, John, *The College: A History of Queen's/University College Cork, 1845–1995* (Cork UP, 1995)

235 *Musical Times* (London)

236 NICHOLSON, Robert, *The ULYSSES Guide: Tours through Joyce's Dublin* (Methuen, 1988)

237 NORMAN, E. R., *The Catholic Church and Ireland in the Age of Rebellion, 1859–1873* (Longmans, 1965)

238 NORRIS, Margot, *Joyce's Web: The Social Unraveling of Modernism* (University of Texas Press, 1992)

239 O'BRIEN, Conor Cruise (ed.), *The Shaping of Modern Ireland* (Routledge & Kegan Paul, 1960)

240 O'BRIEN, Conor Cruise, *Parnell and his Party, 1880–90* (Clarendon Press, 1957)

241 ——*Ancestral Voices: Religion and Nationalism in Ireland* (Poolbeg, 1994)

242 O'BRIEN, Joseph V:, *'Dear Dirty Dublin': A City in Distress, 1899–1916* (University of California Press, 1982)

243 O'BRIEN, R. Barry, *The Life of Charles Stewart Parnell* (Smith, Elder & Co, 2 vols, 1898)

244 O'BRIEN, William, *Irish Fireside Hours* (M. H. Gill, 1928)

245 ——*The Lost Opportunites of the Irish Gentry* ('Freeman's Journal' Office, 1887)

246 ——*Evening Memories* (Maunsel, 1920)

247 ——*When we were Boys: a Novel* (Longmans Green, 1890)

248 ——*Recollections* (Macmillan, 1905)

249 O'BROIN, Leon, *The Prime Informer: A Suppressed Scandal* (Sidgwick & Jackson, 1971)

250 *O'Connell Centenary Record 1875* (O'Connell Centenary Committee, 1878)

251 *O'Connell School Centenary Record 1828-1928* (Christian Brothers, 1928)

252 O'CONNOR, Ulick (ed.) *The Joyce we Knew* (Mercier, 1967)

253 O'DONNELL, E. E., *The Annals of Dublin: Fair City* (Wolfhound, 1987)

254 O'DONNELL, F. H., *A History of the Irish Parliamentary Party* (Longmans, 2 vols, 1910)

255 O'DUFFY, R. J., *Historic Graves in Glasnevin Cemetery* (James Duffy, 1915)

256 O'FLANAGAN, J. R., *The Blackwater in Munster* (Jeremiah How, 1844)

257 Ó GRÁDA, Cormac, *Ireland: A New Economic History, 1780-1939* (Clarendon Press, 1994)

258 O'LEARY, Peter, *My Own Story* (trans. Sheila O'Sullivan) (Gill and Macmillan, 1971)

259 O'NEILL, Michael J., 'The Joyces in the Holloway Diaries', in Marvin Magalaner (ed.), *A James Joyce Miscellany: Second Series* (Southern Illinois UP, 1959)

260 O'SHEA, Michael J., *Joyce and Heraldry* (SUNY Press, 1986)

261 OSTEEN, Mark, *The Economy of ULYSSES: making both ends meet* (Syracuse UP, 1995)

262 O'SULLIVAN, Seumas, *Essays and Recollections* (Talbot Press, 1944)

263 *Our Boys* (Dublin)

264 PAKENHAM, Thomas and Valerie, *Dublin* (Constable, 1988)

265 PARRINDER, Patrick, *James Joyce* (CUP, 1987)

266 PEARL, Cyril, *Dublin in Bloomtime: The City James Joyce Knew* (Angus & Robertson, 1969)

267 PEASE, Alfred, *Elections and Recollections* (John Murray, 1932)

268 PETTIT, S. F., *This City of Cork, 1700-1900* (Studio Publications, 1977)

269 PIERCE, David, *James Joyce's Ireland* (Yale UP, 1992)

270 POTTS, Willard (ed.), *James Joyce: Portraits of the Artist in Exile* (Wolfhound, 1979)

271 ——'Joyce's Notes on the Gorman Biography', *IcarbS*, Vol. IV No. 2 (Spring–Summer 1981), pp. 83–99

272 POWER, Arthur, *Conversations with Joyce* (Millington, 1974)

273 PRESCOTT, Joseph, 'Local Allusions in Joyce's *Ulysses*', *PMLA* 68 (December 1953), pp. 1223–28

274 *Proceedings of the Royal Irish Academy*

275 'Public Health of Dublin' *Parliamentary Papers 1900*, Vol. XXXIX [Cd 244] (HMSO, 1900)

276 *Punch* (London)

277 Queen's University of Ireland *Calendars*, 1866–74

278 RALEIGH, John Henry, *The Chronicle of Leopold and Molly Bloom* (University of California Press, 1977)

279 ——'On the Chronology of the Blooms', *JJQ* (14), pp. 395–407

280 ——' "Afoot in Dublin in Search of the Habitations of Some Shades" ' *JJQ* (8), pp. 129–41

281 REID, B. L., *The Man from New York: John Quinn and His Friends* (OUP, 1968)

282 ——*The Lives of Roger Casement* (Yale UP, 1976)

283 RESTUCCIA, Frances L., *Joyce and the Law of the Father* (Yale UP, 1989)

284 'Returns of Local Taxation in Ireland for the Year 1881', *Parliamentary Papers 1882*, Vol. LIX [Cd 3367] (HMSO, 1882)

285 REYNOLDS, Mary T., 'Joyce and his Brothers: The Process of Fictional Transformation', *JJQ* (25), pp. 217–25

286 ROBBINS, Alfred, *Parnell: The Last Five Years* (Thornton Butterworth, 1926)

287 RODGERS, W. R. (ed.), *Irish Literary Portraits* (BBC, 1972)

288 RONAN, Myles V., *The Most Reverend W. J. Walsh* (1927)

289 'Royal Commission of the Arrest and Subsequent Treatment of Mr Francis Sheehy Skeffington [et al.]' *Parliamentary Papers 1916*, Vol. XI [Cd 8376] (HMSO, 1916)

290 RYAN, John, *Remembering How We Stood* (Lilliput Press, 1987)

291 RYAN, John (ed.), *A Bash in the Tunnel: James Joyce by the Irish* (Clifton Books, 1970)

292 SAVAGE, Gail, ' "The Wilful Communication of a Loathsome Disease": Marital Conflict and Venereal Disease in Victorian England', *Victorian Studies*, Vol. 34 No. 1 (Autumn 1990), pp. 35–54

293 SCHOLES, Robert (comp.), *The Cornell Joyce Collection: A Catalogue* (Cornell UP, 1961)

294 SCHOLES, Robert, *In Search of James Joyce* (University of Illinois Press, 1992)

295 SCHOLES, Robert, and Kain, Richard, *The Workshop of Daedalus: James*

Joyce and the Raw Material for A PORTRAIT OF THE ARTIST AS A YOUNG MAN (Northwestern UP, 1965)

296 SCOTT, Bonnie Kime, *Joyce and Feminism* (Indiana UP/Harvester, 1984)

297 SHANNON, Richard, *The Crisis of Imperialism, 1865–1915* (Paladin, 1976)

298 SHEEHAN, Patrick A., *Under the Cedars and the Stars* (Browne & Nolan, 1903)

299 ——*The Blindness of Dr Gray* (Longmans & Co, 1909)

300 ——*Geoffrey Austin, Student* (M. H. Gill & Son, 1902)

301 SHEEHY, Eugene, *May It Please the Court* (C. J. Fallon, 1951)

302 SHILLMAN, Bernard, *A Short History of the Jews in Ireland* (printed: Cahill, 1945)

303 SCHLOSS, Carol Loeb, 'Joyce's Will', *Novel*, Vol. 29 No. 1 (Fall 1995), pp. 114–127

304 *Slater's Royal Directory*, 1881

305 SMEDLEY, Frank E, *Frank Fairlegh* (Downey & Co, 1899)

306 ——*Harry Coverdale's Courtship, and what came of it* (George Routledge, 1854)

307 ——*Lewis Arundel, or the Railroad of Life* (Downey & Co, 1899)

308 SMITH, Charles, *The Antient and Present State of the County of Kerry* (1760)

309 SPIELBERG, Peter, *The James Joyce letters and manuscripts at the University of Buffalo* (University of Buffalo, 1962)

310 SPILKA, Mark, 'Leopold Bloom as Jewish Pickwick: A Neo-Dickensian Perspective', *Novel*, Vol. 13 No. 1 (Fall 1979), pp. 121–46

311 SPOO, Robert, *James Joyce and the Language of History: Dedalus's Nightmare* (OUP, 1994)

312 STERN, James, 'James Joyce: A First Impression', *Listener*, Vol. LXVI No. 1696 (September 28th 1961), pp. 461–3

313 *Strand Magazine*, 'Crime and Criminals: No 1 – Dynamite and Dynamiters', January–June 1894

314 STRONG, L. A. G., *The Sacred River: An Approach to James Joyce* (Methuen, 1949)

315 SULLIVAN, Kevin, *Joyce Among the Jesuits* (Columbia UP, 1958)

316 SULTAN, Stanley, *The Argument of ULYSSES* (Wesleyan UP, 1987)

317 SULLIVAN, T. D., *A Guide to Dublin* (T. D. Sullivan, 1888)

318 SUZUKI, Takashi, 'James Joyce's Unpublished Letters in the National Library of Ireland', *Notes and Queries* (1988), pp. 337–8

319 SVEVO, Livia Veneziani, *Memoir of Italo Svevo* (trans. Isabel Quigly) (Libris, 1989)

320 Thom's *DIRECTORY* (Dublin) 1860–1949

321 TIERNEY, Mark, *Croke of Cashel: the Life of Archbishop Thomas William Croke* (Gill and Macmillan, 1976)

322 *The Times*, 'Action Against B.B.C.', October 9th 1954

323 TOMKINSON, Neil, 'Bloom's Job', *JJQ* (2), pp. 103–7

324 TYMOCZKO, Maria, *The Irish Ulysses* (University of California Press, 1994)

325 TYRRELL, George, *Autobiography and Life of George Tyrrell* (Edward Arnold, 2 vols, 1910, 1912)

326 ——*Through Scylla and Charybdis* (Longmans, 1907)

327 VAUGHAN, W. E. (ed.), *A New History of Ireland, Vol. VI: Ireland Under the Union, II: 1870–1921* (Clarendon Press, 1996)

328 VOGEL, Jane, 'The Consubstantial Family of Stephen Dedalus', *JJQ* (2), pp. 109–32

329 WALDRON, Jarlath, *Maamtrasna: The murderers and the mystery* (Edmund Burke, 1993)

330 WALKER, Brian M. (ed.), *Parliamentary Election Results in Ireland, 1801–1922* (Royal Irish Academy, 1978)

331 WALKER, Brian M., O'Broin, Art, & McMahon, Seán, *Faces of Ireland: A photographic and literary picture of the past* (PRC, 1992)

332 WALSH, F. R., 'New Light on James Joyce's Medical Problems', *Irish Medical Times*, May 9th 1975

333 WARD, C. S., *Ireland (Part II.)* (Dulau & Co/ Through Guides, 1891)

334 WATSON, Richard B., with Lewis, Randolph, *The Joyce Calendar* (HRHRC Austin, 1994)

335 WATTERS, Eugene, and Murtagh, Matthew, *Infinite Variety: Dan Lowrey's Music Hall, 1879–97* (Gill and Macmillan, 1975)

336 WICKHAM, Harvey, *The Impuritans* (Lincoln Mac Veagh – The Dial Press/Longmans, Green, 1929)

337 *Wine Trade Review* (London)

338 WITEMEYER, Hugo, 'He Gave the Name': Herbert Gorman's Rectifications of *James Joyce: His First Forty Years*', *JJQ* (32), pp. 523–32

339 WORTHINGTON, Mabel P., 'Gilbert and Sullivan Songs in the Works of James Joyce', *Hartford Studies in Literature*, Vol. I No. 3 (1969) pp. 209–18

340 YEATS, W. B., *Autobiographies* (Macmillan, 1927)

341 YOUNG, Arthur, *A Tour in Ireland* (1780)

342 YOUNGER, Calton, *Ireland's Civil War* (Frederick Muller, 1968)

ADDENDUM OF OTHER SOURCES

343 AINSWORTH, Fr Godrey, Interviews with Sister Gertrude (Margaret 'Poppie' Joyce), 1961–3, copy at James Joyce Cultural Centre, Dublin'.

344 LACY, C. R., Letters at the James Joyce Foundation, Zürich, and personal correspondence with JWJ.

345 MACCARVILL, Eileen, Photocopies of disbound proofs at James Joyce Foundation, Zürich.

Source Notes

These, deliberately kept relatively sparse, usually refer the reader to the bibliographical list above, which specifies the edition used. Each note gives the number there of the book or other source used, followed by page number, date, or other identifying reference. Thus, a note reading 'q. *82*, p 666' signifies 'Quoted on page 666 of Richard Ellmann's *James Joyce* (Oxford UP, 1982 edition)'. Details of items already indicated in the text are not usually repeated below, while individual notes may cover more than the specific passages indicated by the short quotations. Two previous books, *James Joyce: The Years of Growth* by Costello and *James Joyce's Annotated Dubliners* by Jackson and McGinley have been drawn upon silently here: if desired, further details may perhaps be gleaned from those volumes. Any material that has come solely from fictional sources is indicated as such: while it is evident that real life gave James Joyce much of the information he used, it is important to bear in mind that the members of the D(a)edalus family were always subject to his literary designs.

INTRODUCTION

xv . . . audacious and incomplete: *121*, p. ix

1 Ancestral Joyces

3 . . . *Afin d'éterniser*: *98*, p. 74
3 . . . Stephen Joyce remembers: *49*, p. 98
5 . . . the Joyces of Corgary: *39*, pp. 294–5
7 . . . William Fitzmaurice: *6*; *14*, p. 174; *60*; *308*, *passim*
8 . . . Lord Lansdowne: *92*, vol. I, pp. 1–9
9 . . . everything in ruins: *341*
9 . . . the idlest ostentation: *Last Journal* (Horace Walpole), October 1774

9 . . . a careful and prudent man: Archives Nationales Fonds T. 451, Paris (copy in National Library of Ireland)

10 . . . an Honour from his Majesty: *293*, 686

10 . . . nineteen Joyce households: *159*

10 . . . Riobeárd an Gaelgóir: *157*, *158*

11 . . . My home in Glenosheen: *161*, Introduction

12 . . . the very first Bloomsday expedition: *66*, *290* and John Ryan in conversation

13 . . . drunk and unsteady: *151* p. 199

13 . . . a sea-blue: *262*, p. 104

14 . . . John Anderson: *35*, *passim*

14 . . . Elizabeth Bowen: *26*

14 . . . stay the night here: *145*, p. 198

15 . . . alluded to in *Ulysses*: *149*, 8:971

16 . . . tales of the local hunt: *256*

16 . . . once possessed extensive holdings: *110*, p. 18

19 . . . a deed of 16 July 1830: This and subsequent similar details come from the Registry of Deeds: Index of Grantors, under 'Joyce', 'O'Connell' *et al.*, and from the Lands Index, under 'Cork City' (Public Record Office papers)

20 . . . to steady the young man: *162*, p. 44

21 . . . a matter of her own choosing: q. *172*

22 . . . the symbol of culture: *162*, p. 44

23 . . . I'm his grandmother: *162*, p. 44

2 The Son of a Gentleman

Background details for this chapter come from *64*, *162* and *82*.

26 . . . Griffith's *Rates Valuation:* Griffith's Valuation and Tithe Applotment Books are indexed in the National Library of Ireland

30 . . . in an interview: *8*

3 At St Colman's

32 . . . aspiring to the ecclesiastical states: *97*

32 . . . James F. X. O'Brien: *128*, p. 20

33 . . . the great Dr Croke: *321*, *passim*

33 . . . humility and obedience: Keane Papers, Cloyne Archive, Croke to Keane, 8.4.1864

33 . . . Fr Peter O'Leary: *258*, *passim*

34 ... *When We Were Boys:* 247, pp. 15ff
34 ... piano and singing lessons: 82, p. 12, quoting records supplied by Revd Duggan, President of St Colman's
36 ... beside him at dinner: 110, p. 9
36 ... *Geoffrey Austin:* 300
37 ... Fermoy had some distractions: 37, *passim*
37 ... a public meeting: *Cork Examiner,* 14.12.1859
38 ... he sang at concerts: 162, p. 45
39 ... bathed him: Richard Ellmann papers, Tulsa

4 Learning to Swear

40 ... when I was a nipper: 144, p. 3
40 ... the Harbour Master of Cork: 162, p. 45
40 ... pilots employed about Cork Harbour: *Annual Returns Relating to Pilots and Pilotage, for the Year Ending 31 December 1861* (Board of Trade); *Report of the Ports and Harbours Tribunal* (Dublin: Government Publications, 1930), p. 238
41 ... ozone round the Head: 145, p. 26
42 ... Fort Carlisle: 149 16:416–8
43 ... a mock Fenian password: 149, 10.400
43 ... mooncarole: 149 11:849–53

5 His Father's Son

46 ... the estate of Castlehyde: 201, pp. 2off; Grove White vol. II, p. 98
46 ... James Stern: 312
47 ... following the hounds: 214
48 ... a long and severe illness: *Cork Examiner,* 30.10.1866
48–9 ... the first act of *Exiles:* 147, pp. 128–9
49 ... the *Southern Reporter:* 30 October, 1 & 20 November 1866 etc.

6 The Queen's College, Cork

52 ... inquiry by Parliament: Return of Numbers of Matriculated Students ... in the Queen's Colleges 1868–9 (1870), LIV 605, p. 440; Return of Professors ... (1873), LII 435, p. 54
52 ... *University Calendar: Calendars* (Queen's University of Ireland) 1866–74

53 ... Ay, bedad!: *145*, p. 96
54 ... Poor Mick Lacy!: *145*, p. 94
54 ... Dick Tivy bald?: *149*, 6:556–63
55 ... bloody good honest Irishmen too: *145*, p. 97
57 ... *The Blindness of Dr Gray: 299*
57 ... THE MUMMY: *Cork Examiner*, 16.4.1869
57 ... the fancy of the audience: *Cork Constitution*, 16.4.1869
58 ... racy of the soil: *162*, p. 46
58 ... John Murphy: *234*
60 ... the mountain road by night: *248*, p. 57
60 ... the handsomest man in Cork: *145*, p. 98

7 Young Man About Town

63 ... papers and tobacco: *8*
63 ... In 'Circe': *149* 15:3941–50
64 ... Dr Walsh: *332*
64 ... After a long dispute: *227*, *passim*

8 Something in a Distillery

For this chapter, information on the distillery comes from *337*, 1873 onwards, and from various standard works on the drinks trade. See also *204*, pp. 191–210. *320* has been widely drawn upon from this point in the narrative.

70 ... *The House by the Churchyard:* first published 1861
72 ... used to play bowls: *162*, p. 48
73 ... a little sailing boat: *162*, p. 49
74 ... McGuckin was a tenor: *8*
75 ... The *Athenæum*: 23.1.1886
76 ... John sang, unabashed: *162*, pp. 49–50
77 ... A judge would later comment: *Irish Times*, 2.2.1878
78 ... a sleeping dog: *162*, pp. 48–9
80 ... mineral water papers: q. *82*, p. 540
81 ... a transparent bellshade: *149*, 17:1336–7
82 ... a few real friends: *163*, p. 8
82 ... Philip Moisel: *139*, p. 181

9 A Shouting Politician

10 John and May

11 Another Joyce

123 . . . thundered past: *162*, p. 56–7
123 . . . cornet player: *163*, p. 13
123 . . . medieval intensity: *143*, p. 115
124 . . . Morrison's Hotel: *195*, p. 246
125 . . . nyumnyum: *149*, 8:394–5

12 Being a Gentleman

126 . . . hole in his sock: *149*, 18:1089
127 . . . William Desmond: *64*, p. 62
129 . . . arms without authority: *260*, p. 49, & *passim*
130 . . . a cottonball one: *82*, p. 21
131 . . . Twine me a bower: *162*, p. 38
131 . . . to the *backbone: 12*, vol. I, p. 79
131 . . . out of bed entirely: *12*, vol. I, p. 206
131 . . . the bloody globe: *149*, 15:2679–81
131 . . . Dr Achmet Borumborad: *12*, vol. I, p. 128
134 . . . Cork people would adopt: q. *45*, p. 108
136 . . . after-dinner oratory: *162*, p. 49
136 . . . Unless he tells a lie: *144*, p. 183
137 . . . under his mahogany: *145*, p. 37
138 . . . pretty young lady: *162*, p. 58

13 Bray

139 . . . an S like that: q. *243*
141 . . . cad with a pipe: *9*, p. 264
141 . . . shillelagh: *162*, p. 63
141 . . . that part of the Park: *151*, p. 396 (& see *150*, pp. 35–47)
143. . . . morning to midnight: *162*, p. 63.
143 . . . in Rathgar: *145*, p. 3
144 . . . on the level sea: *162*, p. 28
144 . . . that never went to mass: *145*, p. 34
145 . . . James Healy: *7*, *passim*
146 . . . mahogany sideboard: *149*, 18:724
146 . . . linsey-woolsey: *149*, 14:1371
146 . . . a celebrated bowler: *8*
147 . . . 'Joycean setting': reproduced in *64*, p. 69
147 . . . Fr Charles: *54*, *passim*
147 . . . a Dutchman: *8*

171 . . . two years earlier: *Irish Press* (Dublin), 14.1.1941
172 . . . tall blackbearded: *149*, 6:252
173 . . . another bank: *110*, p. 11
174 . . . the Merrion Road: *145*, p. 68
175 . . . a cutting: *2*, pp. 76ff
176 . . . the best pantomime: *114*, p. 114
177 . . . unveiling of a statue: *147*, p. 345
178 . . . figure in the school: *29*, p. 84
179 . . . to school with him: Reuben Dodd quoted in Francis Aylmer 'Reuben Didn't Admire James Joyce', *Irish Digest* (December 1957), pp. 50–1
179 . . . The summer trip: *145*, pp. 91ff
180 . . . much too low: letter: Sister Mary Ita to May Monaghan, 26.3.1955, at James Joyce Cultural Centre, Dublin
180 . . . notes for *Stephen Hero:* q. *295*
181 . . . the dicky bird: *163*, p. 14
181 . . . I am now desirous: reproduced in *64*, pp. 126–7

16 Halcyon Days

184 . . . hopping and trotting: *162*, p. 81
185 . . . Intermediate Examination: *345*
185 . . . an expensive restaurant: *82*, p. 40
186 . . . into the Irish Sea: *162*, pp. 77–8
187 . . . Your tea is served: JWJ telephone interview with Paddy Joyce (Patrizio Schaurek), July 1996
187 . . . burying her: *301*, p. 24
189 . . . Are you going to win?: *162*, p. 92
189 . . . further sums: *162*, p. 83
189 . . . time to finish it: *162*, p. 74
192 . . . three months' renewal: *149*, 7:120ff
193 . . . Tom the Devils ad: *149*, 18:1342
193 . . . I won't let him: *162*, p. 86
193 . . . jiggled furiously: q. *82*, p. 418
193 . . . *je n'ose pas dire:* letter: James Joyce to Paul Léon, 31.7.1932 (see *88*)
194 . . . in the Church: *137*, p. 22
194 . . . able to do something: q. *132*, p. 103
194 . . . friend of all nationalists: *87*, 14.4.1896
195 . . . blow where it listeth: *United Irishman* (Dublin), 18.1.1896
195 . . . Mr John G. Joyce: *87*, 17.4.1896

195 ... prosperous bulk: *149*, 6:739
197 ... true Irish heart: *255*, p. 144
197 ... *whoever done it: 149*, 6:717–731
197 ... Dublin Castle: Irish National Archives: Secret Police File
197 ... stripped parlour: *162*, p. 78
198 ... a dancing bear: *343*
198 ... safely housed: *144*, p. 21
199 ... a good turn: *163*, p. 78
199 ... a big kite: *151*, p. 393
199 ... Madame de Vere: *293*, 913
200 ... even Zola: *162*, p. 89
200 ... Madame Marie Tallon: *82*, p. 375
200 ... the rest of the group: *162*, p. 81
201 ... middle of the Sahara: see *82*, p. 28
201 ... word-painting of Dublin: *191*
202 ... sandwiches and tea: *137*, p. 25
202 ... halcyon days: *162*, p. 81

17 A Little Learning

203 ... 92 Windsewer Ave: *150*, p. 420
203 ... the Civil Service: 2, p. 32
204 ... a surreal note: *149*, 10:881–954
204 ... my young days: *149*, 15:4701
205 ... not to have suffered: *162*, p. 141
205 ... cut above buttermilk: typescript by Ken Monaghan in James Joyce Cultural Centre, Dublin
205 ... one of the breed: *151*, p. 199
206 ... an easy mind: *146*, p. 16
206 ... his cockiness: *343*
206 ... the Dublin firm, Maunsel's: *126*, p. 479.67
207 ... at the Gaiety: from 22.10.1897
207 ... remembers seeing it: *149*, 18:1111–7
207 ... to mark the occasion: 9, p. 151
207 ... the millentury: *150*, p. 32
208 ... list of subscribers: *87*, 20 & 23.10.1897
209 ... I remember it well: *343*
209 ... a slap-up meal: *82*, p. 751 n. 14
210 ... a slab of granite: *175*, pp. 112–14
212 ... he has done very well: *8*
213 ... reproachful eyes: *295*

213 . . . fill up my can: *143*, p. 49
213 . . . Going in for competitions: *301*, p. 24
213 . . . general culture: *162*, p. 106
214 . . . David Patrick Moran: see *228*, *passim*
215 . . . an old sailor: *162*, p. 93
215 . . . Captain Weldon: *126*, p. 393.10

18 A Travelling Man

216 . . . women had a vote: see *242*, pp. 78ff
217 . . . made Presiding Officer: *162*, p. 80
217 . . . the Sheriff's office: *143*, p. 155
217 . . . His Lordship: *59*, p. 51
218 . . . The mountain dew: *145*, p. 93
218 . . . entrance form: *345*
219 . . . genius breaking out: *162*, p. 102
220 . . . wage-slavery: *143*, p. 53
220 . . . a Dame Street office: *143*, pp. 90–3
220 . . . On the jury: *87*, 21.10.1899; *2*, p. 174
220 . . . taking notes: *82*, p. 91
221 . . . dislike of the Murrays: *143*, p. 115
221 . . . Bossinet: *68*, p. 69
221 . . . until the small hours: *64*, p. 163; *143*, p 165
223 . . . 'Drama & Life': *146*, pp. 38ff
223 . . . raving mad: *301*, p. 13
223 . . . well-whipped: *82*, p. 70
223 . . . Dublin's Darlin: *Modern Society* (London), 14.4.1900
223 . . . South African War: *162*, p. 70
223 . . . rectal complaints: *126*, p. 468.10
223–4 . . . long round end: *149*, 17:1833
224 . . . vocabulary be revealed: *68*, p. 70
224 . . . a whoite-arsed bugger: *148*, p. 195
225 . . . Paul Kruger: *162*, p. 110
226 . . . a reptile people: letter: Maria Jolas to May Monaghan 21.9.1965, in James Joyce Cultural Centre, Dublin
226 . . . exorbitant sums: *143*, p. 155
227 . . . the ashpit: *162*, pp. 113–15
228 . . . Pat of Mullingar: *16*, p. 70
228 . . . Mr Tobin: *148*, p. 169; *71*, *passim*
228 . . . 'sinful': *141*, 1894
229 . . . Matilda Pender: *Westmeath Examiner* (Mullingar) 21.7.1900

229 ... A *Brilliant Career:* *162*, pp. 126ff
230 ... Constable Henry Flower: *144*, p. 47
230 ... the River Liffey: *149*, 10:875–7
231 ... a sentimentalist: *162*, p. 95

19 The Boer Constructor

233 ... legitimate work: *143*, p. 61
233 ... tragic consequences: 72, p. 56
234 ... beef to the heel: *149*, 14:502–3
235 ... on his flesh: Eva Joyce q. in *82*, p. 65
235 ... the matter with you: *82*, p. 93
236 ... 'James Clarence Mangan': *146*, pp. 73ff
236 ... a boer constructor: *150*, p. 180
237 ... not fit to be washed: *8*
237 ... a regular young pagan: *163*, p. 16
238 ... dying upstairs: *137*, p. 36
238 ... very young to die: *162*, p. 143
239 ... death very deeply: *162*, p. 143
239 ... keep her spirits up: *143*, p. 169
240 ... a parti-cularly stupid boy: *162*, p. 191
240 ... make a quick fortune: *68*, p. 43
242 ... Jim Tully: *100*, p. 41
242 ... a pigeon's egg: John Stanislaus Joyce q. by Alfred Bergan q. by Niall Sheridan q. by Richard Ellmann, *82*, p. 106
242 ... Mrs McBride: *343*
242 ... failed to see the joke: *Irish Society* (Dublin), 8.10.1902, p. 4664; *Irish Figaro* (Dublin), 8.10.1902, p. 761
243 ... *Cavalleria Rusticana:* *155*, p. 399
244 ... got back from McKenna: *68*, p. 64
244 ... brown and healthy and neat: *154*, p. 39

20 A Loving Pair of Sons

Over the next decade or so, biographical information and small quotations unless otherwise indicated come from *154* or are catalogued in *293*. Misdatings are corrected where appropriate.

245 ... Matthew F. Kane: *154*, p. 32
247 ... Pappie, 'toned down: *162*, p. 205
248 ... bad or indifferent: *144*, pp. 116–17

248 ... priest-ridden: *242*, p. 88
249 ... unbecoming a gentleman: *154*, p. 26
250 ... beginning to cry out: *154*, p. 33
250 ... sold a carpet: *154*, p. 29
250 ... false teeth: *154*, p. 22
250 ... poor old Thornton: *154*, p. 39
250 ... *Intransigeant*: *186*, pp. 262–3
250 ... a blatant refugee: D. Ryan, *The Fenian Chief* p. 341
251 ... green fairy's fang: *149*, 3:226
251 ... fumbling shamefacedly: *162*, p. 223
252 ... a little chat with him: *163*, pp. 105–6
253 ... a 'new warmth': *149*, 9:826
253 ... she was no drinker: *197*, p. 100
253 ... florid letter of thanks: *271*; *110*, p. 108 n. 1
254 ... imaginary buttercups: *149*, 1.211
254 ... babbled in gibberish: *144*, p. 32
254 ... Die and be damned to you: *162*, p. 230
255 ... escaped through the window: *82*, pp. 136 & 769 n. 25
255 ... soon be stretched: *149*, 6:645
256 ... You don't understand, boy: 162, p. 232
256 ... under the sofa: *154*, p. 382
257 ... her locked drawer: *149*, 1:255–6
258 ... what survives is enlightening: *163*, *passim*
259 ... her mother had appeared: *343*
259 ... its loose graveclothes: *149*, 1:270–3
260 ... the skull: *154*, p. 51
260 ... consulting a priest: *343*
260 ... slobbery-mouthed: *162*, p. 241
261 ... Her milky breast: *197*, p. 99
261 ... briefly engaged: *163*, p. 19
262 ... ridiculed in *Ulysses*: *149*, 9:727–34
263 ... to make nuns of: Papers of Lily & Lollie Yeats

21 Shite and Onions

264 ... Sighing Simon: *163*, p. 12
264 ... no kettle: *163*, pp. 24–5
265 ... Ye dirty pissabed: *163*, p. 28
265 ... balking little rat: *163*, p. 37
265 ... the peacemaker: *154*, p. 33
265 ... fondling Baby: *163*, p. 32

22 Parting Drinks

283 . . . only ten shillings: *293*, 613
283 . . . an inside lavatory: *293*, 706
283 . . . drank several pairs of boots: *293*, 613
283 . . . porter into seed: *293*, 615
284 . . . The day Pappie was paid: *293*, 613
285 . . . paws, ears or arse: *293*, 616
286 . . . the poltroons: *293*, 616
286 . . . something to eat: *293*, 915
286 . . . his first letter to Jim: *154*, pp. 228–9, 16.5.1906 (misdated 1909)
286 . . . never apologise: *162*, p. 52
287 . . . they got drunk together: *293*, 606
287 . . . very bad use: *293*, 916
287 . . . a journal: *293*, 618
290 . . . owed money by Tom Kernan: *149*, 6:456
290 . . . potential employers: *154*, p. 145
290 . . . a collection had to be taken: *293*, 618
291 . . . of the poorest class: *98*, 23.12.1909
291 . . . a bathroom with hot water: *293*, 706 & 707
291 . . . red herrings on the Saturday: *222*, p. 108 (*293*, 669)
292 . . . he had a cold: *293*, 616
292 . . . the biggest 'Stink': *293*, 668
292 . . . this 'Bastard': *293*, 669
293 . . . decayed ambitions: *154*, p. 216
293 . . . a Kaffir kraal: q. *113*, p. 29
293 . . . nibbling cabbages: *154*, pp. 208–9
293 . . . Todd Burns: *293*, 718, 25.2.1907 (misdated 1906)
293 . . . the Telephone Office: *293*, 721
293 . . . a Corporation job: *293*, 669
294 . . . Perhaps in years to come: *154*, pp. 221–3
294 . . . an Italian daily paper: *82*, p. 260
294 . . . Hugh McNeill: *293*, 673
295 . . . the old sheet of tissue paper: *293*, 625
295 . . . Jim was 'quite mad': *293*, 710
296 . . . he'd see stars: *293*, 625
296 . . . a terrible little no-good: *293*, 721
297 . . . ran into Pat Casey: *293*, 722
297 . . . the same paupers: *293*, 722
297 . . . poverty-stricken geniuses: *293*, 722
298 . . . corner boys: *293*, 671
298 . . . the child is mine: *293*, 626
299 . . . Slough of Cadism: *293*, 671

23 The Language of Music

300 . . . splendid salary: *293*, 672
301 . . . something wrong with his waterworks: *100*, p. 40
301 . . . feet foremost: *293*, 672
302 . . . John shared the mourning carriage: *293*, 673
303 . . . too bright to live: *293*, 627
303 . . . 'rather crazy': *293*, 724
304 . . . like a 'found Ass': *293*, 673
305 . . . Colum could not remember what it was: *59*, p. 79
305 . . . peculiar rapport: *105*, pp. 103–4
306 . . . courteously hospitable: *154*, p. 284
307 . . . had to get a servant: *154*, p. 247
307 . . . out of mischief: *293*, 724
307 . . . the jaunty 'Kildare' angle: *137*, p. 79
308 . . . that was my sacrifice: *343*
308 . . . on the broad of his back: *154*, p. 263
308 . . . conjunctivitis and slight iritis: *154*, p. 267
308 . . . that hairy mechanic: *137*, p. 79
309 . . . He is an Irish suicide: q. *295*, 'Alphabetical Notebook': 'Pappie'
310 . . . The lines on Conservio: *149*, 15:2664–7
310 . . . reused in 'Eumaeus': *149*, 16:175–6
310 . . . representations on the screen: *24*, Autumn–Winter 1909

24 A Shout in the Street

311 . . . A strange land: *154*, p. 266
311 . . . such a dreadful house: *154*, p. 280
311 . . . black bandages: *154*, p. 285
313 . . . a £20 commission: *154*, p. 286
313 . . . much to Pappie's annoyance: *293*, 727
313 . . . *all alone*: *293*, 676
314 . . . his 'pal': *293*, 675
314 . . . a long letter: *82*, *passim*
314 . . . what any of those messages had been: *82*, p. 300
316 . . . views of Fermoy: *293*, 677
316 . . . 'The Home Rule Comet': *146*, pp. 209–13
318 . . . particularly dirty and shaby: *293*, 646
319 . . . when we went into the ward: *293*, 727
319 . . . I can't go into the details: *293*, 679
320 . . . There is one thing I know: *293*, 727

321 . . . 'the surage in Hishon's': *293*, 646
322 . . . he goes to bed again: *293*, 727

25 The Old Story

324 . . . her accommodation expenses: *293*, 647 & 729
324 . . . When I ask Pappie: *293*, 648
324 . . . the city at night: *293*, 729
325 . . . severe emotional problems: *293*, 913
325 . . . visit a doctor: *293*, 729
325 . . . difficulty articulating his words: *293*, 653
325 . . . in a madhouse: *293*, 727
326 . . . coming to the wall: *293*, 727
327 . . . she needed a stool: *293*, 731
327 . . . too bad to describe: *293*, 651
328 . . . some sort of a suit: *293*, 653
329 . . . 'The Shade of Parnell': *146*, pp. 223–8
329 . . . an old pair of trousers: *154*, p. 296
330 . . . a good three-cornered fight: *154*, pp. 295–6
330 . . . really 'all about Jim': *154*, p. 303
331 . . . seemed 'quiet happy': *154*, p. 303
332 . . . through his own fault: *154*, pp. 298 & 304
334 . . . a blackguard production: *154*, p. 307
334 . . . what kind of individual: *162*, pp. 79–80
334 . . . His Grace was made an archbishop: *154*, pp. 306–7
335 . . . up 'all night' listening: *154*, p. 304
335 . . . prostitutes: *154*, p. 307
335 . . . the end of her apprenticeship: *293*, 632
335 . . . nearly asphyxiated: *2*, pp. 92–3
336 . . . as big as the eyes of a cow: James Stephens, in the *Listener* (London), XXXVI (24.10.1946), p. 315
337 . . . smoke from the pages: *105*, p. 97
337 . . . wrapping around other books: *137*, p. 87

26 The Patriarch Game

341 . . . The anchor's weigh'd: *27* pp. 238–9
341 . . . out and out ruffian: *82*, p. 337
342 . . . to go back: *293*, 734
342 . . . change his mind: *293*, 734

27 'Let Me Like a Soldier Fall'

374 ... a typewritten list: Curran papers, U.C.D.
374 ... an amusing screed: *151*, p. 174

28 Learning to Die

376 ... an impressive list: *11*, pp. 104–5
377 ... He's a nice sort of blackguard: *82*, p. 530
378 ... Dan Flavin's: *Irish Digest*, c.1957
379 ... only enlivening feature: *151*, p. 191
379 ... one sure five!: The metaphor is from billiards
381 ... 'Pop': *120, passim*
382 ... Tristan and Isolde: now *150*, pp. 383–9
383 ... James wrote Pappie: *82*, pp. 540–1
383 ... chateaubottled Guiness's: now *150*, p. 382
385 ... John's repertoire: *190*
385 ... Jean de Reszke's: *181*, p. 244
386 ... an obstinate artist: *137*, p. 148
387 ... keenly criticised: *11*, p. 46
387 ... Christian name was Simon: *74*, pp. 309–10
388 ... Piaras Beaslai: *Irish Digest*, September 1962
388 ... George Lashwood: *252*, p. 20
388 ... Constantine Curran: *68*, pp. 68–70
388 ... Another witness: *59*, p. 201
390 ... late in the day to start: *293*, 933
390 ... institutional hostility: British Library Add. MSS.57346/102–3
390 ... realized insurance: *59*, p. 200
390 ... only Eileen visited: *197*
390 ... 'Monto': *62*, p. 9, Ch. 8
392 ... gone off his head I am afraid: *151*, p. 235
392 ... a great flow of language: *8*
392 ... He sat up in bed: *203*
393 ... expressions of gratitude': BL Add. MSS.
394 ... more children before the end: *203*
394 ... I have at least one son: *82*, p. 610
395 ... clotted nonsense: *220*
395 ... that Antichrist: Ken Monaghan, lecture in Trieste, 1.7.1997
396 ... jacket-over-waistcoat style: *270*, p. 78
398 ... Old Dedalus swears admirably: *112*, p. 92 and cover

29 Old Man Gone

30 Recirculation

422 ... master of English vernacular: *Chicago Tribune*, 2.1.1932 (Paris edition)
422 ... more and more as he grew older: *155*, pp. 239–40
422 ... 'The Groves of Blarney': see *150*, pp. 126–168
423 ... an intense love for him: *151*, p. 311
423 ... being a sinner myself: *156*, p. 361
423 ... extravagant licentious disposition: *151*, p. 312
423 ... GRANDSON BORU TODAY: *155*, p. 241
423 ... 'Ecce Puer': *147*, p. 111
423 ... most important thing: 272, p. 110
424 ... £36.12s.1d: *216*
426 ... exquisite calligraphy: *110*, p. 108n. Joyce also insisted (at best ambiguously) that his father 'never ceased to write to him in Trieste' (*110* p. 269)
426 ... be better deleted: *215*, p. 11
426 ... a patient ghost: *110*, p. 10
427 ... Pappappaparrassannuaragheallachnatullaghmonganmacmac macwhackfalltherdebblenonthedubblandaddydoodled: *150*, p. 332

EPILOGUE

431 ... Tom Devin: death cert. February 1937; notices of death and funeral in *Irish Independent*; family members
431 ... Bergan: death cert.; also Charles family and City of Dublin Cancer Hospital; testamentary records for Bergan family 1870–1955
432 ... Charles Joyce: death cert., obituary in *Belvederian* 1942; local records Hastings and St. Albans
433 ... Frederick Joyce: professional records and family sources
434 ... Hutchins: note on Stephen Joyce among Hutchins Papers TCD
435 ... Eva Joyce: death cert.; Glasnevin records
435 ... Eileen Schaurek: *Evening Herald* 9 and 16.7.1963
435 ... waistcoat: *Irish Times*, 26.1.1963
437 ... George Joyce: from Adrian Kenny and J. B. Lyons
437 ... Florence Joyce: *Irish Times*, 5.9.1973
438 ... Jolas: *Irish Times*, 16.6.1977
438 ... bench: *Irish Times* 18.5.1976; 14.6.1977

Index

'JJ' indicates James Joyce and 'JSJ' John Stanislaus Joyce.

MAP
OF THE
CITY OF DUBLIN AND ITS ENVIRONS.

REFERENCES.

THE CITY IS DIVIDED INTO TWENTY WARDS, VIZ :—

North Dock Ward,	marked	A	coloured		Inns Quay Ward,	marked	K	coloured	
South Dock Ward,	„	B	„		Wood Quay Ward,	„	L	„	
Mountjoy Ward,	„	C	„		Arran Quay Ward,	„	M	„	
Trinity Ward,	„	D	„		Ushers' Quay Ward,	„	N	„	
Rotunda Ward,	„	E	„		Merchants' Quay Ward,	„	O	„	
North City Ward,	„	F	„		Clontarf Ward West,	„	P	„	
South City Ward,	„	G	„		Drumcondra Ward,	„	Q	„	
Royal Exchange Ward,	„	H	„		Glasnevin Ward,	„	R	„	
Mansion House Ward,	„	I	„		New Kilmainham Ward,	„	S	„	
Fitzwilliam Ward,	„	J	„		Clontarf Ward East,	„		not shown	

Ward Boundaries marked thus ——————
Township Boundaries ——————
Railways ——————
Tramways ——————

SCALE – SIX INCHES TO ONE STATUTE MILE

A. THOM & CO., LTD., 87 ABBEY STREET, DUBLIN.

COPYRIGHT, ENTERED AT STATIONERS' HALL